PREFACE

INTRODUCTION
How to use this Study Text - syllabus - tutor's guidance no[...]
the examination paper - study checklist

   BPP Publishing

CIM
Study Text

Advanced Certificate

Marketing Operations

First edition 1994
Second edition September 1995

ISBN 0 7517 4032 2 (previous edition 0 7517 4020 9)

British Library Cataloguing-in-Publication Data
A catalogue record for this book
is available from the British Library

Published by

BPP Publishing Limited
Aldine House, Aldine Place
London W12 8AW

Printed in Great Britain by
WM Print Ltd
Frederick Street
Walsall
West Midlands WS2 9NE

BPP would like to thank Professor Geoff Lancaster, who prepared the first
edition of this Study Text.

We are grateful to the Chartered Institute of Marketing for permission to
reproduce in this text the syllabus, tutor's guidance notes, and specimen
examination paper of which the Institute holds the copyright.

We are also grateful to the Chartered Institute of Marketing for permission to
reproduce past examination questions. The suggested solutions to both the
specimen paper questions and the past examination questions have been
prepared by BPP Publishing Limited.

PREFACE

The examination syllabus of the Chartered Institute of Marketing changed radically with effect from the December 1994 examination. The new syllabus is a demanding test of each student's knowledge and skills.

Thorough, up-to-date and effective learning and practice material is crucial for busy professionals preparing for professional exams. All our study texts are written by educators and professionals who have themselves experienced the pressures of having to study as well as to work. Our material is therefore *comprehensive* - covering the *whole* syllabus - *on-target* - covering *only* the syllabus - and *up-to-date* at the month of publication. All our books are fully revised annually: we do not believe in mere topic supplements.

This Study Text has been written specifically for the CIM Advanced Certificate paper *Marketing Operations* with the active involvement of the Senior Examiner. The syllabus on pages (viii) and (ix) has been cross-referenced to the text, so you can be assured that coverage is complete. The tutor's guidance notes on pages (x) to (xiv) give more substance to the syllabus. This is followed by details of the examination paper format and an analysis of questions set in the specimen paper and all papers set to date under the new syllabus. There is also a study checklist so you can plan and monitor your progress through the syllabus.

The main body of this Study Text takes you through the syllabus in easily managed stages, with plenty of opportunities for skill - and exam question - practice. All examinable topics are covered in full. For a brief guide to the structure of the text, and how it may most effectively be used, see pages (vi) to (vii).

The September 1995 edition of this Study Text

This Study Text has been updated and improved in the following ways.

(a) We have taken a fresh look at the structure of the Study Text. While this edition continues to follow the layout of the syllabus, we have re-organised and revised some material. We have performed a thorough review of the content of each chapter, particularly those on marketing opportunities and marketing planning, and added sections explaining how the individual activities and considerations referred to in the 'tutor's guidance notes' fit into the overall process. At the same time we have cut out or abridged some of the more detailed material dealt with more fully in other papers. This will make these chapters easier to work through and allow students to focus on core topics.

(b) We have expanded and updated our coverage of ACORN and MOSAIC and added new material on regional trade alliances and markets and on consumer and community issues.

(c) Each part of the text has a case example putting its subject matter in a wider context.

BPP Publishing
September 1995

For details of other BPP titles relevant to your studies for this examination, including our exam-oriented Practice & Revision Kits, and for a full list of books in the BPP CIM range, please turn to pages 327 and 328. If you wish to send in your comments on this Study Text, please turn to page 329.

HOW TO USE THIS STUDY TEXT

This Study Text has been designed to help students and lecturers to get to grips as effectively as possible with the content and scope of *Marketing Operations*.

Syllabus coverage in the text is indicated on pages (viii) and (ix) by chapter references set against each syllabus topic. Syllabus topics are also identified within each chapter of the text. It is thus easy to trace your path through the syllabus.

As a further guide - and a convenient means of monitoring your progress - we have included a *study checklist* on page (xvi) on which to chart your completion of chapters and their related illustrative questions.

Chapter format and contents

Each *chapter* of the Study Text is divided into *sections* and contains:

- learning objectives, cross-referenced to the syllabus
- an Introduction, indicating how the subject area relates to others in the syllabus
- clear, concise topic-by-topic coverage
- examples and exercises to reinforce learning, confirm understanding and stimulate thought
- a 'roundup' of the key points in the chapter
- a test your knowledge quiz
- a recommendation on illustrative questions to try for practice. These are provided in a bank at the end of the text, with suggested solutions; there are some further 'class questions' to be attempted under supervision.

Exercises

Exercises are provided throughout the text to enable you to check your progress as you work through the text. A suggested solution is usually given, but often in abbreviated form to help you avoid the temptation of merely reading the exercise rather than actively engaging your brain. We think it is preferable on the whole to give the solution immediately after the exercise rather than making you hunt for it at the end of the chapter, losing your place and your concentration. Cover up the solution with a piece of paper if you find the temptation to cheat too great!

Examples can also often be used as exercises, if not the first time you read a passage, then certainly afterwards when you come to revise.

Chapter roundup and Test your knowledge quiz

At the end of each chapter you will find two boxes. The first is the *Chapter roundup* which summarises key points. The second box is a quiz that serves a number of purposes.

(a) It is an essential part of the chapter roundup and can be glanced over quickly to remind yourself of key issues covered by the chapter.

(b) It is a quiz pure and simple. Try doing it mentally on the train in the morning to revise what you read the night before.

(c) It is a revision tool. Shortly before your examination sit down with pen and paper and try to answer all the questions fully. Many of the questions are typical of the four- or five-mark-earning opportunities that feature so regularly in examination questions.

Illustrative questions

Each chapter also has an illustrative question, in the bank at the back of the Study Text. Initially you might attempt such questions with reference to the chapter you have just covered. Later in your studies, it would be helpful to attempt some without support from the text. Only when you have attempted each question as fully as possible should you refer to the suggested solution to check and correct your performance.

Glossary and Index

Finally, we have included a glossary to define key terms and a comprehensive index to help you locate key topics.

A note on pronouns

On occasions in this Study Text, 'he' is used for 'he or she', 'him' for 'him or her' and so forth. Whilst we try to avoid this practice it is sometimes necessary for reasons of style. No prejudice or stereotyping according to sex is intended or assumed.

 BPP Publishing

SYLLABUS

Aims and objectives

- to build on the knowledge of marketing fundamentals which the student is already expected to have

- to provide students with a sound understanding of the process of marketing operations (analysis, planning, implementation and control) and the process of marketing decisions. This will enable them to perform effectively in any single functional area of marketing at the junior management level

- in particular to enable students to gain a good grasp of the details of marketing operations and be able to adapt and apply them in their own job situation and in a variety of practical situations

- to encourage students to test and apply modern marketing theory to the understanding and solution of practical marketing problems and situations

- to demonstrate the contribution of marketing operations in a variety of business, governmental, charitable and not for profit organisations

Learning outcomes

Students will be able to:

- work effectively in a marketing organisation

- make a contribution within a specific marketing function

- be sensitive to the forces of consumer and organisational buyer behaviour

- make a contribution to the process of planning marketing operations

- make a contribution to the process of making marketing decisions

- understand the process of providing customer service

- understand the organisation and allocation of marketing resources

- contribute to the planning and control of marketing budgets

- understand the application of marketing operations in a number of private sector and public sector organisations

- understand the application of marketing operations in differing regional, national and international situations

- understand the contribution of information technology to marketing operations at a tactical level

- appreciate the role of business ethics in marketing operations

Indicative content and weighting

		Covered in Chapter
1	**Analysis of marketing opportunities: the basics (20%)**	
1.1	What is meant by marketing opportunity	1
1.2	Analysis of organisation's internal capabilities	1
1.3	Analysis of organisation's marketing environment	1
1.4	Segmenting markets, targeting and positioning	2

BPP Publishing

TUTOR'S GUIDANCE NOTES

1   Analysis of marketing opportunities: the basics (20%)

1.1   What is meant by marketing opportunity

- when an opportunity exists
- what an opportunity allows an organisation to do
- factors which an organisation must consider

1.2   Analysis of organisation's internal capabilities

- strengths and weaknesses: Marketing (marketing mix, branding, information); Engineering: R & D; Operations; People; Management; Resources (people, money)

1.3   Analysis of organisation's marketing environment

- macro: legal, regulatory, political, societal (cultural), technological, economic

- micro: direct competition/substitutes, supplier power, buyer power, company's resource base

1.4   Segmenting markets, targeting and positioning

- mass market (total market) approach or segmentation
- segmentation (bases and descriptors)
- targeting (which, why and how)
- positioning (criteria and attributes)

2   The marketing planning process: an introduction (20%)

2.1   The marketing planning process defined

- analysis of markets and trading environment opportunities

- determination of core markets; competitive edge/differential advantage; statement of goals and desired brand positioning

- determination of marketing programmes for implementation

2.2   Relationship to corporate planning

- corporate strategy helps determine an organisation's mission

- corporate goals relating to R & D, Engineering, Production, Finance, Personnel and Sales, as well as to Marketing used to invoke this mission

2.3   Conducting a marketing audit (or marketing analyses)

- review of activities/results/performance
- information on customers, competitors, the marketing environment
- exploration of opportunities/threats
- provision of database or marketing databank

2.4   Developing marketing objectives and strategies

- marketing objectives as simple goal statements

- marketing strategy defines target markets, competitive edges and desired brand positionings

2.5   Detailed plans and programmes document

- company mission
- product/market background information
- SWOT analysis
- statement of objectives
- strategies (target markets, competitive edge brand positionings)
- marketing programmes, (sales targets, detailed marketing mixes)
- allocation of resources, tasks, responsibilities
- financial implications/budgets
- operational implications and implementation
- appendices (supportive information)

2.6   Constraints on marketing decisions

- legal/regulatory constraints (eg contracts)
- voluntary constraints (eg codes of practice)
- ethics/social responsibilities

3   Marketing organisation (10%)

3.1   -   Marketing in the organisation structure

- centralisation or decentralisation (delegation)
- marketing's role sales led, product led or marketing led organisation

3.2   Alternative ways of organising marketing activities

- marketing can be organised by function, region, product, type of customer

3.3   The role of marketing personnel

- marketing manager (general responsibilities for a variety of products and tasks)
- product manager (responsible for related lines)
- a brand manager (handles just one brand)

3.4   Marketing control and evaluation

- the marketing control process: Establish performance standards; Evaluate actual performance; Reduce the differences between actual performance and performance standards

  evaluating performance: Sales analysis (sales figures); Marketing cost analysis (cost per activity to gain a certain level of sales)

4   Managing outside resources (10%)

4.1   Types of outside resources and when to use them

- range of supplies/suppliers
- presale/postsale
- ad hoc/repeat

4.2   Competitive tendering/selection

- tendering/bid pricing
- organisational buying process

4.3   Briefing and working with outside suppliers

- specifying needs/time span/budgets

4.4   Control and review of external suppliers

- setting standards/benchmarks
- rating and measuring performance

5 Selected marketing applications: an overview (25%)

5.1 Industrial/business to business marketing applications

- relative ease of target marketing (SIC classes, input/output data, trade directories, location)

- marketing mix differences (eg bid and negotiated pricing, role of personal selling, etc)

- creation of competitive edge increasingly important: price no longer the key; service, etc

5.2 Services marketing

- growth of services in economy (employment/GNP)

- basic characteristics (intangibility, inseparability, perishability, heterogeneity)

- importance of quality in services

- extended marketing mix (product, price, promotion, place plus people, process, physical evidence)

- difficulties creating a competitive edge (eg lack of product tangibility and the role of people)

- importance of people as employees/customers; motivation and training

5.3 Charity and not for profit marketing

- negotiation and persuasion rather than selling

- objectives differ from consumer/industrial

- target publics (client publics and general publics)

- marketing mix differences (eg product usually ideas and services rather than goods; short distribution channels; different approach to pricing; promotion emphasis on PR and face to face fund raising)

- performance hard to measure

5.4 International marketing

- marketing information needs are great

- marketing environment differences must be known

- regional trade alliances and markets (eg the EU) present difficulties and opportunities

- adaptation of marketing mixes necessary, particularly distribution and pricing

- structure choices: Exporting; Licensing; Joint ventures; Trading companies; Direct ownership

6 Legal, ethics and wider Issues (15%)

6.1 The importance of marketing ethics and social responsibility

- customer service/customer loyalty are central to successful marketing; lack of ethics spoil both

- ethics for marketing executives and within the marketing mix

- awareness by organisations and consumers of ethical and social responsibility issues

- codes of ethics and disciplinary action

- social responsibility issues: consumer, community, green

- proactive, reactive or passive strategies to social responsibility

6.2 Wider issues

- marketing as a profession, responsibilities etc

- contribution of information technology to marketing operations, the role of information systems and the marketing databank

- topical marketing issues such as privatisation and the creation of internal markets

Senior examiner's comments

The examination paper comprises two parts. Part A is a minicase study with compulsory questions for all students to answer. This part carries 50% of the marks. Part B requires the student to answer any two questions from five. The two questions in Part B will carry equal weight and 50% of the marks for the paper will be allocated for this part.

The *Marketing Operations* subject is a new course, which has been designed to incorporate a range of important new developments in the marketing field. The principal aim of the *Marketing Operations* course is to build on the material covered in *Marketing Fundamentals*, adding depth to certain areas and introducing new principles to others. However, there are also important linkages between *Marketing Operations* and *Promotional Practice, Management Information for Marketing and Sales*, and *Effective Management for Marketing*, all Advanced Certificate subjects. It is often difficult to build artificial divides between different aspects of marketing, so it is important that students develop an awareness of marketing as a single discipline and that they understand the interactions between the Advanced Certificate subjects.

The *Marketing Operations* course aims to provide a broad base of expertise which is particularly geared towards the needs of those employed in marketing operations jobs. There is also specific emphasis on the areas of services marketing, the role of people, ethics and social responsibility in marketing and international issues. These aspects of marketing are having a major impact on the way marketing is practised today and will increasingly affect how marketing practitioners carry out their jobs. It is appropriate, therefore, to ensure that students receive a sound grounding in these areas.

In terms of teaching strategy, it is essential that the development of theoretical concepts is based on the application of real cases and current marketing campaigns, and that students learn to apply relevant marketing theories in an analytical way. Students should understand both the scope and limitations of the theories and concepts taught and should be able to apply them in an appropriate manner. All too often marketing concepts, such as market segmentation and aspects of marketing planning, are applied blindly in business situations with little attention to practical considerations or potentially damaging consequences. Above all, the theoretical component of the *Marketing Operations* subject, should not allow the practical side of marketing to become obscured. Put simply, on completion of the course students should be better able to apply marketing concepts and theories in practical situations.

The policy for examining the subject involves assessing the student's basic understanding of marketing operations under the headings of the syllabus. The examiners are keen to reward candidates who demonstrate they can use the text material in an intelligent manner, in real marketing situations. There should be less emphasis on lengthy expositions of theory. To impress highly, the candidate should show the ability to combine the theory with real life experience and practical understanding of how it can be effectively applied. In the examination this will involve careful interpretation of case material and good use of supporting examples. Above all, the *Marketing Operations* course should result in marketing practitioners who carry out their jobs as effectively as possible with a heightened awareness of some nuances of the subject of marketing.

THE EXAMINATION PAPER

Assessment methods and format of the paper

	Number of marks
Section A: one minicase study with compulsory questions	50
Section B: any two questions from five (equal marks)	50
	100

Time allowed: 3 hours

Analysis of past papers

June 1995

Part A

1   *Minicase: Ben & Jerry's takes on Haagen-Dazs*
     (a)   Social responsibility issues and the benefits of involvement in such issues
     (b)   Marketing planning and its use in becoming established in an overseas market
     (c)   Areas covered by a detailed marketing plan

Part B

2   Market segmentation and its practical benefits
3   Using Ansoff's matrix as the basis for seeking out new marketing opportunities
4   Services marketing: characteristics, the extended marketing mix and the role of people in the service organisation
5   Approaches to marketing control and evaluation
6   International expansion and the impact of the marketing environment on the marketing mix.

December 1994

Part A

1   *Minicase: Computer games for all*
     (a)   Categories of information required for a marketing audit to provide input into the marketing planning process
     (b)   Legal, regulatory, ethical and social responsibility constraints
     (c)   Opportunities arising from co-operative deals

Part B

2   The effect on marketing programmes of variables in the marketing environment
3   Ethics and social responsibility issues
4   Market segmentation and its benefits; base variables appropriate in the motor industry
5   Characteristics of industrial markets
6   Organising marketing activities in the UK and overseas

Analysis of specimen paper

The questions in the specimen paper published by the CIM are included in the bank of illustrative questions at the end of the text with BPP's suggested solutions. They cover the following topics

STUDY CHECKLIST

This page is designed to help you chart your progress through the Study Text, including the illustrative questions at the back of it. You can tick off each topic as you study and try questions on it. Insert the dates you complete the chapters and questions in the relevant boxes. You will thus ensure that you are on track to complete your study before the exam.

	Text chapters *Date completed*	Illustrative questions *Question numbers*	*Date completed*

PART A: ANALYSIS OF MARKETING OPPORTUNITIES

1	Marketing opportunities		1	
2	Segmenting markets, targeting and positioning		2	

PART B: THE MARKETING PLANNING PROCESS

3	Introduction to marketing planning		3	
4	Developing marketing objectives and strategies		4	
5	The detailed planning process		5, 6	

PART C: MARKETING ORGANISATION

6	Organising marketing activities		7	
7	Marketing control and evaluation		8	

PART D: MANAGING OUTSIDE RESOURCES

8	Managing outside resources		9	

PART E: SELECTED MARKETING APPLICATIONS

9	Business-to-business, services and charity marketing		10 - 12	
10	International marketing		13	

PART F: LEGAL, ETHICS AND WIDER ISSUES

11	Marketing ethics		14	
12	Marketing and social responsibility		15	
13	Wider issues		16	

 BPP Publishing

Part A
Analysis of marketing opportunities

Chapter 1

MARKETING OPPORTUNITIES

This chapter covers the following topics.

1   Marketing opportunity

2   Factors to consider in analysing marketing opportunities

3   Using SWOT analysis

4   Analysis of an organisation's internal capabilities

5   Analysis of an organisation's marketing environment

6   Macro-environmental factors

7   Mircro-environmental factors

Introduction

Planning is a central aspect of the marketing manager's role. Effective planning enables the organisation to co-ordinate resources and direct their use towards the achievement of clearly defined goals. Planning aims to establish control and to reduce uncertainty and 'surprises' by marshalling knowledge and analysing the factors which are at work in a particular situation.

Beginning to plan involves, in the first instance, a careful and systematic appraisal of where the firm is at the moment. This usually involves looking first at the internal situation, at those factors which are directly under managerial influence, and then at the external environment, at competitors, customers, marketing, economies, the society itself, and sometimes beyond.

In this chapter, we explain how an organisation analyses the internal situation and the external environment. Important techniques introduced here are SWOT analysis and PEST analysis

1   MARKETING OPPORTUNITY

1.1   A marketing opportunity exists whenever there is a gap between demand and supply. When there is an unfulfilled demand, an opportunity exists for an enterprising marketer to fulfil this by supplying suitable goods and services at the right time, at the right place and at the right price. For example, in the UK a demand may exist for alcoholic beverages outside normal pub opening hours, especially during hot weather. A pub which opens earlier, subject to the constraints of current licensing laws, can make a profit by fulfilling this demand, ie exploiting this marketing opportunity.

1.2   The tightening of the drink/drive laws in Europe, and an awareness of possible negative effects of alcohol has led to an increase in demand for low alcohol beers and lagers. This provided a marketing opportunity for those brewers who were able to identify and close this gap between demand and supply.

1.3   Marketers need to recognise that demand changes over time, due to changes in the so-called environmental factors (sometimes classified as Political, Economic, Sociological, Technological) and competition. For example, increased concern over health in the western world has provided marketing opportunities for all sorts of diets, sporting equipment and health clubs, as well as for books on how to keep healthy and a great variety of lotions and potions.

1.4   Equally, demand for existing goods and services will normally diminish over time due to technological advances and/or changes in fashion. To stay in business therefore, a company needs to modify its goods and services or provide new goods and services in order to meet changing customer wants and needs.

1.5   Alternatively a company may identify new markets for existing goods and services, for example a demand for British bread in Paris and a demand for British stores such as Marks and Spencer and Sainsbury in France.

1.6   Companies need to be continuously on the lookout for marketing opportunities if they wish to grow. Marketing growth opportunities have been classified by Ansoff as falling under four general categories. (We will develop these ideas further when we look at marketing planning.)

(a)   *Market penetration,* selling existing products into existing markets.
(b)   *Market development,* selling existing products into new markets.
(c)   *Product development,* selling new products into existing markets.
(d)   *Diversification,* selling new products into new markets.

1.7   Would-be marketers and firms wishing to stay in business must be capable of both recognising and exploiting marketing opportunities, ideally before competitors do so. They must also be capable of analysing these opportunities so as to quantify demand and to determine an appropriate marketing mix. These requisites imply an adequate and continuous supply of marketing information ideally formalised in a MkIS (Marketing Information System).

1.8   In summary, a marketing opportunity exists whenever circumstances allow an organisation to take advantage of demand from particular group of people or indeed from other organisations.

Capitalising on marketing opportunities

1.9   Marketing opportunities may present themselves, or be identified, in several ways, but unless an organisation is well organised, it will be unable to capitalise on these opportunities. While remaining flexible enough to adjust to opportunities when they arise, successful organisations must:

(a)   be in control of their direction and development as much as possible;

(b)   have a realistic knowledge of themselves, of their capacities and limitations;

(c)   be aware of the environment within which they operate, and use that knowledge effectively.

2   FACTORS TO CONSIDER IN ANALYSING MARKETING OPPORTUNITIES

2.1   The main factors to be taken into account by the marketing manager can be represented by the 'four P's' of the marketing mix. Other managers might well be concerned with other factors, for instance, sales or production managers might well be concerned with technological aspects, raw material prices or competitor activity.

2.2   In addition, marketing planning is directed by corporate planning, although the two are intimately connected. The corporate audit of product/market strengths and weaknesses, and much of its external environmental analysis is directly informed by the marketing audit. The marketing department is probably the most important source of information for the development of corporate strategy, and represents the starting point for developing the marketing plan, and identifying the key marketing controllables which can be manipulated in pursuit of objectives. (We will examine the relationship between marketing planning and corporate planning further when we look at marketing planning in more detail.)

2.3   As a first step, an internal audit is carried out to examine the present position of the organisation in terms of its internal strengths and weaknesses. Internal factors are classified as the *controllable variables,* that is to say, those which can be influenced by actions taken by managers.

The position and situation audit at corporate level

2.4 At a corporate level the internal factors are sometimes described as the five M's, representing the functional areas of the business.

  (a) Men and women - its human resources and organisation
  (b) Money   - its financial health
  (c) Materials   - supply sources and products
  (d) Machines   - the production facilities, its fixed assets, capacity etc
  (e) Markets   - its reputation, position and market prospects

2.5 Within this list you also need to remember the less obvious intangibles like goodwill, brand names, patents, trademarks and development work in progress.

2.6 Gathering this information involves obtaining answers to the following sort of questions.

  (a) *Men and women*

      (i) *Labour.* What is the size of the labour force? What are their skills? How much are they paid? What are total labour costs? What proportion of the organisation's added value or sales revenue is accounted for by labour costs? How efficient is the workforce? What is the rate of labour turnover? How good or bad are industrial relations?

      (ii) *Management.* What is the size of the management team? What are its specialist skills? What management development and career progression exists? How well has management performed in achieving targets in the past? How hierarchical is the management structure?

  (b) *Money*

      (i) *Finance.* What are the company's financial resources? What are its debt and gearing ratios?

      (ii) *Working capital.* How much working capital does the organisation use? What are the average turnover periods for stocks and debtors? What is the credit policy of the organisation? What credit is taken from suppliers? What is the level of bad debts? How is spare cash utilised by the treasury department? How are foreign exchange transactions dealt with? How profitable is our product portfolio?

  (c) *Materials*

      Where do they come from? Who supplies them? What percentage of the total cost of sales is accounted for by materials? What are wastage levels? Are new materials being developed for the market by suppliers?

  (d) *Machines*

      Fixed assets. What fixed assets does the organisation use? What is their current value (on a going concern value and on a break-up value basis)? What is the amount of revenue and profit per £1 invested in fixed assets? How old are the assets? Are they technologically advanced or out of date? What are the organisation's repairs and replacement policies? What is the *percentage fill* in the organisation's capacity? This is particularly important for service industries, such as cinemas, football grounds and trains, where fixed costs are high and resources need to be utilised as much as possible to earn good profits. R & D experience and level of technological expertise should also be assessed.

  (e) *Markets*

      Market share, reputation, level of competition, deals with distributors and the level of goodwill etc. is the company customer oriented and how is the customer contact/service perceived?

2.7 The audit of the company's resources involves asking '*What have we got, and how is it being used?*' Assessment of a 'random collection' of resources is insufficient however; resources are of no value unless they are organised into systems. A resource audit needs to consider how well or how badly resources are being used, and whether or not the organisation's systems are effective and efficient.

2.8   The resource audit should also assess how well resources are being *controlled*. Some resources might be used both efficiently and effectively, but *control* of the resources could still be poor because, for example:

(a)   not enough of the resources were obtained, and even better results could be achieved if more of the resources were obtained and utilised;

(b)   key resources could have been used even more efficiently and effectively if they had been diverted to a different purpose.

Limiting factors

2.9   Every organisation operates under resource constraints. There is never enough money or skilled labour or key components supplies etc. It is very important that any such limiting factors be identified and quantified.

2.10   A limiting factor or *key factor* is anything which limits the activity of an entity. An entity seeks to optimise the benefit it obtains from the limiting factor. Examples are a shortage of supply of a resource and a restriction on sales at a particular price.

2.11   Finance seems always in (relatively) limited supply, but there could well be other resources or other factors which restrict the effective use of what finance is available, to limit the ability of the organisation to achieve its objectives. For example, a shortage of skilled labour, deterioration in roads or railways, problems with raw material suppliers, etc might put an organisation at a serious disadvantage against competitors and so restrict the ability of the organisation to improve its profitability and return on capital.

2.12   Other examples of limiting factors include the following.

(a)   A shortage of suitable plant.

(b)   A limited number of key personnel, such as salespeople with technical knowledge.

(c)   A restricted distribution network which may be inadequate for a national market coverage.

(d)   A very small number of managers with knowledge about finance, or overseas markets.

(e)   Inadequate design resources to develop new products or services.

2.13   In strategic planning, once limiting factors have been identified, planners need to develop plans which make use of the resources which are actually available, in order to counter this problem.

Environmental analysis

2.14   This environmental analysis is an extension of a position audit. Instead of getting answers to the question 'Where are we now?' (position audit), environmental analysis asks the question '*What is the environment in which we operate going to be like?*'

2.15   It is this recognition of what factors in the *external* environment are relevant, in conjunction with a realistic assessment of how the external environment is *changing*, which ensures that the organisation is fully aware of both the emergent opportunities and also threats posed by that environment.

3   USING SWOT ANALYSIS

3.1   Collecting the information about the current position and environment is one thing, but to be of real value to the planners it needs to be *assessed*. There are a number of factors to be considered and one of the most useful tools for sorting and analysing information is a SWOT analysis.

3.2   This stands for strengths, weaknesses, opportunities and threats. SWOT analysis is a management tool which can be used in a wide variety of situations. *Its value is as a technique to help you sort information* and it does not, in itself, provide ready made answers. A SWOT analysis can usefully be carried out at corporate, marketing or product levels or when trying to compare alternative projects or courses of action.

3.3   SWOT analysis is undertaken as part of the preparation in planning. The quality of a recommendation will reflect the thoroughness of the analysis, but it is important to realise that the quality of the information which is used, and the pre-suppositions of the manager, will determine the value of the analysis it provides.

3.4   At a corporate level, SWOT analysis helps by providing a framework to build up the full picture using the information and evaluations available to the manager.

3.5   Corporate appraisal has been defined as 'a critical assessment of the strengths and weaknesses, opportunities and threats in relation to the internal and environmental factors affecting an entity in order to establish its condition prior to the preparation of the long- term plan.'

(a)   *Strengths and weaknesses analysis* involves looking at the particular strengths and weaknesses of the organisation itself and its product/service range. It is an *internal appraisal*.

(b)   An analysis of *opportunities and threats* is concerned with profit-making opportunities in the business environment, and with identifiable threats, for example falling demand, new competition, government legislation etc. It is therefore an *external appraisal*. (*Note*. Opportunities and threats would require similar treatment for organisations in the non-profit making sector, but the nature of such factors would be necessarily different.)

SWOT analysis

3.6   This simple technique provides a method of organising information in identifying possible strategic direction. The basic principle is that an organisation or its environment can be described in terms of features, each described as either a Strength, Weakness, Opportunity or Threat. An *opportunity* is simply any feature of the external environment which creates conditions which are advantageous to the firm in relation to a particular objective or set of objectives. A *threat* is any environmental development which will present problems and may hinder the achievement of organisational objectives. An opportunity to some firms may constitute a threat to others.

3.7   A *strength* may be a particular skill or distinctive competence which the organisation possesses and which will aid it in achieving its stated objectives. Examples may include experience in specific types of markets or specific skills possessed by employees, or factors such as a firm's reputation for quality or customer service. A *weakness* is simply any aspect of the company which may hinder the achievement of specific objectives. This may be, for example, limited experience of certain markets/technologies, or the extent of financial resources available.

3.8   This information is presented as a matrix of strengths, weaknesses, opportunities and threats. There are several points to note about presentation and interpretation. First, effective SWOT analysis does not simply require a categorisation of information, but also requires some *evaluation* of the relative importance of the various factors. These features are only relevant if they are actually perceived to exist by the consumers.

Producing a listing of corporate features which internal personnel regard as strengths/weaknesses is of little relevance if they are not perceived as such by the organisation's consumers. In the same vein, threats and opportunities are conditions presented by the external environment and they should be *independent* of the firm.

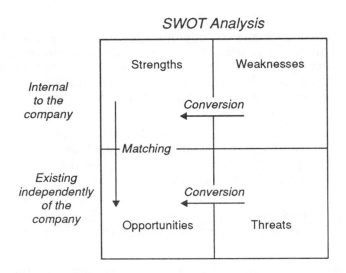

The practice of corporate SWOT analysis

3.9 Internal and external appraisals are brought together in the form of SWOT analysis. Potential strategies are evaluated and alternative strategies emerge from this analysis. Exploitation of competitive edge or identification of competitor weaknesses will provide the opportunity to develop appropriate products or services. At the same time, major weaknesses and threats should be countered, or a contingency strategy or corrective strategy developed.

3.10 SWOT analysis is often presented using a cruciform chart, as in the diagram above. This involves a tabular listing of the significant strengths and weaknesses and opportunities and threats to present the conclusions of the analysis. In the example below, the development of a single, simple potential strategy from the analysis is illustrated.

Strengths	*Weaknesses*
£10 million of capital available. Production expertise and appropriate marketing skills.	Heavy reliance on a small number of customers. Limited product range, with no new products and expected market decline. Small marketing organisation.
Threats	*Opportunities*
Major competitor has already entered the new market.	Government tax incentives for new investment. Growing demand in a new market, although customers so far relatively small in number.

3.11 Here, it might be possible to surmise that the company faces the danger of losing its existing markets and must diversify its products and markets. The new market opportunity exists to be exploited and since the number of customers is currently few, the relatively small size of the existing marketing force would not be an immediate hindrance. A strategic plan could be developed to buy new equipment and to use existing production and marketing to enter the new market, with a view to rapid expansion. Careful planning of manpower, equipment, facilities, research and development etc. would be required and there would be an objective to meet the threat of competition so as to obtain a substantial share of a growing market. The cost of entry at this early stage of market development should not be unacceptably high.

3.12 In this example, a strategy emerges readily from our simplified cruciform chart. Reality is likely to be much less clear-cut. In practice, a combination of individual strategies and a complete analysis and evaluation of all the alternatives would be required.

4   ANALYSIS OF AN ORGANISATION'S INTERNAL CAPABILITIES

4.1 As we have already seen, an internal appraisal seeks to identify the following.

(a) Shortcomings in the company's present skills and resources.
(b) Strengths which the company should seek to exploit.

4.2 Strengths and weaknesses analysis is internal to the company and is intended to shape its approach to the external world. For instance, the identification of shortcomings in skills or resources could lead to a planned acquisition programme or staff recruitment and training. First, the strengths and weaknesses analysis involves looking at the findings of the position audit.

4.3 The analysis seeks to express, qualitatively or quantitatively, which areas of the business have strengths to exploit, and which areas have weaknesses which must be improved. Although every area of the business should be investigated, only the areas of significant strength or weakness should warrant further attention.

4.4 The appraisal should give particular attention to the following.

(a) *A study of past accounts and the use of ratios*. By looking at *trends*, or by comparing ratios (if possible) with those of other firms in a similar industry, it might be possible to identify strengths and weaknesses in major areas of the business. This is a key area of strengths and weaknesses analysis, and here, financial data and techniques of assessment provide 'hard' data for decision making.

(b) *Product position and product-market mix*.

(c) *Cash and financial structure*. If a company intends to expand or diversify, it will need cash or sufficient financial standing in order to acquire subsidiaries or for investing in new capacity.

(d) *Cost structure*. If a company operates with high fixed costs and relatively low variable costs, it might be in a relatively weak position with regards to production capacity. High volumes of production and sale might be required to break even. In contrast, a company with low fixed costs might be more flexible and adaptable so that it should be able to operate at a lower breakeven point.

(e) *Managerial ability*. While objective data should be used, the danger is that management may well overestimate their own ability or be unable to form a useful evaluation.

4.5 Typically, the analysis would use information from the following areas of company activity.

(a) *Marketing*

   (i)   Success rate of new product launches.

   (ii) Advertising campaigns - evaluating advertising strategies and the success of individual campaigns.

   (iii) Market shares and market sizes - is the organisation in a strong or weak position?

   (iv) Portfolio of business units in various types of markets - new, growth, mature and declining markets.

   (v)   Sales force organisation and performance.

(vi)   Service quality.

(vii) Customer care strategies: nature of markets targeted.

(b) *Products*

(i)   Sales by market, area, product groups, outlets etc.

(ii)   Margins and contributions to profits from individual products.

(iii) Product quality.

(iv)   Product portfolio - age and structure of markets in which products are placed.

(v)   Price elasticity of demand of products - price sensitivity of demand for products.

(c) *Distribution*

(i)   Delivery service standards - lead times for competitors and products.
(ii)   Warehouse delivery fleet capacity.
(iii) Geographical availability of products.

(d) *Research and development (R & D)*

(i)   R & D projects in relation to marketing plans.
(ii)   Expenditure on R & D relative to available assets.
(iii) Evaluation of R & D in new products/variations on existing products.
(iv)   Appropriateness of R & D workload and schedules to competitor activity.

(e) *Finance*

(i)   Availability of short term and long term funds, cash flow.

(ii)   Contribution of each product to cash flow.

(iii) Returns on investment from individual products.

(iv)   Accounting ratios to identify areas of strength or weakness in performance (for example asset turnover ratios, liquidity ratios etc).

(f) *Plant and equipment and other facilities. Production*

(i)   Age, value, production capacity and suitability of plant and equipment.

(ii)   Valuation of all assets.

(iii) Location of land and buildings, their value, area, use, length of lease, current book value.

(iv)   Achievement of 'critical mass' of output capacity, so that it can achieve maximum economies of scale and minimum production costs.

(v)   Asset evaluation (age, condition, quality, property etc)

(g) *Management and staff*

(i)   Age profile.
(ii)   Skills and attitudes.
(iii) State of industrial relations, morale and labour turnover.
(iv)   Training and recruitment facilities.
(v)   Manpower utilisation.
(vi)   Management team strengths and weaknesses.

(h) *Business management: organisation*

(i)   Organisation structure in relation to the organisation's needs and functional divisions (for example production, marketing, finance etc) or product/market profit centres.

(ii)   Appropriateness of management style and philosophy.

(iii) Communication and information systems.

(i) *Raw material and finished goods stocks*

(i)   The sources and security of supply.
(ii)   Number and description of items.
(iii) Turnover periods.

(iv)   Storage capacity .
(v)   Obsolescence and deterioration.
(vi)   Pilfering, wastage.

Example: report

4.6   When the analysis has been carried out, the following type of report might be produced.

Strengths

(a)   Marketing, products and markets
   (i)   Products A, B and C are market leaders.
   (ii)   Product D, new product launch, high profit potential.
   (iii)   Good brand images.
   (iv)   Good relations with suppliers and dealers.
   (v)   Good packaging and advertising appeal.

(b)   Production
   (i)   New factory in North West, fully operational for next year.
   (ii)   Thorough quality inspection standards.

(c)   Finance
   (i)   £0.5 million cash available from internal resources.
   (ii)   Further £2.0 million overdraft facility, so far unused.

(d)   Management and staff
   (i)   High skills in marketing areas of packaging, sales promotion, advertising and sales generally.
   (ii)   Good labour relations, except at one plant which has low productivity.

Weaknesses

(a)   Marketing
   (i)   Products X, Y and Z contribute no profit.
   (ii)   Products P, Q and R are declining and will lose profitability in three years.
   (iii)   Sales of product D are dependent upon a high level of sales of complementary products (for example razor blades and razors).
   (iv)   No new products, except for D, have been successfully launched in the last two years.

(b)   Research and development
   (i)   No major new products have been derived from R & D for two years. Becoming too dependent on acquisition for additions to product range.
   (ii)   Little control over R & D budget.

(c)   Production
   (i)   Plant at most factories has an average age of 8.7 years.
   (ii)   New developments could threaten ability to compete.
   (iii)   High level of spoiled goods on lines 3, 7, 9 at one location.
   (iv)   Low productivity on all lines at one plant.

(d)   Management and staff
   (i)   Poor labour relations at plant with low productivity.
   (ii)   Senior executives approaching retirement with no clearly recognisable successor.
   (iii)   Success of the organisation too dependent on senior executive charisma.

5   ANALYSIS OF AN ORGANISATION'S MARKETING ENVIRONMENT

5.1   The internal appraisal highlights areas within the company which are strong and which might therefore be exploited more fully, and weaknesses where some 'defensive' planning might be required to protect the company from poor results. Following the position audit and the environmental analysis, external appraisal aims to identify profit-making *opportunities* which can be exploited using the company's strengths and also (in order) to anticipate environmental *threats* (a declining economy, competitors' actions, government legislation, industrial unrest etc) against which the company must protect itself.

5.2   This is the 'opportunities and threats' part of SWOT analysis.

5.3   *Opportunities* involve analysis of the following.

(a)   Opportunities in the environment within which the firm operates.
(b)   Evaluation of profit-making potential.
(c)   The capacity of organisations to exploit identified opportunities.
(d)   Strength of competition in capacity to exploit opportunities.
(e)   The company's comparative performance potential in this field of opportunity.

The opportunities might involve product development, market development, market penetration or diversification. Realism is particularly important in the evaluation process.

5.4   *Threats* involve the following issues.

(a)   Threats to the company or its business environment.

(b)   Competitors' position in relation to these threats.

(c)   Effects on the company: capacity to resist threats, corrective action, use of contingency strategies.

5.5   Opportunities and threats may arise in the following areas.

(a)   *Economic:* unemployment, the level of wages and salaries, the expected total market behaviour for products, total customer demand, the growth and decline of industries and suppliers, general investment levels etc. At an international level, world production and the volume of international trade, demand, recessions, import controls, exchange rates.

(b)   *Government:* legislation involving, for example, pollution control or a ban on certain products would be a *threat* to various industries, but also an opportunity for selling, eg lead-free petrol and suitable   cars. Taxation incentives, rent-free factory buildings, or investment grants might be available for exploitation. Government policy may be to increase expenditure on housing, defence, schools and hospitals or roads and transport and this gives opportunities to private companies and the relevant government organisations alike. Political upheaval might damage market and investment prospects, especially overseas.

(c)   *Technology:* new products appearing, or cheaper means of production or distribution will clearly have profound implications in these types of analysis.

(d)   *Social*

(i)   Social attitudes will have a significant effect on customer demand and employee attitudes.

(ii)   Social issues such as environmental pollution, women's roles, and the needs to solve social problems offer opportunities for new products and services.

(iii)   Demographic change and population structure will provide continuing product opportunities. There are recognised opportunities for growth in the personal pensions market.

(iv)   Unemployment will strongly affect the total spending power of consumers. This has been chronic and long term in certain parts of the UK.

5.6   Macro-environmental factors which cannot be controlled are as follows.

(a)   **P**olitical (and legal)
(b)   **E**conomic

(c) Social

(d) Technological

Mnemonic alternatives for this list are PEST or SLEPT (social, legal, economic, political, technological). It should be noted that *competitor activity* is also vitally important. This has resulted in some people using the mnemonic SLEPT/C.

Competitors

5.7 The micro-environment should not be ignored. A complete analysis of current and potential competitors, the market situation and degree of competition and their comparative strengths and weaknesses should be undertaken. Michael Porter suggests that analysis of competitors should involve the following.

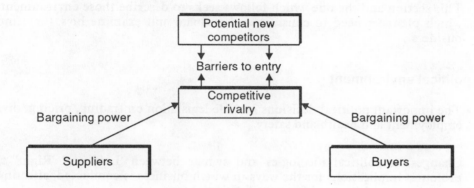

5.8 Future competitors' strategies must be anticipated. It is especially important to identify competitors' weaknesses in export markets, or where foreign competitors might penetrate home markets. British industry in recent years has called for protection against Japanese cars, foreign textiles and imported fish, in the face of external threats. Certain industries and individual firms have successfully resisted these threats, however.

5.9 To decide whether it is under threat of a takeover bid by any other company, comparison of strengths and weaknesses of any potential buyers is needed.

6   MACRO-ENVIRONMENTAL FACTORS

External factors influencing planning

6.1 Business plans are always developed within a wider environment within which the organisation is operating. They must necessarily take into account the opportunities and threats which are emerging and, in order to ensure plans will be effective, this necessitates a thorough appraisal of the relevant environment. This *situational audit* ensures that plans are relevant, realistic and achievable for the organisation.

6.2 External influences impact on both corporate and marketing plans. Consequently the following steps are essential.

(a) We must recognise which aspects of the environment impact on the organisation.

(b) We must identify which environmental changes might create threats, opportunities and organisational problems - and develop appropriate responses to these.

The environment: definition

6.3 The term 'environment' covers all the economic, political, social, cultural, legal, technological and demographic influences acting on the markets within which the organisation operates. It also encompasses influences on customers and the behaviour of competitors in these 'markets'. All these factors have an impact on the performance of the organisation, but cannot be controlled by management actions. They are therefore often referred to as the 'uncontrollable' factors.

6.4   Strategic planners must firstly take account of the environmental influences which exist, and try to forecast how these might develop, so as to produce plans that are realistic and achievable. As the environment constantly changes, this is difficult. Michael Porter has written the following.

   (a)   'The essence of formulating competitive strategy is relating a company to its environment.'

   (b)   'Every industry has an underlying structure or set of fundamental economic and technical characteristics ... The strategist must learn what makes the environment tick.'
                                                                         (Porter, *Competitive Strategy*)

6.5   This section and the one which follows seeks to describe those environmental variables which planners need to consider and evaluate and examine how they impact on the business.

The political environment

6.6   The important political decisions include legislation on trading, pricing, dividends, tax, employment and health and safety.

6.7   Changes in political ideologies and swings between 'Left' and 'Right' clearly have profound implications for the ways in which business is conducted, affecting the power of managers and the workforce, and their rights.

6.8   In the UK under 'Thatcherism', small business enterprise and competition were all championed. Public sector firms were privatised and services put out to competitive tender. Wide ranging changes that affected many business sectors.

6.9   Other areas that are under political influence in a mixed economy include the following.

   (a)   The government controls much of the economy, being the nation's largest supplier, employer, customer and investor. Changes in policy can affect various industries. For example, aerospace and defence are particularly vulnerable to shifts in political decisions.

   (b)   Nationalism can impact in various ways. Shipping and airline industries have been affected as many countries build up their own fleets. Other effects include resistance to the power exercised by multinationals in some countries, and the policies which insist on nationals being given positions of responsibility where multinationals are operating.

Political change

6.10   Planning needs to take account of changes in the political climate.

6.11   Some political changes cannot easily be planned for. There was, for instance, a world-wide call for economic sanctions against South Africa during the apartheid period. Suggestions were made that all British Airways flights to and from South Africa should be banned. British Airways could not develop long-term plans to respond to specific political decisions such as this, but given the likelihood that national airlines will be subjected to political pressures and restrictions, organisations such as British Airways could develop the strategy objective of not relying on a small number of routes for their profitability. In the event of a political ban on a part of its business, an organisation would still be able to fall back on its remaining business without undue worries about profitability and survival. Conflict can be sudden and unpredicted; the Gulf War, Rwanda and Yugoslavia are recent examples.

6.12 Strategic planners should try to take the following into account.

(a) The possible impact of political change on their organisation.

(b) The impact such political change might have.

(c) How far reaching any such change might be.

(d) The likelihood of change taking place and the possible need for contingency plans.

(e) What needs to be done to cope with the change - sometimes called scenario planning.

The economic environment

6.13 The economy affects all organisations, both commercial and non-commercial. The rate at which it grows affects the rate at which demand for goods and services changes. Growth is a likely indicator of increasing demand. An increase in gross national product per head of the population might result in a greater demand for private cars and decreased demand for public transport. Alternatively, it might lead to a greater demand for certain domestic consumer goods, such as video recorders, dishwashers and compact disk players - ie luxury goods.

6.14 Regional variations in growth rate will result in differential demand. If growth is accompanied by an increase in the size of the public sector, funded by higher taxation, then increased demand may manifest itself in public sector areas, eg in demand for new school buildings, roads or more police cars.

6.15 Economic influences include the following.

(a) *At a regional or national level*

(i) The rate of inflation.
(ii) Unemployment and the availability of manpower.
(iii) Interest rates.
(iv) The balance of trade and foreign exchange rates.
(v) The level and type of taxation.
(vi) The propensity to save within the community.
(vii) The availability of credit.

(b) *At an international level*

(i) Comparative growth rates, inflation rates, interest rates and wage rates in other countries.

(ii) The extent of protectionist measures against imports.

(iii) The nature and extent of exchange controls in various countries.

(iv) The development of international economic communities such as the European Community and the prospects of international trade agreements between countries.

(v) The levels of corporate and personal taxation in different countries.

6.16 The state of the economy will inevitably be taken into account in the planning process. Increased demand during periods of expansion will create a planning need to satisfy demand. In times of recession, contracting demand will place the emphasis on cost-effectiveness, continuing profitability, survival and competition.

The strategic planning process depends heavily on economic forecasts and information about economic trends.

Economic trends - regional, national and international

6.17 Three levels of economic trend analysis need to be considered; regional (area) trends, national trends and international trends.

6.18   The *local* geographical environment is important, whether it is in a growth area full of modern thriving industry, such as Milton Keynes, or an area of urban decay like parts of the North East, Clydeside or Merseyside. This will affect wage rates, availability of labour, disposable income of local consumers, unemployment, the provision of roads and other services etc.

6.19   Relevant *national* economic trends may include the prospects for national economic growth and growth in national income per head of population, trends in price inflation, unemployment, international trade, the balance of payments and taxation levels. These are factors over which an organisation has no direct control. They are referred to as 'exogenous' variables (ie external, or arising from outside).

6.20   These must be located within the context of *world trends*. These can have an important influence on the future of any company with plans to trade abroad, whether in buying imports or selling as exporters. More and more markets are being opened to international competition, throughout Europe and also in the rest of the world.

6.21   Four economic groupings (described below) within the world are often identified. Other writers see important distinctions between the North and the South.

Category	*Characteristic*
Western democracies (including Japan)	Stable economic growth although variable between different countries; politically stable; low population growth; low growth in basic industries; emphasis more on high technology industries, service industries (for example leisure) and personal care; increased market segmentation and choice for the consumer.
Former Eastern bloc countries	This includes Eastern Europe and the successor states to the USSR. Bias toward heavy industry, technologically backward, a primitive service sector, and undergoing economic upheaval. The privatisation of many state industries and the opening of economies mean that major potential new opportunities and risks are emerging for Western organisations.
Less developed countries (LDCs)	Living standards are low, with little hope of improvement; rising population; low education standards; inadequate infrastructure of roads, telecommunications, financial markets etc.
Developing nations	Fast growth in GNP; low wages by Western standards; consumer goods are scarce; infrastructure being provided.

6.22   Argenti identifies one particular factor which translates world trends and national trends down to the level of the small and medium-sized company, and that is the implication of economic trends upon organisation size itself. Two developments in particular seem evident.

(a)   For standard, basic goods in mass markets, there is a trend towards larger organisations, with a few companies supplying virtually the entire world demand (for example motor cars).

(b)   At the other end of the size spectrum, there is a continuing emergence of products and services with an individual personal appeal, leading to product differentiation and market segmentation. Here the trend may well be towards small company operations and greater specialisation.

Economic change

6.23   The economic environment changes continually, through cycles of growth and recession in which interest rates and foreign exchange rates fluctuate.

6.24   Recent changes to the European Community, including the formation of the European Union, aim to move towards the creation of a single market. These will have a number of implications.

(a)   Certain technical barriers to the free movement of goods between countries in the EU are removed. Technical barriers fragment the market, and force producers to manufacture modified goods, at higher cost, for each separate fragment. Barriers are created by differences in:

(i)   national product standards for the quality and safety of goods. Harmonised European standards are being established;

(ii)   food laws, for example on food labelling, and safety and hygiene standards;

(iii)   regulations for controlling the access of pharmaceuticals (medicines) to the market.

(b)   *Public purchasing.* EU rules will open up the market for goods purchased by governments of member countries, by making sure that all companies in the Community have an equal chance to seek individual public contracts.

(c)   *Telecommunications.* The EU is hoping to open up telecommunications markets by eliminating differences in national standards for telecommunications equipment.

(d)   *Information technology.* The EU is promoting the creation of a common set of standards for IT equipment (OSI standards).

(e)   *Financial services.* Harmonisation measures in the provision of financial services between EU countries include the liberalisation of capital movements, common regulations for banks and banking activities and removal of barriers preventing the provision of cross-border insurance services.

(f)   *Capital movements.* The EU has nearly achieved the complete liberalisation of capital movements within the Community.

(g)   *Transport.* Measures are being taken to liberalise transport services, so as to increase competition and make it easier for companies in one EU country to compete in other EU countries. Liberalisation measures are being applied to road haulage, shipping and civil aviation.

(h)   *Professional services.* Most restrictions on the free movement of labour applied to accountants, lawyers and teachers have now been removed.

6.25   Before the Single European Market a domestic UK firm had a home market of some 56 million people; since 31 December 1992 it has grown to 350 million.

6.26   The Department of Trade and Industry listed seven key questions of business strategy, which UK firms (and other EU firms) should face up to, in view of these changes.

(a)   How has the market changed for our business?

(b)   Should we shift from being a UK firm with a UK market, to a European firm with a European market?

(c)   If we became a European firm with a European market, would this alter the *scale of our operations*?

(d)   In what ways will we become vulnerable in our existing markets to new or greater competition?

(e)   Is our management structure suitable for exploiting new opportunities, and taking defensive measures against new threats?

(f)   Should we be seeking mergers or takeovers to strengthen our market position, broaden our product range, or spread our financial risk?

(g) Who in the firm is going to be responsible for making the key decisions about how to exploit the single market opportunities?

The social and cultural environment

6.27 Social change involves changes in the nature, attitudes and habits of society. Social changes are continually happening, and *trends* can be identified. Such changes include the following.

(a) A fall in the length of working week, falling demand for labour and so high unemployment in the long term, earlier retirement etc. There have also been changes in housing characteristics, and there are continuing changes in the nature and standard of education.

Rising standards of living may result in wider ownership of automatic dishwashers, microwave ovens, compact disk players and sailing boats. All these changes have implications for sports, leisure and holiday industries. But perhaps the most significant recent social change in the UK has been the emergence of 'green issues' and public concern for the world's environment.

We will look at green issues in Chapter 12.

(b) Society's attitude to business and companies: in the UK, increasing social obligations and responsibilities are being heaped on to companies, not least with respect to environmental protection and ethical conduct (towards customers, employees etc). At the present time there is an unresolved debate about Sunday trading.

We will look at ethical behaviour in marketing in Chapter 11.

(c) The workforce itself. There has been a decline in 'blue collar jobs' and an increasing proportion of people employed hold 'white collar' clerical, supervisory or management jobs. The potential implications to firms of (social) trends among the workforce should be readily identifiable. Some commentators have detected hostility to manufacturing industry, as opposed to the professions or financial services, as a cultural factor leading to the UK's relative decline in the manufacturing sector.

We will look at services marketing in Chapter 9.

6.28 B R Jones (1979) classified the social factors in strategic planning in a slightly different way, as follows.

(a) *Underlying factors:* population trends, education policy and the educational standards of the workforce, attitudes to acquiring skills.

(b) *People at work:* the labour market, trade unions and work attitudes. These aspects relate to a politically sensitive area in which organisations are very much at the mercy of legislation and political pressures. For example legislation on equal treatment for men and women, on racial discrimination, minimum wages, redundancy pay, unfair dismissals, laws on strike action and so on.

(c) *Individuals and society:* this is wide ranging although it would include challenges to the existing social order, involvement by junior employees in decisions taken within their organisation, the social responsibility of employers, income and wealth distribution, and spending patterns.

6.29 A key area of change so far as business is concerned has been in the area of consumer credit growth. There has been substantial growth in consumer credit in recent years, with credit card lending accounting for much of the growth. A rapid growth in consumer credit can have significant economic and social implications. Businesses affected could include the following.

(a) Firms that provide credit, for example banks, or retail stores with their own in-store credit cards.

(b) Firms that produce goods which are commonly bought with credit finance, for example house builders and property developers, motor car manufacturers, producers of other consumer durable goods.

6.30 The volume of consumer credit has grown in most developed countries. In the UK, for example, the following characteristics can be observed.

(a) Consumer credit grew substantially in real terms during the 1980s. There were two main aspects.

(i) Credit card borrowing.

(ii) Mortgage borrowing, owing to increases in house prices and 'equity withdrawal' (ie people obtaining extra finance by adding to their existing mortgage).

(b) Credit cards are also commonly used to spread the costs of common transactions, or defer payment.

(c) Social attitudes to borrowing and debt vary from culture to culture, and change over time.

Cultural changes

6.31 Culture refers to the way of living followed within a particular society - its rules, norms, beliefs, actions and so on. Each society has its own culture. There are also specific culture groups.

(a) *Ethnic* and *racial* cultures.

(b) *Religious* cultures.

(c) *Corporate* cultures. Most companies have a distinctive culture, which employees, management in particular, are expected to adopt. This is also something which many companies try to influence and develop.

(d) *Class* cultures. Class is a particularly sensitive issue in the context of UK business.

Cultural variables are particularly significant for marketing in foreign countries. Cultural factors may be represented by the following chart.

The impact of culture

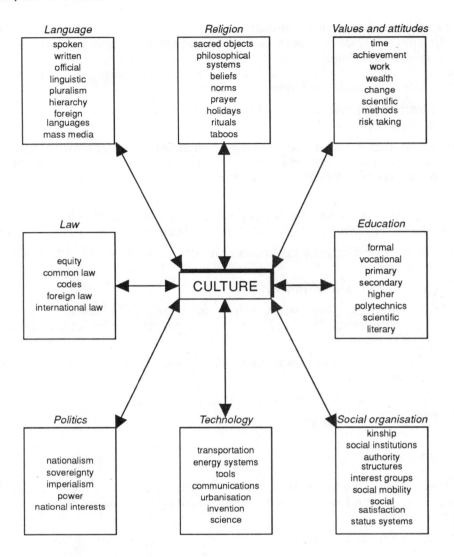

6.32   There is also some variation within cultures. 'Sub-cultures' may be based on a number of different factors such as ethnicity, religion, age etc. Culture varies between countries but also within countries (subculture). Not only do we have restaurants in the UK offering ethnic food (such as Chinese or Indian) but within the UK there are major (although declining) regional differences in the food we eat, haggis in Scotland being one obvious example.

6.33   Language differences have clear marketing implications. For example brand names have to be translated, often leading to entirely different (and sometimes embarrassing) meanings in the new language.

Cultural differences may affect buying patterns in many ways, including the following.

(a)   *What* is bought (style, colours, types of goods/service)?
(b)   *When* are things bought (for example, is Sunday shopping approved of)?
(c)   *How* are things bought (bartering, haggling about price)?
(d)   *Where* are things bought (type of retail outlet)?
(e)   *Why* are things bought (influence of culture on needs and hence motives)?

6.34   Other socio-cultural factors which might be important include the following.

Socio-economic groups

6.35   These are seen by marketers as 'natural' segments. Marketing interest stems from the observable fact that members of particular groups have similar lifestyles, beliefs and values which can and do affect their purchasing behaviour. Socio-economic classification involves taking factors such as occupation, education and income into account. It can be misleading however. In terms of disposable income (the take-home pay of workers) C2 members often have more money than do C1, which obviously affects buying capability.

6.36   Because of criticisms of the A - E classification, more sophisticated measures of socio-economic (SE) group membership have been devised. Other types of SE classification are discussed under segmentation.

6.37   'Psychographic' classifications based on socio-economic groups have been developed which add the person's activities, interests and opinions to the analysis. These analyses identify specific clusters of individuals with similar activities, interests and opinions and putatively, purchasing behaviour.

Family

6.38   Family background is a very strong influence on purchasing behaviour. Family groups 'socialise' future members of society and teach them how to behave in different settings. Family influences are stronger than any others in this respect.

6.39   Family structure is changing in most of the developed world. There are more single person and single family households due to increased divorce rate and population ages. There are now more single person households of all ages. The traditional nuclear family of husband, wife and two children beloved of TV advertisements actually represents a relatively small proportion of all families rather than being the 'norm'.

6.40   The family is a 'purchasing unit' with one member (the buyer) buying on behalf of all members (users) but others in the family influencing the decision (influencers). Joint husband and wife purchasing decisions for major items are common.

6.41   The family is a reference group in that, in marketing decisions, it is used as a reference point. Socio-economic groups are also reference groups in this sense. The immortal phrase 'keeping up with the Jones's' is a useful reminder of a further point: that other groups to which a person belongs or aspires can be strong influences on purchasing and other behaviour. Examples abound. Yacht clubs are synonymous with a particular style of dress (club blazer, for example) whereas working men's clubs conjure up different but no less potent images (such as the cloth cap). Different marketing approaches by suppliers would be necessary for each type of reference group.

Socio-cultural factors which influence consumer behaviour include the following.

(a)   *Economic*

   (i)   Income
   (ii)   Occupation
   (iii)   Career prospects
   (iv)   House type

(b)   *Social*

   (i)   Family
   (ii)   Socio-economic group
   (iii)   Culture
   (iv)   Reference groups
   (v)   Education

(c) *Psychological*

    (i)   Needs
    (ii)   Motivation
    (iii) Personality

(d) *Socio-psychological*

    (i)   Attitudes

(e) *For organisational buyers: organisational*

    (i)   Company needs
    (ii)   Inter-departmental rivalries
    (iii) Performance
    (iv) Buying committee/purchasing officer.

6.42   Various attempts have been made to produce models of how these factors operate.

Models of customer behaviour

6.43   Models attempt to express simply the fundamental elements of a complex process, in this case, to express the interrelationship between variables which influence consumer behaviour. They provide a means for the marketing manager to understand the buying process in order to develop strategies which fit the analysis.

6.44   A simple model attempts to simplify and clarify the purchase decision process by showing it as a series of sequential steps. This type of model is useful to the marketing manager in trying to influence the process. For example, advertising and promotional activity is aimed at the information search stage and after sales service is aimed at the post-purchase evaluation stage.

6.45   The theoretical model tries to show the interrelationship between the various behavioural and economic factors which are involved. The aim is to give the marketing manager a better understanding of the buying process. Here is an example of a well known theoretical model, the Howard-Sheth model of consumer behaviour.

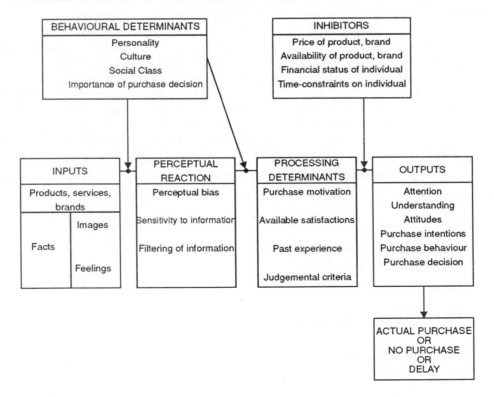

6.46   Culture also operates within the organisation, of course, and corporate cultural change may involve conflicts in, for example:

(a)   a large public company taking over a smaller private company;

(b)   a multinational company establishing a new subsidiary in a different country.

6.47   The integration between 'head office' and the subsidiary might be the critical issue here. For example, the following issues might be relevant.

(a)   How can employees in an acquired company adjust to the culture of the dominant groups?

(b)   What concessions, if any, should head office allow to the 'local' culture of the subsidiary's country? How can language differences be overcome?

The technological environment

6.48   Rapid, and accelerating, technological change has been a feature of the late twentieth century. Technological change has affected organisations as follows.

(a)   *The type of products or services that are made and sold.* Within consumer markets we have seen the emergence of home computers, compact discs and satellite TV; industrial markets have seen the emergence of custom-built microchips, robots and local area networks for office information systems; government markets have seen space rockets and space shuttles. Even minor technological changes, such as the introduction of tennis and squash rackets with graphite frames, fluoride toothpaste and quartz wrist watches are nevertheless vitally important to the firms involved.

(b)   *The way in which products are made.* Modern labour-saving production equipment, and the use of automated systems of design and manufacture have revolutionised manufacturing (so called 'CAD/CAM' systems). This has changed the size and also the nature of labour forces involved.

(c)   *The way in which services are provided.* Computerised cash dispensers and point of sale terminals are examples of this trend.

(d)   *The way in which markets are identified.* Database systems make it easier to analyse the market place. New types of marketing strategy, and new organisational structures, have been developed from these changes.

(e)   *The way in which employees are mobilised.* Computerisation might encourage the 'delayering' of management hierarchies and less workforce skills. It has been said that this 'de-skilling' has shifted the balance of power between workforce and management.

6.49   The effects of technological change are wide-ranging.

(a)   Cuts in production costs and other costs of sale. This may afford the opportunity to reduce prices.

(b)   The development of better quality products and services.

(c)   Developing products and services that did not exist before.

(d)   Provision of improved products or services to customers.

Ethics and social responsibility

6.50   A business must give some consideration to social trends when developing its corporate plan. The activities of businesses also have ethical dimensions. A business has a responsibility to the society within which it operates.

Argenti defines *ethos* as 'how a company thinks it should conduct itself in society'.

Exercise

List the areas in which you think that a company should give consideration to the ethical dimensions of its operations.

Solution

A company should give consideration to the *ethics* of the following aspects of its operations.

(a) Employment policies (including attitudes to employing and paying women, minority groups, disabled people etc).

(b) Attitudes towards customers, competitors, suppliers, bankers, creditors, the government (national and local), foreign subsidiaries.

(c) Dealings with foreign governments, especially where those governments have earned disapproval and condemnation from the international community.

(d) Relationship with environmentalist groups.

(e) Its position in relation to local communities.

6.51 Recently, there have been fierce debates concerning the impact of business activities on the natural environment. The damage wrought by industrial pollution, and the depletion of natural resources have generated fierce political conflicts. The previous indifference of business to such issues is now unacceptable. All strategic planning now needs to take account of public responses to these environmental issues.

6.52 There is concern that many traditional energy sources may soon be exhausted and as a consequence restrictions on the use of oil and gas for electricity generation have been introduced in some parts of the world. We can expect this to increase, and businesses will have to live up to environmental standards such as BS 7750/ISO 9000.

6.53 Organisations can expect to plan for change, developing products and production methods that are less damaging and harmful. At the same time, the emerging demands for environmentally friendly products have resulted in new product/market opportunities for 'green' products, often at premium prices. Consumer priorities in this area may well be affected by, for instance, economic recession.

The legal environment

6.54 The legal framework within which organisations operate may affect the way in which they do business in the following ways.

(a) How the laws of contract, laws on unfair selling practices and the safety of goods, the law of agency and so on operate. What laws operate to restrict price increases, and which legislation affects promotional activities.

(b) How an organisation treats its employees (employment law, trade union law etc).

(c) How an organisation deals with its owners and gives information about its performance (for example the Companies Act).

(d) Criminal law.

6.55 In the UK, governments publish a Green Paper discussing a proposed change in the law, before issuing a White Paper and passing a Bill through Parliament. If such changes are likely to have an impact on what an organisation can do, contingency plans should be formulated. Within the EU, it is also important to monitor areas of legal change likely to impact on business activity.

Demography

6.56 Demography is the study of population and population trends. The following demographic factors are important to planners and have an impact on market segmentation.

(a) Changes in national population and in regional distribution.

(b) Changes in the age distribution of the population. All over the developed world populations are ageing, with improved health and falling birth rates.

(c) The concentration of population into certain geographical areas.

6.57 Demographic change affects:

(a) the services and products consumers demand and the size of market. An ageing population may demand certain kinds of leisure activities and health care services.

(b) Certain countries are seeing movements of population from cities into smaller towns.

7   MICRO-ENVIRONMENTAL FACTORS

Competition within the economic environment

7.1 The nature of competition is a key element in the environment of commercial organisations. The main issues here are:

(a) identifying the competitors;
(b) the strength of the competition;
(c) characteristics of the market;
(d) the likely strategies and responses of competitors to the organisation's strategies.

7.2 Porter (*Competitive Strategy*) identifies five basic forces which influence the state of competition in an industry.

(a) The threat of new entrants to the industry.
(b) The threat of substitute products or services.
(c) The bargaining power of customers.
(d) The bargaining power of suppliers.
(e) The rivalry amongst current competitors in the industry.

7.3 The intensity of competition relates to the following factors.

(a) *Whether there is a large number of equally balanced competitors*. Markets involving a large number of firms are likely to be very competitive, but when the industry is dominated by a small number of larger firms, competition is likely to be less intense.

(b) *The rate of growth in the industry*. Fast growth is likely to benefit a larger number of firms, and so their rivalry will be less intense. Rivalry is intensified when firms are competing in a market where growth is slow or stagnant.

(c) *Whether fixed costs are high*. If fixed costs are high, and variable costs are a relatively small proportion of the selling price, it is often tempting for firms to begin to compete on prices and to sell at prices above marginal cost, even though this may mean a failure to cover fixed costs and make an adequate return in the longer run.

7.4 *The rivalry amongst current competitors in the industry*. Intensity of competition within an industry will affect the profitability of the industry as a whole. Competitive actions might take the form of price competition, advertising battles, sales promotion campaigns, introducing new products for the market, improving aftersales service or providing guarantees or warranties.

7.5   Competition may:

    (a)   help the industry expand, stimulating demand for new products and advertising. Industry here is stimulated by the competition;

    (b)   leave demand unchanged, so that individual competitors will simply be spending more money, charging lower prices and so making lower profits. The only benefits involve maintaining market share.

Competitive moves/response models

7.6   In competitive market situations (for instance the oligopoly) firms are influenced by the actions of competitors and are likely:

    (a)   to respond to actions of those competitors;
    (b)   to take competitor responses into account in the formulation of their own strategy.

7.7   Unpredictability in competitor response creates a dilemma.

    (a)   Should firms act in the best interests of the *industry*, though that may not maximise their own profits or achievements?

    (b)   Should they take aggressive actions which offer, potentially, great rewards but which risk retaliation and thus lower levels of achievement than would be gained by taking the less aggressive first option?

7.8   In an industry, firms which co-operate can make reasonable profits, but a single firm taking an aggressive strategy can do even better, as long as the others do not retaliate.

7.9   If the competitors do retaliate everyone will be worse off than if all had co-operated. Price wars often result in falling profits for all firms. In this 'lose/lose' scenario the only group to benefit are the customers who gain the short term advantage of lower prices produced by competition.

7.10   Assessing the likely industry response is an important dimension in the process of strategic planning. Two aspects are important.

    (a)   What moves might others make and how will that affect our business? (What is our response to them?)

    (b)   How might others react to our strategies? (What is their response to us?)

7.11   Porter identifies a number of specific competitor responses which can be summarised under three broad categories.

    (a)   *Neutral moves* cause no real offence, and are co-operative or at least non threatening.

       (i)   *Hospitable moves* are visible but cause no real threat.

       (ii)   *Blind spot moves* are not recognised or perceived to be important perhaps because the firm is not felt at that time to be real competition.

    (b)   *Offence moves* are calculated to improve the firm's position and therefore may well elicit a response from competitors.

    There are two types of offence moves.

       (i)   *Superior strength moves* come from a privileged position, for example location or technical superiority. The firm must enjoy clear superiority for such a 'brute force' approach to be effective.

       (ii)   *Asymmetric cost moves*, where matching the move involves a substantial cost. Firms may be prepared to make short term losses to gain strategic advantage.

    (c)   *Defensive moves* are made to protect the firm's position, for instance preventing other firms actually entering into battle.

(i) *Readiness moves* are moves made in anticipation of competition. Pro-active product development, undertaken and communicated to competitors can in effect 'warn them off'.

(ii) *Leverage moves* are moves made so that the firm is ready to retaliate should it be necessary.

7.12 The nature of competition and the decisions of other firms affect both directly and indirectly the success of the organisation. The competition cannot be taken for granted. Managers must get to know its characteristics, strengths and weaknesses nearly as well as they know their own.

The impact of environmental change

7.13 To summarise this section and the previous one, the environmental influences on a business are complex and varied, but an awareness of their impact and forecast changes is critical to the survival of any organisation. If planners ignore the external influences on the business they are operating in the dark and the risks of being unprepared for an unexpected environmental threat are immense. The ability to produce plans in the context of a realistic appraisal of the current and forecasted business environment is dependent on adequate information being available to the planners at the right time and in a useable format.

7.14 Managers who are alert to forecast environmental changes and develop their strategies in advance of these changes are pro-active. These organisations are most likely to thrive and prosper. Those who are forced to change after the event are reactive and run the risk of failing to survive.

7.15 The response of competitors, both in general and to specific strategies must be considered when assessing the opportunities and threats facing the firm.

Chapter roundup

- A marketing opportunity exists whenever there is a gap between demand and supply. When there is an unfulfilled demand, an opportunity exists for a marketer to fulfil it.

- The first stage in the creation of a marketing plan is an analysis of the organisation's own (internal) strengths and weaknesses and of the (external) environment in which it operates. This provides answers to the 'where are we now?' question.

- As a first step, an internal audit is carried out to examine the present position of the organisation in terms of its strengths and weaknesses. Internal factors are classified as controllable variables, or those which can be influenced by management actions. This is an audit of the company's resources, which are sometimes classified as the five Ms.

- The external audit involves an analysis of opportunities in the environment and an identification of threats in the environment. These factors are uncontrollable variables and can be classified under the heading PEST, SLEPT or SLEPT/C.

- The internal and external appraisals can be brought together by means of a SWOT analysis.

- Competition is a key element of the environment. Michael Porter's work is instructive in this area.

Test your knowledge

1   What are the five Ms, which describe the internal factors of an organisation's resources? (see para 2.6)

2   Give four examples of limiting factors. (2.10 - 2.12)

3   What is a SWOT analysis? (3.1, 3.2)

4   What does PEST stand for? (5.6)

5   What is meant by the term 'environment'? (6.3)

6   Give four examples of each of national and international economic influences. (6.15)

7   In the light of the extension of the UK's 'domestic' market following creation of the Single European Market, what key questions should an organisation consider, according to DTI guidance? (6.26)

8   Why is 'family' a strong influence on purchasing behaviour? (6.38 - 6.41)

9   What is demography? (6.56)

10 What are the five forces identified by Porter as influencing the shape of competition in an industry? (7.2)

11 What are the three categories of competitor response identified by Porter? (7.11)

Now try illustrative question 1 at the end of the Study Text

Chapter 2

SEGMENTING MARKETS, TARGETING AND POSITIONING

This chapter covers the following topics.

1　The mass market approach

2　Market segmentation

3　Segmenting consumer markets

4　ACORN and MOSAIC

5　Segmenting industrial markets

6　Targeting

7　Positioning

8　A segmentation and positioning study

Introduction

As we saw in Chapter 1, the analysis of marketing opportunities begins with an analysis of the organisation's internal capabilities and of the marketing environment. The second part of the overall analysis involves segmenting markets, targeting and positioning. These activities are described in this chapter.

A market is not a mass, homogeneous group of customers, each wanting an identical product. Market segmentation is based on the recognition that every market consists of potential buyers with different needs, and different buying behaviour. These different customer attitudes may be grouped into segments and a different marketing approach will be taken by an organisation for each market segment.

1　THE MASS MARKET APPROACH

1.1　The mass or total market approach is seen where an organisation opts not to distinguish between customers on the assumption that majority needs can be satisfied with a single marketing mix, ie the same product at the same price, promoted to everyone in the same way and using a single method of distribution. In highly developed countries this approach becomes increasingly less effective as people's wants and needs grow in variety and sophistication. Fewer people aspire to 'go with the crowd', more people want to 'do their own thing' and so more opportunities are open to organisations which are willing to satisfy needs with a differentiated marketing mix.

1.2　This approach had greater applicability in the past before the advance of branding and the increased saliency of wants/needs brought about largely by more widespread education and travel. Thus consumers brought 'commodities' or 'staples' such as sugar, butter, lard and milk in totally unbranded wrappings. Items such as sugar were ladled from larger 'sacks' into thick blue paper bags by assistants at corner grocery shops at the point of sale to consumers. This approach is still partially tenable in some markets, although increasingly less so. For example, in the fresh vegetable market, most of us are happy to buy unbranded items such as cabbages, cauliflowers, peas and beans. However, even here we find ourselves drawn to buying/specifying English, Spanish or Italian tomatoes.

1.3   Examples of the total market approach are perhaps more prevalent in industrial 'commodity' markets. For example, in the building industry, customers might buy sand, cement and timber with scant regard for brand. Also in the metals market, where copper, steel, iron ore etc are bought on a commodity basis, the same might apply.

1.4   The segmentation approach, on the other hand, recognises that people have different wants and needs and that some are willing to pay more or go to greater lengths to satisfy these. Where a sufficient number of people have affordable wants, if one manufacturer fails to satisfy them, another will.

2   MARKET SEGMENTATION

2.1   Market segmentation may be defined as follows.

> 'The subdividing of a market into distinct and increasingly homogeneous subgroups of customers, where any subgroup can conceivably be selected as a target to be met with a distinct marketing mix. ... The danger of thinking in terms of single, mass homogeneous markets has been recognised. Market segmentation, as an approach, emerged from the recognition of this danger.'   (Tom Cannon, *Basic Marketing: Principles and Practice*)

> 'Market segmentation is the subdividing of a market into distinct subsets of customers, where any subset may conceivably be selected as a target market to be reached with a distinct marketing mix.'   *(Kotler)*

2.2   Customers differ according to age, sex, income, geographical area, buying attitudes, buying habits etc. Each of these differences can be used to segment a market.

2.3   Consumer and industrial buyers may be influenced by a wide range of factors and be in a variety of buying situations. A whole range of situational and background factors determine the outcome of a particular purchase opportunity.

2.4   Marketing activity is more effective if groups can be identified and 'targeted' according to the marketing objectives of the company. This is done by the process of *market segmentation* which groups potential customers according to identifiable characteristics relevant to their purchase behaviour.

2.5   What segments are identified and selected depends on the objectives pursued.

2.6   There are many possible characteristics of buyers which could be chosen as 'segmentation variables' and a variety of criteria which can be used to identify the most effective characteristics for use in market segmentation.

2.7   Irrespective of the approach, there are a number of requirements for effective market segmentation.

(a)   *Measurability* refers to the degree to which information exists or is cost effectively obtainable on the particular buyer characteristics of interest. Whilst a car manufacturer may have access to information about location of the customers, personality traits of buyers are more difficult to obtain information about, because the tests which are required may be impossible or unfeasible to administer - or too expensive.

(b)   *Accessibility* refers to the degree to which the company can focus effectively on the chosen segments using marketing methods. While we may be able to select what seems like the most appropriate target segment very clearly, we may not be able to identify the individual or households involved, or communicate with them cost-effectively. Thus whilst a new car dealer may be able to access potential corporate customers in their area, by direct mail or tele-sales, identifying individual customers with family incomes in excess of £30,000 pa would not be easy.

(c)   *Substantiality* refers to the degree to which the segments are large enough to be worth considering for separate marketing cultivation. The target segment must be large enough to offer profitable returns, over and above the cost of investment in marketing of promotional activities directed specifically at them. Devising and mounting different marketing approaches is expensive, so a minimum size of a segment depends on profits. Thus, whilst a large number of people in social group DE aged over 65 could be identified, their potential *profitability* to a retailer is likely to be less in the long term than a smaller number of 17-18 year olds. This latter group might be worth cultivating using a specially devised marketing approach whereas the former might not be.

Steps in the analysis of segmentation

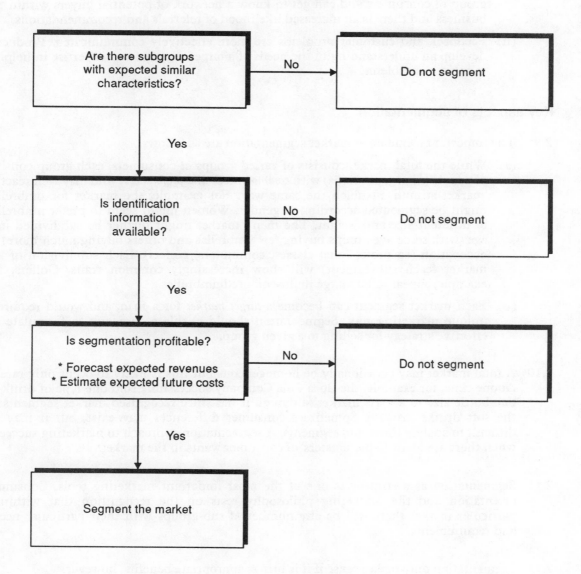

Non-profit benefits of segmentation

2.8   (a)   The identification of new marketing opportunities as a result of better understanding of consumer needs in each of the segments.

(b)   Specialists can be developed and appointed to each of the company's major segments. Operating practices then benefit from the expertise of staff with specialist knowledge of the segment's business.

(c)   The total marketing budget can be allocated more effectively, according to needs and the likely return from each segment.

(d) Precision marketing approaches can be used. The company can make finer adjustments to the product and service offerings and to the marketing appeals used for each segment.

(e) Specialist knowledge and extra effort may enable the company to dominate particular segments and gain competitive advantage.

(f) The product assortment can be more precisely defined to reflect differences between customer needs.

(g) Improved segmentation allows more highly targeted marketing activity. For instance, the sales team develops an in-depth knowledge of the needs of a particular group of consumers and can get to know a network of potential buyers within the business and there is an increased likelihood of referrals and recommendations.

(h) Feedback and customer problems are more effectively communicated. Producers develop an understanding in the needs of a target segment and expertise in helping to solve its problems.

Key aspects of segmentation

2.9 The important elements of market segmentation are as follows.

(a) While the total market consists of varied groups of consumers, each group consists of people (or organisations) with *common needs and preferences*, who may well react to 'market stimuli' in much the same way. For example, the market for umbrellas might be segmented according to gender. Women might seem to prefer umbrellas of different size and weight. The men's market might further be subdivided into age (with some age groups buying few umbrellas and others buying much more) or occupation (eg professional classes, commuters, golfers). Each subdivision of the market (each subsegment) will show increasingly common traits. Golfers, for example, appear to buy large multi-coloured umbrellas.

(b) Each market segment can become a *target market* for a firm, and would require a unique marketing mix. Segmentation should enable a company to formulate an effective strategy for selling to a given group.

2.10 A total market may occasionally be homogeneous but this is likely to occur only rarely. At one time, for example, the Coca Cola Company successfully sold one type of drink in one bottle size to a mass market (although it has since recognised market segments in the soft drinks market). Sometimes consumer differences may exist, but it may be difficult to analyse them into segments. A segmentation approach to marketing succeeds when there are identifiable 'clusters' of consumer wants in the market.

2.11 Segmentation as a strategy is one of the most important marketing tools. Consumer orientation and the marketing philosophy rests on the recognition that within a particular market there will be any number of sub-groups with their particular needs and requirements.

2.12 Segmentation only makes sense if it is brings appropriate benefits, however.

(a) Segmentation should increase benefits to consumers by providing products, product features or attributes more closely matching their identified needs.

(b) Segmentation enables the firm to identify those groups of customers who are most likely to buy. This ensures that resources will not be wasted, and marketing and sales activity can be highly focused. The result should be lower costs, greater sales and higher profitability.

(c) Across the industry, segmentation will provide greater customer choice by generating a variety of products within a particular class from which consumers can choose.

3   SEGMENTING CONSUMER MARKETS

3.1   There are a number of ways which a consumer market can be segmented. Segmentation decisions have clear implications for other decision areas however, for instance, choice of and medium for advertising, and allocation of resources.

Geographic segmentation

3.2   This is based on geographic location. It may be important, for instance, for retailers who need to get to know about the different groups of customers within their catchment area. Segmentation by location can also be a feature of international marketing strategy, where marketing strategy is formulated around the different needs of various cultures, countries or regions. Needs and motives will be significantly influenced by a range of factors including climate, religion, culture and even geography. The opportunity to design an appropriate marketing mix and use sales staff familiar with a particular international market is vital for marketing success.

3.3   A national chain of supermarkets will use geographic segmentation because it interacts closely with the chain's outlet strategy. Each branch or group of retail outlets could be given mutually exclusive areas to service and so the method enables the supermarket chain to make more effective use of target marketing and cover the market available. The obvious advantage to customers is convenience of access, which is a primary motivation to retailers when considering ways of segmenting the grocery shopping market. Of course, this customer benefit needs to be considered against the cost of provision of retail branches. Research has shown that one of the major reasons why customers choose particular stores in which to shop is convenience of access.

Demographic segmentation

3.4   The total size of the population defines the total possible level of demand for a product. With the formation of the Single European Market in 1992 the *home* market for UK companies becomes comparable in size to the US market.

3.5   The population is usually broken down into groups defined by demographic characteristics such as sex or 'age' (eg the baby market, teenage market and senior citizens market). The total size of each segment will suggest possible levels of demand for corresponding products (rattles and prams, bicycles and motor cycles, retirement cottages and sea cruises).

Social class (socio-economics)

3.6   The social class of a person is also likely to influence his/her buying habits and preferences. Although there are a number of factors involved in social class position (income, education, background, status) the most commonly used classification, in the marketing world, is the JICNARs scale, based on occupation of the main wage earner in the household. This involves the following classification scheme.

Social grade	Social status	Occupation
A	Upper middle class	Higher managerial, professional or administrative jobs.
B	Middle class	Middle managerial, professional or administrative jobs.
C1	Lower middle class	Supervisory or clerical jobs, junior management.
C2	Skilled working class	Skilled manual workers.
D	Working class	Unskilled and semi-skilled manual workers.
E	Those at the lowest level of subsistence	Pensioners, the unemployed, casual or low grade workers.

3.7 This scheme lacks precision as it divides the total population into just six large groups. It is very difficult to make significant distinctions between a B and a C1 class person. Also, because it is based on the occupation of the 'chief income earner' only (an improvement nonetheless on the original focus on head of the household only), it does not reflect the income of the whole family unit, or the background and aspirations of members.

3.8 Computer databases using census details, market research and commercial data has over recent years made possible the use of segmentation systems based on a number of different household characteristics, from the *names* of occupants to the types of houses they occupy. By linking this to postcode data it is possible to identify very precisely the characteristics of consumers in a particular location, or to build up a *profile* of the types of people sending for goods by mail order, or completing hire purchase forms.

3.9 We will look at two approaches to geo-demographic segmentation, ACORN and MOSAIC, in the next section of this chapter.

Family characteristics

3.10 Another form of segmentation is based on the size and constitution of the family unit. As the following table illustrates, there have been changes in the characteristics of the family unit in the last few decades.

	Percentages				
	1961	1971	1981	1991	1993
One person households					
Under pensionable age	4	6	8	11	11
Over pensionable age	7	12	14	16	16
Two or more unrelated adults	5	4	5	3	3
One family households					
Married couple[1] with:					
No children	26	27	26	28	28
1 - 2 dependent children[2]	30	26	25	20	20
3 or more dependent children	8	9	6	5	5
Non-dependent children only	10	8	8	8	7
Lone parent[1] with:					
Dependent children[2]	2	3	5	6	7
Non-dependent children only	4	4	4	4	3
Two or more families	3	1	1	1	1
Number of households (=100%)(millions)	16.2	18.2	19.5	21.9	22.9

1 Other individuals who were not family members may also have been included.

2 May also include non-dependent children.

3.11 A rising divorce rate is one of the factors underlying an increase in single-parent families and a decline in the incidence of the 'nuclear' family of working husband, wife and dependent children. Declining traditional industries and the increasing employment of females in service orientated industries, often involving part rather than full-time work, has produced more households in which the sole breadwinner is female rather than male, and households with two or more wage earners.

3.12 Structural changes have been accompanied by a trend towards later marriage and delayed child bearing. Rising house prices plus high interest rates have meant that many newly formed households often contain partners who both work. Greater financial independence for women is also growing as a result of the economic and social changes of the 1980s.

Family life cycle

3.13 *Family decision making units* represents a widely accepted classification of consumer 'units' which make buying decisions. It is based on the family situation of the consumers. These are described as:

(a) young and single;
(b) young, married, no children;
(c) young, married, youngest child under six years old;
(d) young, married youngest child over six years old;
(e) older, married, with children;
(f) older, married, no children under eighteen;
(g) older and single;
(h) other.

3.14 The *family life cycle* (FLC) is a summary demographic variable. It brings together factors of age, marital status, career status (income) and the presence or absence of children. As a consequence, it is able to characterise the various stages through which households progress, with each stage involving different needs and resources.

3.15 The FLC's enduring appeal as a segmentation technique has been maintained because it is based on the central premise of birth and death and the various stages between these two events, although a wide range of formulations have been produced, and various factors cited.

3.16 Demographic segmentation methods are powerful tools especially when each of the bases is combined with other methods. The bases for demographic segmentation are clearly interdependent. Age and family life cycle stage are patently linked, as are housing and socio-economic group. Using a combination of these bases it is possible to define targets for marketing campaigns and sales activities.

THE FAMILY LIFE CYCLE

No	Stage	Characteristics
I	*Bachelor Stage.* Young single people not living at home.	Few financial burdens. Fashion/opinion leader led. Recreation orientated. Buy: basic kitchen equipment, basic furniture, cars, equipment for the mating game, holidays. Experiment with patterns of personal financial management and control.
II	*Newly married couples.* Young, no children	Better off financially than they will be in the near future. High levels of purchase of homes and consumer durable goods. Buy: cars, fridges, cookers, life assurance, durable furniture, holidays. Establish patterns of personal financial management and control.
III	*Full nest I.* Youngest child under six	Home purchasing at peak. Liquid assets/saving low. Dissatisfied with financial position and amount of money saved. Reliance on credit finance, credit cards, overdrafts etc. Child dominated household. Buy necessities - washers, dryers, baby food and clothes, vitamins, toys, books etc.
IV	*Full nest II.* Youngest child six or over	Financial position better. Some wives return to work. Child dominated household. Buy necessities - foods, cleaning material, clothes, bicycles, sports gear, music lessons, pianos, holidays etc.
V	*Full nest III.* Older married couples with dependent children.	Financial position still better. More wives work. School and examination dominated household. Some children get first jobs; other in further/higher education. Expenditure to support children's further/higher education. Buy: new, more tasteful furniture, non-necessary appliances, boats, holidays.etc
VI	*Empty nest I.* Older married coupes, no children living with them, head of family still in labour force	Home ownership at peak. More satisfied with financial position and money saved. Interested in travel, recreation, self-education. Make financial gifts and contributions. Children gain qualifications and move to Stage I. Buy: luxuries, home improvements eg fitted kitchens etc.
VII	*Empty nest II.* Older married couples, no children living at home, head of family retired.	Significant cut in income. Keep home. Buy: medical appliances or medical care, products which aid health, sleep and digestion. Assist children. Concern with level of savings and pension. Some expenditure on hobbies and pastimes.
VIII	*Solitary survivor I.* In labour force	Income still adequate but likely to sell family home and purchase smaller accommodation. Concern with level of savings and pension. Some expenditure on hobbies and pastimes. Worries about security and dependence.
IX	*Solitary survivor II.* Retired	Significant cut in income. Additional medical requirements. Special need for attention, affection and security. May seek sheltered accommodation. Possible dependence on others for personal financial management and control.

Psychographic segmentation

3.17 Psychographics or *life style* segmentation seeks to classify groups according to their values, opinions, personality characteristics, interests and so on. Its inherent nature should be very dynamic. This ability to introduce various new dimensions to existing customer information, for example customers' disposition towards savings, investment and the use of credit, general attitude to money, leisure and other key influences makes it extremely flexible and relevant to the needs of changing markets.

Lifestyle dimensions

Activities	Interests	Opinions	Demographics
Work	Family	Themselves	Age
Hobbies	Home	Social issues	Education
Social events	Job	Politics	Income
Vacation	Community	Business	Occupation
Entertainment	Recreation	Economics	Family size
Club membership	Fashion	Education	Dwelling
Community	Food	Products	Geography
Shopping	Media	Future	City size
Sports	Achievements	Culture	Stage in lifecycle

(Joseph Plummer, *'The Concept and Application of Lifestyle Segmentation'*, *Journal of Marketing (January 1974), pp 33-37*)

3.18 Where innovation is the key to improved organisational performance as competition increases the new perspectives introduced by the system are worthy of investigation. Life style segmentation fits this criterion because it deals with the *person* as opposed to the *product* and characterises the unique life style patterns of customers, in order to provide a richer insight into their preferences, motivation and usage behaviour. Consequently, strategists will be better able to direct their marketing energies to meet the future needs of these identified groups.

3.19 Lifestyle refers to distinctive ways of living adopted by particular communities or sub-sections of society. Lifestyle involves factors such as motivation, personality and culture, and depends on accurate description. When a group has been identified and accurately characterised, marketers can produce products and target promotion towards this particular target lifestyle group. Lifestyle is a controversial issue, and it is important to understand that different characterisations of psychographic groups are perfectly possible, and that in no sense are we 'describing' what is there in a substantive sense. It is perfectly possible for the same person to belong to several different psychographic groups at the same time. How the groups are characterised depends on the nature of the market being addressed. It is possible, in theory, to generate endless categorisations of different lifestyle groups - some very small.

3.20 One simple example generalises life style in terms of four categories.

(a) *Upwardly mobile, ambitious*. People seek a better and more affluent lifestyle, principally through better paid and more interesting work, and a higher material standard of living. Persons with such a lifestyle will be prepared to try new products.

(b) *Traditional and sociable*. Compliance and conformity to group norms bring social approval and reassurance to the individual. Purchasing patterns will therefore be 'conformist'.

(c) *Security and status seeking*. 'Safety' needs and 'ego-defensive' needs are stressed. This lifestyle links status, income and security. It encourages the purchase of strong and well known products and brands, and emphasises those products and services which confer status and make life as secure and predictable as possible. These would include insurance, membership of the AA or RAC etc. Products that are well established and familiar inspire more confidence than new products, which will be resisted.

(d) *Hedonistic preference*. The emphasis is on 'enjoying life now' and the immediate satisfaction of wants and needs. Little consideration is given to the future.

3.21 An alternative scheme involves reference to environmental awareness. Companies segment according to whether clients are 'pale' or 'dark' green in their attitude to the environment and therefore how significant environmentally friendly product attributes will be to the purchasing decision.

Benefit segmentation

3.22 This form of segmentation relates to different benefits being sought from a product or service by customer groups. Individuals are segmented directly according to their needs. In this form of segmentation, it is usual for varying customer groups to share the same benefits from the product or service. Benefit segmentation includes:

(a) benefits sought;
(b) usage rates;
(c) attitudes.

3.23 Segmenting the market in terms of *benefits sought*, there is a need to identify common characteristics which the customer requires from the product or service. Amstrad, the computer manufacturer, has developed its strategy around the principle of benefit segmentation. The requirement for basic word processing and spreadsheet packages has been synonymous with small businesses, students, home use and the professional. Amstrad has been able to meet these common needs, albeit with technology which is not necessarily at the leading edge.

3.24 Individuals can be categorised by usage patterns - whether they are light, medium or heavy users of a product or service. The TGI (Target Group Index) helps to identify these groups for a wide range of products and services. This form of segmentation assists the marketer in developing distinct and personalised strategies aimed at specific users, based upon their existing consumption of a product or service. For example, banks and other financial institutions have introduced incentive schemes for customers when using their credit cards. This allows heavy users of the service to amass points and convert them into gifts.

Benefit segmentation of the toothpaste market

Segment name	Principal benefit sought	Demographic strengths	Special behavioural characteristics	Brands dis-proportionately favoured	Personality characteristics	Lifestyle characteristics
The sensory segment	Flavour, product appearance	Children	Users of spearmint flavoured toothpaste	Colgate, Stripe	High self-involvement	Hedonistic
The sociables	Brightness of teeth	Teens, young people	Smokers	Macleans, Ultra Brite	High sociability	Active
The worrier	Decay prevention	Large families	Heavy users	Crest	High hypo-chondriasis	Conservative
The independent segment	Price	Men	Heavy users	Brands on sale	High autonomy	Value-oriented

Examples of segmentation

3.25 A few illustrative examples follow, but you should appreciate that these examples merely try to indicate an approach to the more general problem.

(a) *Adult education.* The market for adult education (say, evening classes) may be segmented according to:

    (i)   age (younger people might prefer classes in, say, yoga);

    (ii)   sex (women might prefer self defence courses);

    (iii) occupation (apprentices may choose technical classes);

    (iv) social class (middle class people might prefer art or music subjects);

    (v)   education (poorly educated people might prefer to avoid all forms of evening class);

    (vi) family life cycle (the interests of young single people are likely to differ from those of young married people with children).

(b) *Magazines and periodicals.* In this market the segmentation may be according to:

    (i)   sex (Woman's Own);
    (ii)   social class (Country Life);
    (iii) income (Ideal Home);
    (iv) occupation (Accountancy Age, Computer Weekly);
    (v)   leisure interests;
    (vi) political ideology;
    (vii) age ('19', Honey);
    (viii) lifestyle (Playboy).

(c) *Sporting facilities:*

    (i)   geographical area (rugby in Wales, ski-ing in parts of Scotland, sailing in coastal towns);

    (ii)   population density (squash clubs in cities, riding in country areas);

    (iii) occupation (gymnasia for office workers);

    (iv) education (there may be a demand from ex-schoolboys for facilities for sports taught at certain schools, such as rowing);

    (v)   family life cycle or age (parents may want facilities for their children, young single or married people may want facilities for themselves).

3.26   The salesperson needs to understand both the basis of segmentation and the characteristics of the various segments. For instance, a car sales person should appreciate that the couple with a young family will have different needs from those of a retired couple. Segmentation enables the sales staff to get 'clues' about buyer behaviour and motives to use as part of their sales approach.

3.27   When dealing with an individual customer, care needs to be taken to avoid stereotypes and not jump to conclusions. Sales staff may use segmentation as a benchmark, but should act cautiously on their assumptions.

Fragmented industries and market segmentation

3.28   Industries begin to fragment and market segments proliferate when:

(a)   entry barriers are low and new firms can enter the market relatively easily;

(b)   economies of scale or learning curve effects are few, and so it is difficult for big firms to establish a significant overall cost leadership;

(c)   transport and distribution costs are high, and so the industry fragments on a geographical basis;

(d)   customer needs are extremely diverse;

(e)   there are rapid product changes or style changes, which small firms might succeed in reacting to more quickly than large firms;

(f)   there is a highly diverse product line, so that some firms are able to specialise in one part of the industry;

(g)   there is scope for product differentiation, based on product design/quality differences or even brand images.

4   ACORN AND MOSAIC

4.1   In this section, we continue our review of segmentation of consumer markets by looking at two well-known approaches to geo-demographic segmentation.

(a)   ACORN (A Classification of Residential Neighbourhoods) was the first geo-demographic method of segmentation classification. It was originally based on 1971 census data and was developed by CACI Ltd.

(b)   MOSAIC is a rival system marketed by CCN Marketing.

ACORN

4.2   ACORN divides up the entire UK population in terms of the type of housing in which they live. For each of these areas, a wide range of demographic information is generated and the system affords the opportunity to assess product usage patterns, dependent upon the research conducted within national surveys. There are 54 separate groupings.

4.3   Although the census is only conducted once every ten years, the ACORN database is updated annually to take account of latest population projections. The 1995 classification is given below.

THE ACORN TARGETING CLASSIFICATION: FULL LIST

A Thriving (19.7% of population)

A1 Wealthy Achievers, Suburban Areas (15.0%)

		% of population
1.1	Wealthy Suburbs, Large Detached Houses	2.5
1.2	Villages with Wealthy Commuters	3.2
1.3	Mature Affluent Home Owning Areas	2.7
1.4	Affluent Suburbs, Older Families	3.7
1.5	Mature, Well-Off Suburbs	3.0

A2 Affluent Greys, Rural Communities (2.3%)

2.6	Agricultural Villages, Home Based Workers	1.6
2.7	Holiday Retreats, Older People, Home Based Workers	0.7

A3 Prosperous Pensioners, Retirement Areas (2.4%)

3.8	Home Owning Areas, Well-Off Older Residents	1.4
3.9	Private Flats, Elderly People	0.9

B Expanding (11.6% of population)

B4 Affluent Executives, Family Areas (3.8%)

4.10	Affluent Working Families with Mortgages	2.1
4.11	Affluent Working Couples with Mortgages, New Homes	1.3
4.12	Transient Workforces, Living at their Place of Work	0.4

B5 Well-Off Workers, Family Areas (7.8%)

5.13	Home Owning Family Areas	2.6
5.14	Home Owning Family Areas, Older Children	3.0
5.15	Families with Mortgages, Younger Children	2.2

C Rising (7.8% of population)

C6 Affluent Urbanites, Town and City Areas (2.3%)

6.16	Well-Off Town and City Areas	1.1
6.17	Flats and Mortgages, Singles and Young Working Couples	0.7
6.18	Furnished Flats and Bedsits, Younger Single People	0.4

C7 Prosperous Professionals, Metropolitan Areas (2.1%)

7.19	Apartments, Young Professional Singles and Couples	1.1
7.20	Gentrified Multi-Ethnic Areas	1.0

C8 Better-Off Executives, Inner City Areas (3.4%)

8.21	Prosperous Enclaves, Highly Qualified Executives	0.7
8.22	Academic Centres, Students and Young Professionals	0.7
8.23	Affluent City Centre Areas, Tenements and Flats	0.4
8.24	Partially Gentrified Multi-Ethnic Areas	0.7
8.25	Converted Flats and Bedsits, Single People	0.9

D   **Settling (24.1% of population)**

D9 Comfortable Middle Agers, Mature Home Owning Areas (13.4%)

		% of population
9.26	Mature Established Home Owning Areas	3.3
9.27	Rural Areas, Mixed Occupations	3.4
9.28	Established Home Owning Areas	4.0
9.29	Home Owning Areas, Council Tenants, Retired People	2.6

D10 Skilled Workers, Home Owning Areas (10.7%)

10.30	Established Home Owning Areas, Skilled Workers	4.5
10.31	Home Owners in Older Properties, Younger Workers	3.1
10.32	Home Owning Areas with Skilled Workers	3.1

E   **Aspiring (13.7% of population)**

E11 New Home Owners, Mature Communities (9.7%)

11.33	Council Areas, Some New Home Owners	3.8
11.34	Mature Home Owning Areas, Skilled Workers	3.1
11.35	Low Rise Estates, Older Workers, New Home Owners	2.8

E12 White Collar Workers, Better-Off Multi-Ethnic Areas (4.0%)

12.36	Home Owning Multi-Ethnic Areas, Young Families	1.1
12.37	Multi-Occupied Town Centres, Mixed Occupations	1.8
12.38	Multi-Ethnic areas, White Collar Workers	1.1

F   **Striving (22.7% of population)**

F13 Older People, Less Prosperous Areas (3.6%)

13.39	Home Owners, Small Council Flats, Single Pensioners	1.9
13.40	Council Areas, Older People, Health Problems	1.7

F14 Council Estate Residents, Better-Off Homes (11.5%)

14.41	Better-Off Council Areas, New Home Owners	2.4
14.42	Council Areas, Young Families, Some New Home Owners	3.0
14.43	Council Areas, Young Families, Many Lone Parents	1.6
14.44	Multi-Occupied Terraces, Multi-Ethnic Areas	0.9
14.45	Low Rise Council Housing, Less Well-Off Families	1.8
14.46	Council Areas, Residents with Health Problems	1.9

F15 Council Estate Residents, High Unemployment (2.7%)

15.47	Estates with High Unemployment	1.1
15.48	Council Flats, Elderly People, Health Problems	0.7
15.49	Council Flats, Very High Unemployment, Singles	0.9

F16 Council Estate Residents, Greatest Hardship (2.8%)

16.50	Council Areas, High Unemployment, Lone Parents	1.9
16.51	Council Flats, Greatest Hardship, Many Lone Parents	0.9

F17 People in Multi-Ethnic, Low-Income Areas (2.1%)

17.52	Multi-Ethnic, Large Families, Overcrowding	0.6
17.53	Multi-Ethnic, Severe Unemployment, Lone Parents	1.0
17.54	Multi-Ethnic, High Unemployment, Overcrowding	0.5

4.4   CACI, in its ACORN User Guide, suggests the following as possible applications of the ACORN classifications.

(a) *Site Location Analysis:* using ACORN profiles of the purchasing behaviour and socio-economic status of people living in the catchments of your most successful trading outlets, you can identify sites with similar profiles for new stores or branches.

(b) *Sales Planning:* defining a sales territory by ACORN Type shows you immediately which areas are best suited to your range of products and services.

(c) *Media Planning:* an ACORN analysis of various media gives you the tool for understanding which media you should use to target the consumers who buy your products.

(d) *Market Research Sample Frames:* ACORN can help you generate the most representative sample frames for market research, identifying areas with the right consumer mix.

(e) *Planning for Public Services:* healthcare and government services can be focused more effectively with an ACORN analysis of a local area revealing the likely needs of the population.

(f) *Database Analysis:* ACORN can be used to profile both your own in-house customer files or bought-in lists by ACORN Type, providing essential information which can be used to target people with similar characteristics.

(g) *Direct Mail:* by selecting form CACI's Electoral Roll database of 40 million names and addresses (the ACORN List) according to the ACORN Types relevant to your products, we can identify new prospect lists for your direct mailings

(h) *Door-to-Door Leaflet Campaigns:* ACORN can segment and define your target market by postal sector for effective and customised distribution planning in door-to-door promotions.

(i) *Coding:* once your in-house list has been coded by ACORN Type, existing customers can be approached for cross-selling into other products from your range with a suitable ACORN match.

MOSAIC

4.5   This system analyses information from various source including the census, which is used to give housing, socio-economic, household and age date; the electoral roll, to give household composition and population movement data; post code address files to give information on post 1981 housing and special address types such as farms and flats; and the CCN files/Lord Chancellor's office to give credit search information and bad debt risk respectively.

4.6   MOSAIC can provide information at three levels of detail.

(a) *Unit postcodes.* A unit postcode is a full six or seven character code such as W12 8AW. There are some 1.5 million unit postcodes containing an average of 15 addresses each.

(b) *Census enumeration districts.* These are based on census data and contain around 180 addresses each.

(c) *Pseudo enumeration districts.* These are areas created by MOSAIC and each contains a number of unit postcodes within a single census enumeration district.

4.7   The current MOSAIC classification includes 52 separate neighbourhood types.

Other geo-demographic classifications

4.8   Recent classifications launched include the following.

(a)   PORTRAIT, developed by Equifax Europe (UK) Ltd and NDL to combine geo-demographic and lifestyle date. It is not census-based, but uses a range of other data sources including county court judgements, unemployment statistics, loan applications, births and deaths registers, electoral registers and credit searches.

PORTRAIT uses a four-digit classification based on

(i)   gradations of income, from 'extremely affluent' to 'very low income' in ten roughly equal groups;

(ii)   gradations of age, in four roughly equal groups;

(iii)   lifestyle clusters, of which there are 175.

(b)   PSYCHE is based on consumer values, which are assumed to affect purchasing behaviour. It is based on a continuous rolling survey and uses *social value groups* (SVGs).

(a)   *Self-explorers*. Motivated by self-expression and self-realisation. Less materialistic than other groups, and showing high tolerance levels.

(b)   *Social resisters*. The caring group, concerned with fairness and social values, but often appearing intolerant and moralistic.

(c)   *Experimentalists*. Highly individualistic, motivated by fast-moving enjoyment. They are materialistic, pro-technology but anti-traditional authority.

(d)   *Conspicuous consumers*. They are materialistic and pushy, motivated by acquisition, competition, and getting ahead. Pro-authority, law and order.

(e)   *Belongers*. What they seek is a quiet, undisturbed family life. They are conservative, conventional rule followers.

(f)   *Survivors*. Strongly class-conscious, and community spirited, their motivation is to 'get by'.

(g)   *Aimless*. comprises two groups,

(i) the young unemployed, who are often anti-authority, and
(ii) the old, whose motivation is day-to-day existence.

5   SEGMENTING INDUSTRIAL MARKETS

5.1   Industrial markets are usually smaller and more easily identified than consumer markets. Segmentation may still be worthwhile, however, identifying and targeting specified groups within the total market.

5.2   Various segmentation schemes for industrial markets exist and may, once again, be used in combination. Databases have been developed to provide additional intelligence information which allows much tighter targeting of industrial customers. Industrial markets may be targeted as follows.

(a)   *By location*. Many business sectors are concentrated in particular locations for example, steel in Sheffield, computer companies along the M4 corridor etc.

(b)   *Company size* either by turnover or employees. This can give a good indication of their possible needs for products or services.

(c)   *Usage rates*. Heavy, medium or light users. This is most relevant in raw material and parts markets and the market for some industrial services example telecommunications and travel.

(d)   *Industry classification* indicates the nature of the business and may provide a useful method to prioritise and classify sales leads.

(e)   *Product use*. An industrial organisation may buy a fleet of cars for use by its salesforce, or to hire out to the public as the basis for its service. Different uses are likely to be associated with different needs.

5.3   Segmenting markets enables companies to devise strategies which more closely match the identified needs of customers.

5.4   These smaller subgroups allow the marketing and sales team to get to know customers much better and resources and efforts to be channelled towards the most profitable segments.

5.5   Remember that, as we saw in section 2 of this chapter, to be effective, segments need to be:

(a)   measurable;
(b)   accessible;
(c)   substantial.

6   TARGETING

6.1   Limited resources, competition and large markets make it ineffective and inappropriate for companies to sell to the entire market; that is, every market segment. For the sake of efficiency they must select target markets. Marketing managers may choose one of the following policy options.

(a)   *Undifferentiated marketing* aims to produce a single product and get as many customers as possible to buy it. Segmentation is ignored.

(b)   *Concentrated marketing* attempts to produce the ideal product for a single segment of the market (eg Rolls Royce cars, Mothercare mother and baby shops).

(c)   *Differentiated marketing* attempts to introduce several versions of a product, each aimed at a different market segment (for example, the manufacture of several different brands of washing powder).

6.2   *Concentrated marketing* runs the risk of relying on a single segment of a single market. This can lead to problems. For example, the de Lorean sports car firm ran into irreversible financial difficulties in 1981-82 when the sports car market contracted in the USA. Specialisation nonetheless can enable a firm to capitalise on a profitable, although perhaps temporary, competitive edge over rivals (such as Kickers specialising in leisure footwear).

6.3   The main disadvantage of *differentiated marketing* is the additional cost of marketing and production (extra product design and development costs, the loss of economies of scale in production and storage, extra promotion and administrative costs and so on). When the costs of further differentiation of the market exceed the benefits from further segmentation and target marketing, a firm is said to have *over-differentiated*. Some firms have tried to overcome this by aiming the same product at two market segments (so, for example, Johnson's baby powder is sold to adults for their own use).

6.4   The choice between these three approaches will depend on the following factors.

(a)   The degree to which the product and/or the market can be considered homogeneous.

(b)   How far the company's resources are overextended as a consequence of differentiated marketing. Small firms, for example, may perform better by concentrating on only one segment.

(c)   How far the product is advanced in its 'life cycle' in order to attract a substantial total market. If it is not, segmentation and target marketing is unlikely to be profitable, because each segment would be too small.

6.5   The potential benefits of segmentation and target marketing are as follows.

(a)   *Product differentiation,* so that a particular product might be thought better than its rivals by this segment. Different segments of the market may not value this distinguishing feature, and would not prefer it to a rival product.

    (b) The seller will have increased awareness of how product design and development stimulates demand in a particular section of the market.

    (c) The resources of the business will be more effectively employed, since the organisation should be more able to make products which the customer demands.

7 POSITIONING

7.1 Brands can be 'positioned' in relation to competitive brands on product maps in which space is defined in terms of how buyers perceive key characteristics.

7.2 Wind provides a comprehensive list of the characteristics which may be used.

    (a) *Positioning by specific product features*. The most common approach to positioning, especially for industrial products, price and specific product features being used as the basis for positioning. Most car advertisements for example stress the combination of product features available and usually also stress good value for money.

    (b) *Positioning by benefits, problems, solutions, or needs*. Benefits are emphasised. This is generally more effective than positioning on product features independent of benefits. Pharmaceutical companies position their products to relative doctors by stressing effectiveness and side effects. Other examples include Crest, which positions its toothpaste as a cavity fighter, and DHL, which uses its worldwide network of offices as a basis for its positioning.

    (c) *Positioning for specific usage occasions*. Similar to benefit positioning but this uses the specific occasion of usage as the main basis for the positioning. Johnson's Baby Shampoo is, thus, positioned as a product to use if you shampoo your hair every day, and Hennessy Cognac is for special occasions.

    (d) *Positioning for user category*. 7-Up's use of the Fido Dido character to target urban adolescents illustrates how age has been used as a basis for positioning. Many breakfast cereal producers have also positioned by age.

    (e) *Positioning against another product*. Although Avis never mentions Hertz explicitly in its advertising, its positioning as Number 2 in the rent-a-car market is an example of positioning against a leader. 'Me too' products can always be related to leaders in this way.

    (f) *Product class disassociation*. A less common basis for positioning, but effective when introducing a new product clearly distinct from standard products in an established product category. For example, lead-free petrol is positioned against leaded petrol.

    (g) *Hybrid basis*. On occasion, a positioning strategy may be founded on several of these alternatives, incorporating elements from more than one positioning base. Porsche, for example, use a combination of the product benefits and user characteristics.

7.3 A basic perceptual map is to plot brands in perceived price and perceived quality terms.

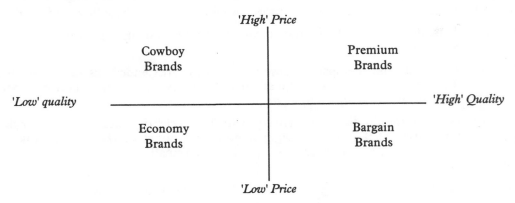

7.4 Price and quality are clearly important elements in every marketing mix, but, in the customer's opinion, they cannot be considered independent variables. A 'high' price will almost always be associated with high quality and equally low price with low quality. Thus, while everybody would like to buy a bargain brand, there is a problem to overcome. This is a question of belief: will customers accept that a high quality product can be offered at a low price?

7.5 MFI would claim to be in the 'bargain' quadrant. Many consumers perceive them to be at the lower end of the economy segment. Frequent sales and discounts in the store has the effect of overcoming at least some of the difficulties resulting from individuals using price as a surrogate for assessment of quality. Thus the price label shows the higher pre-discounted price and the low sale price. Customers appear to use the pre-sale price in order to confirm promotional claims about quality.

7.6 Public concern about such promotional pricing has resulted in the introduction of restrictions on the use of these techniques. Promotions have to be part of a genuine 'sale', and stores must provide evidence of this fact.

Gaps in the market

7.7 Market research into consumer perceptions can determine how customers locate competitive brands on a matrix.

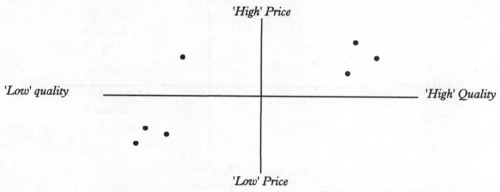

Restaurants in Anytown

7.8 The hypothetical model above shows a gap in the market for a moderately priced reasonable quality eating place. This is evident between clusters in the high price/high quality and the low price/low quality segments.

7.9 It would be wise to think before acting on this assumption. Why does the gap exist? Is it that no entrepreneurial restaurateur has noticed the opportunity? Or is it that, while there is sufficient demand for gourmet eating and cheap cafes, there are insufficient customers to justify a restaurant in the middle range segment? There may well be other factors, such as these, to be taken into consideration in this case. More research would be needed to determine which of these conditions apply.

7.10 As Kotler demonstrates, perceptual maps can also indicate how customers perceive competitive brands performing on key product user benefits. Kotler provides the following hypothetical examples. He starts by considering the various products that serve the US breakfast market.

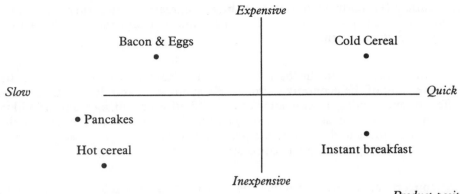

Product-positioning map:
Breakfast market

7.11 A producer might be interested, for example, in entering the instant breakfast market. This is a sub-section of the breakfast market as a whole. It is necessary to plot the position of the various instant breakfast brands.

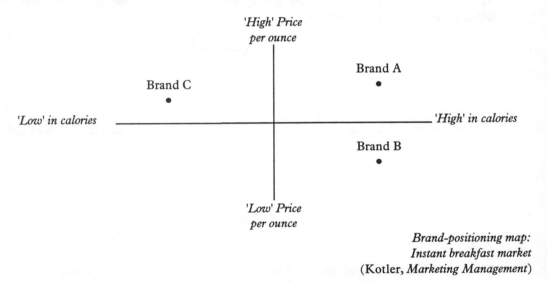

Brand-positioning map:
Instant breakfast market
(Kotler, *Marketing Management*)

Exercise

The analysis above indicates that there is an apparent gap which would suit what type of brand? What is the major consideration after identifying the gap?

Solution

The analysis indicates a gap for a modest priced slimmers brand. It would be necessary to establish that demand for the product is sufficient for it to be profitable.

7.12 In the case of the Ford Fiesta, market research showed that although potential customers thought highly of the new car's performance and considered it economical, perceptions of safety were less satisfactory. Its small size was seen as a safety drawback in the event of a crash. Ford believed their product to be safe and so, when the Fiesta was relaunched, intended the advertising copy line to change people's perception. One such advertisement showed the Fiesta braking in wet conditions, another showed a pregnant woman being raced to hospital.

Competitive positioning

7.13 Competitive positioning is concerned with 'a general idea of what kind of offer to make to the target market in relation to competitors' offers' (Kotler). Product quality and price are obviously important for competitive positioning, but Kotler identified a 3 × 3 matrix of nine different competitive positioning strategies.

Product quality	High price	Medium price	Low price
High	Premium strategy	Penetration strategy	Superbargain strategy
Medium	Overpricing strategy	Average quality strategy	Bargain strategy
Low	Hit and run strategy	Shoddy goods strategy	Cheap goods strategy

8   A SEGMENTATION AND POSITIONING STUDY

8.1   Texas Instruments, the US electronics manufacturer, aimed to be the market leader in the world's semiconductor industry, continuing to compete with the Japanese in the commodity microchip market long after other US chip manufacturers had given up competing and had begun to concentrate on custom-made and original design chips for specific customers or specific uses, which earn a higher profit margin on sales.

8.2   In 1980s, the price of dynamic random access memory (DRAM) chips fell sharply, and Texas Instruments' record profits turned to record losses. Reassessment of its marketing strategy led to the following policy decisions.

8.3   Texas realised that within its generic product market, there were specific segments with clearly identifiable needs. It was then able to evaluate those segments and to position products aiming to exploit those markets. Most attractive segments, for Texas, would be those whose needs could be met by building on the company's strengths and where demand, profitability and growth forecasts were favourable.

8.4   Evaluating a market opportunity begins with the estimation of market demand. It is extremely important to decide on:

(a)   the precise nature of the product;
(b)   the characteristics of consumers;
(c)   usage aspects of the product;
(d)   the time sale involved;
(e)   the location and scale of the market.

Kotler identifies 90 possible combinations of market demand definitions based on product level, geographic area and time horizon.

8.5   The definition of market demand must be clearly specified in terms of customer group, geographic area and time period. Any forecast of future demand must also include consideration of the expected level of marketing activity within the industry.

MARKET ATTRACTIVENESS

	High	Medium	Low
High			
Medium			
Low			

COMPETITIVE ADVANTAGE

8.6   When the attractiveness of each identified segment has been evaluated it can be considered along with the relative strengths which determine the potential advantages the organisation would have in each segment. In this way preferred target segments can be targeted.

8.7   Given that the risks and investment of resources required are very similar for each segment, then the company will choose to concentrate its resources and efforts in the segments which provide the best combination of market attractiveness and competitive advantage.

8.8   The needs of the targeted segment can then be identified and a marketing mix strategy developed in order to provide the relevant benefits package.

(a)   Texas Instruments decided to stay in the DRAM business, because the skills and technical expertise obtained in this industry would spill over into other parts of the business, and keep the company in the forefront of technological developments. The company no longer aimed to be the world's market leader in the DRAM business. Sales growth was no longer a number one priority.

(b)   In order to cut costs in its DRAM business, TI's workforce was cut by 10%, and two semiconductor factories were closed down, as part of a strategy for reorganisation and improving productivity.

(c)   A more marketing oriented approach was needed, since customers were now expecting better service from microchip manufacturers. The philosophy that superior technology will sell itself was abandoned, and instead the company began to recognise that customers didn't necessarily want the 'best' microchips; they wanted the chips that would solve their particular processing problems. The president of TI was reported as saying:

> 'There is a new emphasis across the corporation on strengthening our customer relationships. This will be a key to our long-term success. We must and will be market-oriented. Profitability will only come as a result of identifying and satisfying the real needs of our customers.'

(d)   The company targeted four specific segments of the market:

   (i)   microchips tailored to the needs of specific customers - custom-made chips;

   (ii)   'application processors' - microprocessors for special uses such as graphics and local area networks;

(iii)   highly integrated standard logic chips;

(iv)   military uses.

8.9   Other parts of the company portfolio, such as oil exploration and home computers, were also subject to cost-cutting measures. Two programmes of R & D, in artificial intelligence and factory automation, with large research and development budgets, were developed as part of a long term strategy. The president of TI has again been quoted as follows.

'Artificial intelligence and industrial automation both have the potential of becoming important businesses to TI. But a significant, additional advantage will come from our ability to focus these skills, strengthen them and infuse them back into our core businesses.'

Chapter roundup

- A market is rarely a mass, homogeneous group of customers, each wanting an identical product. Market segmentation is based on the recognition that every market consists of potential buyers with different needs, and different buying behaviour. These different customer attitudes may be grouped into segments and a different marketing approach will be taken by an organisation for each market segment.

- A total market may occasionally be homogenous, but this is rare. Each market segment becomes an individual target market for the organisation, and requires a unique marketing mix. The organisation can formulate a marketing strategy for each target market. Segmentation is an extremely important marketing tool.

- There are a number of ways in which a consumer market can be segmented, for example by location, by demography, by social class or by life style. Industrial markets can also be segmented.

- Limited resources and competition in large markets make it impossible for companies to sell to the entire market. For the sake of efficiency they must select target markets. There are three basic options in marketing products for target markets.

- Brands can be positioned in relation to competitors on 'product maps', on which space and positioning is defined in terms of how key characteristics of products are perceived by buyers.

Test your knowledge

1   What is Kotler's definition of market segmentation? (see para 2.1)

2   What are the three requirements for effective market segmentation? (2.7)

3   What is the most commonly used classification in segmentation by social class? (3.6)

4   Give examples of recent trends (over the last 20 - 30 years) in the characteristics of the family unit. (3.11)

5   What is psychographics? (3.17)

6   What is ACORN? (4.2)

7   Give four examples of how industrial markets might be segmented. (5.2)

8   What is concentrated marketing? (6.1)

9   Give five examples of characteristics which may be used to position products. (7.2)

10   Draw Kotler's 3×3 matrix of different competitive positioning strategies, plotting price against product quality. (7.13)

Now try illustrative question 2 at the end of the Study Text

MARKETING OPERATIONS IN ACTION

At the end of each part of this Study Text, we take a look at the subject matter covered in the light of real companies, either to offer more detail or to give an understanding of the wider corporate context.

In this first part of the Text we have explored some issues relating to the analysis of marketing opportunities. We have seen that the analysis of the organisation's marketing environment is a key part of this process and that, within the environment, the nature of competition and the state of rivalry amongst current competitors should be monitored. You should find the following material interesting both in the context of what you have read and in the context of asking yourself what constitutes ethical behaviour something we will be looking at later in this Study Text.

Increased competition and the development of the global marketplace have led to many organisations demanding more and more information about their competitors. Whereas in the UK and Europe, organisations are largely content to carry out primary and secondary research, using recognised methods such as customer satisfaction surveys, product literature, newspaper articles and annual reports, the situation in the US and in Japan is rather different. Competitive intelligence, or CI, is becoming an acceptable business practice, even though it has been likened by some to corporate espionage.

A number of organisations in the US have now crossed the line from traditional market research and analysis to competitive intelligence. The Marketing Audit of Philadelphia, Pennsylvania and Fuld & Co, Inc of Cambridge, Massachusetts are just two companies which specialise in CI. Jonathan Lax, managing partner of TMA, is quoted in *Marketing Business* (March 1994) as follows. 'About four years ago, three independent clients simultaneously came to me with the same request. They said that we were very good at getting people on the phone and structuring research projects and interviewing their customers and suppliers, but could we do this with their competitors?'

Lax's team of 'intelligence agents' use the telephone as their primary weapon. Although it may seem strange that staff in an organisation would willingly discuss confidential company information with strangers, the experience is that this is exactly what happens. Many employees simply do not recognise the value of the data which they possess, and junior staff who are privy to data intended for their bosses may pass it on either because they are unwary or because they are not used to being asked to divulge or discuss it.

One of TMS's assignments was performed for DuPont. DuPont was investigating the feasibility of entering the soda bottle recycling market and TMA staff carried out telephone interviews with existing players in the market and performed generic market research in order to identify potential opportunities.

TMA was able to glean precise information on the following.

(a)   Volume per site
(b)   Volume per month
(c)   Spot prices for sorted and unsorted materials
(d)   Advantages of sites and locations

Using the results of this summary, DuPont decided to enter the soda bottle recycling market.

The CI companies claim that their work is both legally and ethically correct and some publish ethics statements claiming that they will not lie, bribe or steal in gathering confidential information. They might, for example, describe themselves on the telephone as industry researchers without disclosing that they are working for a specific client.

You might wish to revisit this page after you have studied the chapter on Marketing Ethics later in this Text.

Part B
The marketing planning process

Chapter 3

INTRODUCTION TO MARKETING PLANNING

This chapter covers the following topics.

1   The marketing planning process

2   The relationship of marketing planning to corporate planning

3   The marketing planning cycle

4   Conducting a marketing audit

5   Using ratio analysis

Introduction

Once the analysis of marketing opportunities has been completed, as described in Part A of this Study Text, the marketing planning process can begin. This is an analysis of markets and trading environment opportunities. It will usually involve a determination of an organisation's core markets, a search for competitive advantage and a statement of goals and desired brand positioning. It will result in the determination of marketing programmes for implementation.

In this chapter, we look at marketing planning and its relationship to corporate planning, see how a strategy might be formulated and introduce the marketing audit. In Chapter 4 we develop the links between strategy and objectives and in Chapter 5 we will examine the planning process itself.

---

1   THE MARKETING PLANNING PROCESS

1.1   Marketing planning is a systematic process that involves the identification and assessment of marketing opportunities, the assessment of current and likely future resources and distinctive competences, the development of strategies and objectives and the implementation of detailed marketing programmes. In the syllabus, this process is defined and categorised in three main stages as follows.

(a)   Analysis of markets and trading environment opportunities

(b)   Determination of core markets; competitive edge/differential advantage, statement of goals and desired brand positioning.

(c)   Determination of marketing programme for implementation.

1.2   Further insights into how the market planning process actually works are afforded by Dibb, Simkin, Pride, Ferrell:

'The marketing planning process *combines* the organisation's overall marketing strategy *with* fundamental analyses of trends in the marketing environment; company strengths, weaknesses, opportunities and threats, competitive strategies; and identification of target market segments. Ultimately the process *leads to* the formulation of market programmes or marketing mixes *which facilitate* the implementation of the organisation's strategies and plans.

1.3   The emphases in key words (which are added, not the authors') serve to highlight the nature of the process, which is also cyclical.

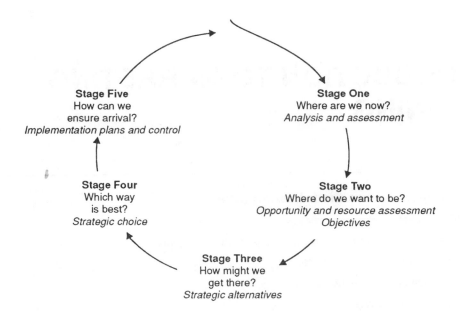

1.4   *Stage 1* is analytical rather than decisive. We can't decide where we want to be until we know where we are now. Examples of the sort of analyses required start with sales, market share and environmental analysis. We should also want to know our position relative to competitors and so competitor analysis is also pertinent.

1.5   *Stage 2* is more decisive than analytical and moves us deeper into the planning process. However, coming to the right decision depends upon further analysis, both of the opportunities emerging from stage 1's environmental scanning and of our organisation's strengths, weaknesses, resources and distinctive competences. This part of the process is the *combines* stage referred to in the Dibb et al definition and *leads to* the setting of achievable/realistic objectives.

1.6   *Stage 3* involves achieving of objectives and now we are at the heart of the process. Achieving objectives is normally split into two sub-stages.

(a)   How are we going to get there in broad terms: = *strategy*
(b)   How are we going to get there in detailed terms: = *tactics (or operations)*

There are choices at both of these sub-stages which have to be evaluated and decisions made. At strategic level a suitable choice framework might be Ansoff, whereas at the more detailed level it is likely to be the marketing mix (which *facilitates* the implementation of strategies)

1.7   We can see from these examples that all the stages of the planning process, although being distinctive, tend to merge into the process as a whole, which is in itself iterative in nature.

2   THE RELATIONSHIP OF MARKETING PLANNING TO CORPORATE PLANNING

2.1   Although marketing has in the past been seen as a separate distinct activity with a primarily *tactical* role to play in business development, this view is largely being replaced by the recognition that marketing has a key *strategic* role. Planning at the corporate level is now employing a totally new notion of this strategic role of marketing. *Strategic planning* sets or changes the *objectives* of an organisation. *Tactical planning* is concerned with decisions about the efficient and effective use of an organisation's resources to achieve these objectives and strategic targets.

2.2   At the same time, consumers are becoming more sophisticated and quality conscious. Consequently, planning is more important than ever, to allow a business to guide its development in an increasingly unknown and uncertain future. Effective planning will establish a *proactive* stance to its markets and to anticipate changes to ensure that it sustains a competitive position. It is crucial that plans are flexible and adaptable in these circumstances.

2.3   *Corporate strategic plans* aim to guide the overall development of an organisation. Specific plans regarding marketing strategies will be determined within these parameters. These plans, to be effective, will inevitably be interlinked and interdependent with those for other functions of the organisation. This chapter focuses on marketing planning, recognising that this will involve both strategic and operational components. The *strategic* component of marketing planning focuses on the direction which an organisation will take in relation to a specific market or set of markets in order to achieve a specified set of objectives. Marketing planning also requires an *operational* component which defines specific tasks and activities to be undertaken in order to achieve the desired strategy.

2.4   Developing a planned, strategic approach ensures that marketing activities are consistent with organisational goals, are internally coherent and are tailored to the needs of identified consumer markets. It should also ensure that the resources available are systematically allocated and are consistent with specified objectives.

3   THE MARKETING PLANNING CYCLE

3.1   Any marketing plan should follow a logical structure, from historical and current analyses of the organisation and its market, on to a statement of objectives, on to the development of a strategy suitable for that market (both in general and on the way to developing an appropriate marketing mix) and finally to an outline of the appropriate methods for implementation. Implementation often appears briefly at the end of any discussion of marketing plans; and yet, arguably, the process of monitoring and controlling marketing activities is *the* crucial determinant of whether a plan is successful or not.

3.2   The plan aims to offer management a coherent set of clearly defined guidelines, but at the same time remain flexible enough to adapt to changing conditions both within the organisation and also in relation to its markets. The stages in strategic planning are shown below.

Development of the organisation's mission statement

↓

Statement of objectives

↓

Situational analysis

↓

Strategy development

↓

Specific plans

↓

Implementation

Mission statement

3.3   The company mission statement is simply a statement of what an organisation is aiming to achieve through the conduct of its business. In a sense, it can be thought of as a statement of the organisation's reason for existence. The purpose is to provide the organisation with *focus* and *direction*.

3.4   The corporate mission depends on a variety of factors. Corporate history will often influence the markets and customer groups served - thus, in the banking sector Credit

Agricole retains strong links with its farming depositors, while Coutts concentrates primarily on high income consumers in its retail banking activities.

3.5   What approaches are taken to markets and customers is also influenced by corporate culture and organisational structures. The commonest approach to the corporate mission relies on the product/market scope. The mission statement then rests on customer groups, needs served and technology employed. From the perspective of marketing this is useful since it forces managers to 'foreground' the customer groups and the needs/wants which the firm aims to satisfy.

3.6   It is insufficient for a bank to identify its mission as being 'banking' - it would be more appropriate to identify that mission as being, for example, 'meeting consumer needs for financial transactions.' A mission statement in this form can offer guidelines to management as to how the business should develop and in which directions. A clear mission statement enables future growth strategies to rely on what are regarded as distinctive competences and aim for synergies by dealing with similar customer groups, similar customer needs or similar service technologies.

3.7   We look at mission statements further in Chapter 4.

Statement of objectives

3.8   Objectives are part of the planning process both at the corporate and at the market level. Corporate objectives define specific goals for the organisation as a whole. This may be expressed in terms of profitability, returns on investment, growth of asset base, earnings per share etc. These will permeate the planning process and be reflected in the objectives for marketing and other functional plans. Clearly, the objectives specified for marketing will be subordinate to those specified at the corporate level. An important component of the marketing planning process is the translation of corporate (often financial) objectives into market specific marketing objectives. This may well involve targets for the size of the customer base, growth in the usage of certain facilities, gains in market share for a particular product type etc. Any objectives must conform to three criteria; they must be achievable, they must be consistent and they must be stated clearly and preferably quantitatively.

3.9   We look at objectives further in Chapter 4.

3.10   Once the corporate mission has been formulated and corporate objectives have been specified, this information, in conjunction with further detailed analysis of the environment, provides the input for the next stage in the planning process.

Situation analysis

3.11   Environmental factors will have affected the mission statement and the identification of objectives, but a much more comprehensive analysis is necessary as a basis for overall and market specific strategies. Situation analysis involves a thorough study of the broad trends within the economy and society, and a comprehensive analysis of markets, consumers and competitors. In particular, the nature and extent of *market segmentation* must be taken into account as well as an understanding of the organisation's internal environment and its particular strengths and weaknesses. Market research and the use of external databases provide the main source of information relating to the external environment. An audit of the organisation's marketing activities provides information on the internal environment. A *marketing information system* is the ideal means for processing and analysing this type of data, while techniques such as SWOT analysis (see earlier) are of use in organising and presenting the results.

3.12   This situation analysis was largely the subject of Chapter 1.

Strategy development

3.13 The process of strategy development links corporate level plans and market level plans. In developing strategy, most large organisations will be required to make important *resource allocation* decisions. Balancing a range of products, divisions, financial and human resources requires that they be allocated in a manner consistent with the achievement of corporate objectives. Some areas will be designated for expansion, others perhaps for contraction. This process of resource allocation is a key component of corporate strategy and it indicates the direction in which specific markets or products are expected to develop. It therefore provides direction for the development of *market level plans*.

3.14 We look at strategy in detail in Chapter 4.

Specific plans

3.15 Market specific plans express the organisation's intentions concerning particular markets, or in some cases, particular products. These are linked to the corporate plan through the statement of objectives and the resource allocation component in strategy development. Situation analysis at the market level can provide information on patterns of competition, consumer behaviour and market segmentation, as an input to the development of marketing objectives and market specific strategies.

3.16 Market specific variables, typically under the control of the marketing department, are product, price, promotion and place. The development of the marketing mix aims to ensure that the product is appropriate to the market in terms of its features, its image, its perceived value and its availability.

3.17 Marketing expenditure will depend on resource allocation decisions at corporate levels, but any marketing plan will include, as a matter of course, a statement of the budget required and the way it is to be spent.

3.18 We look at detailed plans in Chapter 5.

Implementation

3.19 This involves identifying the specific tasks to be performed, the allocation of those tasks to individuals and putting in place a system which can monitor their implementation - specifying any short term marketing research which needs to be undertaken to determine how appropriate the product is, the nature of customer reactions etc. The implementation procedure may also include some elements of contingency planning. The market is always changing so that even the most well formed marketing plan will need to be changed and certain planned activities may turn out to be inappropriate or ineffective.

4 CONDUCTING A MARKETING AUDIT

4.1 Marketing management aims to ensure the company is pursuing effective policies to promote its products, markets and distribution channels. This involves exercising strategic control of marketing, and the means to apply strategic control is known as the marketing audit.

4.2 A marketing audit is not a legal requirement, nor does it involves formal procedures, as does an external financial audit does. In order to exercise proper strategic control, however, a marketing audit should:

(a) be conducted regularly;

    (b)   take a comprehensive look at every product, market, distribution channel, ingredient in the marketing mix and so on and should not be restricted to areas of apparent ineffectiveness such as an unprofitable product, a troublesome distribution channel, or low efficiency on direct selling;

    (c)   be carried out according to a set of predetermined, specified procedures: it should be systematic.

The 'auditors' should, if possible, be independent and not be coloured by particular job interests, or distorted by a particular perspective.

The audit procedure

4.3   A marketing audit should consider the following. An alternative framework is offered at the end of this section.

(a)   *The marketing environment*

    (i)   What are the organisation's major markets, and how are these markets segmented? How are these market segments likely to change?

    (ii)   Who are our customers, what is known about their needs, intentions and behaviour?

    (iii)   Who are our competitors, and what is known about them?

    (iv)   Have there been any significant developments in the broader environment (eg economic or political changes, population or social changes).

(b)   *Marketing objectives and plans*

    (i)   What are the organisation's marketing objectives with respect to its products or services and how do they relate to overall corporate objectives?

    (ii)   Is allocation of resources being committed to marketing sufficient to enable the objectives to be achieved? Are the costs arising between products, areas etc satisfactory?

    (iii)   Is expenditure allocated to direct selling, advertising, distribution etc appropriate for the objectives being pursued?

    (iv)   What procedures are in place for formulating marketing plans and exercising management control of these plans; are they satisfactory?

    (v)   Are marketing organisations (and personnel) operating efficiently?

(c)   *Marketing activities*

This involves the following.

    (i)   A review of sales price levels (looking at, for example, supply demand, customer attitudes or the use of temporary price reductions).

    (ii)   A review of the state of each individual product (its market 'health') and of the product mix as a whole.

    (iii)   A critical analysis of the distribution system.

    (iv)   A review of the size and organisation of the personal sales force.

    (v)   A review of the effectiveness of advertising and sales promotion activities.

4.4   The following diagram illustrates the relation between planning at corporate level and marketing planning, and shows the position of the marketing audit.

Corporate plan

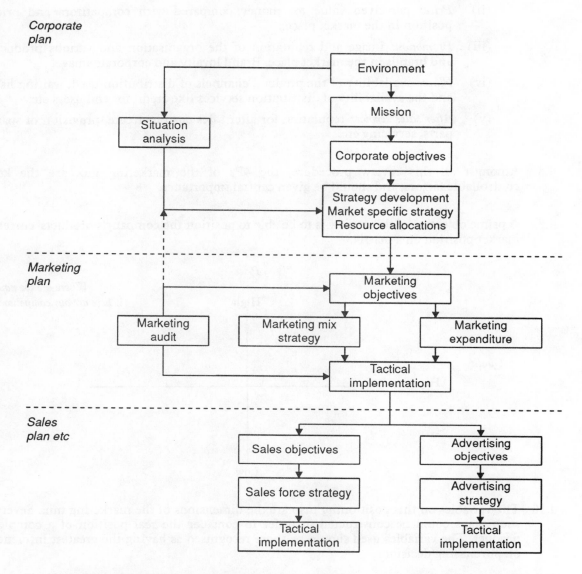

Marketing plan

Sales plan etc

4.5   As we can see, it is easy to confuse marketing with corporate level planning. Corporate audit of product/market strengths and weaknesses and much of the external environment analysis should, of course, be informed by information gathered during the marketing audit. The marketing department is probably the most important source of 'bottom up' information, opinions and views used in the development of corporate strategy. The marketing audit is the starting point for developing the marketing plan. 'Where are we now?' is formulated in terms of marketing controllables.

4.6   A marketing audit involves 'taking stock' of all marketing activity. It must be undertaken regularly to monitor progress and changes in marketing performance. It must be systematic and thorough and a thorough audit at this level needs to review much more than just operational effectiveness of the marketing activity.

4.7   Among the elements reviewed, the following are particularly important.

(a)   Marketing strategy - looking at the quality and effectiveness of marketing plans in the past.

(b)   The marketing organisation - marketing systems, organisation structure, degree of market orientation in the corporate philosophy and the quality of marketing information available, should all be taken into account.

(c)   The strengths and weaknesses of the organisation's marketing mix (ie operational effectiveness) should be evaluated, particularly the following.

(i)   *Products:* range, quality, competitive advantage, stage of the life cycle and technical reputation etc.

    (ii)   *Price:* perceived value for money compared with competitors and price position in the market place.

    (iii)   *Promotion:* image and reputation of the organisation and various products and brands in the market place. Brand loyalty and corporate image.

    (iv)   *Place:* availability of the product, channels of distribution used, waiting lists and the availability of distribution services like credit for end users etc.

    (v)   *After sales service:* reputation for after sales customer care, provision of spare parts, servicing etc.

4.8   Amongst all this review procedure, the 4Ps of the marketing mix are the key controllable factors, and should be given central importance.

4.9   A prime objective of this review is to be able to position the company's products' current market position on a matrix.

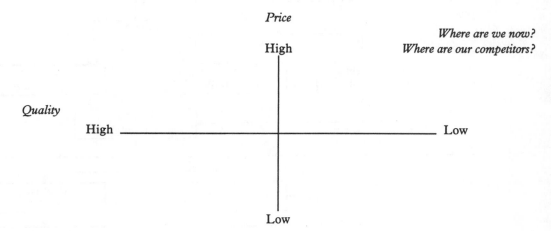

4.10   The variables on this positioning map are the dimensions of the marketing mix. Several such maps could be constructed in order to consider the real position of a complex product. The variables used should be those recognised as having the greatest influence on purchasing decisions.

4.11   External aspects of the marketing audit are the product/market opportunities and threats which evolve from changes in the macro environment identified at the corporate level. For example a demographic shift increasing the proportion of older customers for overseas holidays may have been identified as the environmental audit of a package holiday company. At marketing level this raises a number of possibilities.

(a)   A marketing opportunity to sell existing holidays to this new target market.

(b)   A marketing opportunity to develop new products specifically developed to meet the needs of this emerging segment.

(c)   The option of diverting resources from segments showing less growth potential.

4.12   The Ansoff matrix can provide a formulation of options and opportunities available. In relation to the example, the matrix reveals the following.

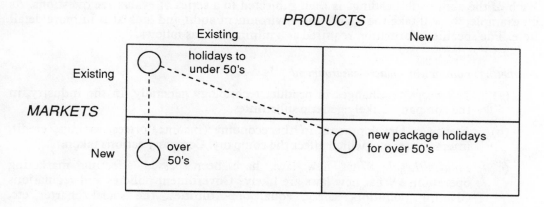

A framework for the marketing audit

4.13 To conclude this section we look at a possible framework for the marketing audit. As regards a suitable framework, Kotler's is often cited as the definitive version, whose outline is generally as follows:

(a) *Marketing environment audit*

    (i)   Macro-environment
        (1) economic-demographic
        (2) technological
        (3) political/legal
        (4) cultural
        (5) ecological

    (ii) Task environment
        (1) markets
        (2) customers
        (3) competitors
        (4) distribution and dealers
        (5) suppliers
        (6) facilitators and marketing firms
        (7) publics

(b) *Marketing strategy audit*

        (1) business mission
        (2) marketing objectives and goals
        (3) strategy

(c) *Marketing organisation audit*

        (1) format structure
        (2) functional efficiency
        (3) interface efficiency

(d) *Marketing systems audit*

        (1) marketing information system
        (2) marketing planning systems
        (3) marketing control system
        (4) new product development system

(e) *Marketing productivity audit*

        (1) profitability analysis
        (2) cost-effectiveness analysis

(f) *Marketing function audit*

        (1) products
        (2) prices
        (3) distribution
        (4) advertising/ sales promotion/publicity
        (5) salesforce

4.14 Each of the above sub-headings is then subjected to a series of evaluative questions. As an example, we will take the Marketing environment audit and look at it in more detail here. The specific information required as a minimum is as follows.

4.15 *Marketing environment - macro-environment*

(a) *Technological.* Changes in product technology generally, in the industry, in the company. Likely generic substitutes.

(b) *Economic.* Developments in the economy (income, prices, savings, credit, interest rates etc) which affect the company. Company actions taken.

(c) *Political/Legal.* What new laws have been passed affecting marketing operations? What new laws are likely? Government policies and regulations covering pollution, safety, equal opportunities, the social charter etc, affecting strategies and the mix.

(d) *Sociological.* What major demographic changes have occurred or are likely to occur? Company responses to these. What public/consumer concerns are being expressed regarding conservation pollution of the environment, generally? Company responses to these. What are our publics' attitudes towards us and our products/services? What changes in consumer/business lifestyles and values have occurred which might affect our marketing?

4.16 *Marketing environment - task environment*

(a) *Markets.* What changes are occurring in market trends - sales, profits, geographic distribution? What changes are occurring in market segments and niches?

(b) *Distributors.* What are the major distributive channels in our markets? What are the channels' efficiency levels and growth trends?

(c) *Suppliers.* Outlooks for future supplies. Trends in patterns of buying/selling. Changes in power bases. Evaluations of suppliers against buying/ marketing criteria

(d) *Agencies.* What are the costs/availability outlooks for transportation services, for warehousing facilities, for financial resources etc? Just how effective are our advertising, PR and marketing research agencies?

(e) *Publics.* What publics offer particular opportunities or problems for us? What steps have we taken to deal effectively with each public?

(f) *Customers.* How do customers/potential customers rate us on aspects such as reputation, product quality, service, salesforce, advertising/price etc, relative to our competitors? What sorts of customers do we have? Are they changing? What is our customers' buying behaviour? Is it changing? How well do we understand our customers and their buying motives?

(g) *Competitors.* Who are our major competitors? What are their market shares? What are their strengths and weaknesses? Competitors' marketing strategies and likely responses to our marketing actions. Future changes in competition.

5   USING RATIO ANALYSIS

5.1 Although the marketer is not usually concerned with financial accounting matters, some knowledge of performance measurements can be a useful tool in carrying out a marketing audit. Ratio analysis involves comparing one figure against another to produce a ratio, and assessing whether the ratio indicates a weakness or strength in the company's affairs. There is a wide range of ratios which can be calculated, ranging from profitability and liquidity through to shareholders' investment ratios.

5.2 Each individual business must be considered separately and those ratios which are important for particular companies identified. Also, a ratio that is meaningful for a manufacturing company may be completely meaningless for a financial institution.

5.3   Meaningful information can be obtained from ratio analysis by a process of *comparison*. This may involve comparing ratios over time within the same business to establish whether things are improving or declining, and comparing ratios between similar businesses to see whether the company you are analysing is better or worse than average.

Exercise

Like SWOT analysis, ratio analysis on its own is not sufficient for understanding a company's operations. What other items of information in a set of company accounts should be examined?

Solution

Other items of information which should be looked at include the following.

(a)   Comments in the chairman's report and directors' report.

(b)   The age and nature of the company's assets.

(c)   Current and future developments in the company's markets, at home and overseas, recent acquisitions or disposals of subsidiaries by the company.

(d)   Extraordinary items in the profit and loss account.

(e)   Any other noticeable features of the report and accounts, such as post balance sheet events, contingent liabilities, a qualified auditors' report, the company's taxation position, and so on.

Profitability ratios

5.4   In assessing a company's profitability, profit on ordinary activities *before* taxation is generally thought to be a better figure to use than profit after taxation, because there might be unusual variations in the tax charge from year to year which would not affect the underlying profitability of the company's operations.

5.5   PBIT, profit before interest and tax, is the amount of profit which the company earned before having to pay interest to the providers of loan capital. By providers of loan capital, we usually mean longer-term loan capital, such as debentures and medium-term bank loans, which will be shown in the balance sheet as 'creditors: amounts falling due after more than one year'.

Liquidity

5.6   Although profitability is an important aspect of a company's performance, it does not address directly the key issue of liquidity.

5.7   Liquidity is the amount of cash a company can put its hands on quickly to settle its debts (and possibly to meet other unforeseen demands for cash payments too). Liquid assets are current asset items that will or could soon be converted into cash, and cash itself. Liquid assets consist of the following.

(a)   Cash.

(b)   Short-term investments for which there is a ready market.

(c)   Fixed-term deposits with a bank or building society.

(d)   Trade debtors (those who will pay within a short period of time).

(e)   Bills of exchange receivable (also amounts of cash due to be received within a relatively short period of time).

Liquidity ratios

5.8 The 'standard' test of liquidity is the current ratio. It can be obtained from the balance sheet, and is the ratio of:

$$\frac{\text{current assets}}{\text{current liabilities}}$$

5.9 A ratio comfortably exceeding 1 should be expected, but what is 'comfortable' varies according to the business involved.

5.10 Often companies are unable to convert all their current assets into cash very quickly, for example, manufacturing companies may hold large quantities of raw material stocks. Where stock turnover is slow, most stocks are not very 'liquid' assets, because the cash cycle is so long. For these reasons, we calculate an additional liquidity ratio, known as the quick ratio or acid test ratio.

5.11 The quick ratio, or acid test ratio is:

$$\frac{\text{current assets less stocks}}{\text{current liabilities}}$$

Other performance ratios

5.12 A range of performance ratios may be employed, for a variety of reasons. For a marketing manager, the performance of a brand or a product range is particularly important. *Market share* shows the volume of sales for the organisation's own product as a percentage of total sales for the market as a whole.

5.13 Other performance ratios may be relevant when measuring the effectiveness of different aspects of marketing performance - for instance, the distribution system, the efficiency of employees or the value of a particular promotional strategy. Cost or revenue performance measures may also include non-monetary data, such as:

(a) value added per employee;

(b) wages per employee;

(c) sales per cubic metre of shelf space;

(d) sales per square metre of floor space;

(e) sales per £1 of advertising;

(f) sales per employee in the sales force;

(g) contribution per cubic metre of shelf space, per square metre of floor space or per employee;

(h) net profit per cubic metre of shelf space, square metre of floor space or per employee;

(i) occupancy costs per square metre of floor space;

(j) cost per call of a salesperson;

(k) value of sales per call;

(l) cost per ton/mile or tonne/kilometre of delivering goods.

This list is by no means exhaustive and ratios to measure both the effectiveness and efficiency of a business can and are calculated within each business because they are specific to that business and provide a good yardstick for comparative purposes.

Chapter roundup

- Marketing planning is a systematic process that involves the identification and assessment of marketing opportunities, the assessment of current and likely future resources and distinctive competences, the development of strategies and objectives and the implementation of detailed marketing programmes.

- Corporate planning should include the formulation of specific marketing strategies. Marketing planning involves strategic and operational components. It is important that marketing activities are consistent with organisational goals.

- *Marketing audits* are a means of applying strategic control to ensure that marketing policies are optimal. They should be carried out regularly, comprehensively and as far as possible objectively. The audit should consider the marketing environment existing marketing objectives and plans, and marketing activities, and use various kinds of performance measure.

- Performance measures are also an important aspect of the audit, planning and strategy formulation process. A wide range of measures are available, both quantitative and qualitative, and which ones need to be employed will depend on the particular objectives, and problems, faced by a manager, as well as the nature of the business involved.

Test your knowledge

1   What are the three stages of marketing planning? (see para 1.1)

2   What is a mission statement? (3.3)

3   How does the setting of objectives fit into the planning process? (3.8)

4   What does implementation of the marketing plan involve? (3.19)

5   What are the features of a good marketing audit? (4.2)

6   Explain the use of the price/quality matrix. (4.9)

7   Sketch the Ansoff matrix (4.12)

8   What are the contents of Kotler's framework for the marketing audit? (4.13)

9   What is liquidity? (5.7)

10 Give five examples of performance ratios. (5.13)

Now try illustrative question 3 at the end of the Study Text

Chapter 4

DEVELOPING MARKETING OBJECTIVES AND STRATEGIES

This chapter covers the following topics.

1   The mission statement

2   Objectives

3   Non-financial objectives

4   Gap analysis

5   What is a strategy?

6   Strategy formulation

7   Competitive strategies

8   Growth strategies

9   Boston Consultancy Group

10 PIMS

11 Evaluating the strategy

Introduction

In this chapter we develop some of the ideas introduced in Chapter 3. As we have seen, the marketing strategy defines target markets, competitive edges and desired brand positioning. Marketing objectives, on the other hand, are simple goal statements. Strategic planning requires the development of strategies to enable the organisation to achieve its objectives: we describe later in the chapter a number of techniques used for this.

---

1   THE MISSION STATEMENT

1.1   As we saw briefly in the last chapter, a mission statement sets the scene and provides the broad parameters within which management is expected to operate. The firm's mission is a clear statement of the business it identifies itself as being in or intending to be in.

1.2   A mission statement such as 'we are in the business of making profits' does not give guidance on the nature of the business involved.

1.3   If mission statements are too narrow they tend to blinker management thinking, so that threats and opportunities are missed. British Rail are accused of getting the mission statement wrong for decades in seeing themselves as being in the business of 'running a rail network'. Their image of their business, it is claimed, resulted in failure to respond strategically to the development of motorways, the growth of car ownership and the developing domestic airline network.

1.4   Arguably, it would have been more appropriate to see themselves as being in the business of 'transporting people and freight throughout Britain', since this would have given them a different view of threats.

1.5   The mission should encompass the opportunities for diversification and development which will encourage synergy within the total operation.

1.6   Mission statements can be changed and should be challenged if there is a good case for doing so, but not too often, because they act as a broad umbrella statement under which managers can plan medium-term strategy, forming an important anchor for the business.

1.7   A good mission statement should be concise. It should clearly answer the question, 'what business are we in?'. Financial or profit dimensions can be left out as these are contained much more specifically in the corporate objectives.

2   OBJECTIVES

2.1   Objectives are clear statements of what the business or department intends to achieve. They are created in hierarchical order. The lower objectives contribute to the achievement of primary objectives.

2.2   *Corporate objectives* are those which are concerned with the firm as a whole. Objectives should be explicit, quantifiable and capable of being achieved. They outline the expectations of the firm. The *strategic planning* process is concerned with the *means* of achieving these objectives.

2.3   Corporate objectives often relate to key financial factors including the following.

   (a) Profitability (return on investment)
   (b) Market share
   (c) Growth
   (d) Cash flow

2.4   *Unit objectives* are specific to individual units of an organisation, and are often 'operational' objectives, for example, marketing or production. Examples would include the following.

   (a) *From the commercial world*

   (i)   Increasing the number of customers by X% (an objective of a sales department).

   (ii) Reducing the number of rejects by 50% (an objective of a production department).

   (iii) Producing monthly reports within five working days of the end of each month (an objective of the management accounting department).

   (b) *From the public sector*

   (i)   To reduce the cost of travel by introducing an X% subsidy on bus travel.
   (ii) To introduce 1,000 more nursery education places.
   (iii) To reduce the response times to emergency calls by two minutes.

Primary and secondary objectives

2.5   In the hierarchy of objectives, a *primary corporate objective* (restricted by certain constraints on corporate activity) is more important than *secondary objectives* which are strategic objectives which should combine to ensure the achievement of the overall corporate objective.

2.6   If a company sets itself a primary objective of growth in profits, it will then have to develop *strategies* by which this primary objective can be achieved. An objective must then be set for each individual strategy. Many secondary objectives may simply be targets by which the success of a strategy can be measured.

2.7 Although profitability must be the primary objective for a profit-making commercial organisation, there are different ways of measuring profitability. Argenti cited the creation of customers, servicing society, providing employment and maximising profits as various objectives, and concluded that an objective must be expressed as follows.

(a) It must identify the beneficiaries.
(b) It must state what the nature of the benefit is to be.
(c) It must state the size of the benefit.

Trade-off between objectives

2.8 When there are several key objectives, some might be achieved only at the expense of others. For example, a company's objective of achieving good profits and profit growth might have adverse consequences for the cash flow of the business, or the quality of the firm's product and vice versa.

2.9 In a trade-off between objectives when strategies are formulated, a choice will have to be made.

Long-term and short-term objectives

2.10 Objectives may be long-term and short-term.

2.11 Secondary objectives will range from short-term to long-term. Planners will formulate secondary objectives within the guidelines set by the primary objective, after selecting strategies for achieving the primary objective.

2.12 Objectives, targets and plans are inter-related aspects of the strategic planning process. Targets cannot be set without an awareness of what is realistic. Quantified targets for achieving the primary objective, and targets for secondary objectives, must therefore emerge from a realistic 'situation audit' of the organisation's position and resources, and from the planning process.

> 'Organisations should set realistic objectives; these should be related both to short-term and long-term goals. Since marketing is concerned with the efficient use of corporate resources to meet specific market needs, these targets, short- or long-term, should be based on budgets which are tied in with levels of forecasted demand.'
>
> (P M Chisnall, *Strategic Industrial Marketing*)

Trade offs between short-term and long-term objectives

2.13 There might be a need to make trade offs between short-term and long-term objectives. This is referred to as S/L trade-off.

2.14 Managerial performance is usually judged by short-term achievements.

(a) Middle and senior management are criticised if they do not achieve budgetary aims.

(b) The board of directors of a public company are expected to achieve a certain growth in profits and EPS each year. Failing this, the share price will be marked down, and the board will be criticised for poor corporate results.

2.15 The emphasis on short-term achievements creates pressure for managers to sacrifice longer term aims in order to achieve short-term targets. Ideally, an organisation should try to control S/L trade-offs, to ensure that the most suitable decisions are taken in each situation.

2.16 Typical examples of decisions which sacrifice longer term objectives include the following.

(a)   Postponing or abandoning capital expenditure projects, which would eventually contribute to (longer term) growth and profits, in order to protect short term cash flow and profits.

(b)   Cutting R&D expenditure to save operating costs, and so reducing the prospects for future product development.

(c)   Reducing quality control, to save operating costs.

(d)   Reducing the level of customer service, to save operating costs.

2.17   Control of S/L trade-offs, might include the following.

(a)   Realistic short term targets. If budget targets are unrealistically tough, a manager will be forced into making S/L trade-offs.

(b)   Providing sufficient management information. Managers must be kept aware of long term aims as well as shorter term (budget) targets.

(c)   Evaluating managers' performance related to long term objectives.

Open objectives and aims

2.18   An objective should be expressed as a measurable quantity, and fitted in to an appropriate timescale. These are sometimes called *closed objectives*.

2.19   In contrast, an aim might be stated in non-quantified terms, such as:

(a)   providing high quality products that satisfy customer needs; or

(b)   providing sound investment opportunities for shareholders and worthwhile job prospects for employees.

2.20   Non-quantified objectives are sometimes referred to as *open objectives* or *aims*.

2.21   Aims (open objectives) and goals or targets (closed objectives) can be illustrated by referenced to one of John F Kennedy's declared *aims* in 1960, which was to re-establish and maintain America's role as a leader in the fields of science and technology, whereas one of his *objectives* was to land a man on the moon and return him safely before the end of the decade. Thus a *goal* had a *time constraint* attached to it and had a specific *end in view*.

2.22   One school of thought maintains that an *objective* must be expressed as a *target*, ie in quantitative terms, if it is to have any practical value for planning and the only practical objective is therefore a closed one.

2.23   Once objectives have been quantified, control criteria can easily be established and resources allocated.

Alternative primary financial objectives

2.24   The primary objective for a company must be a financial objective based on earning profits, but there are different ways of expressing such an objective. Various financial objectives might be expressed in terms of the following.

(a)   Profitability.

(b)   Return on capital employed (ROCE) or return on investment (ROI).

(c)   Survival.

(d)   Earnings per share and dividends to shareholders.

(e)   Growth

(f)   Return on shareholders' capital with an allowance for the element of risk.

(g) Several of these objectives simultaneously, so that there are multiple targets of 'equal' importance.

Profitability

2.25 Although a company must make profits, *profitability* on its own is not satisfactory as an overall long-term corporate objective because it fails to allow for the size of the capital investment required to make the profit.

2.26 Further drawbacks to the use of profitability as a primary overall objective are as follows.

(a) Capital is often in restricted supply, so profitability must always be measured in terms of the limiting factor, ie in terms of the scarce financial resources that a company will have at its disposal.

(b) It is not always possible to measure and compare profits over time. Long-term profitability requires investment of short-term gains. Since *long-term* profitability would be the central objective, there would inevitably be confusion due to the conflict between expenditure for long term benefits (for example R & D) and short-term demands on the limited resources available.

Return

2.27 *Return on investment (ROI)* or *return on capital employed (ROCE)* might be a more appropriate objective than profitability. They take into account the funds actually required to generate given levels of profit.

Survival

2.28 Drucker (*Theory of Business Behaviour* 1958) suggested that the *prime objective* of a company is not simply financial, but is one of *survival*. There are five major areas in which to decide objectives for survival.

(a) A need to anticipate the social climate and economic policy in those areas where the company operates and sells. A business must organise its behaviour in such a way as to survive in respect to both.

(b) A business is a human organisation and must be designed for joint performance by everyone in it.

(c) Survival also depends on the supply of an economic product or service.

(d) A business must *innovate*, because the economy and markets are continually changing.

(e) Inevitably, a business must be *profitable* to survive.

2.29 The needs and opportunities in each of these five areas in turn affect performance and results in the others. 'Success, like failure, is multi-dimensional.' Note that survival is not widely accepted as a corporate objective. Argenti, for example, has argued that the owners of a company might choose, in some circumstances, to wind up their business or sell out to another company in a takeover bid, and so their objectives would obviously be better served by *not* surviving.

EPS and dividends

2.30 *Earnings per share* or *dividend payments* are often used as a basis of re-establishing corporate objectives. They are both measures which recognise that a company is owned by its shareholders and the ultimate purpose of a company must be to provide a satisfactory return for its owners. Failure to provide a satisfactory EPS or dividend would presumably lead the shareholders to sell their shares and perhaps eventually to sell off the company's assets. When earnings and dividends are low, the market value of shares will also be depressed unless there is a strong prospect of dividend growth in the future.

Growth

2.31 Some argue that a company should make *growth* its prime objective - growth in EPS, growth in profits, growth in ROCE or growth in dividends per share. The problems, however, include the following.

(a) Growth of what? Some businesses and some aspects of businesses grow much faster than others.

(b) Growth might lead to diseconomies of scale and inefficiencies. The idea that a company must grow to survive is no longer widely accepted.

(c) Survival is a perfectly reasonable state for a company to be in.

Financial growth must be a high priority for many companies. Growth should be expressed, more suitably, as growth in profits, returns, earnings, dividends or capital value etc.

Return on shareholders' capital (ROSC)

2.32 Ansoff suggested that *return on equity* should be the overall corporate objective. This should be a measurable target over the 'proximate' period, ie for the next three to ten years, when forecasts can be made with reasonable accuracy. Beyond this period, however, when accurate forecasts are impossible, Ansoff suggested that a variety of long-term subsidiary objectives should be substituted for return on equity because they are more easily measurable and contribute towards the overall return.

2.33 Argenti also suggested that return on shareholders' capital (ROSC) should be the prime corporate objective and he specified the method whereby a target ROSC could be derived.

2.34 Both Ansoff and Argenti agreed the need to allow for *risk* in deciding the size of return as the target for the corporate objective.

Multiple objectives

2.35 A firm may identify several objectives. Linneman argues that a firm should be concerned with its risk posture, and that its objectives should therefore have regard to its financial risk, expressed as its debt/equity ratio. He suggests that there is a 'golden mean' or optimum combination of the following.

(a) Scope for *growth* and enhanced *corporate wealth*, through a suitable balance between equity and debt finance.

(b) Maintaining a policy of paying attractive but not over-generous *dividends*.

(c) Maintaining an acceptable, but flexible, *gearing ratio*. The acceptable norm will vary from industry to industry.

2.36 Linneman also discusses *relative* ranking in the market. This is really a subsidiary marketing objective, concerned with market position and market share. Most top executives of a company are interested in maintaining or achieving a certain rank relative to other competitors in their market.

Subsidiary objectives

2.37 Whatever primary objective or objectives are set, subsidiary objectives will then be developed beneath them. The diagram below illustrates this process in outline.

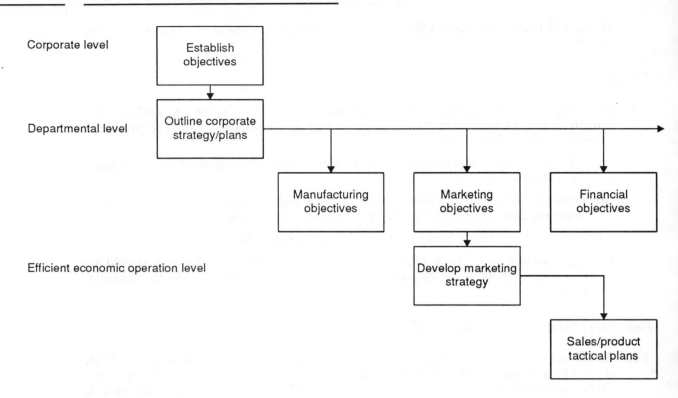

2.38 Unless an organisation is so small that it is a single unit, without functional departments, the overall objectives of the organisation must indicate different requirements for different functions.

2.39 Functional objectives must be specific and clear cut.

Ranking objectives in order of importance

2.40 While some objectives are clearly subordinate to others (departmental objectives are subsidiary to corporate objectives) problems of ranking arise where there are multiple corporate objectives, and multiple departmental objectives.

  (a) Resources, including time, are always limited.
  (b) Specifying numerical objectives builds in the possibility of failure.

2.41 Kepner and Tregoe rank objectives in the following way.

  (a) Objectives should be divided into two categories: *must* and *want* objectives. 'Must' objectives are absolutely essential, whereas 'want' objectives are not. 'Must' objectives rank equally, with no hierarchy or ranking since they all have to be achieved and so resources must somehow be committed to achieving them.

  (b) A minimum level of achievement should be specified for each 'must' objective.

  (c) Anything beyond the minimum level of achievement for 'must' objectives are 'want' objectives, and should be ranked in order of preference. There may not be enough resources to achieve all the 'want' objectives, and management must ensure that resources are not diverted away from achieving the 'must' objectives. If commitment to 'must' objectives is threatened, then 'want' objectives are best forgotten.

The monitoring and revision of objectives

2.42 Successful planning requires a commitment to objectives, and so objectives should not be subject to too frequent change. A planning review, in which objectives should be reassessed and planning horizons reviewed, should be held regularly, perhaps once a year.

3   NON-FINANCIAL OBJECTIVES

3.1   Although primary and subsidiary corporate objectives are often financial or commercial, other objectives which are non-financial may be identified. These can act as a brake or constraint on the organisation's pursuit of its primary targets.

Social and ethical obligations: social responsibility

3.2   As well as overall financial objectives, expressed as a quantifiable target, there are certain social or ethical obligations which a company must fulfil.

3.3   A company is an integral part of society and is subject to the pressures of that society. Most companies seek a good public image and to take account of the points on 'green marketing' and social responsibility raised in Part F of this Study Text.

3.4   Ansoff proposed the following objectives.

(a)   A primary objective, which is economic, aimed at optimising the efficiency and effectiveness of the firm's 'total resource-conversion process'.

(b)   Social or non-economic objectives, which are secondary and modify management behaviour. These social objectives are the result of the inter-action among the individual objectives of the differing groups of 'stakeholders'.

(c)   In addition to economic and non-economic objectives, there are two other factors exerting influence on management behaviour.

(i)   *Responsibilities:* these are obligations which a company undertakes, but which do not form a part of its 'internal guidance or control mechanism'. Responsibilities would include charitable donations, contributions to the life of local communities etc.

(ii)   *Constraints:* these are rules which restrict management's freedom of action, and would include government legislation (on pollution levels, health and safety at work, employment protection, redundancy, monopolies, illegal business practices etc) and agreements with trade unions.

3.5   The stakeholder view or the consensus view of corporate objectives would suggest that an organisation will sometimes make decisions which are not purely in the interests of shareholders and which mean that an objective of achieving growth or maximising profits will sometimes be compromised.

4   GAP ANALYSIS

4.1   Strategic planners must develop new strategies needed to enable the organisation to achieve its objectives. One technique whereby this can be done is gap analysis. This rests on the following information.

(a)   What are the organisation's targets for achievement over the planning period?

(b)   What would the organisation be expected to achieve if it 'did nothing' and did not develop any new strategies, but simply carried on in the current way with the same products and selling to the same markets?

The difference between the targets in (a) and expected achievements in (b) is the 'gap'. New strategies must then be developed which will close this gap, so that the organisation can expect to achieve its targets over the planning period.

4.2   The following activities are all relevant.

(a)   *Forecasting* is 'the identification of factors and quantifications of their effect on an entity, as a basis for planning.'

(b) A *projection* is 'an expected future trend pattern obtained by extrapolation. It is principally concerned with quantitative factors whereas a forecast includes judgements.'

(c) *Extrapolation* is 'the technique of determining a projection by statistical means'.

(d) *Gap analysis* is 'the comparison of an entity's ultimate objective with the sum of projections and already planned projects, identifying how the consequent gap might be filled.'

A forecast or projection based on existing performance: F_0 forecasts

4.3 This is a forecast of the company's future results assuming that nothing changes. The company is expected to continues to operate as at present without any changes in its products, markets, organisation, assets, human resources, research spending, financial structure, purchasing and so forth.

4.4 Argenti calls such forecasts 'F_0 forecasts' and identifies four stages in their preparation.

(a) The analysis of revenues, costs and volumes.

(i) Revenues are analysed by units of sale and price.
(ii) Costs are analysed into variable, fixed, and semi-variable costs.

(b) Projections into the future, based on past trends, should be made up to the end of the planning period.

(c) Other factors affecting profits and return. Examples include the following.

(i) What is the likelihood of strikes and what might they cost the company in lost profits or higher wages?

(ii) What is the likelihood that machinery will break down more in future than in the past, and what would it cost in lost production, sales and profit?

(iii) What is the likelihood that raw materials will be difficult to obtain, that their prices might rise dramatically, or that new materials or new sources of supply will become available?

(d) Finalising the forecast.

4.5 Arguably the F_0 forecast is unrealistic since it unrealistically allows the company no new products or markets and no other new strategies. But the purpose of the F_0 forecast and gap analysis is to determine the size of the task facing the company if it wishes to achieve its target profits. The gap must be filled by new strategies and since the gap is quantifiable in money terms, it is essential to estimate the extent to which any individual strategy or group of strategies might close the gap.

The profit gap

4.6 The profit gap is the difference between the target profits (according to the overall corporate objectives of the company) and the profits on the F_0 forecast.

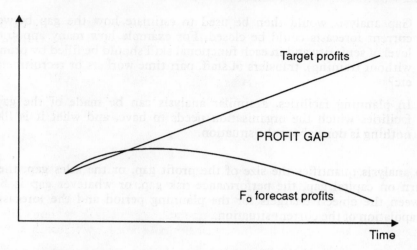

4.7   The options for bridging the gap need to be identified. The gap indicates how much extra profit has to be generated by the decisions and the commitments to be made over the next few years.

Other forms of gap analysis

4.8   Gap analysis as outlined here relates to the context of achieving the overall objective of the organisation, whether it be quantified in terms of return on shareholders' capital, or even simply sales growth (sales gap analysis). There are other forms of gap analysis.

The sales gap

4.9   Sizer (1968) described a *sales gap* that could be filled by new product-market growth strategies as follows.

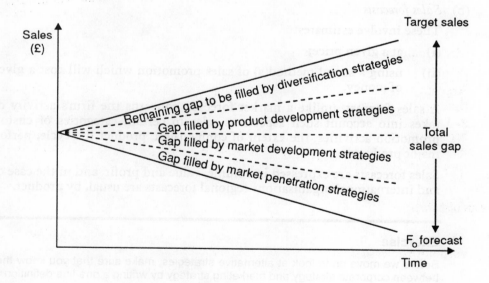

4.10 The same basic technique can serve as the basis for formulating any particular strategy.

(a) In planning for human resources, for example, gap analysis would be used to assess the difference over time between the following.

(i)   What the organisation *needs to have* in terms of staff of differing skills and seniority.

(ii) What the organisation is *likely to have*, allowing for 'natural wastage' of staff, assuming that it does nothing to train staff or appoint new staff as vacancies arise.

Gap analysis would then be used to estimate how the gap between target and current forecasts could be closed. For example how many appointments at each level of seniority and in each functional skill should be filled by promotion (with or without training), transfers of staff, part time workers or recruitment from outside etc?

(b)   In planning facilities, a similar analysis can be made of the gap between the facilities which the organisation needs to have, and what it is likely to have if nothing is done about the situation.

4.11   Gap analysis quantifies the size of the profit gap, or the sales gap, the EPS gap, the return on capital gap, the performance-risk gap, or whatever gap is being measured between the objective/targets for the planning period and the forecast based on the extrapolation of the current situation.

Market forecasts and sales forecasts

4.12   Market forecasts and sales forecasts are complementary and should not be undertaken separately. A market forecast covering a longer period of time should be carried out first.

(a)   *Market forecast*

This involves assessment of environmental factors, outside the organisation's control, which will affect the demand for its products/services. There are three main elements:

(i)   the economic review (national economy, government policy, covering forecasts on investment, population, gross national product, etc);

(ii)   specific market research (to obtain data about specific markets and forecasts concerning total market demand);

(iii)   evaluation of total market demand for the firm's and similar products, for example profitability, market potential etc.

(b)   *Sales forecasts*

These involve estimates:

(i)   at a given price;

(ii)   using a stated method(s) of sales promotion which will cost a given amount of money.

A sales forecast, unlike a market forecast, concerns the firm's activity directly. It takes into account such aspects as sales to certain categories of customer, sales promotion activities, the extent of competition, product life cycle, performance of major products.

Sales forecasts are expressed in volume, value and profit, and in the case of national and international organisations regional forecasts are usual, by product.

Exercise

Before we move on to look at alternative strategies, make sure that you know the difference between corporate strategy and marketing strategy by writing a one-line definition of each.

Solution

Corporate strategy involves decisions and direction for all functions of the operation.

Marketing strategy incorporates decisions relating to the positioning of the marketing mix to exploit and develop product/market opportunities.

---

5   WHAT IS A STRATEGY

5.1   Strategies develop at a number of levels. *Corporate strategy* is concerned with the overall development of an organisation's business activities, while *marketing strategy* is concerned with the organisation's activities in relation to the markets which it serves. Strategy takes two main forms.

(a) *Deliberate strategies* are the result of conscious, planned activities.

(b) *Emergent strategies* are patterned, but unsystematic: they are the outcome of activities and behaviour which develop unconsciously.

5.2   Most strategies are part deliberate and part emergent. To the extent that they are deliberate, typically they are the outcome of a planning process.

5.3   Within the marketing plan, strategic marketing has three key components:

(a)   the *designation* of specific, desired *objectives*;
(b)   commitment of *resources* to these objectives;
(c)   evaluation of a range of *environmental influences*.

5.4   Strategy does not just focus on organisational *efficiency*; arguably, its more important function is enabling the organisation to be *effective*. Where strategy and planning are concerned, *efficiency* simply relates to doing a task well, but *effectiveness* relates to doing the *right* task - having the right products in the right markets at the most appropriate times.

5.5   An organisation can only be effective, however, if it is aware of, and responsive to, the environment in which it operates. It might be argued that marketing is, by definition, 'strategic', since to be able to market a product successfully ultimately requires that the firm has the right type of product and is operating in the right markets.

5.6   The concept of strategy also has a dynamic component. While strategy is important in enabling an organisation to be effective, to be truly effective the organisation should not only be 'doing the right things now', it should also be aware of, and oriented towards the anticipation of, future changes. Planning and strategy in themselves do not give the organisation the ability to predict the future. Rather, planning enables managers to think through the possible range of future changes, and as a consequence be better prepared to meet the changes that actually occur.

6   STRATEGY FORMULATION

6.1   When developing a marketing strategy, a company is seeking to discover where it should be located in its operating environment. This may mean adjusting the company's strategy to fit into the existing market environment, although it may involve changing the environment to fit with the company's strategy. The strategy must enable the company to meet the specific needs of its consumers and to do so more effectively than its competitors.

6.2   It is likely that a strategy will be formulated in the early stages of the planning cycle and that it will need to be revisited when the situational (SWOT) analysis has been completed.

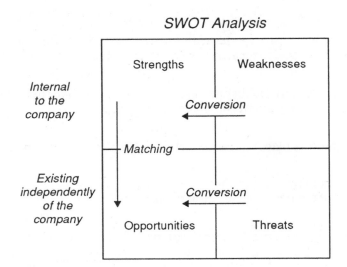

SWOT Analysis

6.3   You should remember the above matrix from Chapter 1. This matrix can be used to guide strategy formulation. The two major strategic options are as follows.

(a)   *Matching* involves finding, where possible, a match between the strengths of the organisation and the opportunities presented by the market. Strengths not matching any available opportunity are of limited use while opportunities which do not have any matching strengths are of little immediate value from a strategic perspective.

(b)   *Conversion* requires strategies to convert weaknesses into strengths to take advantage of an opportunity, or converting threats into opportunities which can then be matched by existing strengths.

6.4   SWOT is useful in suggesting a direction to take, but more specific aspects of strategies such as how best to *compete*, how to *grow* within the target markets etc need to be considered. There are a number of analytical techniques which can be used, not to offer definitive statements on the final form that a strategy should take, but rather to provide a framework within which ideas and information can be organised and analysed. No single technique can always provide the most appropriate framework and those discussed in the sections which follow can and should be regarded as complementary rather than competitive.

7   COMPETITIVE STRATEGIES

Competitive advantage

7.1   Competitive advantage is anything which gives one organisation an edge over its rivals in the products it sells or the services it offers. This could be:

(a)   a dealer network;
(b)   quality;
(c)   price;
(d)   age.

7.2   Firms constantly strive for competitive advantage as competitors seek to share in the obvious benefits. This involves a continuous search for new product/market opportunities as an indispensable part of a firm's strategy.

7.3   The management must swiftly identify the way in which it will compete with other organisations and what it perceives as the basis of its competitive advantage. Michael

Porter argues that strategy is essentially a method for creating and sustaining a profitable position in a particular market environment. The profit made by the firm depends first on the nature of its strategy and second on the inherent profitability of the industry in which it operates. With this in mind, it follows that an organisation in a basically profitable industry can perform badly with an unsuitable strategy while an organisation in an unprofitable industry may perform well with a more suitable strategy.

7.4 Profitability depends on the structure of the industry and specifically on five key features:

(a) bargaining power of suppliers;
(b) bargaining power of consumers;
(c) threat of entry;
(d) competition from substitutes;
(e) competition between firms.

7.5 A competitive strategy is based on a thorough analysis of these factors. Using this analysis the organisation must decide whether to compete throughout the market or only in certain segments (*competitive scope*) and also whether to compete through low costs and prices or through offering a differentiated product range (*competitive advantage*). Four possible strategies, as outlined below, follow from this decision.

Competitive strategies

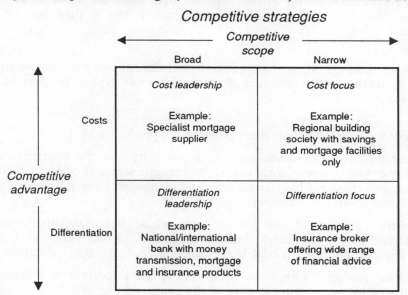

(Source: Ennew, Watkins and Wright, *Marketing Financial Services*)

(a) *Cost leadership* attempts to control the market through being the low cost producer. Typically, the product is undifferentiated, although differentiation cannot be ignored, since the cost savings for the consumer must compensate for the loss of product features, while the discount offered by the firm should not be so high as to offset cost advantages.

(b) *Differentiation* aims to offer products which can be regarded as unique in areas which are highly valued by the consumer. It is the products' uniqueness and the associated customer loyalty that protects the firm from competition. However, the price premium received must outweigh the costs of supplying the differentiated product for this strategy to be successful; at the same time, the customer must feel that the extra features more than compensate for the price premium.

(c) *Focus/nicheing* uses either costs or differentiation but rather than serving the entire market, the organisation looks to operate only in particularly attractive or suitable segments or niches. Differentiation focus is the most common form of focus strategy and implies producing highly customised products for very specific consumer groups.

This approach points strongly to the need to avoid being 'stuck in the middle' - trying to be all things to all consumers. It advocates the need to make choices. The firm trying to perform well on costs and on differentiation is likely to lose out to firms concentrating on either one strategy or the other.

7.6   Competitive strategy can be defined as follows.

> 'Taking offensive or defensive actions to create a defendable position in an industry, to cope successfully with ... competitive forces and thereby yield a superior return on investment for the firm. Firms have discovered many different approaches to this end, and the best strategy for a given firm is ultimately a unique construction reflecting its particular circumstances.'
>
> (Porter, *Competitive Strategy*)

7.7   Competitive strategy is only required where organisations face competition.

7.8   Firms with a monopoly must also compete to retain their monopoly position, and prevent encroachments from competitors.

The choice of competitive strategy

7.9   Competitive strategy may be based on product/market strategies or manufacturing strategy. As we saw above, Porter suggests that there are three broad competitive strategies. One of them is a manufacturing strategy, two of them are product/market strategies.

7.10   The type of competitive strategy adopted will depend on the competitive strategies adopted by rivals and the structure of the business and type of product or service that the firm is producing.

7.11   A distinction can be made into three categories of product.

(a)   *Search products.* These are products whose attributes the consumer can discern, evaluate and compare fairly easily, for example size and colour, as with a style of dress, and these easily-assessed 'searched attributes' form the major factors in the consumer's purchase decision.

(b)   *Experience products.* These are products whose important attributes cannot be discerned by the consumer until the consumer has had some experience of using the product, for example taste in the case of food, and product durability.

(c)   *Credence products.* These are products whose important attributes cannot be evaluated by the consumer, even if the consumer has purchased it before, either because the product's attributes might vary the next time (for example quality of service in a restaurant) or because the product's attributes cannot easily be evaluated (for example pet food, the competence of professional advice from a solicitor or insurance broker etc). The consumer must therefore show 'faith' or 'credence' in the product.

Cost leadership strategy

7.12   A cost leadership strategy aims to be lowest-cost producer. The manufacturer can then compete on price with every other producer in the industry, and earn the highest unit profits.

7.13   This requires the following.

(a)   Setting up production facilities for mass production, so as to obtain economies of scale.

(b)   Using the latest technology.

(c)   In high-technology industries, and in industries depending on labour skills for product design and production methods, there will be a *learning curve effect* (also called a *cost experience curve*). By producing more items than any other competitor, a firm can benefit more from the learning curve, and achieve lower average costs.

(d) Concentrating on productivity objectives, and seeking productivity improvements and cost reductions in various ways (for example zero base budgeting, value analysis programmes etc).

(e) Cost minimisation in areas of overhead costs - such as R & D, the sales force, advertising costs etc.

(f) Favourable access to sources of raw materials supply would also contribute towards overall cost leadership.

7.14 Where there is a low *critical mass* of production output because maximum economies of scale are achievable, cost leadership would be difficult to achieve, because many rival firms should be able to achieve similar low costs too. Only when the critical mass of production is high is a cost leadership strategy likely to be effective.

7.15 This strategy clearly has implications for pricing, product quality and marketing, especially in the case of *search products*.

(a) Pricing. To achieve high volumes of sales, the firm may need to keep prices low, if the price elasticity of demand for a product is high. The importance of low prices suggests the need for low-cost production.

(b) *Product quality*. A cost leadership strategy is well suited to search products, where consumers can readily compare the attributes of competing products from rival firms. With such products, firms must be able to match the product quality of rivals, otherwise they will lose customers to these rivals. On the other hand, firms should not incur costs to improve quality attributes which have little, if any, impact on the consumer's purchasing decision.

(c) *Marketing*. Advertising may be used to boost sales volume, especially where advertising emphasises price discounts, or 'unbeatable prices'. In the case of search products, advertising should be informative about the key attributes of the product (for example price) and persuasive advertising is unlikely to have much effect on demand.

7.16 A strategy for overall cost leadership would call for the following.

(a) High capital expenditure on top quality and up to date equipment.

(b) Aggressive pricing and a capacity to bear large losses initially in order to build up market share.

7.17 The drawbacks to this strategy are as follows.

(a) Technological change, which may nullify all the cost advantages so far achieved.

(b) Resources needed to stay up to date in technology.

(c) Competition from other low cost economies compared with Europe and the USA. Selling on price always means that the organisation is in danger of being undercut and is not an effective strategy if demand is price inelastic.

(d) Market fragmentation.

(e) Cost inflation.

Differentiation strategy: product differentiation

7.18 Differentiation strategy seeks to add value to the product, and in doing so, to raise the product's cost and sales price. The improvements in quality should be of more value to the customer than the price increase, so that the customer is willing to pay more for the superior quality: there must be perceived added value.

7.19 A differentiation strategy is therefore aimed at achieving an optimal balance for the customer between quality and price. ('Quality' is a term used to refer to desirable attributes, including customer service.) Firms try to provide greater quality relative to price than rival firms are offering. Given a limit on what a consumer will pay for a product, there will be a trade-off by the consumer between quality and price.

7.20 A differentiation strategy assumes that competitive advantage can be gained through particular characteristics of a firm's products. Products may be categorised as follows.

(a) *Breakthrough products* offer either a radical performance advantage over competition, a drastically lower price, or ideally, it may offer both.

(b) *Improved products* are not radically different to their competition but are obviously superior in terms of better performance at a competitive price. It will usually be the result of incorporation of recent advances in technology, applied to a particular product. Examples would be the much-improved capabilities of pocket calculators in the 1980s and colour televisions in the 1970s, and personal computers over recent years. A problem for producers is that product improvements are quickly copied by competitors.

(c) *Competitive products* show no obvious advantage over others, but which derive their appeal from a particular compromise of cost and performance. The car industry provides excellent examples of competitive products. Cars are not all sold at rock-bottom prices, nor do they all provide immaculate comfort and performance. Nearly all makes of car are a compromise between price, comfort and performance, and they compete with each other by trying to offer a more attractive compromise than rival models.

7.21 A successful differentiation strategy builds up loyalty to the firm's products and so the firm can sell its products at prices that are higher than the least-cost producer in the market. A firm which uses a strategy of differentiation is unlikely to be the market leader.

7.22 A differentiation strategy risks customers not wanting to pay higher prices for the different product. In times of recession when customers are more price sensitive this is a big risk, and the quality of the marketing strategy will be a critical success factor.

7.23 A *critical success* factor is any factor which is essential to the success of the strategy, plan or organisation. Organisations which identify these critical factors are able to concentrate management attention on these essential factors, ensuring their performance is on target.

Focus strategy

7.24 The third type of competitive strategy identified by Porter is a focus strategy, whereby a firm concentrates its attention on one or more particular segments or niches of the market, and does not try to serve the entire market with a single product.

7.25 A focus strategy is based on segmenting the market and focusing on particular market segments. The firm will focus on a particular type of buyer or geographical area.

'The strategy rests on the premise that the firm is thus able to serve its narrow strategic target more effectively or efficiently than competitors who are competing more broadly. As a result, the firm achieves either differentiation from better meeting the needs of the particular target, or lower costs in serving this target, or both.'   (Porter)

(a) A *cost-focus* strategy involves selecting a segment of the market and specialising in a product (or products) for that segment.

(b) A *quality-focus* strategy involves selecting a segment of the market and competing on the basis of quality (through product differentiation) for that segment. Luxury goods are the prime example of such a strategy.

7.26   A focus strategy is appropriate for new entrants. The implications of a focus strategy for product quality, price and advertising will be:

(a)   for a cost-focus strategy, similar to a cost leadership strategy;
(b)   for a quality-focus strategy, similar to a differentiation strategy.

7.27   The risk is that the market segment might not be large enough to be profitable.

7.28   The niche marketing of the 1980s (eg Sock Shop, Tie Rack) illustrates focus strategy, but few of the niche retailers survived the recession of the early 1990s indicating that their market segments may have been too narrow to cover a burgeoning cost base. Body Shop, reflecting the growing appeal of its positioning as a 'caring' company as far as the environment is concerned, and its exploitation of the widespread belief that 'natural' equals 'healthy', has survived. Also, Body Shop focused on a customer segment, rather than a product.

7.29   Although there is a risk with any of the three broad competitive strategies he identified, Porter argues that a firm must pursue one of them. A 'stuck-in-the-middle' strategy is almost certain to make only low profits. 'This firm lacks the market share, capital investment and resolve to play the low-cost game, the industry-wide differentiation necessary to obviate the need for a low-cost position, or the focus to create differentiation or a low-cost position in a more limited sphere.'

8   GROWTH STRATEGIES

8.1   Ansoff's Product/Market matrix, used for the analysis and determination of growth strategies, suggests that the strategy decision rests on whether to use new or existing products in new or existing markets. Four possible options are suggested.

(a)   *Market penetration*. This involves increasing sales of the existing products in existing markets. This may include persuading existing users to use more (so a credit card issuer might try to increase credit card use by offering higher credit limits or gifts based on expenditure); persuading non-users to use (for example, by offering free gifts with new credit card accounts); or attracting consumers from competitors. Market penetration will, in general, only be viable in circumstances where the market is not already saturated.

(b)   *Market development*. This entails expansion into new markets using existing products. New markets may be 'new' geographically, addressing new market segments or may entail finding new uses for products amongst existing consumers. Opportunities for market development may arise in circumstances such as opening up of Eastern European markets or in the development of markets in China or Africa. This strategy requires swift, effective and imaginative promotion, but can be very profitable if markets are changing rapidly.

(c)   *Product development*. This approach requires the organisation to operate in its existing markets but redesign or reposition existing products to appeal to those markets. Recent developments in the mortgage market, for example, illustrate product development as the traditional standardised mortgage account is rapidly being supplemented by variants which offer lower starting rates, special terms for particular types of customer, particular mixes of fixed and flexible repayment rates etc. This strategy relies on good service design, packaging and promotion and on company reputation to attract consumers. By tailoring the products personally to the needs of existing consumers and new consumers the organisation can strengthen its competitive position.

(d)   *Diversification*. The fourth strategy - diversification (new products, new markets) is much more risky than the other three because the organisation is moving into areas in which it has little or no experience. Instances of pure diversification are consequently rare and as a strategic option it tends to be used in cases when there are no other possible routes for growth available. Diversification in the financial services sector, for example, typically involves the introduction of new (as opposed to modified) products for the same broad market.

8.2   Porter's three generic strategies for success are useful positioning strategies which involve corporate strategy to some degree but they do not directly address the central marketing issues of customers and products in a specific operational way. Ansoff's competitive strategy framework (sometimes called *strategies for growth* or the *Ansoff matrix*) fills this gap and also relates well to the sub-strategies of the marketing mix.

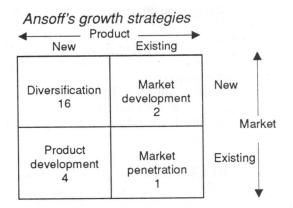

Ansoff's growth strategies

8.3   Most companies adopt, at least initially, a strategy of market penetration which carries the lowest risk (the figures in the boxes indicate notional levels of risk). However, when current market saturation is reached a company needs to consider entering into new markets with existing products to maintain growth. Technological advance and competitive pressures will normally force companies into some degree of product development (ranging from cosmetic alterations to tangible product improvements to revolutionary new products). Diversification does not necessarily mean merger or takeover. For example the UK's Royal Mail, which is an acknowledged leader in efficiency/effectiveness, could offer a new service (consultancy) to new markets (European countries' postal organisations) without the need for takeover or merger.

8.4   Ansoff's matrix then leads naturally into marketing operations such as research to identify new markets and new products and the deployment of the marketing mix in exploiting these product/market opportunities for growth.

9   BOSTON CONSULTANCY GROUP

9.1   The Boston Consultancy Group's Product Portfolio Analysis is a tool for determining marketing strategy and is based upon the premise that relative market share (ie relative to competitors) and market growth are important strategic choice criteria. Just as a wise investor will hold a portfolio of shares, some with high growth but high risk, some with low risk but low growth, so an astute company will hold a balanced portfolio of products. The tool is perhaps best explained by use of a 2×2 diagnostic matrix.

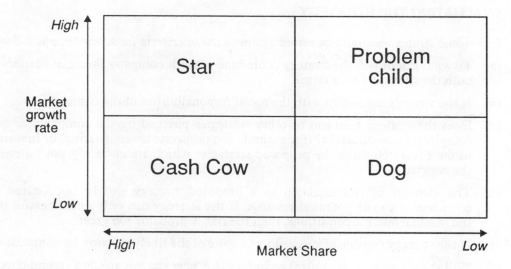

(a) *Stars* are SBUs or products with high market share and high growth, ie leaders, but often needing a large cash investment in order to maintain growth in face of competition, which may offset cash generation.

(b) *Cash cows* are typically former stars entering a period of low growth, still generating large amounts of cash but needing relatively little cash investment. Because of high market share over a period of years, cash cows enjoy economies of scale and high profit margins.

(c) *Dogs* have low market shares in a low-growth market and tend to generate either a loss or a relatively low profit. They typically take up more management time than warranted and, unless they can be strategically justified, are candidates for withdrawal.

(d) *Problem children* are sometimes alternatively labelled *question marks*, because, with a low share but high growth prospects, they need considerable investment for initially low returns. They are therefore cash users but *potential* stars. Management must choose between further speculative investment or withdrawal.

10   PIMS

10.1 Pims or Profit Impact on Marketing Strategy, is a large database covering more than 3,000 SBUs, developed largely in America but now adding a considerable number of European businesses to the portfolio. It is 'owned' by the Strategic Planning Institute which has a London office. Clients input detailed confidential data on their expenditure and returns which are then computer-analysed to determine norms for groups of like businesses (like businesses in terms of data characteristics rather than type of product-markets). This diagnostic tool thus enables a business to compare its own strategic performance (outputs relative to inputs) with 'par for the course', ie the norm. The data is claimed to show in what respects the business is under-performing and how its performance might be improved.

10.2 The factors which have been persistently revealed as being the most influential determinants of profitability are as follows.

(a) The business' competitive position including market share and relative product quality.

(b) The attractiveness of its served market as indicated by growth rate and customer characteristics.

(c) Its production structure including operational productivity and investment intensity.

11   EVALUATING THE STRATEGY

11.1   Individual strategies should be tested against a list of criteria for acceptance as follows.

(a)   To what extent will the strategy contribute towards company financial objectives in both the short and long term?

(b)   Is the strategy consistent with the social responsibilities of the company?

(c)   Does the strategy conform to other strategies pursued by the company, or is it a completely new direction? (for example conglomerate diversification, or investment in pure research might be proposed strategies which are currently not pursued by the company).

(d)   The element of risk attached to a proposed strategy should not be too high compared with the potential rewards. If the strategy can only be successful under the most favourable conditions, then the risk is probably too great.

(e)   Is the strategy capable of succeeding in spite of the likely reaction by competitors?

(f)   Will there be adequate control techniques? A new strategy needs a careful check on performance to put any necessary remedial steps into effect, particularly in the early stages. The lack of an adequate control system may be serious hindrance to effective decision making.

(g)   Is the strategy preferable to other, mutually exclusive strategies? Is there an option to combine two separate strategies into one action? 'While it is often sufficient to solve problem A by taking action A, and to solve problem B by taking action B, greater economy in effort and in cost would be achieved if one could take action C to solve both problem A and problem B at the same time - two birds with one stone, as it were.' *(Argenti)* Argenti used the example of one department buying a computer for £50,000 for accounting work, a second department buying a £30,000 computer for scientific work, when a £60,000 computer would have been capable of handling the workload of both departments.

11.2   Argenti produces six criteria for testing strategy.

(a)   Can it be shown that the strategy gives the company an expected return with a given business risk attached, similar to the one expected by its shareholders?

(b)   Does the company have the necessary competence to carry out the strategy?

(c)   Does the strategy eliminate all the significant weaknesses of the company, as identified by the internal appraisal?

(d)   Does the strategy exploit any opportunities which have been identified as possibly arising in the future?

(e)   Does the strategy reduce the impact of any significant external threats?

(f)   Does the strategy call for action by the company which is objectionable on social or moral grounds?

Evaluating strategy: financial considerations

11.3   The financial objectives of the firm are paramount and so strategies will be evaluated by considering how far they contribute to return on investment, profits, growth, EPS and cash flow.

Evaluating strategy: synergy

11.4   A strategy for product or market development, or for diversification, should be evaluated in terms of whether it is likely to result in synergy.

Evaluating strategy: company image

11.5   Investment decisions and other corporate issues are now being taken with an eye to their effect on public opinion. Multinational companies in particular appear to be conscious of their image, perhaps because of their size or perhaps because they feel vulnerable to accusations that they trample roughshod over national interests for the gain of shareholders abroad.

11.6   A good company image may well be essential to continued commercial success. For companies manufacturing consumer goods the continually growing public concern about conservation of natural resources and the environment makes this a very big issue indeed.

Evaluating strategy: customer satisfaction

11.7   A regard for customer satisfaction is becoming the key differentiating factor in competition.

Evaluating strategies: resource utilisation

11.8   Strategies which fail to make use of the existing manpower skills and technical expertise of the company, and which therefore call for new skills to be acquired, might be unacceptable to the corporate planners for the following reasons.

(a)   Acquiring expertise and experience through organic growth of the company would be a long process.

(b)   If a takeover of another company is therefore necessary for faster entry into a new product-market area, the disadvantages of an acquisition policy might outweigh the advantages.

Evaluating strategies: a summary

11.9   Strategies are evaluated to decide whether they will help to achieve the organisation's objectives and so whether they are desirable. The final list of desirable strategic opportunities, if it is not empty, will be a list for ranking in order of priority. Kotler summarises the stages in evaluating a marketing opportunity as follows.

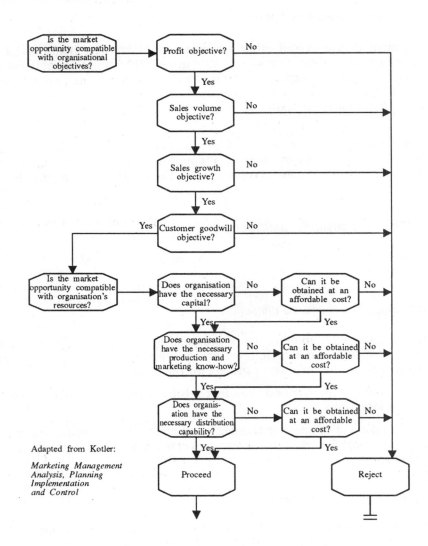

Adapted from Kotler:

*Marketing Management
Analysis, Planning
Implementation
and Control*

11.10 The selection of strategies is formulated in a *policy statement*, which describes the planned long-term strategy of the company, identifying the objectives, constraints and strategies to be pursued over the corporate planning period. This statement should be short, and restricted to identifying a few key strategies. However, to 'sell' the plan to junior managers and employees, the ideas in the statement might need to be internally marketed with explanations for presentation and communication to staff.

Risk appraisal in strategy evaluation

11.11 Risk has been mentioned before. It is clearly important, in view of the uncertainty about the future. Some strategies will be more risky than others.

11.12 One of the problems arising when evaluating alternative strategies is the reliability of the data used. Since the figures are compiled on estimates of the future, there must be considerable uncertainty about the final accuracy of the figures. Business planners frequently use various operational research techniques to measure the degree of uncertainty involved. These include the simple 'rule of thumb' methods of expressing a range of values from worst possible result to best possible result with a best estimate lying between these two extremes. Also, there is the use of basic probability theory to express the likelihood of a forecast result occurring. This would evaluate the data given by informing the decision maker that there is, for example, a 50% probability that the best estimate will be achieved, a 25% chance that the worst result will occur and a 25% chance that the best possible result will occur. This evaluation of risk might help the executive to decide between alternative strategies, each with its own risk profile.

11.13 Ansoff suggests that decision theory is of limited relevance in measuring risk, and *sensitivity analysis* should be used in preference. This involves identifying each variable factor in the calculation and assessing what would be the effect on the final result if the variable was amended by x% up or down. This will highlight those variables which are most likely to have a significant effect on the final result.

11.14 When evaluating a strategy, management should consider the following.

(a) Whether an individual strategy involves an unacceptable amount of risk. If it does, it should be eliminated from further consideration in the planning process.

(b) However, the risk of an individual strategy should also be considered in the context of the overall 'portfolio' of investment strategies adopted by the company. If you have already studied portfolio theory you will be aware of the following.

(i) If a strategy is risky, but its outcome is not related to ('correlated with') the outcome of other strategies, then adopting that strategy will help the company to spread its risks. (Diversification, after all, is intended to 'put more eggs into different baskets'.)

(ii) If a strategy is risky, but is negatively correlated with other adopted strategies, so that if strategy A does well, other adopted strategies will do badly and vice versa, then adopting strategy A would actually reduce the overall risk of the company's strategy portfolio.

Chapter roundup

- Objectives are goal statements. Strategic planning requires the development of strategies to enable the organisation to achieve its objectives. Strategies are usually formulated early on in the planning cycle and may need revision when the SWOT analysis has been completed.

- To develop a strategic plan, an organisation's management must be aware of the current position of the organisation, the threats and opportunities it faces, and the weaknesses or 'gaps' in its position. Strategies should be developed which fill gaps in any area, ie remove weaknesses or develop strengths and exploit opportunities and counter threats.

- Gap analysis quantifies the size of the profit gap, or other appropriate 'gap' between the objective/targets for the planning period and the forecast based on the extrapolation of the current situation. The organisation must then identify different actions or strategies which would help to fill the identified gap.

- The purpose of competitive strategy is to provide the organisation with a competitive advantage. A number of alternative approaches to competitive strategy exist, but Porter suggests three basic types.
  o Overall cost leadership
  o Differentiation
  o Segmentation

- Ansoff's product/market matrix is used for the analysis and determination of growth strategies. It suggests four possible options.

- The BCG's product portfolio analysis is a tool for determining marketing strategy.

- PIMS is a diagnostic tool based on a database. It allows organisations to compare their strategic performance with that of other organisations.

- Strategies need to be evaluated annually against a list of carefully considered criteria. Potential strategies need to be carefully evaluated to identify those which will fill the identified planning gap within the limits of the resources and strengths of the organisation. A number of financial and marketing tools are available to help managers make their strategic evaluations.

Test your knowledge

1   What is an objective? (see para 2.1)

2   What is a unit objective? (2.4)

3   Distinguish between primary and secondary objectives. (2.5, 2.6)

4   What is S/L trade-off? (2.13)

5   What do both Ansoff and Argenti recommend is used as the overall corporate objective? (2.32, 2.33)

6   Distinguish between 'must' objectives and 'want' objectives, as ranked by Kepner and Tregoe. (2.41)

7   What does gap analysis involve? (4.2)

8   What is meant by matching and conversion respectively? (6.3)

9   Distinguish between search products, experience products and credence products. (7.11)

10   What three types of products can be categorised in a differentiation strategy? (7.20)

11   What four options are suggested by Ansoff's product/market matrix? (8.1)

12   Sketch a diagram of the Boston Consultancy Group's product portfolio analysis. (9.1)

13   What criteria does Argenti suggest for testing strategy? (11.2)

Now try illustrative question 4 at the end of the Study Text

Chapter 5

THE DETAILED PLANNING PROCESS

This chapter covers the following topics.

1   Planning

2   Control

3   The planning framework

4   Preparing the marketing plan

5   The detailed plans and programmes document

6   Constraints on marketing decisions

Introduction

In this chapter, we look at the marketing planning process in more detail. The relationship between planning and control is an important one, not just in marketing; it is explored here. We then move on to look at the detailed planning framework and set out the contents of the detailed plans and programmes document. We round off this part of the syllabus by identifying some typical constraints upon marketing decisions.

---

1   PLANNING

1.1   Planning is a fundamental part of the manager's role. It involves co-ordinating resources and channelling them towards the achievement of pre-determined goals.

1.2   Plans give direction to an organisation. Without plans, events will be left to chance.

1.3   Planning seeks to influence an uncertain future. By deciding what you want to achieve or what you want to happen in the future, you can take logical steps which will help you to achieve this goal.

1.4   The purpose of planning is:

(a)   to decide objectives for the organisation;

(b)   to identify alternative ways of achieving them; and

(c)   to select, from amongst these alternatives, the best option for both the organisation as a whole, and also for individual departments, sections and groups within it.

1.5   Planning therefore involves decisions about the following factors.

(a)   What to do in the future (objectives).
(b)   How to do it (strategy).
(c)   When to do it (tactics).
(d)   Who is to do it (tactics).

1.6   We looked at objectives and strategy in Chapter 4. Here we are concerned with *tactics*.

1.7   Planning may involve a system whereby opportunities are exploited as they arise, judged on their individual merits and not within the rigid structure of an overall corporate strategy. This approach contrasts with the generally accepted principles of disciplined strategic planning and is sometimes called *freewheeling opportunism*.

1.8   The advantages of this approach are as follows.

   (a)   Opportunities can be seized when they arise, whereas a rigid planning framework may impose restrictions and cause opportunities to be lost.

   (b)   It is flexible and adaptable.

   (c)   It might encourage a more flexible, creative attitude among lower-level managers, unlike formal planning.

Exercise

Given the advantages of freewheeling opportunism set out above, what disadvantages of the approach can you think of?

Solution

   (a)   It fails to provide a co-ordinating framework for the organisation as a whole. There is consequently a tendency for large organisations to break up into many fragments.

   (b)   Not all opportunities are identified and appraised. Strategic planning depends on its managers to design strategies and a formal system aims to exploit this creativity to the full.

   (c)   It over-emphasises the profit motive.

Barriers to good planning

1.9   Many managers are reluctant to make formal plans, and prefer to operate without them, dealing with problems only when and if they arise. There may be many reasons for their reluctance to plan. These include the following.

   (a)   A lack of knowledge (or interest) about the purpose and goals of the organisation.
      (i)   Duplication of effort.
      (ii)   Conflicts.
      (iii)   Extraneous effort.
      Good planning encourages the co-ordination of efforts within an organisation.

   (b)   A reluctance to be committed to one set of targets.

   (c)   A fear of blame or criticism for failing to achieve planned targets.

   (d)   A manager's lack of confidence in performing the job efficiently and effectively.

   (e)   A manager's lack of information about what is going on in the 'environment'.

   (f)   A manager's resentment of plans made for the department.

1.10   Attempts to overcome these problems might involve the following.

   (a)   All levels of staff involved in the planning process.

   (b)   Planners to be adequately provided with the information they need (and access to sources of future information, when it arises).

   (c)   A system of rewards for successful achievement of plans.

   (d)   Managers should be taught the virtues of planning and the techniques of good planning.

2   CONTROL

2.1   Planning and controlling are often seen as two separate activities. However, Robert N Anthony argued in his book *Planning and Control Systems: a Framework for Analysis (1956)* that:

> 'the trouble essentially is that, although planning and control are definable abstractions and are easily understood as calling for different types of mental activity, they do not relate to separable major categories of activities actually carried on in an organisation either at different times, or by different people, or for different situations.'

2.2   Many managers plan and control at the same time.

2.3   Koontz (1958) argues:

> 'Planning and control are so closely interconnected as to be singularly inseparable activities' and

> 'The fact that there seem ... to be so many fewer principles of control than principles of planning indicates the extent to which control depends upon planning and how it is largely a technique for assuring that plans are realised.'

The cycle of control

2.4   The basic control process or control cycle has six stages.

(a)   Making a plan; deciding what to do and identifying the desired results.

(b)   Recording the plan formally or informally, in writing or by other means, statistically or descriptively. The plan should incorporate standards of efficiency or targets for performance.

(c)   Carrying out the plan, or having it carried out by subordinates, and measuring results achieved.

(d)   Comparing actual results against the plans. This is sometimes referred to as the provision of 'feedback'.

(e)   Evaluating the comparison, and deciding whether further action is necessary to ensure the plan is achieved.

(f)   Where corrective action is necessary, this should be implemented. Alternatively, the plan itself may need adjusting (for example if targets were unrealistic or have been overtaken by events, or if actual results are better than planned).

2.5   The control cycle rests on:

(a)   feedback on performance; and
(b)   flexibility of response.

2.6   Planning and control systems must be developed together.

3   THE PLANNING FRAMEWORK

Definitions

3.1   *Objectives* and *strategy* were defined earlier.

3.2   *Tactics*, the third element, refers to details of the strategic plan. For example, we will substitute defender Y with attacker X after 25 minutes or we will increase our sales push with a telesales campaign, operated by an agency and targeted at 6,000 client leads over three months from January.

Levels of planning

3.3   As before, it is vital to distinguish levels of organisational activity.

(a)   At corporate level the focus is on the organisation as a whole. Objectives will be expressed in financial terms, for example return on investment or profit, and strategy has to provide direction to the functional areas of the business, finance, operations and marketing. The details of implementing this strategy are tactics to the managing director, but represent strategic direction to the functional heads.

(b)   At marketing department level the focus is on the marketing activity. Objectives are shaped against the corporate objectives and strategy and they are expressed in marketing terms, for example market share or sales volume. Marketing strategy indicates how the marketing mix will be set to achieve these objectives and the marketing tactics include details of their implementation. In turn these details are expressed in terms of distribution, research, advertising and sales objectives and strategies.

The planning process

3.4   At what management level are you positioned? The process and framework of planning is the same whether you are the managing director, marketing manager or sales manager. The focus does differ and it is essential that you retain a clear picture of who you are and what your area of authority is.

3.5   Planners must decide what the planning period ought to be. It ought to be the period of time which is most suitable for business requirements and which enables the decision making and control processes to be most effectively exercised.

3.6   A failure to take a long enough view to planning can be risky. Short termism can lead to missing long-term opportunities and/or failing to identify emerging threats.

Defining the long and short term

3.7   *Long term* is usually five years. *Short term* is usually annual and forms part of a long-term plan.

3.8   The problem is that the further ahead you look the more imprecise planning becomes.

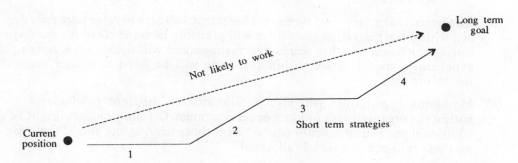

3.9   Long-term planning, even beyond the planning horizon (the furthest time ahead for which plans can be usefully quantified) is still a useful activity as it provides managers with a picture of how the organisation should be developing, a vision for the future.

3.10   It is instructive to quote the businessman, Sir James Goldsmith.

> 'Muddling through is a euphemism for failing to plan forward. It means acting tactically and without strategy; it means confusing the means with the end. If we continue to avoid facing the facts ... the epitaph on the graves of our democracy will be: "They sacrificed the long term for the short term, and the long term finally arrived." '

Contingency and scenario planning (What if? ...)

3.11   Planning within the planning period but based on unexpected and dramatic changes in the environment is known as scenario planning. Based on the idea of 'What if...':

(a)   interest rates doubled?
(b)   there was a vote of no confidence in the government? or
(c)   a war broke out in a key market area?

More futuristic versions of scenario planning might include planning for a future with no motor cars.

3.12   A contingency is an event that is liable, but not certain, to occur. For corporate planners, a contingency is a possible future event which, on the balance of probabilities, they do not expect to happen, but if it were to happen, there would be nothing the organisation's management could do to stop it.

Contingencies which are anticipated events

3.13   Where contingencies are known about, *contingency plans should be prepared in advance* to deal with the situation if and when it arises. Such plans might be prepared in detail, or in outline only, depending on the likelihood that the contingency will become a reality. Such plans can be prepared to deal with adverse exchange rate movements, for example.

4   PREPARING THE MARKETING PLAN

4.1   Arriving at a marketing plan in detail involves several inter-related decisions.

(a)   *Sales targets* must be set for each product and each sales division (with sub-targets also set for sales regions, sales areas and individual salesmen). Sales targets may be referred to as *sales quotas*.

(b)   The *total marketing budget* must be set.

(c)   Given an overall marketing budget, resources (cash) must be allocated between:

(i)   salaries and other staff costs;

    (ii)   above the line expenditure (advertising);

    (iii)   below the line expenditure (sales promotion items, price reduction allowances etc).

(d)   The overall sales target set by top management will also involve *sales price decisions*; but within the marketing plan there will probably be some room for manoeuvre in setting the price. In other words, top management will decide on a 'rough pricing zone' and a specific price within this zone will be fixed at a later stage in the marketing plan.

(e)   Marketing expenditure will also be allocated to different products or services within the organisation's product or service range. Certain products might be given additional marketing expenditure; whereas those nearing the end of their life cycle may lose resources previously allocated.

4.2   Marketing planning decisions - concerning targets, total marketing expenditure budget, the marketing mix and the allocation of expenditure to products - are the principal aspects of *marketing programming*. They are closely inter-related, and a marketing plan cannot be arrived at without due consideration of alternative choices.

4.3   Three types of annual budget planning are commonly used when planning a marketing budget:

(a)   top down planning involves high management setting goals for lower management;

(b)   bottom up planning involves employees setting their own goals and submitting them for higher management approval;

(c)   'goals down - plans up' planning mixes the two styles; top management sets overall goals and subordinates then formulate plans for achieving those goals. This type of planning is often used in the formulation of sales budgets.

4.4   Setting budgets to accommodate sales revenue and selling costs is plagued with uncertainty. Complex wide-ranging variables are difficult to accommodate, even within a wide tolerance (largely because of competitive action and changing customer habits and tastes). Consequently, both setting budgets and marketing budgetary control are different from the more 'mechanical' approach which can be adopted with other budgets.

4.5   Clearly high detailed and specific cost control systems in production are pointless if all other costs (eg research, distribution, sales) are left without planning and strategy. A sales and marketing budget is necessary because:

(a)   it brings together all the activities of the business within the overall strategic plan of the business (the master budget);

(b)   if sales and other non-production costs are a significant aspect of total costs, it is financially expedient to forecast, plan and control them;

(c)   uncertainty in the factors influencing selling makes the need for good forecasts and plans greater, and the more uncertain the budget estimates are, the more budgetary control is necessary when budgets are being used for control.

Forecast demand matched to estimated available capacity

4.6   Matching the forecast demand from customers with the estimated available capacity is a budgeting problem. There are three aspects to this problem.

(a)   Accurate forecast of demand is difficult.

(b)   Predicting available capacity accurately is difficult too, given uncertainties in relation to:

    (i)   efficiency and productivity levels;

    (ii)   the availability of staff, or cash;

    (iii)   the likely down-town or time lost through industrial disputes;

(iv)   whether overtime or double shift working will be available;

(v)   the likelihood that changes in equipment (eg introduction of new equipment and replacement equipment) will take place in the budget period.

(c)   Practical difficulties exist in matching demand with capacity. A number of factors militate against this, including seasonality of demand, or if services or non-standard products are required, it will not be possible to build up inventories in periods of slack demand in anticipation of periods of high demand.

4.7   Matching demand with capacity requires management to be flexible, and be prepared to take action:

(a)   to suppress demand if it exceeds capacity, by raising prices, for example;

(b)   to stimulate demand if there is excess capacity, such as by advertising or price reductions;

(c)   to reduce excess capacity by selling off surplus assets;

(d)   to supplement production when there is undercapacity by subcontracting work to other organisations, and perhaps to take steps to increase capacity (by acquiring new premises, equipment and labour, or by negotiating for more overtime from existing employees).

Advertising budget decisions

4.8   The theory behind the setting of an advertising budget is the theory of diminishing returns. This maintains that for every extra £1 of advertising spent, the company should earn an extra £x of profit. Further expenditure on advertising is justified until the marginal return £x diminishes to the point where £x < £1.

4.9   In practice, marginal returns from additional advertising cannot be measured easily because:

(a)   advertising is only one factor within the overall marketing mix;

(b)   advertising effects, at least in part, are *long-term*, and go beyond the limits of a measurable accounting period;

(c)   if the advertising budget is fixed as a percentage of sales, advertising *costs* tend to follow *sales levels* and not vice versa.

4.10   The UK, most advertising budgets are fixed by some rule of thumb, non-scientific method, such as:

(a)   a percentage of the previous year's sales;
(b)   a percentage of the budgeted annual sales;
(c)   a percentage of the previous year's profit.

There is no reason, however, why advertising costs should relate directly to either total turnover or profits.

4.11   Other possible methods of setting the advertising budget include the following.

(a)   Fixing advertising expenditure in relation to the expenditure incurred by *competitors*. This is unsatisfactory because it presupposes that the competitor's decision must be a good one.

(b)   The *task method*. The marketing task for the organisation is set and an advertising budget is prepared which will help to ensure that this objective is achieved. A problem occurs if the objective is achieved only by paying out more on advertising than the extra profits obtained would justify.

(c)   *Communication stage models*. These are based on the idea that the link between advertising and sales cannot be measured directly, but can be measured by means of intermediate stages (increase in awareness, comprehension, and then intention to buy). An example of such a model is Colley's *DAGMAR* model (Defining

Advertising Goals for Measured Advertising Results). A major problem with the use of such models is that it is not yet clear how the use of indices of customer opinion will enable management to set an effective advertising budget.

4.12 Recommended practice for fixing advertising cost budgets would be the use of:

(a) *empirical testing* (for example, in a mail order business or in retail operations, since it may be possible to measure the effect of advertising on sales by direct observation);

(b) *mathematical models* using data about media and consumer characteristics, desired market share, and using records of past results. Regression analysis can be conducted to find out the likely cost of advertising (through several media) to achieve a given target.

Control

4.13 Once the plan has been implemented, the task of management is to control the use of resources. Aspects of control include:

(a) a comparison of actual sales against the budget;

(b) a comparison of actual marketing costs against the budgeted expenditure levels and against actual sales;

(c) analysis of the profitability of individual products, and distribution outlets;

(d) strategic control, ie checking whether the company's objectives, products and resources are being directed towards the correct markets.

5 THE DETAILED PLANS AND PROGRAMMES DOCUMENT

5.1 A marketing plan is a written document covering all an organisation's marketing activities, their implementation and control.

5.2 The detailed plans and programmes document is described (in the syllabus) as comprising:

(a) company mission;
(b) product/market background information;
(c) SWOT analysis;
(d) statement of objectives;
(e) strategies (target markets, competitive edge, brand positionings);
(f) marketing programmes (sales targets, detailed marketing mixes);
(g) allocation of resources, tasks, responsibilities;
(h) financial implications/budgets;
(i) operational implications and implementation; and
(j) appendices (supportive information).

5.3 It is therefore quite clearly a very comprehensive document indeed, containing as it does both detailed analyses and the complete marketing plan including its resource, financial and operational implications.

5.4 It can be seen to build on, ie to include but expand considerably upon the marketing planning process (outlined earlier). It is a blueprint for the marketing function in an organisation for the period covered by the document.

5.5 Expanding now upon the above outline:

(a) *Company mission*. This is basically a clear statement of what business the company is in and what its ambitions are.

(b) *Product/market background information*. Comprehensive data on product portfolio and market segments including historical trends and future projections.

(c) *SWOT analysis.* A multi-sourced statement of company strengths, weaknesses, opportunities and threats, ideally with scores and degrees of importance as recommended in Kotler, or at least some indication of rank order.

(d) *Statement of objectives.* Normally expressed in terms of sales/market shares/gross margins for given periods of time but often extended to include sub-objectives of, say, levels of awareness, degrees of distribution outlet penetration etc

(e) *Strategies.* Target markets, new product developments, building up distinctive competences, determining brand positioning, internal marketing and relationship marketing.

(f) *Marketing programmes.* Sales targets over time periods for each product and market, together with detailed action programmes for each element/sub-element of the marketing mix. Also action programmes for marketing research.

(g) *Allocation of resources, tasks, responsibilities.* For each action on above programmes including timings.

(h) *Financial implication/budgets.* Estimated costs for each action programmed together with anticipated gains. Control mechanisms.

(i) *Operational implications and implementation.* What needs changing in terms of people, job descriptions, equipment etc. Problems envisaged and potential solutions.

(j) *Appendices.* Detailed supporting information: tables, graphs, product descriptions, marketing research data etc.

6   CONSTRAINTS ON MARKETING DECISIONS

Legal constraints

6.1 *Legal constraints* are those imposed by law, mainly by competition legislation and consumer protection laws, contained in Acts of Parliament in the UK. Regulatory constraints normally arise from legal constraints and comprise the rules which are drawn up for enforcement by regulatory agencies in the UK such as the Ministry of Agriculture, Fisheries and Food, and the Department of the Environment.

6.2 Other regulatory constraints can arise from legally binding agreements in contract such as conditions of sale and conditions of purchase. The essential point about the first group of constraints is that organisations have to abide by them or suffer legal penalties such as fines or even imprisonment, and the second group raises issues of being sued for damages (compensation).

Voluntary constraints

6.3 *Voluntary constraints,* by contrast, carry no legal penalties and are not enforceable in law. They are simply guiding principles such as Codes of Practice, normally drawn up by institutions or industries to guide members on how to operate responsibly. The CIM, for example, has its own Code of Practice which, if broken by a member can lead to that member's expulsion. Quite often, voluntary constraints are entered into to pre-empt or forestall legal constraints and/or in response to complaints from consumer associations or media pressure. They are a form of self-regulation.

Ethics and social responsibilities

6.4 *Ethics* relate to moral values and commonly accepted principles of right and wrong. Organisations which offend these values are likely to receive adverse publicity in the media and by word of mouth. *Social responsibilities* are akin to ethics but involve the impact of an organisation's behaviour upon society. For example, a company like Boots the Chemists considering selling off its pharmaceutical division to a German company will offend no laws but places 2,000 jobs in jeopardy. This would reflect upon Boots' caring image and long-standing record of social responsibility. Social responsibility is like an unwritten contract with society, both locally and at large, whilst ethics are reasoned-out rules based on moral values that guide individual/group decisions.

6.5   Neither ethics nor social responsibilities are written down in 'tablets of stone' like Codes of Practice or Acts of Parliament although companies may of course adopt their own codes on these matters. They differ from both legal/regulatory constraints and voluntary constraints by being non-specific and rooted in culture/tradition rather than contractual documentation.

Summary

6.6   Marketing managers need to consider carefully what issues arise from these different forms of constraint and how they affect marketing decisions. Clearly costs are involved in complying with these constraints and the degree of latitude increases as one moves from decisions bound by legal constraints to those based on ethical or social responsibilities.

6.7   We will return to these issues in part F of this Study Text.

Chapter roundup

- Planning is a fundamental part of the manager's role. It involves co-ordinating resources and channelling them towards the achievement of pre-determined goals. The purpose of planning is as follows.

    o   To determine objectives for the organisation
    o   To identify alternative means of achieving those objectives
    o   To select, from among the alternatives, the 'best' option for achievement of the plan.

- Planning and control are often seen as two separate activities. However, Anthony has argued that although they call for different types of mental activity, they do not relate to separable categories of activity carried on at different times. Many activities may contain elements of planning *and* control.

- The control cycle, which depends on feedback of performance and flexibility of response, has six stages.

- Strategic planning starts with the setting of corporate objectives, expressed in quantitative terms, and runs through to implementation and evaluation of the chosen strategy. Planning requires consideration of the long term as well as the short term; even though long-term planning is imprecise in nature, it is a useful activity.

- A detailed plans and programmes document is a document covering all aspects of an organisation's marketing activities, their implementation and control.

- There are a number of areas of constraints upon marketing decisions.

Test your knowledge

1   What are the barriers to good planning? (see para 1.9)

2   Identify the six stages of the control cycle. (2.4)

3   What is a contingency plan? (3.12)

4   How is a marketing plan usually set? (4.1)

5   How is an advertising budget arrived at? (4.10, 4.11)

6   List the contents of a detailed plans and programmes document (5.2)

7   Give an example of a voluntary constraint which could affect marketing activities. (6.3)

Now try illustrative questions 5 and 6 at the end of the Study Text

MARKETING OPERATIONS IN ACTION

At the end of each part of this Study Text, we take a look at the subject matter covered in the light of real companies, either to offer more detail or to give an understanding of the wider corporate context.

In Part B of the Text we have focused on the marketing planning process. We have seen that the impetus for the setting of objectives and the formulation of strategies for achieving those objectives may come from an organisation's mission statement. Many organisations develop a mission statement but leave it at that. The mission statement remains a collection of words, and business carries on as usual with no changes. What is important is that these words permeate into the day-to-day working practices of the organisation and become a way of life.

Writing in *Marketing Business* (July 1994), Philip Forrest suggests a model for accomplishing the mission. An organisation starts with a strategic intent, which represents the long-term goal. This is the organisation's mission, or 'vision'. The next step is to define values and beliefs; if everyone believes the same things and understands the strategic intent, they are more likely to behave in the same way. Once this has been done, objectives can be set and a gap analysis carried out. It is now that strategic options for achieving desired outcomes (objectives) become clearer and a plan developed for achieving the strategy.

Forrest suggests that City analysts, who have traditionally focused on financial performance measurements, have leaned to understand brands, products and marketing, but have still to master the concepts of an organisation's mission and values. These elements are becoming increasingly important to analysts.

An example of the difficulties and dangers in following strategic intent is shown by the attempts of a number of UK firms to break into the US food sector. The example of United Biscuits (UB) is described in an article in *Marketing Week* (July 28 1995) by George Pitcher.

The history of UB 'demonstrates the dangers of the UK food industry's over-reaching ambition when it comes to dealings in US.' UB is not the only firm to suffer in this way.

The heart of UB's problem lies in its US subsidiary, Keebler, purchased by UB in 1974. At the time of purchase, Keebler was considered a success story; 'But the point about success stories in business is knowing when they end ... a happy ending amounts to quitting when you're ahead'.

In the 1980s, Keebler's 'distributive power harmed the mighty Nabisco and PepsiCo. But the business was racing close to its limit ... it had to trade extremely high volumes or its heavy overhead structure would immediately start eroding margins. It only needed the market to change its characteristics in some power-shift and Keebler would be exposed. This happened in the late 1980s when Procter and Gamble tried to enter the market, and fought competitive wars with PepsiCo. Keebler survived quite well.

However, Keebler's 'next move was the big mistake. UB, through Keebler, sank $130m (£83m) into the US salty-snack manufacturing business, and took PepsiCo on in one of the world's most viciously competitive markets'.

PepsiCo's vulnerability was only temporary, and Keebler suffered huge falls in profits; however a three year recovery programme was put in place.

Keebler was dealt another blow when 'new products from other rivals took away much of the traditional snack market'. In other words, Keebler (and UB) had paid insufficient attention to its core business, and its failed diversification into salty-snacks weakened it disastrously.

A general point is that UK businesses find the US food market almost fatally attractive. George Pitcher suggests that failure might be caused by the organisational decision to run the US business from the UK.

Part C
Marketing organisation

Chapter 6

ORGANISING MARKETING ACTIVITIES

This chapter covers the following topics.

1 Organisation structure

2 Centralisation and decentralisation

3 Sales-led, product-led and marketing led organisations

4 Alternative approaches to organisation structure

5 Alternative ways of organising marketing activities

6 The role of marketing personnel

Introduction

One of the effects of a move towards a marketing orientation is that the marketing department, or function, increases in prominence. This has obvious effects on the structure of the organisation. In this chapter, we examine typical organisation structures and look at the place of marketing within the organisation. An organisation may typically be sales-led, product-led or marketing-led, and within this framework there are different ways of organising the marketing department.

We conclude the chapter with a look at the role of the marketing department and the responsibilities of the various personnel.

---

1 ORGANISATION STRUCTURE

1.1 Organisations function to:

(a) link individuals in an established network of relationships so that authority, responsibility and communications can be controlled;

(b) group together (in any appropriate way) the tasks required to fulfil the objectives of the organisation, and allocate them to suitable individuals or groups;

(c) give each individual or group the authority required to perform the allocated functions, while controlling behaviour and resources in the interests of the organisation as a whole;

(d) co-ordinate the objectives and activities of separate units, so that overall aims are achieved without 'gaps' or 'overlaps' in the flow of work required;

(e) facilitate the flow of work, information and other resources required, through planning, control and other systems.

1.2 The advantages of having a formal organisation structure therefore include the following.

(a) Unity or 'congruence' of objectives and effort.

(b) Control over interpersonal relationships, exercise of authority, use of resources, communication and other systems (for example promotion, planning, reward, discipline), offering predictability and stability for planning and decision making.

(c) Controlled information flow throughout the structure to aid co-ordination and (arguably) employee satisfaction.

(d) The establishment of precedents, procedures, rules and norms to facilitate decision making and interpersonal relations in recurring situations.

1.3 Many factors influence the structural design of the organisation.

(a) *Size*. As an organisation gets larger, its structure gets more complex: specialisation and subdivision are required. The process of controlling and co-ordinating performance, and communication between individuals, also grows more difficult. Large organisations tend to generate more *informal* groupings within the formal structure.

(b) *Task*, ie the nature of its work. Structure is shaped by the division of work into functions and individual tasks, and how these tasks relate to each other, depending on the nature of the work. The nature of the market will influence how tasks are grouped into functions, 'sales territories' etc.

(c) *Staff*. The skills and abilities of staff will determine how the work is structured.

(d) Legal, commercial, technical and social *environment*.

(e) *History:* how an organisation has developed over time.

(f) *Culture* and *management style:* the willingness of management to delegate authority at all levels, skill and the approach the company takes to staff and customers.

Organisational culture

1.4 Every organisation is different. Even though two organisations may be similarly structured and involved in similar activities, they may *still* be quite different to work for, or deal with. This is often referred to as 'organisational culture'.

1.5 Culture may be defined as a complex body of shared values and beliefs. Handy sums up 'culture' as 'that's the way we do things around here'. He uses classical analogies to describe the cultural factors found in different organisation types.

(a) Zeus or the club culture (entrepreneurial boss, snap decisions).
(b) Athena or the task culture (get the job done, multi-functional teams).
(c) Apollo or the role culture (bureaucracy, everyone in his or her place).
(d) Dionysus or the existential culture (management based on personal relations).

1.6 For Edgar Schein, culture is the 'pattern of basic assumptions that a given group has invented, discovered, or developed, in learning to cope with its problems of external adaptation and internal integration, and that have worked well enough to be considered valid and, therefore, to be taught to new members as the correct way to perceive, think and feel in relation to these problems.'

> 'I believe that the real difference between success and failure in a corporation can very often be traced to the question of how well the organisation brings out the great energies and talents of its people. What does it do to help these people find common cause with each other? And how can it sustain this common cause and sense of direction through the many changes which take place from one generation to another?... I think you will find that it owes its resiliency not to its form of organisation or administrative skills, but to the power of what we call beliefs and the appeal these beliefs have for its people.'
>
> Watson (IBM) quoted by Peters and Waterman

1.7 Schein brings together corporate culture and management by objectives when he suggests that for culture to support an organisation's strategy, there needs to be a high degree of consensus between managers and employees. He identified five specific areas where this tacit agreement is essential.

(a) Consensus on the mission and primary task of the business.
(b) Consensus on what everyone is meant to do - goals.
(c) Consensus on how tasks should be tackled, allocation of work and rewards.
(d) Consensus on how to measure progress.
(e) Consensus on how and when to intervene if things are going wrong.

1.8   The culture of the organisation is clearly important. It is influenced and shaped as follows.

  (a) *Economic conditions.* In prosperous times organisations will either be complacent or adventurous, full of new ideas and initiatives. In recession they may be depressed, or challenged.

  (b) *Nature of the business and its tasks.* The types of technology used in different forms of business creates a set of working conditions - shop floor, office, department etc.

      Some organisations contain many tasks, so there may be task-related cultural differences between departments (eg the sales department and the finance department).

  (c) *Leadership style* in the exercise of authority will determine the extent to which subordinates feel alienated and uninterested or involved and important. Leaders are also the creators and 'sellers' of organisational culture: it is up to them to put across the vision.

  (d) *Policies and practices.* The level of trust and understanding which exists between members of an organisation can often be seen in the way policies and objectives are achieved. The balance between 'custom' and 'formal rules' is also an important factor.

  (e) *Structure.* The way in which work is organised, authority exercised and people rewarded will reflect an emphasis on freedom or control, flexibility or rigidity.

  (f) *Characteristics of the work force.* Organisation culture will be affected by the demographic characteristics of the workforce, for example manual/clerical division, age, sex, personality. For example all-male or all-female workforces have distinct cultures.

1.9   Culture is clearly not something which will influence eventual success or failure of plans when they are implemented. Each organisation generates its own culture, as the outcome of natural processes, and also the more active guidance of a positive managerial strategy.

1.10 A managerial culture involves three elements.

  (a) The *basic, underlying assumptions* which guide the behaviour of the individuals and groups in the organisation, for example customer orientation, or belief in quality, trust in the organisation to provide rewards, freedom to make decisions, freedom to make mistakes, and the value of innovation and initiative at all levels. Assumptions will be reflected in the kind of people employed (their age, education or personality), the degree of delegation and communication, whether decisions are made by committees or individuals etc.

  (b) *Overt beliefs* expressed by the organisation and its members, which can be used to condition (a) above. These beliefs and values may emerge as sayings, slogans, mottos etc. such as 'we're getting there', 'the customer is always right', or 'the winning team'. They may emerge in a richer mythology - in jokes and stories about past successes, heroic failures or breakthroughs, legends about the 'early days', or about 'the time the boss ...'. Organisations with strong cultures often centre themselves around almost legendary figures in their history. Management can encourage this by 'selling' a sense of the corporate 'mission', or by promoting the company's 'image'; it can reward the 'right' attitudes and punish (or simply not employ) those who aren't prepared to commit themselves to the culture.

  (c) *Visible artefacts:* the style of the offices or other premises, dress 'rules', display of 'trophies', the degree of informality between superiors and subordinates etc.

1.11 Examining the structure of the organisation and understanding its characteristics is an essential first step in successful planning. It will help you to assess the likely reaction of both superiors and subordinates. With this insight you will be able to forecast more accurately the resources required and the time necessary for the implementation of your plans. Case studies will frequently provide you with clues about the organisation and its culture. Recognising these and taking them into account in developing your strategies is an important aspect of the realistic approach the examiners will expect.

1.12 For example a company with a *risk averse* culture is unlikely to adopt a strategy based on speculative land deals and one with a strong religious base to its culture is unlikely to be happy to diversify into casinos or betting shops.

2 CENTRALISATION AND DECENTRALISATION

2.1 A *centralised organisation* is said to be one where very little decision-taking responsibility is delegated downwards by top management. It tends to be autocratic in nature and to be characterised by a head office, perhaps located away from the remainder of the organisation, normally in a big city. All major marketing decisions are made 'centrally' by top management and passed downwards for implementation by lower management. People below top management are expected to carry out decisions made above with little or no right to participate in or indeed question these decisions (except for clarification). A centralised organisation is therefore though to be a more disciplined structure where all marketing staff know what is expected of them. The decision taking process is clearly laid down.

2.2 There are however disadvantages in this approach. Clearly if no-one except the top managers can take decisions, damaging delays can occur in their absence. Centralising can also destroy initiative and certainly de-motivate lower management who might otherwise make a significant contribution to the decision-taking process.

2.3 A *decentralised organisation* is by contrast one where decision-taking authority is delegated outwards from head office to the regions and downwards from top management to middle management. Such an approach encourages initiative and allows decisions to be taken where the action is taking place. It does also allow for quicker and some would say more effective decision taking, since decisions do not have to be continually referred upwards to a senior manager who might be unavailable at that time.

2.4 However, in a decentralised organisation there is the danger of overlap and/or contradictory decisions as well as the possibility of confusion. Senior management may also have to accept a reduced degree of control.

2.5 Most organisations seek to achieve a balance between centralised and decentralised decision taking so as to gain the benefits of both. This may mean clearly identifying and communicating the types of decisions which may be taken at the various levels and giving guidance in the attempt to avoid contradictions between one region and another.

2.6 For example, in a large retail organisation, major product/brand decisions may be made centrally, but individual branch managers may be allowed some discretion with regard to stocking and pricing decisions according to local conditions.

3 SALES-LED, PRODUCT-LED AND MARKET-LED ORGANISATION

3.1 When a company becomes marketing oriented, a number of changes take place.

(a) Long term orientation.

(b) Preoccupation with planning:

(i) the right products;
(ii) the right channels;
(iii) the right level of service;
(iv) the right marketing strategy to meet the customer's long term needs.

3.2   The marketing approach, according to Lancaster and Massingham:

> 'challenges every member of a company, whatever his or her specialist function, to relate his or her work to the needs of the marketplace, and to balance it against the firm's own profit needs. Nowhere is this more important than in the area of product design, where customers' views, rather than the views of production, should be the starting point'.

Marketing led organisations

3.3   The *marketing oriented company* is obsessed with marketing, and if it is staying faithful to the principles involved, the marketing department will be very prominent indeed within the organisation.

3.4   A market-led organisation is one which first of all determines what customers want and then sets about providing goods/services which meet customers' wants and needs, at the right price, at the right time, at the right place and communicates effectively with these customers. The organisation will do this in a way consistent with achieving its own objectives.

3.5   The market-led organisation is therefore characterised by an emphasis on marketing research so that decisions on the marketing mix are based upon a continual flow of information from customers and potential customers.

Sales-led organisations

3.6   The *sales oriented company* is very likely to be organised into specialised departments, charged with carrying out company tasks. Each of these specialist departments will have an impact on the customer through the actions and decisions which they take. The marketing concept requires that these activities should be co-ordinated, since customer satisfaction depends on these different departments acting in unison. The change from sales to marketing orientation, then, means that marketing will have much greater power within the company, and much greater influence and authority to make other departments fall in line with the dominant policies - which foreground marketing concerns. Integrated, co-ordinated marketing is the aim.

3.7   A sales-led organisation is one where the selling function is dominant and marketing, if indeed it is practised at all, is regarded as subservient to sales. It is typically found where capacity exceeds demand and where the organisational aim is to sell what it makes rather than make what it can sell. A sales-led orientation tends to follow a previous period of production-led orientation when the organisation has concentrated on increasing its production capacity without necessarily improving its products. When the decline stage of the product life cycle begins, the organisation finds itself 'over-planted' and emphasis switches to selling. Unfortunately some organisations adopt what has become known as the 'hard-sell approach' where products/services are pushed onto prospects irrespective of their real needs and building up considerable badwill (as has recently occurred in the holiday market with timeshares and, it is claimed, in the insurance market with PEPs).

3.8   Clearly, some kinds of conflicts are likely to arise. In a marketing oriented company, however, senior personnel are much more likely to come from a marketing background. The marketing manager is usually given a position of authority which is equal to that of production or financial directors.

The organisation of a marketing-oriented firm

3.9 While the position of marketing personnel, and the organisational structure of this type of company, is vital for the marketing orientation to have a deep and lasting effect, the ideas which it represents must become articles of faith within the culture and values of the organisation.

3.10 The respective emphases within sales and marketing oriented companies can be depicted as follows.

Department	Sales Emphasis	Marketing emphasis
Sales	Short-term sales Sales most important One department	Long-term profits Customer satisfaction most important Whole organisation
Purchasing	Narrow product line Standard parts	Broad product line Non-standard parts
Finance	Hard and fast budgets Price to cover costs	Flexible budgets Market-oriented pricing
Accounting	Standard transactions	Special terms and discounts
Manufacturing	Long runs Few models Standard orders Long production lead times	Short runs Many models Custom orders Short production lead times

Product-led organisations

3.11 There is also a third type of organisation: the product-led organisation. A product-led organisation is one which concentrates on the product itself and tends to de-emphasise other elements of the marketing mix. It tends to take the view that if the product is right it will self itself and the world will beat a path to its doorstep. The product-led approach is typically adopted by companies in high technology or small companies set-up to exploit a new invention. Product-led organisations can develop 'marketing myopia' to the extent that they forget the need. As Levitt says 'people who buy ¼" drills want ¼" holes'. If someone comes along with a better way of making ¼" holes, such as a laser beam, the drill becomes redundant. Design tends to be decided by the technicians rather than the customers.

The development of marketing departments

3.12 Although every organisation is different, common patterns appear in the structure of all organisations. The position occupied currently by departments of marketing evolved from the existence of sales departments. Traditionally all dealings with a marketplace would have been the responsibility of a sales director who would typically report direct to senior management. As a marketing orientated approach developed a marketing director might appear in parallel to the sales director, but with two distinct *functional* departments. As fuller recognition of the marketing approach to business was granted, sales and marketing would become a single functional department, with sales as a sub group within marketing.

3.13 Within organisational structures emphasis has shifted from a sales department to a marketing department. In the banking sector, for example, the traditional disapproval of sales and selling - and indeed the view that it was not necessary - means that the pattern of development was slightly different. In the case of banking the development often came from Publicity or Public Relations managers or perhaps even advertising managers to marketing managers. This simply reflected a different balance of activities in terms of relationships with a market.

3.14 In its current format, the marketing department plays a key role in co-ordinating marketing activities. The marketing manager in particular is responsible for planning, resource allocation, monitoring and controlling the marketing effort. In fact, in order to ensure that the marketing effort has maximum effectiveness, this co-ordinating role is crucial, involving co-ordination of marketing efforts for different products in different markets, in addition to ensuring that individual marketing campaigns are co-ordinated. The marketing function tends to be thought of as a staff management function with a co-ordinating role, rather than a line management function.

3.15 Marketing affects all of a company's activities. This means, in service industries, that the structure of operations is increasingly being designed, not so much around administrative convenience, but around the customer.

   (a)   For example, a British Telecom advertisement showed one member of staff dealing with a variety of queries from one caller, as opposed those enquiries being re-routed to several different departments.

   (b)   Banks, too, have personal bankers dealing with many affairs of individual customers. These individuals might simply play a co-ordinating role, but it is one greatly valued by the customer. Moreover, it is possible that a bank's marketing department, by enquiring as to what customers want, will affect the *physical layout* of the branches in which services are delivered.

3.16 In financial services companies information flow is crucial as financial 'products' can change very swiftly. A rise in interest rates will swiftly affect the 'price' element of the marketing mix, to the extent that consumers are price sensitive. It is no use to the marketing function promoting financial products when the conditions which have made these profitable have changed.

3.17 The adoption of a marketing philosophy by a business leads inevitably to involvement of the marketing function in other business activities.

3.18 Our section on 'internal markets' later deals with this issue in more detail.

4   ALTERNATIVE APPROACHES TO ORGANISATION STRUCTURE

4.1   The grouping of organisational activities (usually in the form of 'departments') can be done in different ways. It is important to appreciate these before we move on to look at organisation of marketing activities.

Function

4.2   Primary functions in a manufacturing company might be production, marketing, finance and general administration.

4.3   Functional organisation is logical and traditional and accommodates the division of work into specialist areas. Apart from the problems which may arise when 'line' management resents interference by 'staff' advisers in their functional area, the drawback to functional organisation is that more efficient structures might exist which would be more appropriate in a particular situation.

4.4   Functionally organised institutions can have communication problems caused by these functional 'corridors'. Communication goes up and down the function, but is less effective across the company - this leads to problems of focus and resource allocation. The result is a move towards teams and other forms of organisation structures.

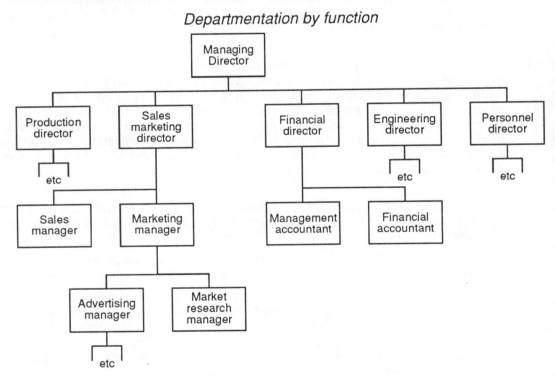

Departmentation by function

Region

4.5   This method of organisation is suitable when similar activities are carried out in widely different locations. Many sales departments are organised territorially. The branch structure of a bank works in the same way, to offer local provision of services.

4.6   The *advantage* of territorial departmentation is better local decision-making at the point of contact. Localised knowledge can be an important competitive advantage, as can close contacts with local communities (for example, in services marketing).

4.7   The *disadvantage* of territorial departmentation is possible over-complexity in channels of communication.

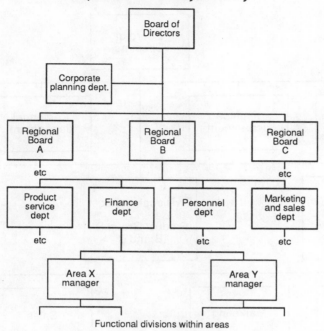

Departmentation by territory

Functional divisions within areas

Product

4.8   Some organisations group activities on the basis of products or product lines. Functional division of responsibility remains, but a manager is given overall responsibility and control of the product, product line or brand.

4.9   The *advantages* of product departmentation are as follows.

(a)   Individual accountability for the *profitability* of each product.

(b)   Specialisation and valuable expertise can be developed amongst sales and support staff.

(c)   Different functional activities and efforts can be co-ordinated and integrated by the product manager.

4.10   The *disadvantage* is that this increases the overhead costs and organisational complexity.

Departmentation by product

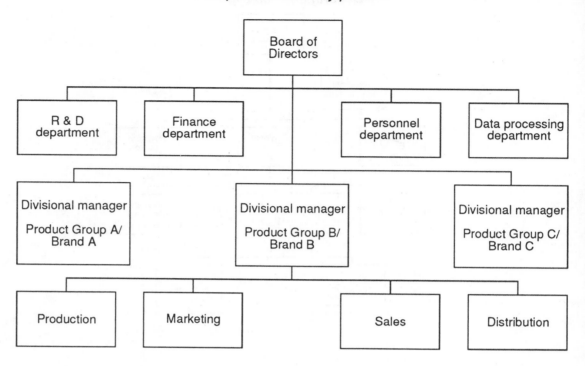

Customer type

4.11 Departmentation by customer is commonly associated with marketing departments and selling effort, but might also occur at the product development stage. Such an approach encourages cross selling across the whole product range and the orientation of activities to meet the needs of client groups.

Common processes or technology

4.12 The most obvious example is the data processing department of large organisations. Batch processing operations are conducted for other departments at a computer centre (where it is controlled by DP staff) because it would be uneconomical to provide each functional department with its own large mainframe computer.

Matrix organisation

4.13 In recent years, awareness of internal and external influences on organisational structure and of difficulties created by more 'traditional' forms has led to the need for flexibility and adaptability in organisational design. The pace of the change in the technological and competitive environment has also put pressure on businesses to innovate, to adopt a market orientation.

4.14 Part of this shift in emphasis has been a trend towards task-centred structures, for example multi-disciplinary project teams, which draw experience, knowledge and expertise together from different functions to facilitate flexibility and innovation. In particular, the concept of 'matrix' organisation has emerged, dividing authority between functional managers and product or project managers or co-ordinators - thus challenging classical assumptions about 'one person one boss' and the line/staff dilemma.

4.15 Matrix management first developed in the 1950s in the USA in the aerospace industry. Lockheed-California, the aircraft manufacturers, were organised in a functional hierarchy. Customers were unable to find a manager in Lockheed to whom they could take their problems and queries about their particular orders. As a response, the company began to employ 'project expediters' as customer liaison officials. From this developed 'project co-ordinators', responsible for co-ordinating line managers into solving a customer's problems. Up to this point, these new officials had no functional responsibilities.

4.16   Increasingly heavy customer demand caused Lockheed to create 'programme managers', with full authority for project budgets and programme design and scheduling. This is, as illustrated, a *dual* authority structure.

BOARD OF DIRECTORS

	Design Dept	Production Dept A	Production Dept B	Service Dept X	Service Dept Y	Finance Dept
Project P co-ordinator						
Project Q co-ordinator						
Project R co-ordinator						

4.17   Functional department heads are responsible for the internal organisation of their departments, but project co-ordinators are responsible for the aspects of all departmental activity as it affects their individual projects. Nowadays, many educational establishments use this approach with course teams drawn from a range of subject-based departments. Some proponents argue that the organisation of the future will be chameleon like - changing teams and shape in response to a changing environment.

4.18   The *advantages* of a matrix structure are as follows.

(a)   Greater flexibility.

(i)   *People*. Employees and departments are geared to change.

(ii)   *Tasks and structure*. The matrix structure may be short term (as with project teams) or readily amended.

(b)   Re-orientation. Responsiveness to customer needs is closer to pure market-orientation.

(c)   Responsibility is directly placed on individual managers.

(d)   Interdisciplinary co-operation and a mixing of skills and expertise.

(e)   Arguably, motivation of employees by providing them with greater participation in planning and control decisions.

4.19   The *disadvantages* of matrix organisation are as follows.

(a)   Dual authority creates conflict and confusion of authority between functional managers and product/project managers.

(b)   Rigidity and status concerns may make a matrix structure and the culture of participation, shared authority and ambiguity that it fosters difficult to accept.

4.20   Structure has a direct impact on the culture of the organisation. Attempts to transform the 'culture', say, from product to a more market orientation are often difficult to achieve.

5   ALTERNATIVE WAYS OF ORGANISING MARKETING ACTIVITIES

5.1   In the same way as the development of marketing within organisations has varied, so will the present organisation of marketing departments. There is no one format which can be described as 'best' or 'most effective'; rather the format chosen will depend on the nature of the existing organisational structure, patterns of management and the spread of the firm's product and geographical interests, among other things. Every marketing department must take responsibility for four key areas:

(a)   functions (promotion, pricing etc);
(b)   geographical areas (domestic, EC, International);
(c)   products (current accounts, deposits accounts, personal loans);
(d)   markets (personal, corporate).

5.2   You should notice that these reflect the main organisation structures discussed in the previous section.

Functional organisation

5.3   The department is typically headed by a marketing director who is responsible for the overall co-ordination of the marketing effort. A number of functional specialists such as a market research manager and a sales manager will be found in the second tier of management and they take responsibility for all activities in their functional specialism across all products and markets. This is a very simple format and is relatively straightforward in administrative terms. It also allows individuals to develop their particular specialisms, at the same time imposing a burden on the marketing director who will be required to perform co-ordinating and arbitrating activities to ensure the development of a coherent marketing mix for elements of the product range.

Functional organisation

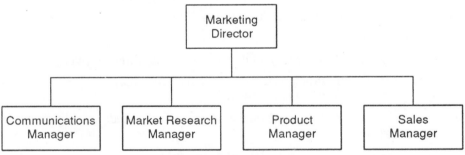

5.4   For a limited range of products, the burden on the marketing director is unlikely to be severe. As the organisation's range of products and markets expands however, this arrangement will tend to be less efficient. Then there is always the danger that a particular product or market may be neglected because it is only one of a great variety being handled by a specific functional manager.

Geographical organisation

5.5   A simple geographical organisation for a marketing department is an extension of the functional organisation in which responsibility for some or all functional activities is devolved to a regional level, through a national manager. Most common in the organisation of a sales force, this also occurs for other functions and indeed, in some organisations, such as financial services, the increase in marketing and sales activities being undertaken at local level can be seen as corresponding to a form of geographical organisation. This type of organisation would probably be more common in firms operating internationally where the various functional activities would be required for each national market or group of national markets.

5.6 The structure tends to be adopted by larger companies with big salesforces that contain too many people to be managed nationally by one person and for where there are perceived regional differences. An FMCG manufacturing company, for example, may supply multiple grocery chains that are organised regionally and therefore develop regional sales/sales promotions managers to link up with customers and regional store managers. Where sales promotion activities are needed quickly in response to competition, then there may be a case for regional promotions managers to decide and implement these in conjunction with regional sales managers.

Geographical organisation

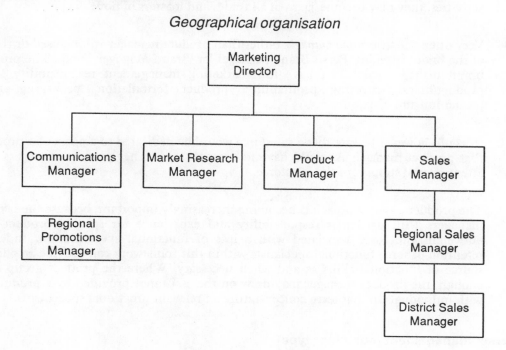

Product-based organisation

5.7 This involves adding an additional tier of management which supplements the activities of functional managers. Product managers take responsibility for specific products or groups of products. This type of approach is likely to be particularly appropriate for organisations with either very diverse products or with a large range of products.

Product management

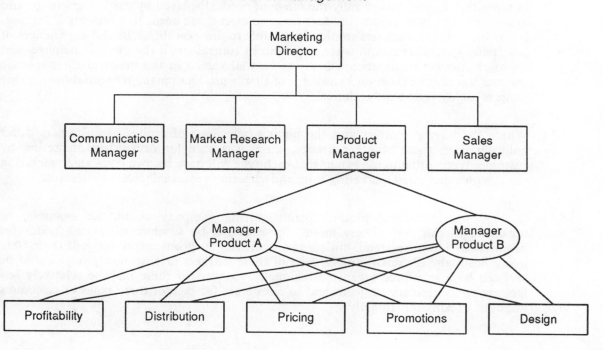

5.8   The individual product manager is responsible for developing plans to suit specific products and ensures that products remain competitive, drawing on the experience and guidance of functional managers. The product manager is effectively responsible for all the marketing activities relating to a particular product group and needs to draw on and develop skills in relation to promotion, pricing and distribution. This allows the individual product managers to build up considerable experience and understanding of particular products groups, invaluable within a rapidly changing competitive environment. Because these managers are responsible for a variety of functional activities, they may become 'jacks of all trades and masters of none'.

5.9   Very often the title *brand manager* rather than product manager will be used or the name of the brand itself, eg 'Persil Brand Manager 'or 'Brand Manager Dreft'. The product or brand manager will often have full marketing management responsibility for that product/brand, covering profitability, product formulation, packaging, pricing, promotion and distribution.

5.10   It would however be rare that a salesforce would be dedicated to a particular product, so that product manager A would have to compete with other product managers for the attention and support of the salesforce.

5.11   The product-based approach is becoming increasingly important, because the benefits of managers with particular responsibility and experience for specific product groups outweighs the costs associated with a loss of functional specialisation. Indeed, the retention of some functional specialists within this framework can provide an additional source of functional skills as and when necessary. Where the product group is large enough, the product manager may draw on the assistance provided by a product team, with individuals in that team concentrating on relevant functional specialisms.

Market management (customer type)

5.12   In a variant on the product management structure, instead of individual managers taking responsibility for particular products, they instead take responsibility for particular markets. The advantage of this approach lies in an organisation offering a variety of different products into particular markets. The understanding of the product here is perceived to be slightly less important than the understanding of the market.

5.13   In the case of services, market management would be consistent with the need to develop relationships with customers, since the individual marketing manager would be in a position to understand fully the range of needs displayed by particular groups and to draw on the organisation's product range to meet those needs in a systematic fashion. Individual market managers would also be able to draw on the skills and experiences of functional specialists as and when required. In contrast with the product management approach, market managers are likely to be well versed in the needs of their specific markets but may be short on knowledge of a large product range, particularly when that range is highly varied and technical.

5.14   Where the buying motives and the buying behaviour of groups of customers differ radically from those of other groups, there is a case for organising marketing by customer type - often to the extent that each type will have its own dedicated marketing mix, its own dedicated marketing team and sometimes even a dedicated salesforce.

5.15   A large pharmaceutical product manufacturing company could, for example, be organised in this way. There might, for example, be separate marketing teams for hospitals/GPs, farmers, retail outlets and veterinary surgeons respectively. If there were many hospitals/GPs/retail outlets, each of these markets or customer groups could be serviced by a salesforce organised regionally. Conversely there may be relatively few farmers and veterinary surgeons and so salesforces for each of these types of customers might be organised nationally.

5.16   Clearly the buying motives and the marketing/selling approach for general practitioners who the organisation wants to persuade to prescribe its drugs differs totally from the motives/approach needed for retail chemists who it wants to stock and display its proprietary products, and again from farmers who want to buy agricultural chemicals in bulk seasonally.

5.17   Companies with such diverse groups of customers will often be organised alternatively by division, for example agricultural products division, retail division etc.

Exercise

What would be the characteristics of a market based approach to organising marketing departments in a banking environment?

Solution

In the case of banking, a market based approach would be characterised by managers with responsibility for personal markets, large corporates, small corporates and so on.

Matrix management

5.18   Matrix management can be thought of as an integration of the product and market management approaches. In an organisation dealing with a variety of products in a variety of markets the product based approach will require managers to be familiar with a wide variety of different markets while the market based approach will require managers to be familiar with a wide variety of products. Nonetheless, expertise may not be fully or efficiently utilised. The matrix based system combines the two. A group of managers deals with markets and a further group with products. The market managers will take responsibility for the development and maintenance of profitable markets while the product manager will focus on product performance and profitability. The system is interlinked with each product manager dealing with a variety of market managers and each market manager dealing with a variety of product managers.

Matrix management

Market Managers

		Corporate	Personal	International
Product Managers	Insurance			
	Investment			
	Lending			

5.19   While this system may seem the ideal approach to resolving the dilemma about the most appropriate form of organisation for a marketing department, it presents certain problems. Cost is likely to be significant because of the extension of the range of management. There are also possible sources of conflict between product and market managers to consider and, particularly, the issue of who should take responsibility for certain activities.

Divisional marketing organisation

5.20   So far we have considered the organisation of marketing within a unitary organisation, but within many organisations larger product groups have developed into separate divisions (what is often called a multi-divisional or 'M' form organisation). These have a high degree of autonomy, but ultimately are responsible to head office. Marketing activity here will often be devolved to divisional level. Some marketing activities will be the responsibility of corporate headquarters, but the extent of corporate involvement can vary a great deal. No particular level of corporate involvement is desirable;

although, it is often suggested that corporate involvement will tend to be more extensive in the early stages of the organisation's development when the divisions are individually quite weak, but as divisions increase their strength, the extent of corporate involvement in marketing declines.

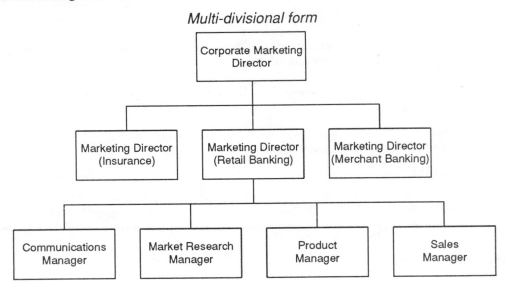

Multi-divisional form

Example: organisation of marketing in the financial services industry

5.21 The organisation of marketing within financial services institutions varies considerably and is still at a relatively early stage of development when compared with many other large business organisations. In the UK clearing banks, the major marketing activities tend to be located centrally in a marketing services department (marketing as a staff management function).

5.22 The manager responsible for the marketing department will essentially be responsible for providing marketing services and support to lower tiers of management with specific responsibility for a variety of line management functions. The typical marketing services manager will be involved in a wide variety of activities which could range from providing an input to the corporate planning procedure, to developing strategies for dealing with changing patterns of competition, and through to identifying the best location for new branches. While many of the functional activities associated with marketing such as advertising, new product development and public relations tend to be managed centrally, in the case of the banks, many of the line management functions, particularly those relating to sales, are the responsibility of general, regional or branch managers.

5.23 The pace of change in the market environment facing banks and the general increase in competition has forced banks to develop an increasingly market orientated approach to their business. These developments have required banks to change their attitudes to doing business and the processes that are involved, and also have consequences for the nature of organisational structure - a change in business philosophy will often necessitate a change in organisational structure. This may create a need to shift from a functional based organisation structure to a flexible one which focuses on products or markets.

5.24 Improved management accounting systems may also be required to enable product profitability and cost control to be effected. Possibilities for cross-selling of the firm's products in a diversified group need to be identified and the mechanism for effecting such co-operation installed, with a need to deal with long standing suspicions and rivalries often a key issue.

5.25   With regard to retail banking, the traditional head office - branch relationship may need to be changed radically to reflect the need to market different products in different ways. Some banks have developed a 'hub and spoke' form of organisation, with the hub being a larger branch offering a full service including responsibility for generating corporate business. The hub may control up to fifteen spoke or satellite branches offering a limited or even automated service concentrating on individuals and small businesses. These aspects of organisational change, which also have direct implications for the role of the branch in distribution are examined further in a later chapter.

5.26   Banks and other financial services firms also need to examine how they ought to interact with their markets. The implementation of a strategic decision to diversify into a new market or enhance a presence in an existing one presents the firm with three main choices:

(a)   the establishment of new outlets;
(b)   joint ventures and links with other service providers (including franchising);
(c)   acquisition (full or partial).

5.27   Firms which perceive a need to build a presence quickly in a market may use a combination of all three possibilities.

5.28   Joint ventures and links with other service providers are a way of extending market reach, or even entering a new market. Some Scottish banks, for example, which do not have a substantial branch presence in England, have pioneered home banking, or have set up arrangements with organisations such as the AA to promote loan and credit card services.

5.29   Building societies have seen substantial further rationalisation by *merger*, the number of societies in the UK falling rapidly in the last decade. Mergers have occurred both amongst the smaller regional societies and between some of the very large ones - the former seeking to strengthen their niche market positions, the latter aiming to have sufficient resources to enable a broader range of services to be provided. Such mergers raise a number of well-known problems concerning the integration of management styles and computer systems, and rationalisation of personnel and branches. Within the UK there are also *legal problems* relating to mergers.

5.30   The pattern in the UK market is being reproduced across Europe as financial services firms seek to take advantage of new opportunities or defend themselves in the light of increased competition.

6   THE ROLE OF MARKETING PERSONNEL

6.1   Now that we have seen how the marketing department fits into the organisation structure, we are ready to look at the role of the department and its personnel. Of particular importance are the marketing manager, who usually has a range of general responsibilities, the product manager, responsible for related lines, and the brand manager, who handles a single brand.

Marketing manager

6.2   A marketing manager's role is to manage marketing, ie to decide marketing objectives (consistent with corporate objectives), marketing strategy and to develop an appropriate marketing mix for implementation. In addition the marketing manager has to obtain information on which to base these decisions from secondary and/or primary data sources as appropriate.

6.3   The marketing manager has to work within agreed budgets and to install suitable control mechanisms to ensure that the marketing plans are being achieved. Finally, the marketing manager needs to lay down and invoke, when necessary, contingency plans when circumstances indicate that the marketing plan proper is 'way off course'.

Segmentation

6.4   When deciding strategy, the marketing manager has to select market segments and a suitable positioning within these segments. Like all managers, marketing managers have a responsibility for working with other functional managers in a corporate team and for the recruitment, training, discipline, remuneration and motivation of their own staff.

Marketing mix

6.5   Marketing mix decisions will include products, pricing, promotion (advertising, selling, sales promotion and PR) and distribution. Marketing managers of services will additionally have to decide on people, process and physical evidence aspects of the marketing mix.

Support

6.6   In a small company the marketing manager may have to carry out all the above responsibilities himself/herself, although it would be usual to delegate sales responsibilities to a sales manager and some of the information gathering and promotional activities to specialised agencies.

6.7   In a larger company, there may be separate marketing managers for particular types of groups of customers, eg one for industrial markets and another for consumer markets.

6.8   Again in large companies the marketing manager will have a number of under-managers specialising in the different marketing functions, eg a marketing research manager or a marketing communications manager. Emphases on particular aspects of the marketing manager's role will vary according to the product-market. For example, a marketing manager in an industrial company might have a heavier emphasis on salesforce support and exhibitions and relatively little emphasis on advertising. By contrast, the marketing manager for a consumer goods company might have a role heavily orientated towards consumer incentives and packaging.

6.9   In large FMCG companies, marketing responsibilities may be delegated to specialists for particularly important products or brands, so as to achieve greater focus in highly competitive markets (as described below).

Product manager

6.10   Where an organisation has many products and particularly when that organisation wishes to have special attention paid to a product, or indeed several interrelated products, it may create the role of product manager.

6.11   A product manager will normally report to, and be responsible to, the marketing manager for the effective marketing of a particular product or group of interrelated products, ie a product line. The product manager receives delegated authority from the marketing manager and is in effect a 'mini-marketing manager' for a particular product or product line. The marketing manager may delegate responsibility for product marketing for the entire range of products to a number of product managers, simply retaining an arbitration and co-ordination role as far as products are concerned. Product managers (rather than brand managers) are perhaps more suitable in industrial concerns where branding is less important. Hence we may find a machine tools manufacturer having separate product managers for drills, lathes, presses etc, all made in different sizes/capacities and marketed under the manufacturer's name rather than under brands.

Brand manager

6.12 In large FMCG companies such as Unilever and Proctor and Gamble it has been found more effective to market brands rather than products and to have brand managers rather than product managers. The brand manager's role is similar to that of a product manager except that it usually carries responsibility for a single brand only. Again the brand manager is responsible to the marketing manager for the complete marketing of that brand, eg Homepride flour or Sensodyne toothpaste.

6.13 However, a brand manager's role carries the extra responsibility of competing (both within the company with other brands and outside the company) for brand leadership. This means building up a strong brand identity and a strong brand loyalty.

6.14 A brand manager (as opposed to a product manager in an industrial concern) for an FMCG company will normally be heavily involved with creative artists and copywriters in an advertising agency in developing favourable brand awareness. Consumer attitudes towards the brand and its packaging are of prime importance. For example, when launching the Yorkie chocolate bar, Rowntree endeavoured to endow it with a strong, filling masculine image by the portrayal of it being eaten by long distance lorry drivers as a snack between meals. The bar was shaped to appear thicker than those of competitors, and the wrapping was shown to be easily removed whilst driving.

Chapter roundup

- Many organisations have a formal organisation structure. There are a number of advantages to adopting a formal structure. Factors influencing structure include size, task, staff, environment, history, culture and management style. The culture of an organisation is also important. It can be defined as a complex set of shared values and beliefs, or 'the way we do things around here'.

- An organisation may be sales oriented, product oriented or marketing oriented. All the key functional departments will have a different emphasis, depending on which orientation is present.

- There is a range of possible organisation structures. The position and prominence of marketing will, to some extent, depend on the structure. Generally speaking, marketing departments must take responsibility for the four key areas of functions, regions, products and markets.

- The concept of matrix management, first developed in the US aerospace industry in the 1950s, is now widely adopted. There are attendant advantages and disadvantages.

- Different marketing personnel have different roles. Important roles include the marketing manager, the product manager and the brand manager.

Test your knowledge

1   What are the advantages of a formal organisation structure? (see para 1.2)

2   Identify five factors which affect the culture of an organisation. (1.8)

3   What are the characteristics of a centralised organisation? (2.1, 2.2)

4   What are the characteristics of a marketing oriented company? (3.3 - 3.5)

5   What are the key distinctions between a sales oriented and a marketing oriented company? (3.10)

6   Describe the features of a typical marketing department. (3.12 - 3.15)

7   Describe the features of a product-based organisation. (4.8 - 4.10)

8   What is matrix organisation? (4.14)

9   What are the advantages of matrix organisation? (4.18)

10   What is the role of the marketing manager? (6.2, 6.3)

11   What is the role of a brand manager? (6.12, 6.13)

Now try illustrative question 7 at the end of the Study Text

Chapter 7

MARKETING CONTROL AND EVALUATION

This chapter covers the following topics.

1 The marketing control process

2 Control of marketing operations

3 Setting targets

4 Measurement and evaluation of performance

5 Efficiency and effectiveness of performance

6 Measuring the effectiveness of the marketing mix

7 Taking control action

Introduction

We round off this part of both the syllabus and the Study Text with a study of marketing control and evaluation. Marketing control involves the application of the control cycle to marketing activities in order to reduce the gap between actual performance and performance standards. Evaluation involves the analysis of sales and marketing cost.

---

1 THE MARKETING CONTROL PROCESS

1.1 The marketing control process is vital to the achievement of marketing objectives and the successful completion of marketing plans. Control is every bit as important a feature of the role of the marketing manager as new product development or promotional creativity.

1.2 The marketing control process can conveniently be broken down into four stages, namely:

    (a) development of objectives;
    (b) establishment of standards;
    (c) evaluation of performance; and
    (d) corrective action.

1.3 Because marketing is essentially concerned with people, and people can be both unpredictable and awkward, controlling marketing activities is particularly problematic. Difficulties arise with information and with timing and cost aspects of marketing plans, to say nothing of competitor activities.

1.4 The marketing control process, or cycle, can be depicted as follows.

The marketing control process

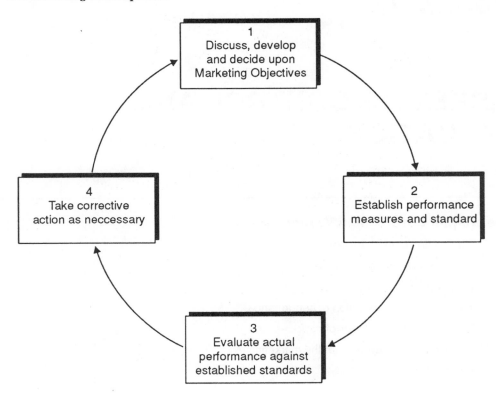

Development of objectives

1.5   The starting point of the marketing control process are the *marketing objectives* which should show clearly where the organisation wants to be, at or by particular points in time. Without knowing clearly where we want to be, we cannot possibly establish the extent to which we are succeeding in getting there or indeed whether we have arrived. Unclear objectives will result in a lack of control. Objectives should therefore have the attributes of quantification and timescales. Objectives should also be achievable given the market conditions and the resources of the organisation. Realistic objectives will be based on past performance moderated by internal and external audits, the latter supplemented by marketing research where necessary. We looked at objectives extensively in an earlier chapter and will not be covering them further here.

1.6   It should be remembered, though, that just as there are formal and informal objectives in the culture of an organisation, so there are formal and informal control processes.

Establishment of standards

1.7   There are a number of *measures by which performance can be judged*, but for a company there are likely to be sales levels, costs and market shares. However, responsible companies will also have ethical and social responsibility standards. The most marketing-orientated organisations will be likely to pursue relationship marketing which entails a high degree of customer care. Thus, in addition to sales measures, many companies will seek to measure customer satisfaction.

1.8   *Performance standards* can now be set at sales of £X for the period, Y% market share and Z% profit, all set against a maximum number of customer complaints.

Evaluation of performance

1.9   The organisation can now *monitor performance* and at given time intervals *compare actual performance with the standards set* to determine whether it is on, above or below these standards.

Corrective action

1.10   Where performance against standard is below a tolerable level then action needs to be taken. This may mean invoking *contingency plans* previously drawn up for this purpose, taking ad hoc actions such as initiating sales promotions, reducing the performance standard or indeed a mix of these possibilities.

1.11   *Information* is needed at all stages of the process, ie information of the right type, in the right place and at the right time. The arrows in the preceding diagram indicate not only the stages and their sequence but also the information flows.

Problems in controlling marketing activities

1.12   A number of problems can occur to 'foul up' the system indicated in the diagram. We have already emphasised the importance of adequate information flow. Information may not be available at the right time - agencies can let you down - or indeed at an affordable cost. Competitors can take retaliatory action, for example aimed at sabotaging a new product launch.

1.13   Unforeseen changes may occur in the environment: new laws may be passed as, for example, regarding Sunday trading; economies can grow or decline and fashions do change.

1.14   In the internal environment, inadequate support may exist from staff both inside and outside marketing. Some may actively resist the performance standards set.

1.15   Last, but not least, there is the element of creativity. Many organisations are in the hands of their advertising agencies in seeking that image breakthrough that can make the difference between success and failure. When first advertising Childrens' World, Boots found that child viewers did not equate themselves with children of similar age on television, they liked to see themselves as older. If child viewers then thought themselves too old for Childrens' World, catastrophe could have resulted. However, Boots were conducting tracking studies during the TV campaign and were able to adjust accordingly.

2   CONTROL OF MARKETING OPERATIONS

2.1   Control and monitoring can be defined as follows.

> 'The continuous comparison of actual results with those planned, both in total and for separate sub-divisions and taking management action to correct adverse variances or to exploit favourable variances.'

2.2   As we suggested in the previous section, this includes the three main underlying components of the control process.

(a)   Setting *targets or standards* which serve as guidelines for performance.
(b)   The *measurement and evaluation* of actual performance.
(c)   Corrective action where it is needed in the form of a control decision.

2.3   Performance measurement, item (b) above, is therefore an essential bridge between planning (item (a)) and control (item (c)). *Performance measurement is an integral part of the planning and control cycle.* Measurement of past performance functions not only to control current activities but also to provide data for making future plans. Plans for the future cannot be made without a realistic assessment of what has happened in the past.

2.4   Targets and standards of performance derive from a decision about what the objectives of the organisation should be. Overall objectives in the planning process serve as a foundation for all subsidiary quantified targets from divisional and departmental targets down to the performance standards for every echelon of manager and employee in the organisation.

Communication in planning and control activity

2.5   There must be effective communication, and certain essential principles should be followed.

(a)   There should be a formal reporting structure, based on the company's organisation structure, and defined by:

   (i)   function; or
   (ii)   product or service; or
   (iii) geographical area;

   or even a combination of all three.

(b)   Duties must be broadly identified, and for control purposes, reporting procedures should be set up. It is necessary to communicate plans so that they can be carried out, but it is also necessary to communicate results, so that achievements can be monitored and reviewed.

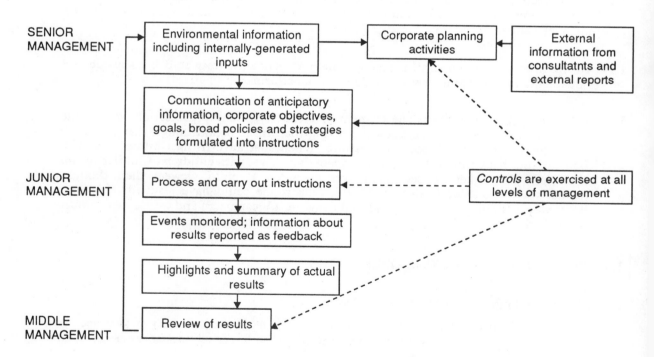

Guidelines for basic strategic control

2.6   Control should take place at three levels - the strategic level, the management control (or tactical) level and the operational control level. The following require attention.

(a)   Distinction between control at different levels in the management hierarchy.

(b)   Individual managers should be identified as having the responsibility for certain matters, and authority to take control measures.

(c) The *key factors for control* should be identified. Managers responsible for taking control action must be informed about what the key factors are, and why they are critical.

(d) Control reporting should be timed sensibly.

(e) Suitable targets and standards should be applied.

(f) Control reports should contain relevant information for the manager receiving the report, and should not contain unnecessary details about irrelevant items.

2.7 Reporting in control reports must be selective, to avoid unnecessary detail and extraneous information. Selective reporting means identifying key points for control.

(a) In the product-market plan, there will be products identified as question marks or potential stars. New products will be planned. The position of each product in the product-market matrix will suggest how much close watching the product needs. High risk/high potential projects should require the greatest amount of monitoring.

(b) A product which performs inconsistently might need close watching and control. However, there is a danger of 'overkill' in monitoring and control of inconsistent performers. Excessive or intensive monitoring in unlikely to change an outcome that is more or less a foregone conclusion. An activity which now appears to have a high probability of indifferent success might respond weakly to control measures, and the product concerned might be drifting into the 'dog' category so that the most appropriate control measure may be to let the product die quietly.

(c) Information and control reporting costs money. The sense of keeping control information down to a minimum is that it saves time and money, and provided that key control measures are identified, nothing is lost by omitting subsidiary detail (which is probably available anyway in routine budgetary control reports).

2.8 If there is a single corporate objective, say profit, this will generate objectives for each divisional function of the organisation and these sub-objectives in turn will be turned into sub-sub-objectives for smaller units of the organisation. There is a clear danger here that the number of key control points will 'mushroom' and so become excessive. If, because of the scale of the organisation's operations, the number of key items is high, the answer is to be even more selective in choosing the critical items which matter more than any others. For example if the key item is to get a new factory built and commissioned, the timing of this project should have control priority over everything else, even current sales levels.

2.9 The key item might be more 'qualitative'. For example within the production function it might be considered vitally important that there should be a rapid and significant improvement in employee commitment and productivity, time lost through stoppages and labour turnover. Control reporting at the corporate planning level should therefore emphasise these points, and shift back to matters such as equipment, tooling and production quantities and costs at a later time, when appropriate.

3 SETTING TARGETS

3.1 The purpose of setting targets or standards is as follows.

(a) To tell managers what they are required to accomplish, given the authority to make appropriate decisions.

(b) To indicate to managers how well their actual results measure up against their targets, so that control action can be taken where it is needed.

3.2 It follows that in setting standards for performance, *it is important to distinguish between controllable or manageable variables and uncontrollable ones*. Any matters which cannot be controlled by an individual manager should be excluded from their standards for performance.

3.3   This is a basic principle of responsibility accounting, ie placing responsibilities fairly and squarely on the right person. Ultimately, it is argued, all costs and revenues are someone's responsibility and so all items of expenditure and income should be appropriately monitored.

3.4   This is especially important in the long-term corporate planning area when even the most ostensibly uncontrollable 'fixed' cost, such as rent, becomes a subject for scrutiny because in the long term, it is negotiable and controllable.

3.5   Higgins argues that as additional shorter term 'objectives' are established, lower levels of the management hierarchy become involved. Each subsidiary 'objective' becomes the standard or benchmark of performance for the manager responsible for its achievement. Additionally, the timing of these events, coupled to the costs involved, add further benchmarks against which to judge actual performance against target.

3.6   With targets or standards for a certain timescale, actual results should be measured with sufficient frequency so that the manager responsible for achieving the targets is aware of the progress being made. She/he should then be able to take control action in good time, so that adverse results can be corrected and the targets still achieved.

3.7   Performance measures should therefore be taken more frequently for targets and standards with a short time scale, and less frequently for longer term targets.

4   MEASUREMENT AND EVALUATION OF PERFORMANCE

4.1   Performance can be measured or evaluated by a management accounting system and other formal reporting systems within an organisation, or by personal observation. The latter is usually the most convenient method for a *qualitative* evaluation of human performance. An experienced supervisor, for example, will be able to judge the pace of the production line, personally inspect the quality of work in progress and also assess workers' morale and motivation by observing their behaviour. Conversely, it is easy for the eye to be deceived and for qualitative judgement to be wrong. Formal reporting systems, such as management accounting systems, provide a much more objective quantitative assessment than the human observer and, once systems are set up, can be much less time-consuming for the controller.

4.2   When performance objectives are not being achieved, the reason will not necessarily be obvious. Before taking corrective action, therefore, it is important to determine the reason for unsatisfactory performance and whether this can be remedied by corrective action. For example if sales in a particular region are low, increasing the sales supervision or sending the representative on additional sales training programmes will be of little effect if the cause of the poor sales is exceptionally high unemployment in the area.

4.3   Performance should be measured and judged by obtaining data about actual results for a direct comparison with the targets or standards set. Performance measures must therefore have the following characteristics.

(a)   They must be measurable, in quantitative or qualitative terms. Not all results are easily measured. For example if a company sets itself an aim of improving customer goodwill, how can the strength of such goodwill be judged, except by relying on the opinion, probably biased, of sales management? Unless an assessment of performance is made, managers will have no information with which to decide whether or not any control action is needed. Ideally, such an assessment should be measured as objectively as possible.

(b)   They must relate directly to the targets or standards set in the plan.

4.4   Targets or standards may be for the long term or short term. Long term targets for achievement will relate to the organisation's *objectives and strategic plans*. Short term targets and standards will be for operational planning and control at a junior management level, and for medium-term planning and budgeting, and budgetary control by middle management.

4.5   The measures and analytical techniques for control at a strategic level are as follows.

Type of analysis	*Used to control*
1 *Financial analysis*	
Ratio analysis	Elements of profitability
Variance analysis	Costs or revenue
Cash budgeting	Cash flow
Capital budgeting and capital expenditure audit	Investment
2 *Market/sales analysis* - overall consideration of size and growth of market segments and corporate market share	
Demand analysis	Competitive standing
Market share or penetration	
Sales targets	Sales effectiveness
Sales budget	Efficiency in use of resources for selling
3 *Physical resource analysis*	
Capacity fill	Plant utilisation
Yield	Materials utilisation
Product inspection	Quality
4 *Human resources analysis*	
Work measurement	Productivity
Output measurement	
Labour turnover	Workforce stability
5 *Analysis of systems*	
Management by objectives	Implementation of strategy
Network analysis	Resource planning and scheduling

Quantitative and qualitative targets

4.6   Performance measurements might be quantitative or qualitative.

(a)   *Quantitative:* ie expressed in figures, and given as cost levels, units produced per week, delay in delivery time, market penetration per product etc.

(b)   *Qualitative:* sometimes called 'judged', which, although not actually and directly measurable in quantitative terms, may still be verified by judgement and observation.

4.7   Where possible performance should be measured in quantitative terms because these are less subjective and biased. Qualitative factors such as employee welfare and motivation, protection of the environment against pollution, and product quality might all be gauged by quantitative measures (for example by employee pay levels, labour turnover rates, the level of toxicity in industrial waste, reject and scrap rates etc).

Financial control information

4.8   Management control information is often expressed in *monetary* terms because this serves as a measurable and readily understandable measure of performance. Money is a useful measure because:

(a) it allows direct performance comparisons of completely different functions and activities: the relative costs and profit contributions of, say, a purchasing manager and sales manager cannot readily be compared without a universal monetary basis;

(b) it facilitates the processing of technical information by non-technical personnel because monetary terms can be understood;

(c) since profitability is the main measure of performance it can serve as a common measure by which corporate and departmental performance can be gauged.

4.9 The disadvantages of using monetary information include the following.

(a) If absorption costing techniques are used, the process of apportioning and absorbing overhead costs is somewhat arbitrary and meaningless.

(b) The common assumption that all costs charged to a product or department are controllable by the manager is actually incorrect. A manager of a production department, for example, cannot control the prices of raw materials, nor the amount of production overhead charged to the department.

(c) Costs and profits may not be the best way of comparing the results of different parts of a business.

(d) Some managers may prefer to quantify information in non-monetary terms, for example:

    (i) the sales manager may look at sales volume in units, size of market share, speed of delivery, volume of sales per sales representative or per call etc;

    (ii) a stores manager might look at stock turnover periods for each item, volume of demand, the speed of materials handling, breakages, obsolescence etc.

(e) Where qualitative factors (notably human behaviour and attitudes) are important, monetary information is less relevant. This is one reason why strategic planning information, which relies more heavily on both external and qualitative factors, is generally more imprecise and not necessarily expressed in money terms.

Evaluation of marketing activities

4.10 The three major ways in which marketing activities may be evaluated could be said to be sales analysis, market share analysis and cost analysis. However there are other analyses which could be almost as important in particular product-market situations. For example when launching a major new FMCG product, it would be crucial to evaluate awareness, trial and re-purchase during the test market. In achieving sales there may also be caveats such as the number of customer complaints received or the number of new customers gained.

Sales analysis

4.11 The table below is a sales analysis for the first quarter of the year.

Month	Actual sales £'000	Budgeted sales £'000	Variance ± £'000	Cumulative variance £'000
1	90	100	− 10	− 10
2	115	120	− 5	− 15★
3	150	140	+ 10	− 5

4.12 We can see that at the start of the period, sales were well below the performance standard. At the point asterisked (★) remedial action was taken which boosted sales above budget for month 3, so that at the end of the quarter the cumulative adverse variance has been greatly reduced.

Market share analysis

4.13 This table shows a comparison of brands over a two year period.

Brand	Sales 1994 £m (est)	Est market share % 1994	Position 1994	Est market share % 1993	Position 1993
Ours	12	20	3	15	3
Brand X	20	33	1	30	2
Brand Y	18	30	2	32	1
Others	10	17	-	23	-
Total	60	100		100	

4.14 In the above table we can see that our position is unchanged from 1993 but that we have increased our market share by 5% over 1993, largely at the expense of the minor players. (Care should be taken with interpretation: it is possible, for example, that in fact we have taken 5% from Brand Y and that Brands X and Y have each taken 3% from 'others'.)

4.15 We can also see that Brand Y has lost its brand leadership to Brand X (1994 versus 1993).

4.16 In order to make this analysis more meaningful we should want to know what our market share objective was for 1994. It would also help to know sales for 1993 so that we can establish whether the total market has risen, fallen or stayed the same.

Marketing cost analysis

4.17 The next table illustrates some of the difficulties in controlling marketing costs.

Period	Cost item	Actual expenditure £'000	Budgeted expenditure £'000	Variance ± £'000	Cumulative ± £'000
Quarter 2	Advertising	100	110	−10	−10
	Exhibitions	50	40	+10	-
	Literature	40	80	−40	−40
	Marketing research	20	5	+15	+5
	Other prom	15	10	+5	+15
	Salesforce	400	440	−40	−60
	Totals	625	685	−60	−90

4.18 At first sight it appears that the performance standards have been poorly set but it should be noted these are only one quarter's figures. Some of the variances might well disappear over the year and some might be easily explained, eg the salesforce is temporarily below establishment, literature is underspent because a new catalogue is late in delivery etc.

4.19 Also, it is good practice to have a contingency reserve, which would normally be added to the year's total at, say, 10% of the total budget.

Special analyses: major new product launch

4.20 Finally we look at an example of a special analysis. This table shows research results for the launch of product X. (*Note*. All figures are percentages of a total target market of 15 million 'housewives')

	Aware-ness Target	Aware-ness Actual	Trial purchase Target	Trial purchase Actual	Repurchase Target	Repurchase Actual
Pre-launch period Weeks 7 and 8	40	30	-	-	-	-
Launch period Weeks 9 and 10	75	60	50	55	-	-
Post-launch period Weeks 11 to 20	80	70	-	-	40	40

4.21 The table shows that the awareness level achieved is less than that targeted. This could indicate a fault in media reach which needs investigation with the media research department of the advertising agency.

4.22 However, despite having reached a smaller target audience than planned, trial purchase was higher than targeted, indicating highly effective advertising content. Due to this and a repurchase rate which is about on target, we have achieved our total sales objective.

4.23 However, it seems clear that if we can improve awareness then we should be able to achieve repurchase sales above target.

5 EFFICIENCY AND EFFECTIVENESS OF PERFORMANCE

5.1 Efficiency and effectiveness are two fundamental ways of measuring performance (preferably in quantitative terms). Drucker wrote:

'Efficiency is concerned with doing things right. Effectiveness is doing the right thing ... Even the healthiest business, the business with the greatest effectiveness, can die of poor efficiency. But even the most efficient business cannot survive, let alone succeed, if it is efficient in doing the wrong things, ie if it lacks effectiveness. No amount of efficiency would have enabled the manufacturer of buggy whips to survive.'

Efficiency

5.2 Efficiency can be defined as the ratio of output quantities to input resources. Efficiency and inefficiency are measures along the same scale, with 'efficiency' referring to a higher ratio of output to input than the norm or standard and 'inefficiency' referring to a lower ratio.

5.3 The fact that most organisations try to achieve certain objectives with limited resources gives rise to the concept of *efficiency* or *productivity*.

5.4 Inputs comprise *all* those factors which contribute to the production of organisational outputs. Drucker points out that efficiency or productivity is now less related to the productivity of manual labour or machinery, and more related to the increasing role of 'knowledge work' ie the work of managers, researchers, planners, designers and innovators - those parts of the organisation often accounted for as 'overheads.' Many managers today believe that the only opportunity left for competitive advantage lies in their human resources.

Effectiveness

5.5 Effectiveness can be defined as success in producing a desired result.

5.6   Two approaches to measuring organisational effectiveness can be suggested.

(a)   *The goal model approach:* this is to express effectiveness in terms of goal attainment, ie. the more an organisation's goals are met or surpassed, the greater is its effectiveness. However, one difficulty with this approach is that most organisations aspire to a number of goals simultaneously and problems arise where realisation of one goal is at the expense of another. Thus, even if an organisation is effective in reaching most of its goals, it may still not be completely effective. Where several goals co-exist, an acceptable ranking of goals must be worked out. When a choice must be made between achieving one goal or another, when it is not possible to achieve both together because resources are insufficient, the ranking process would indicate which goal has priority.

(b)   A second approach to organisational effectiveness focuses on the relationship between the organisation and its environment. This so-called *systems resource approach* defines effectiveness as the degree to which an organisation is successful in acquiring and utilising scarce and valued resources. Organisations take in resources from their environment and 'return' them as output with an economic value. The more effective organisations survive because they can maintain a greater intake of resources than is required to produce their output. An important difficulty with this approach is that it fails to provide guidance as to which resources might be relevant in the assessment of an organisation's effectiveness.

5.7   The goal approach and the systems resource approach are not incompatible and can be taken into account simultaneously. To be effective in the long run, organisations need to be concerned not only with the attainment of internally established objectives (the emphasis of the goal approach) but also with the manner in which objectives are achieved (the emphasis of the systems resource approach).

5.8   Effectiveness can be measured *internally* by establishing whether or not an organisation has achieved the targets set for itself in its planning processes. However, one organisation might set itself easier targets than another and so it might be *effective* in terms of its own targets but not effective when compared with other organisations. This, in fact, highlights the key difference between the goal approach and systems resource approach to measuring effectiveness. If we take the view that comparisons of the effectiveness of different organisations would be useful measures for control purposes, how should yardsticks for measuring effectiveness be set?

5.9   In addition, there are several more general unsolved problems of measuring effectiveness.

(a)   *Effectiveness over time.* Effectiveness has to be measured over time as the organisation and its environment change. The problem is essentially one of how best to balance short term considerations against long term interest.

(b)   *Measurements of effectiveness which relate to the organisation as a whole* are not entirely satisfactory because they ignore the vital role played by individual sub-units of the organisation.

(c)   *Different organisations have different characteristics and goals* and this fact suggests that different criteria of effectiveness ought to apply to different types of organisation. Furthermore, even with similar types of organisation, the appropriate measure of effectiveness may vary according to the stage of development that an organisation has reached or even to the nature of the ownership (for example a public company or a state-owned business etc).

Other aspects of performance

Market share performance

5.10   When a market manager is given responsibility for a product or a market segment, the product or market segment will be a profit centre, and measures of performance for the centre will include profits and cost variances etc. However, another useful measure of performance would be the market share obtained by the organisation's product in the market.

5.11 Changes in market share have to be considered against the change in the market as a whole, since the product might be increasing share simply when the market is declining, but the competition is losing sales even more quickly. The reverse may also be true. The market could be expanding, and a declining market share might not represent a decline in absolute sales volume, but a failure to grab more of the growing market.

5.12 Simmonds concedes that while it may be difficult initially to define the market and the market share of the organisation's products, the approach may be less fraught with theoretical problems than, say, defining capital employed and measuring ROCE.

Monitoring competitor performance

5.13 Budgetary control comparisons will tell the management of an organisation whether the established targets are being achieved, but this sort of comparison can tend to be very inward looking. When an organisation operates in a competitive environment, it should try to obtain information about the financial performance of competitors, to make a comparison with the organisation's own results.

5.14 Financial information which might be obtainable about a competitor from published sources might be as follows.

   (a) Total profits, sales and capital employed.

   (b) ROCE, profit/sales ratio, cost/sales ratios and asset turnover ratios.

   (c) The increase in profits and sales over the course of the past twelve months (and prospects for the future, which will probably be mentioned in the chairman's statement in the report and accounts).

   (d) Sales and profits in each major business segment that the competitor operates in.

   (e) Dividend per share and earnings per share.

   (f) Gearing and interest rates on debt.

   (g) Share price, and P/E ratio (stock exchange information).

5.15 A more detailed comparison of financial performance might be obtainable when there is a scheme of interfirm comparison for the industry.

Monitoring customers

5.16 In some industrial markets or reseller markets, a producer might sell to a small number of key customers. The performance of these customers would therefore be of some importance to the producer: if the customer prospers, he will probably buy more and if he does badly, he will probably buy less. It may also be worthwhile monitoring the level of profitability of selling to the customer.

5.17 Key customer analysis calls for six main areas of investigation.

   (a) *Key customer identity*

      (i)   Name of each key customer
      (ii)   Location
      (iii) Status in market
      (iv)   Products they make and sell
      (v)   Size of firm (capital employed, turnover, number of employees)

   (b) *Customer history*

      (i)   First purchase date.

(ii)   Who makes the buying decision in the customer's organisation?

(iii)   What is the average order size, by product?

(iv)   What is the regularity/ periodicity of the order, by product?

(v)   What is the trend in size of orders?

(vi)   What is the motive in purchasing?

(vii)   What is the extent of the customer's knowledge of the firm's products and of competitors' products?

(viii) On what basis does the customer reorder? How is the useful life of the product judged?

(ix)   Were there any lost or cancelled orders? For what reason?

(c) *Relationship of customer to product*

(i)   Are the products purchased to be resold? If not, for what purpose are they bought?

(ii)   Do the products form part of the customer's service/product?

(d) *Relationship of customer to potential market*

(i)   What is the size of the customer in relation to the total end-market?
(ii)   Is the customer likely to expand, or not? Diversify? Integrate?

(e) *Customer attitudes and behaviour*

(i)   What interpersonal factors exist which could affect sales by the firm and by competitors?

(ii)   Does the customer also buy competitors' products?

(iii)   To what extent may purchases be postponed?

(iv)   What emotional factors exist in buying decisions?

(f) *The financial performance of the customer*

How successful is the customer in his own markets? Similar analysis can be carried out as with competitors.

(g) *The profitability of selling to the customer*

This is an important part of key customer analysis, and must provide answers to questions such as the following.

(i)   What profit/contribution is the organisation making on sales to the customer, after discounts and selling and delivery costs?

(ii)   What would be the financial consequences of losing the customer?

(iii)   Is the customer buying in order sizes that are unprofitable to supply?

(iv)   What is return on investment in plant used? (This will require valuation of the plant and equipment involved in supplying each customer. The valuation might be at historical book value or current cost);

(v)   What is the level of inventory required specifically to supply these customers?

(vi)   Are there any other specific costs involved in supplying this customer, for example technical and test facilities, R & D facilities, special design staff?

(vii)   What is the ratio of net contribution per customer to total investment on both a historic and replacement cost basis?

Such an evaluation would be a part of research into potential market opportunities. Smaller customers should not be ignored and there should be a similar analysis of the organisation's other customers, although a separate analysis for each individual customer may not be worthwhile, and customers may be grouped, for example on the basis of order sizes or another such characteristic such as a geographical basis.

Market performance ratios

5.18   An organisation should study information not only about its share of a particular market, but also the performance of the market as a whole.

(a)   Some markets are more profitable than others. The reasons why this might be so (rivalry among existing firms, the threat of new entrants, the bargaining power of buyers, the bargaining power of suppliers and the threat from substitute products or services) were discussed in an earlier chapter.

(b)   Some markets will be new, others growing, some mature and others declining. The stage in the product's life cycle might be relevant to performance analysis.

5.19   Information about market performance is needed to enable an organisation to plan and control its product-market strategy.

6   MEASURING THE EFFECTIVENESS OF THE MARKETING MIX

6.1   Marketing managers are responsible for monitoring their progress towards the agreed targets and standards. To do this it is necessary to evaluate the effectiveness of the marketing mix.

6.2   This section will consider ways of assessing the effectiveness of four of the mix elements.

(a)   Personal selling
(b)   Advertising and sales promotions
(c)   Pricing
(d)   Channels of distribution

Personal selling

6.3   The effectiveness of personal selling can be measured in three different ways.

(a)   For the sales force as a whole.

(b)   For each group of the sales force (for example each regional sales team, or the 'special accounts' sales staff etc).

(c)   For each individual salesperson.

If there is a telephone sales staff, their performance should be measured separately from the 'travelling' sales staff.

6.4   Measures of performance would compare actual results against a target or standard, and might include any of the following:

(a)   sales, in total, by customer, and by product;

(b)   contribution, in total, by customer and by product;

(c)   selling expenses (budget versus actual), if selling expenses exceeded budget, did actual net sales exceed budgeted sales by a corresponding amount?

(d)   customer call frequency;

(e)   average sales value per call;

(f)   average contribution per call;

(g)   average cost per call;

(h)   average trade discount;

(i)   number of new customers obtained;

(j)   percentage increase in sales compared with previous period;

(k)   average number of repeat calls per sale;

(l)   average mileage travelled per £1 sales.

6.5   While the type of performance standards in this list might seem fairly obvious and sensible, you ought to remember that actual performance is measured in order to compare it against a standard, and it is not an easy task to decide what the standards should be. *How* would an individual's sales quota be set, for example? The standards or budget might be strict or lax. One person might be given an easy quota and another a difficult one to achieve. There is rarely an objectively 'correct' standard or target which seems fair to everyone concerned. It is important not to assume that the 'efficient' sales person who makes ten calls a day is doing a better job by the colleague who makes fewer calls but wins more orders.

6.6   There can be a big difference between (a) net sales (ie sales after returns and discounts) and (b) profits or contribution. The costs of selling and distribution can be a very large proportion of an organisation's total costs, and so the performance of a sales force should be based on productivity and profitability, rather than sales alone.

> 'In recent years the cost of fielding a sales force has increased dramatically ... Faced with such large and continually rising costs, many firms set expense goals all the way down to the territory level. Moreover, although representatives and sales managers tend to focus on the 'top line' (net sales), more and more firms are using profitability and productivity goals (the 'bottom line') to help evaluate the performance of their sales force.'
>
> (P Bennett, *Marketing*)

The effectiveness of advertising

6.7   It is difficult, if not impossible, to measure the success of an advertising campaign, although volume of sales may be a short-term guide.

6.8   A campaign to launch a new product, however, may have to be judged over a longer period of time (ie to see how well the product establishes itself in the market). A comparison of the relative efficiency of different sales promotion methods (price cuts, personal selling, advertising etc.) is also difficult to make, since a combination of different methods is necessary for any successful sales promotion campaign, ie there must be a selling mix, and advertising alone will not sell a product. Shop window displays, for example, may be an important reminder to consumers who have seen a television advertisement. Advertising's main purpose in the communication mix is to create awareness and interest.

6.9   The effectiveness of advertising is therefore usually measured by marketing researchers in terms of customer attitudes or psychological response. Kotler, writing in an American context, commented that:

> 'most of the measurement of advertising effectiveness is of an applied nature, dealing with specific advertisements and campaigns. Of the applied part, most of the money is spent by agencies on *pre-testing* the given advertisement or campaign before launching it into national circulation. Relatively less tends to be spent on *post-testing* the effect of given advertisements and campaigns.'

6.10 Post-testing involves finding out how well people can recall an advertisement and the product it advertises, and whether (on the basis of a sample of respondents) attitudes to the product have changed since the advertising campaign. Post-testing can be conducted over a long period of time, to establish how customer attitudes change over time in response to advertising. This might be particularly relevant in the case of advertising a corporate image: post-testing would help to establish whether an organisation is succeeding in getting the corporate image it is trying to build up in the public mind.

6.11 It would seem sensible too, to try to consider the effectiveness of advertising in terms of cost, sales and profit, but only if the aim of an advertising campaign was directed towards boosting sales. If there is a noticeable increase in sales volume as a result of an advertising campaign, it should be possible to estimate the extent to which advertising might have been responsible for the extra sales and contribution, and the extra net profit per £1 of advertising could be measured.

The effectiveness of sales promotions

6.12   There is often a direct link between below-the-line advertising (sales promotions) and short-term sales volume. For example the consumer sales response to the following is readily measurable.

(a)   Price reductions as sales promotions (for example introductory offers).
(b)   Coupon 'money-off' offers.
(c)   Free sendaway gifts.
(d)   On-pack free gift offers.
(e)   Combination pack offers.

6.13   It might also be possible to measure the link between sales and promotions for industrial goods, for example special discounts, orders taken at trade fairs or exhibitions and the response to trade-in allowances.

6.14   However, there are other promotions where the effect on sales volume is indirect and not readily measurable, for example sponsorship, free samples, catalogues, point-of-sale material and inducements.

6.15   A further problem with measuring the effectiveness of promotions is that they may go hand in hand with a direct advertising campaign, especially in the case of consumer products, and so the effectiveness of the advertising and the sales promotions should then be considered together.

6.16   One problem with sales promotion is its potential expense, if it is not properly controlled. Since many manufacturers have to sell the bulk of their products through supermarket chains or other similar powerful intermediaries, a sales promotion campaign must be planned in consultation with the major intermediaries. Manufacturers will obviously want to restrict their costs, whereas intermediaries might try to persuade the manufacturers to improve their offers (spend more money) in order to make the promotion more attractive to potential consumers.

6.17   There are a number of ways in which a manufacturer can try to control sales promotion costs.

(a)   By setting a time limit to the campaign (for example money off coupons, free gift offers etc must be used before a specified date).

(b)   By restricting the campaign to certain areas or outlets.

(c)   By restricting the campaign to specific goods (for example to only three or four goods in the manufacturer's product range, or only to products which are specially labelled with the offer).

Pricing

6.18   There are several aspects to pricing which should be reviewed. These include discount policy, sales volume, product-market strategy and market positioning.

6.19   *Discount policy* should be directed towards either of the following two aims.

(a)   Encouraging a greater volume of sales.

(b)   Obtaining the financial benefits of earlier payments from customers, which ought to exceed the costs of the discounts allowed.

6.20   Sales prices are set with a view to the total *volume of sales* they should attract.

(a)   New product pricing policy might be to set high 'skimming' prices or low 'penetration' prices. The effectiveness of such pricing policies should be judged in the light of the following.

(i) For skimming prices, whether they have been too high, because the market has grown faster than anticipated, leaving the organisation with a low market share because of its high prices.

(ii) For penetration prices, whether the price level has succeeded in helping the market to grow quickly and the organisation to grab its target share of the market.

(b) Decisions to raise prices or lower prices will be based on assumptions about the elasticity of demand. Did actual increases or decreases in demand exceed or fall short of expectation?

6.21 An aspect of *product-market strategy* is the mixture of product quality and price (both aspects of the marketing mix). An organisation might opt for a *high price and high quality* strategy, or a *low price and average quality* strategy etc. Actual price performance can be judged:

(a) by comparing the organisation's prices with those of competitors, to establish whether prices were comparatively low, average or high, as planned;

(b) by judging whether the mix of product quality and price appears to have been effective.

Channels of distribution

6.22 Some organisations might use channels of distribution for their goods which are unprofitable to use, and which should either be abandoned in favour of more profitable channels, or made profitable by giving some attention to cutting costs or increasing minimum order sizes.

6.23 It might well be the case that an organisation gives close scrutiny to the profitability of its products, and the profitability of its market segments, but does not have a costing system which measures the costs of distributing the products to their markets via different distribution channels.

7   TAKING CONTROL ACTION

Tolerance limits for variances

7.1 No corporate plan has the detail or 'accuracy' that a budget has. Consequently, the tolerance limits giving 'early warning' or deviations from the plan should be wider. For example if tolerance limits in budgetary control are variance ± 5% from standard, then corporate planning tolerance limits might be set at ± 10% or more from targets.

7.2 Whatever the tolerance limits are, the reporting of results which go outside the limits must be prompt. If sales have dropped well below target, the reasons must be established quickly and possible solutions thought about. Tolerance limits should be set on both the favourable and the adverse side of the planning targets. For example if a company's products unexpectedly gain second highest market share, the questions that should be asked are as follows.

(a) How did it happen?

(b) Can profitability targets be maintained or exceeded at the sales volumes supporting that market share?

(c) Can second place be maintained, and if so, what needs to be done to secure the position?

(d) Can the market leader be toppled? (And if so, is this profitable?)

The trade off between the short term and the long term for control action

7.3 We have already introduced the idea of the S/L trade-off in the context of developing marketing objectives. The S/L trade-off is also relevant to control action.

7.4 It is often the case that in order to rectify short-term results, control action will be at the expense of long-term targets. Similarly, controls over longer-term achievements might call for short-term sacrifices. This conflict between controls for achieving short-term and long-term targets, and the need to keep a balance between the short term and long term, is sometimes referred to as the S/L trade-off. (The context will make clear whether S/L trade-off is being discussed in relation to objectives or control; remember that setting objectives is the first stage of the control process, if you find this confusing.)

7.5 Bhattacharya argues that there are times when the long-term targets must be adversely affected by the need for short-term controls, but there should be a control mechanism to ensure that the S/L trade off is properly judged and well balanced.

7.6 He recommends the following.

(a) An organisation should recognise whether or not S/L trade-offs in control action could be a serious problem for it.

(b) Managers should be aware that S/L trade-offs take place.

(c) Controls should exist to prevent or minimise the possibility that short term controls can be taken which damage long term targets, without an appraisal of the situation by senior management.

(d) Senior management must be given adequate control information for long term as well as short term consequences.

(e) The planning and review system should motivate managers to keep long-term goals in view.

(f) Short-term goals should be *realistic*. Very often, the pressure on managers to sacrifice long term interests for short term results is caused by the imposition of stringent and unrealistic short term targets on those managers in the first place.

(g) Performance measures should reflect both long-term and short-term targets. There might be, say, quarterly performance reviews on the achievement of strategic goals.

Revising forecasts

7.7 Real life data can be used to revise forecasts. Managers need information about whether actual results so far show that short term targets have been met. They also need to know whether longer term targets are likely to be met.

7.8 Control at a strategic level calls for the continuous revision of forecasts.

7.9 Control at a strategic level, and the review of strategic plans, should therefore be an iterative process, with revised forecasts for the future serving as an important part of the control information.

Corrective action

7.10 Once it has been decided that control action is going to be taken to reduce a discrepancy between established performance standards and actual performance, two broad options are available.

(a) Marketing managers can take steps to improve actual performance.
(b) Alternatively they can change the performance standard.

7.11 A combination of these two control actions is also possible.

7.12   Improving actual performance can be achieved by a range of methods, depending on the analysis of the reasons for the adverse (negative) variance. The marketing manager might, for example, need to find new ways of motivating marketing personnel or develop better techniques for successful co-ordination of marketing activities.

7.13   Changes to the performance standard are sometimes necessary., The standard might have been unrealistic when it was prepared, or subsequent changes to the marketing environment might have invalidated some of the assumptions made in its preparation so that it has become unrealistic. A major competitor might have left the market leaving an opportunity for the company (and its rivals) to increase market share.

Chapter roundup

- Control is vital if management is to ensure that planning targets are achieved. Control information generated within the organisation is referred to as feedback. The control process involves three underlying components.

    o   Setting standards or targets
    o   Measuring and evaluating actual performance
    o   Taking corrective action.

- Control reports often incorporate selective reporting (exception reporting) in order to minimise volume of information.

- In setting standards, a distinction can be made between controllable and uncontrollable variables.

- Performance should be measured by obtaining data about actual results for a direct comparison with the targets or standards set. In performance evaluation, two terms recur. These are efficiency and effectiveness.

- Monitoring for control purposes should include monitoring of competitor performance, monitoring of customers and monitoring of market performance as a whole.

- Marketing managers should monitor their own progress by evaluating the effectiveness of the marketing mix, in particular personal selling, advertising and sales promotions, pricing and channels of distribution.

- Corrective action should only be taken if variances are outside tolerance levels. It can take two broad forms, involving either steps to improve actual performance or a change to the performance standard.

Test your knowledge

1   What are the four stages in the marketing control process? (see para 1.2)

2   What are the essential characteristics of good communication in control activity? (2.5)

3   What is meant by selective reporting? (2.7)

4   What are the necessary characteristics of performance measures? (4.3)

5   Why are monetary measurements of performance popular? (4.8)

6   What are the three main methods of evaluating marketing activities? (4.10)

7   Distinguish between efficiency and effectiveness. (5.1)

8   What financial information about competitors is publicly available? (5.14)

9   What is post-testing? (6.10)

10   How should managers address the S/L trade off? (7.6)

11   What two options are available for taking corrective action? (7.10, 7.11)

Now try illustrative question 8 at the end of the Study Text

MARKETING OPERATIONS IN ACTION

At the end of each part of this Study Text, we take a look at the subject matter covered in the light of real companies, either to offer more detail or to give an understanding of the wider corporate context.

In this part of the Text we have looked at two main areas: organisation structure and evaluation and control. We have described the characteristics of the marketing oriented organisation and considered some alternative organisation structures. One type of organisation which is demonstrating an increasingly marketing oriented approach is the NHS hospital trust. Many hospitals have now become hospitals trusts with their own boards of directors. According to an article by Clare Crowther in *Marketing Business* (April 1995):

(a)   trusts have to earn a 'return on capital';
(b)   services are charged out to purchasers, although the price at which services are charged must equal the cost of providing them;
(c)   hospitals contract annually with purchasers for health care provision;
(d)   purchasers are either general practitioners or the regional health authorities (who contract for the 'core' items not covered by the general practitioner's needs).

Hospitals are exposed to risk as never before. 'Their income is uncertain because purchasers can place their contracts wherever they can find better quality or a cheaper service. Purchasers may wish to place more weight on primary care, outside of hospitals altogether'. These changes are an opportunity for marketers, who can exercise their skills in a newly-created market. This is because medical consultants have to consider their customers before developing particular interests.

'The cost of increasing speculation means hospitals are having to rethink the range of services they provide. Planning new services and managing alliances with hospitals requires a strategic approach. In particular, while outpatient services are likely to continue in their present location, inpatient services may well be rationalised'.

The author notes that the new hospitals trusts have ten characteristics.

(a)   Hard working employees with little time to analyse the market
(b)   New business and marketing jobs all filled by employees with little experience
(c)   'There is a short term financial perspective'.
(d)   Employees are still on a learning curve.
(e)   'There is reluctance to recognise that those with work experience outside the NHS have transferable skills of value'.
(f)   Costing systems are less than ideal
(g)   Consultants are suspicious of the new system
(h)   Consultants are clinical directors, but with budget responsibilities. They may be unwilling to 'cut'.
(i)   IT has been adapted, rather than designed for the new system
(j)   Internal and external communications are poor

Finally, the environment is highly politicised, as NHS hospitals have a variety of powerful stakeholders.

The authors suggests that to overcome short-termism a marketing perspective is needed. This involves the following.

(a)   Predefining the hospital's catchment area
(b)   Defining who are the customers (general practitioners, regional health authorities, patients) and who are the competition. It is likely that NHS patients are 'consumers' whereas private patients are 'customers'
(c)   'Get closer to customers' (particular GPs)
(d)   Do a risk assessment as some trusts face higher risk from competing hospitals, powerful stakeholders etc than others.
(e)   Marketers should try and generate revenue (eg by helping to win new contracts from GPs) than engaging in 'cosmetic' exercises, such as corporate identity.
(f)   GPs should be treated with more respect than before; as customers they are becoming increasingly powerful.
(g)   Benchmarks of performance should be set, particularly with response to queries from GPs.
(h)   Communications require high priority.

All of this suggests a marketing orientation at corporate level. The author suggests three organisation structures.

(a)   The chief executive champions the marketing orientation, the author's preferred solution.
(b)   A marketing director is appointed
(c)   A clinical director takes over the responsibility of marketing.

Part D
Managing outside resources

Chapter 8

MANAGING OUTSIDE RESOURCES

This chapter covers the following topics.

1 Types of outside resources

2 When to use outside resources

3 Competitive tendering and selection

4 Briefing and working with external suppliers

5 Control and review of external suppliers

Introduction

In this part of the Study Text we are concerned with the management of outside resources. We examine the types of outside resources and when to use them. The purchasing process often starts with some kind of competitive tender; when a supplier or suppliers have been selected, the process continues with the briefing of suppliers and working with them. This involves specifying needs, time spans and budgets. As with any other activity, the process must be subjected to control and review.

---

1 TYPES OF OUTSIDE RESOURCES

1.1 There are almost as many types of outside resources as there are operations' activities. In the modern world, it is possible to outsource everything apart from the broking activity. For example, manufacturing can be sub-contracted, as can distribution and most marketing activities. Recently we have read of an organisation 'exporting' its accounting and financial activities from London to Hong Kong where it can be done more cheaply and efficiently. As the 'information highway' expands internationally, data processing work can be done wherever the computer facilities and expertise exist and the results transferred almost instantaneously to wherever in the world where they are needed.

1.2 In the final analysis, the future of marketing could be said to be in the management of information, ie the bringing together of information on customer needs and wants with information on the best means of supply, in the most efficient and effective way possible, relative to competitors.

1.3 There are so many types of outside resources that it has been thought expedient to list these under the categories of management functions with the major emphasis on marketing within each of the selected areas of operations. Even so this listing can limit itself only to the main types.

Manufacture

1.4 Outside resources can be used in the following areas.

(a) *Manufacturing materials*. These can range from raw materials such as iron ore, to semi-processed materials such as sheet metal, to 'finished' or fully-processed materials such as pressed out car chassis, which may or may not need treating and spraying before/after assembly. There are of course a multitude of suppliers world-wide.

(b) *Assemblies*. Items such as car headlights and car engines can be and often are outsourced.

(c) *Total outside manufacture*. Retailers buy-in their goods fully made, packaged and delivered by the manufacturers, who may well also offer stock control services including auditing and 'Just-in-Time' systems.

(d) *Packaging*. Some manufacturers, eg Boots, will sub-contract out the packaging and/or the filling of containers to local small firms.

(e) *Product design*. In the fashion garments industry it is quite usual for textile manufacturers to use outside designers, some of whom become internationally famous like Christian Dior and Norman Hartnell. Externally sourced design is, however, increasingly used for industrial as well as consumer goods.

Distribution

1.5   Many manufacturers will outsource storage to warehouse space providers and the collection/delivery of their products to transport specialists.

1.6   In international marketing, many exporters will use overseas distributors offering the full range of services from shipping to selling.

Finance

1.7   Most companies, if not all, find it necessary to use outside financial services such as those provided by banks and credit houses.

1.8   In addition, all trading establishments in the UK are required by the Government to provide figures for tax and other reporting purposes, and most use some form of externally sourced auditing and/or accounting services.

Marketing

Consultants

1.9   There are a great many management and marketing consultants in the UK. The CIM, for example, provides a comprehensive service. Some consultants specialise, for example, in design, research or promotion.

Marketing research agencies

1.10   Not many organisations have all the in-house facilities needed to cater for their total information requirements. Nearly all organisations find it necessary from time to time to outsource surveys to specialists.

Promotional agencies

1.11   There are a great variety ranging from advertising agencies to agencies specialising in sales promotion, in PR, in telesales/telemarketing. With sales promotion there is a range of specialists in packaging design, POS display material, exhibition services, mail-order and so on.

Full-service agencies

1.12   These endeavour to supply the full range of marketing services from consultancy to marketing research to promotion.

2   WHEN TO USE OUTSIDE RESOURCES

2.1   A simple rule is to use outside resources whenever:

(a)   external suppliers can provide these better at an equivalent cost; or
(b)   external suppliers can provide these to an equivalent standard at a lower cost.

2.2   The answer is, however, not usually as simple as this. An organisation will be loath to outsource on a long-term basis when it is unsure how long the present circumstances will continue.

2.3   Supposing the organisation was to outsource a substantial telemarketing operation only to find the agency going out of business after a few months. Clearly the degree of risk involved is also an important consideration. Sometimes organisations use outside resources such as design agencies in order to gain new ideas and to avoid over-introspectiveness. When deciding whether to develop and launch a new product, companies find it useful to seek a marketing research agency which will not only be more efficient in conducting surveys but also perhaps more objective. The cost of failure in launching new products is not only the loss of the investment itself but also the risk of loss of goodwill and trust in the market place.

2.4   The case for using advertising agencies is not only to gain their expertise but also the fact that at least some of the cost is defrayed by commission which will only be paid by most of the media to a bona fide agent.

2.5   The use of outside resources can add a great deal of flexibility to an organisation. It reduces the need for investment and offers the possibility of greater profits.

2.6   Outsourcing also reduces the strain on the organisation's limited human resources and frees marketing management to concentrate on the more important strategic rather than the tactical aspects of its marketing plans.

Supplies and suppliers

2.7   Purchasing policy is frequently build around 'what' and 'who' - *what* is to be purchased, and *who* will take the necessary action. 'What' generally refers to the item or service; 'who' means specifically at what level of the company the purchasing action will be taken. Restrictions are often placed on the amount of goods or the value of an order that certain grades within the company can make.

2.8   Although limits must be designated for junior buyers, they must also be in close contact with their superiors so that prompt decisions can be made when substantial economies can be made through a quantity purchase which exceeds the limit within which a junior buyer is confined. For example, when market conditions are favourable to the company - outside suppliers may be offering special prices due to overstocking or competing with each other in a declining market - normal limits may well need to be extended at short notice, and it is important that the company should be flexible. On the other hand, where a company has a limited demand for one or two items, rather than waste buyers' time in negotiating with several suppliers, the company may well prefer to deal with one supplier whom experience tells them can be relied upon to deliver the goods. The 'happy medium' is the general rule, should one be sought. Over-reliance on one supplier can, in the event of a failure, prove utterly disastrous, while a string of orders of small value for the same product from several different sources may increase the administrative costs of purchasing, accounting and payment to levels which are uneconomical.

2.9   Purchasing policy should actively encourage the search for new supplies, and also for new suppliers. Small firms, perhaps lacking the resources to field a large sales team, may nonetheless provide rich resources for a company if they can be located. This type of organisation, often with a minimal amount of capital and overheads, may well undercut larger organisations, particularly where cash-on-delivery terms are on offer. For large companies, complex procedures are often required in order to verify purchases, authorise settlement and actually pay small amounts. This needs adjusting, so that advantage can be taken of purchases for cash.

2.10   Locating the smaller supplier is clearly important. Keeping details of new companies published in the trade press is one useful method. Most will be going concerns, partnerships, sole traders etc, taking on limited liability status.

2.11   The stock levels of the major items that are carried should also be covered by buying policy. Factors such as strikes, weather, seasonal factors, cyclical prices, shipping and handling all require to be taken into account when looking at the stock levels of different items.

2.12   Changes in weather, for instance, are bound to affect the demand for, say, antifreeze or swimming costumes. The purchasing function merits careful consideration when formulating a buying policy. This policy will have a material bearing on the way in which the company is perceived; in terms of relations with outside suppliers, it is best that the company be seen as efficient and friendly. Efficiency serves to deter time wasters and vendors seeking to pass on shoddy goods to the company. If a company is friendly, then a genuine vendor will receive a good hearing and it is more likely that good prices and good quality tenders will be spotted and taken up and that bargains and commercial intelligence are not allowed to escape attention. While, generally, markets for commodities and products tend to favour the buyer, this situation may well change from time to time, and in these circumstances, good relations with suppliers are extremely important.

2.13   For example, an American company operated a harsh and in many circumstances unreasonable purchasing policy, playing off small suppliers against each other. When a world shortage of a specific commodity was exacerbated by a shipping strike, the company's raw material stocks dried up very quickly. Although stocks were available, because of the bad reputation which the company had created, none of the importers were prepared to deal with them. Other companies, who had fostered a reasonable relationship with their suppliers, obtained a continuous supply at only marginally increased prices. A bad purchasing policy cost the company very significant lost custom.

2.14   A good reputation and good relationships with outside suppliers are key elements in the company's purchasing policy. If an outside supplier fails to get an order, but nevertheless feels that he has been fairly treated and given a good hearing, the favourable disposition of that supplier towards the company will bear fruit in the long run. The job of the buyer within the company, particularly in these days of internal markets and 'quality chains', is to act as a representative of the company in just the same way as the salesperson. The buyer is 'selling' his company's ability to trade successfully.

Price

2.15   The right price is a key issue. Nathaniel Rothschild attributed his success to the fact that he never bought shares at the bottom price and never sold at the top. This surely applies to prices in general. At the bottom price, the quality of what we buy is less than perfect, while purchases at the highest price, repeatedly at any rate, may well indicate incompetence or sharp practice.

2.16   Price involves three key areas.

(a)   The purchaser must have a clear idea about the quality, performance and quantity of the product which is being bought. Written specifications or drawings may be required to clarify all these points.

(b)   The purchaser must have a range of target prices that he is prepared to pay relative to the possible alternatives in quality, delivery times, etc.

(c)   The credit terms, quantity bonuses and prompt payment discounts need to be considered so the buyer will be able to select the right price to pay within his range of target prices.

2.17   A perfectly clear idea of what is wanted may not always be communicated to the outside supplier, particularly where non-standard products are concerned. The should not just cover the product, but also refer to its packaging and delivery dates. Standard products and materials are often less costly than speciality items and it is usually worthwhile verifying if special quality products and materials are really required, or whether they are being ordered for some non-practical, historical reason. Guarantees and warranties should also be checked through thoroughly to see how much they are actually contributing to the effective operation of the company.

2.18   With warranty and guarantee terms, what counts as the 'right price' is a matter of the judgement that buyers possess and a good buyer has the ability to make that judgement. If orders are placed at unrealistically low prices for goods which subsequently fail to arrive or come too late with a surcharge to be paid, then this can result in the damaging loss of customer goodwill, and consequently, the loss of sales and profit.

2.19   Price is also a factor in arriving at a correct stock level. What the correct stock level of many products should be in times of inflation, where each new consignment seems to have increased its price, is very difficult to grasp. In the case of a 'rising market' it is necessary for certain kinds of buyers to stockpile raw materials. The cost of carrying stocks should be calculated and make known to buyers. Buying departments need to check at least once every six months in order to clear out redundant stock, which can be sold off. The first loss, hopefully, should be the last too - an exercise like this is a salutary reminder of the waste involved. It is quite apparent too that the costs of this waste are being carried by the other parts of the organisation. Hidden costs that form part of the true price of goods also include, additional to the purchase price, building costs, or the cost of rental or storage space, rates, taxes, insurance and depreciation, together with stockholding charges and administrative expenses.

2.20   In addition to the amount consumed over a given period and price, economic order quantities depend on the costs of acquisition and possession. Skilful buying can afford significant profit making opportunities, and this is well illustrated by the development of 'Just in Time' as a purchasing and stock control system.

Just in Time and the stock control revolution

2.21   Marketing, and the need to be aware of customer needs and respond to them, have now been recognised as a key difference between success and survival on the one hand, and failure on the other, and as a consequence, have been propagated throughout the modern organisation. One of the key areas into which this philosophy has reached is the distribution process. Success nowadays, some commentators have argued, depends on the ability of the company to perform *simultaneously* rather than *sequentially* the processes involved in product development through to product release. Lower investment in goods within this process and faster response to customer needs means reduced costs, better value for customers, and increased benefits for other channel members within the distributive process, enabling everyone within the channel to compete more effectively. Organisational resources, then, form a pool which can be used to counter the challenges of change in competitive markets. Every aspect of the company policy is critical in this effort to maximise competitive capability. At the heart of this is the system by which product and service is made available to the customer.

2.22   Just in Time (JIT) is a system of inventory control invented by the Japanese. The benefit is that it allows 'pull' in the market, in contrast to the traditional system of 'just in case'. JIT is:

'an inventory control system which delivers input to its production or distribution site only at the rate and time it is needed. Thus it reduces inventories whether it is used within the firm or as a mechanism regulating the flow of products between adjacent firms in the distribution system channel. It is a pull system which replaces buffer inventories with channel member co-operation aiming to produce *instantaneously*, with perfect quality and minimum waste'.

2.23   Graham argues that JIT:

'completely tailors a manufacturing strategy to the needs of a market and produces mixes of products in exactly the order required'.

2.24   *Synchronisation* is an essential component of such systems. A successful channel will require precise synchronisation between suppliers, through the production units to retailers and finally suppliers. This depends crucially on *information* freely passed back and forth between channel members. Suppliers need to be informed about raw material deliveries, and also the components delivered to manufacturers. For their part, manufacturers must be confident that their deliveries will arrive on time.

2.25   In the Japanese system, this exchange of information can be supplied throughout the production process by 'Kanban'. This is a very simple 'pull' system which operates at the local level, and is very effective for avoiding stockpiles.

2.26   Information about consumer demand is supplied by retailers, in the form of 'firm' and 'tentative' orders. The effectiveness of this for providing control on distribution costs is demonstrated in the volume car market in Japan. Nearly all cars are made to order and consequently 'lead times' can be as short as ten days!

2.27   If this synchronisation is effectively organised, a JIT system can meet consumer demand while at the same time profits may be maintained or enhanced, because stockpiles and inventory levels - and consequently, the costs of capital tied up unproductively in materials or products which are not being used - are cut dramatically. The supplier/manufacturer interface is, however, crucial to the success of these changes, and a close relationship must be built up. The changes mean that increasing numbers of component parts will be bought from outside the organisation, rather than being manufactured internally.

2.28   When this system is instituted, suppliers become important to the planning process in manufacturing, and may well be brought into production forecasts, schedules and even the design stage. When decisions related to these are being made, the capacities and constraints faced by suppliers is obviously critical. In fact, liaison becomes an important function - their salespersons may well spend less time selling, and become intermediaries conveying information and mediating between buyer, engineering and their own production management. Finding new customers becomes less important than sustaining and improving relations with existing patrons.

2.29   JIT, it can be argued, even improves product quality. If suppliers are being provided with minimum resources, and required to focus on using them to maximum effect, then it becomes even more important to get it 'right first time', since there is very little leeway in the amounts available to do it again. Right first time and Just in Time go together very well indeed.

2.30   However, problems with JIT have been identified, according to some commentators. These include the following.

(a)   *Conflicts over customers.* Suppliers will often, of course, have commitments to other customers, and this may well cause expensive and disruptive delays.

(b)   *Conflicts with the workforce.* Excellent industrial relations are vital to the success of this system, as are flexible, sometimes multi-skilled workforces, with a willingness to accept flexible work routines and hours, so that management can vary manning arrangements. Single union deals, famously, are a *sine qua non* when Japanese companies establish UK operations, and this is a major reason.

(c) *Problems over timescales*. These systems take a very long time to develop. Toyota took 20 years to develop theirs.

2.31 JIT, then, is expanding, as lean production becomes more important. Focusing as it does on customer choice, company profit and strong company-supplier relations, this concept fits comfortably alongside other managerial developments such as TQM and accelerating change in product markets.

3   COMPETITIVE TENDERING AND SELECTION

The tradition of tendering

3.1   Obtaining value for money when work is contracted outside the organisation is of special concern to businessmen everywhere, but particularly guardians of public funds, who are charged with very large numbers of contracts, and very large amounts of money.

3.2   Traditionally, public authorities across the world have attempted to ensure the fairness of this process of obtaining bids for this work by advertising publicly for tenders, and allowing anyone who wishes to do so to submit an offer. For simple supplies of goods, this method is very often employed, even when major constructional works are involved. This practice has been strongly criticised, however, for contracts of any magnitude, or for those in which special technical expertise is involved. Often the low bidder is a firm which has neither the necessary financial backup, nor the technical know-how necessary. The client finds that the firm selected is third-rate, while firms with greater strengths are put off from bidding by the length of the tender list and the fear that their prices would almost certainly be undercut.

Selective tendering

3.3   Under this system, only some firms are invited to bid, while others are not. The difficulty which clients face is the way in which to make that selection in order to obtain a satisfactory completion of the job which is required, while at the same time guaranteeing the fairness and appropriateness of the process of tendering. The aim is to achieve a balance between the price paid and the quality of the job. Two main methods are involved.

(a)   Approved lists
(b)   Pre-qualification

Approved lists and tendering

3.4   There are two ways of operating such a system.

(a)   Public advertising of the particular enquiry, involving a statement that bidding is restricted to those already on the approved list for that category and value of work.

(b)   The firm or authority selects firms from amongst those already on the approved list, seeking to meet criteria of fairness, impartiality etc. This system inevitably causes difficulties and resentments because of the balances which have to be struck between fairness, efficiency and expediency. Only good judgement and fine diplomatic skills on the part of the manager can resolve these problems.

3.5   *EU guidelines* state that in relation to public works contracts, all companies in any one of the EU countries should have the right to participate wherever in the EU these may be located. Evidence suggests that these are largely ineffectual, thanks to the forces which operate to favour local companies and distort the pre-qualification process. However, the legal requirement to advertise such contract is still followed.

3.6   *International lending agencies* such as the World Bank usually underwrite large scale contracts, but the bidder has a contract with the borrower from such agencies, not the agency itself. Preparing a tender, however, involves familiarity with the procurement guidelines which such agencies commonly make available, since they will directly affect the terms under which the borrower operates the contract. These will typically include the following.

(a) Agency objectives (eg due regard for economy and efficiency in the use of their loans).

(b) Length of list. Pre-qualification should be based entirely on the ability of the interested firm to perform the particular work satisfactorily, taking into account:

    (i)   experience and past performance;
    (ii) capabilities with respect to personnel, equipment etc;
    (iii) financial position.

3.7 There should, some guides say, be no limit in theory on the length of the pre-qualification list.

(a) Mandatory associations, between foreign and local firms, are disapproved by some lenders, but not by others.

(b) Turnkey contracts are resisted by many lenders, but large firms who feel that they have the technical and financial ability to take on the responsibility for such contracts often seek to persuade lenders to allow turnkey procurement.

(c) Invitation to bid. All ILA guidelines require that normally, technical analysis and detailed consideration of, for example, the engineering required, should precede invitation to bid. In the exceptional case of turnkey contracts for complex industrial projects, a two step process of first inviting unpriced technical bids, followed by submission of priced proposals is followed.

(d) Comparison of bids should, according to the guidelines, be made on base price, which excludes any consideration of price escalation, and should be expressed in the currency stated in the invitation to tender documents. The strength or weakness of the currency within the bidder's country is obviously, in this case, a highly relevant aspect of the tendering process.

3.8 Since the ILA guidelines require non-price factors such as time of completion, reliability, spares, etc to be taken into account, specified in enquiry documents and expressed in monetary terms, the *lowest evaluated bid* may well not be the lowest price bid.

3.9 Guidelines on *bid price strategy* argue that the opening of bids should be public, and that no bidder shall be allowed to alter his bid after the first bid has been opened. The client may ask any bidder for clarification but should not ask any bidder to change the substance or price of his bid. In many commercial situations, the reverse of these guidelines is followed.

Pre-qualification

3.10 Firms may require potential bidders to fill out a detailed questionnaire in order to be placed on the list of those allowed to tender for certain jobs. This will ask for details of:

(a) previous experience;
(b) organisational structure, showing details of the operation, and its personnel;
(c) lists of facilities;
(d) accounts which illustrate financial health
(e) bankers' letter;
(f) standard documentation in the appropriate language;
(g) names and histories of key personnel;
(h) project control and quality assurance;
(i) sub-contractors pre-qualification criteria.

3.11 These vary widely, and depend on the nature of the contract and the preferences of the client for 'marking schemes'. Bidders would be well advised to find out which criteria are actually applied, and how marking is done.

Evaluation

3.12 Evaluation is normally formal and based on the following sorts of main heading criteria, each of which would be broken down into more detailed sub-criteria and scored on a weighted basis.

- (a) *Reliability:* reputation, performance, finance etc.
- (b) *Technical capacity:* equipment, expertise etc.
- (c) *Managerial capability:* track record, staff qualifications, control mechanisms etc.
- (d) *Project capability:* work schedules, sub-contracts, safety, standards etc.
- (e) *Project experience:* similar projects successfully conducted.

3.13 Evaluation criteria may for example be ranked in the following way.

Evaluation category	Full score
Reliability	
Company profile	1.0
Company staffing	1.0
Construction equipment availability	1.0
Local familiarity	1.0
Line of business	0.5
Performance	0.5
Financial capability	2.0
Insurance	0.5
Interview results	1.0
Reputation	1.5
	10.0
Project attitude	
Workload availability	2.5
Documentation	1.5
Correspondence	1.0
	5.0
Project aptitude	
Capability of settling problems	8.0
Mobilisation capability:	
temporary facility	2.0
construction equipment	2.0
labourer	4.0
Procurement capability	2.0
Contract style	1.0
Business contact	1.0
	20.0
Management capability	
Co-ordination capability	5.0
Schedule control	7.5
Material control	7.5
Cost control	1.25
Manpower control	1.25
Administration	2.5
	25.0

Construction capability	*Full score*
Shift work plan	3.0
Ability of foremen/engineer	6.0
Subcontracting plan	3.0
Construction procedure	3.0
Safety/security	3.0
Transportation	3.0
Quality control	6.0
Field engineering	3.0
	30.0

Project experience	
Last five years experience	3.0
On-going project	3.0
Turn-around/expansion project	4.0
	10.0

4   BRIEFING AND WORKING WITH EXTERNAL SUPPLIERS

4.1   The growth of 'facilities management', the name given to one very important aspect of outsourced externally supplied services since the 1970s has been very rapid - faster, in fact, than any other aspect of middle management. The main reasons for this are as follows.

(a)   There has been a large scale re-sourcing of support services.

(b)   The extension of highly professional standards to the management of the key physical resources upon which the basic performance of company business depends.

(c)   Changing circumstances and the nature of markets has forced change upon those in charge of organisations. Technologies and the very buildings in which business is done are becoming more complex entities, given the way in which they operate and the hardware which is now applied to these tasks, and this has created new needs amongst an increasingly knowledgeable and demanding set of customers.

4.2   Services upon which organisations depend to function properly must be well managed, so that the outside suppliers who are called upon to carry out these tasks are a key aspect of the overall functioning of the organisation. People within organisations interact not only with each other but also with their working environment, and are strongly affected by the services provided by outside suppliers.

Briefing

4.3   The briefing of and working smoothly with outside suppliers are of paramount importance and it could be said that the latter depends upon the former. That is to say that an inadequate brief will lead to misunderstandings between client and supplier to the detriment of the ultimate customer, whose needs both should be working together, in partnership, to fulfil.

4.4   In the event of a dispute, a full brief will leave less room for doubt as to the requirements of the contract agreed to.

4.5   Typical matters to consider in briefing outside suppliers include the following.

(a)   To what extent do we take outside suppliers into our confidence?
(b)   What do they need to know?
(c)   Who will draw up the briefs?
(d)   How often should the brief be reviewed?

Management of externally sourced factors

4.6   Increasingly, companies have begun to 'farm out' their non-essential activities, in order to concentrate on what they see as the core activities of their business. This has been a spur to the growth of 'facilities management', since it has led to the contracting out of key services.

4.7   'Downsizing' has the same consequences. During the shakeouts and privatisations which took place in the UK during the 1980s, many sections or functions within large companies were encouraged to set up as separate external enterprises, providing what were often intermittently needed functions (for example, maintenance of plant, or market research information) on a contract basis. The advantages to the companies concerned were fairly apparent.

4.8   The costs of staffing, training and manning such functions on a long term basis were removed, and the function could be fulfilled on a competitive basis. Other sorts of services, such as cleaning, catering and security began to be fulfilled under the same conditions.

4.9   This practice has been widely extended, and simple sub-contracting has been supplemented by the 'outsourcing' of the management function too. In the UK, a continued commitment to these practices in the 'privatisation' of what were previously public services and utilities sees this development continuing well into the 1990s.

The degree of outsourcing varies from business to business

4.10   Companies vary in what they see as their core business. In smaller companies, many of the functions associated with marketing may actually be sourced from outside the company. Obvious examples would be market research services, advertising, design of packaging, and specialist aspects of product testing (for example, sensory testing of new food products, or safety tests on new electrical goods). Other aspects of organisational function upon which marketing activity depends are also typically subcontracted. For example, when promotional campaigns are being mounted, 'leafleting' is typically the province of small subcontractors. So too would be the teams of promotional staff who dispense free samples during in-store promotional exercises.

Bundling/grouping of outsourced functions

4.11   Often, the functions which have been subcontracted may form natural groups, so that, for example, those working to supply promotional services may also offer market research information, since that kind of information is the lifeblood of such companies. There are obvious attractions, from the point of view of the client, in such arrangements, but it also involves the development of strong ties between large client companies and smaller suppliers of services. It may also create pyramid effects, with suppliers subcontracting and downsizing in order to cut costs and shed risk in a highly competitive market situation. This, of course, can raise great problems in the articulation of the functions which are being served by external suppliers. Subcontractual chains raise severe problems of control and responsiveness to customer needs, so that, typically, new systems are needed to monitor and regulate the way in which client needs are being met. Also, within a service economy, it is increasingly recognised that the perceptions which paying customers have of the company are shaped by the way in which they are treated by personnel identified with the company in question, and there has been a strong movement to regulate and regularise contacts between customers and provider-organisation personnel. As we shall see later, outsourcing creates the need for new systems in order to bring this about, and raises important issues about the internal dynamics of the relationships involved.

Consultants

4.12 The recent move towards privatising public utilities within the UK provides a useful illustration of one of the dangers involved in working with external suppliers. The major managerial problems associated with management of, for example, the National Health Service has led to massive increases in the number of managers employed by the new 'Hospital Trusts', coupled with a reclassification and redeployment of health services. Yet, as a recent report revealed, there was also huge expenditure on the employment of management consultants in order to make recommendations concerning the most efficient deployment of the new management within the organisation.

4.13 Given the large scale of outsourcing, the newly developed structures, and a remit to develop efficient and competitive units based on competition within internal markets, this might seem like a logical move.

4.14 However, a report suggested that there were a number of mistakes involved.

(a) Consultants were given inadequate briefs. Reports showed that too often, consultants would be called into 'fix' an organisation without real guidance as to the areas which needed to be addressed, and without any limits on the scope of the problem with which they were involved. As a consequence, the reports they produced were often inappropriate, unrealistic or ineffective. Often, recommendations were too broad to be implemented, and were used as ammunition when particular interests were being aggressively pursued within the organisation.

(b) Consultants were given too much power. Managers employing consultants in these circumstances were inclined to delegate too wide a range of decisions to them.

(c) Public perceptions were not considered sufficiently.

Total outsourcing

4.15 In the case of facilities management, the general change within the 'enterprise culture' has generated a movement towards downsizing and risk shedding in which what were previously functions within the ambit of large organisations have now been shed or hived off and given over to the control of independent managers. For companies involved in 'core' activities, this means that they can subcontract virtually every other function which they need in order to operate, from cleaning and building security to the plant and fittings which they use from day to day - all will be maintained in the most appropriate and cost effective way by subjection to 'market discipline'.

4.16 The theory underlying this viewpoint is too well known to need restatement, nor is this the place to debate the undoubted successes and failures which have resulted from its widespread implementation. It is worth saying, however, that this notion of autonomous decision making within a downsized free market does actually conflict, in some ways, with another major theme within managerial thinking which emerged during the same period, or rather, reveals an inherent contradiction in the idea that responsiveness to customer needs necessarily produces a more flexible and varied process of service provision.

Exercise 1

What are the main advantages of outsourcing?

Solution

The main advantages are as follows.

(a) Cost savings.

(b) Specialism of the company.

(c) Accountability is tied to specific performance.

(d)   Introduction of desirable outside qualities (such as imagination, fresh ideas etc) into particular sorts of activities.

(e)   Risk shedding.

5   CONTROL AND REVIEW OF EXTERNAL SUPPLIERS

5.1   One of the main potential problems is lack of control, or lack of response to client input. There are some mechanisms, such as staged payments and incentive structure, which attempt to address this issue by making the outsourced function responsible for meeting particular targets, and holding back payment. There is a tendency for this to be seen as somewhat excessive attention in smaller contracts, and there is a feeling that this is a somewhat draconian response if applied too insensitively.

5.2   Control rests, ultimately, upon the market power of the client, and on the quality of the management control system which is being operated within the client organisation.

The control process

5.3   A decision has to be made whether to apply controls selectively. That is to say whether a supplier with which the organisation have a small or spasmodic spend should be subjected to the same degree of control as a supplier with which there is a significant spend.

5.4   However, the answer cannot depend on spend alone. The organisation could, for example, be making a relatively small spend with an agency on concept testing for a proposed new product. However, this proposed new product could be vital to the organisation's future and therefore the agency could require stricter control than say a supplier of raw materials on which there is a large spend but which has proved to be highly dependable for a number of years.

5.5   Then again the nature of the control should perhaps be different according to the nature of the product/service being bought. For raw materials suppliers an organisation might, for example, have scientific tests on quality and maintain records of deliveries late/on time/before time. However, for an advertising agency, control might be more informal and based on frequent personal meetings.

5.6   Bearing in mind the above difficulties in setting standards and the rating of performance, the following might be useful as a typical framework for controls. A fuller list is given later on.

(a)   Supplier's name

(b)   Type of goods/services supplied

(c)   Estimated annual spend

(d)   Record of complaints made by us

(e)   Record of actions taken by supplier

(f)   *Performance standard*   *Rating (scale 0 to 10)*   *Notes*

    (i)   Quality of product/service
    (ii)   Reliability
    (iii)   Prices relative to competitors
    (iv)   Working relationships
    (v)   Overall

(g)   Special terms and conditions relative to this supplier

(h)   Recommended special controls, if any

(i)   Recommended frequency of review

(j)   Person responsible for review, position/department

5.7   There should, following the initial review, be a rolling system of reviewing outside suppliers on the recommended frequencies and against the agreed standards. Formal ratings are preferred to informal measures.

5.8   The frequency of the reviews and the nature of the standards set should be changed in accordance with circumstances.

5.9   In conclusion, a framework for review might look at the following matters.

(a)   Supplier's name, address, telephone number
(b)   Names and positions of contacts
(c)   Description of types of goods and services supplied
(d)   Total annual spend for last three years
(e)   Splits of annual spends by types of product/service where relevant
(f)   Number of years we have been trading with this supplier
(g)   Perceived strengths and weaknesses of supplier
(h)   Record of improvements made by supplier during trading period
(i)   Record of growth of supplier: turnover, staff, number of branches
(j)   List of alternative suppliers
(k)   Perceived strengths and weaknesses of top three alternative suppliers
(l)   Date of last review of this supplier
(m)   Name/position of person conducting this last review
(n)   Recommended date of next review

Quality chains and external suppliers

5.10   The quality movement has recently produced a framework which purports to guide the way in which managers deal with outside suppliers, with customers and with each other.

5.11   This approach argues that the answer is to treat everyone with whom we deal as either a customer for the services or functions we provide for them, or else suppliers of services or functions to us. The whole process then becomes a 'quality chain', with the guidelines for the provision of customer service being applied internally as well as externally and, by implication, extended to the way in which managers relate to the suppliers of external services. The quality chain then extends out into 'satellite companies', and it is suggested that the award of contracts to external suppliers should be dependent on commitments to these standards of service and responsiveness to customer needs. In some cases this might also involve monitoring and verification procedures.

5.12   It has been argued that this represents a kind of *de facto* expansion, with market power being used to suborn the authority and autonomy of managers in (smaller) external companies There is strong support for this approach, however.

A Quality Chain

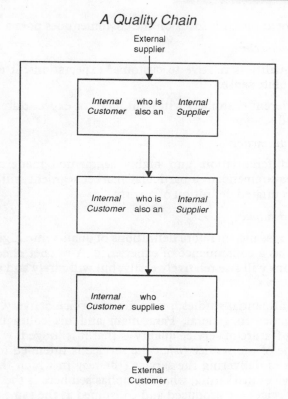

5.13 John Oakland (1989) argues that, when meeting customer requirements, the main focus tends to be in a search for quality, while these requirements would typically include aspects such as availability, delivery, reliability, maintainability and cost effectiveness. In the fact the first priority is to establish what customer requirements actually are. If the customer is outside the organisation, then the supplier must seek to set up a marketing activity to gather this information, and to relate the output of their organisation to the needs of the customer.

5.14 Internal customers for services are equally important, but seldom are their requirements investigated. The quality implementation process requires that all the supplier/customer relationships within the 'quality chain' should be treated as marketing exercises, and that each customer should be carefully consulted as to their precise requirements from the product or service with which they are to be provided. Each link in the chain should prompt the following questions, according to Oakland.

(a) *Of customers*

   (i)   Who are my immediate customers?

   (ii)   What are their true requirements?

   (iii)   How do or can I find out what the requirements are?

   (iv)   Do I have the necessary capability to meet the requirements? (If not, then what must change to improve the capability?)

   (v)   Do I continually meet the requirements? (If not, then what prevents this from happening, when the capability exists?)

   (vi)   How do I monitor changes in the requirements?

(b) *Of suppliers*

   (i)   Who are my immediate suppliers?
   (ii)   What are my true requirements?
   (iii)   How do I communicate my requirements?
   (iv)   Do my suppliers have the capability to measure and meet the requirements?
   (v)   How do I inform them of changes in the requirements?

(from Oakland, 1989)

5.15   It should be noted that this focus on the customer does pose a number of problems.

(a)   *Quality is subjective*

(i)   If quality is relative to customer expectations, it cannot be measured in an absolute sense.

(ii)   Different customers will want, need or expect different things from the same product-type.

(b)   *Quality is distinctive*

Product differentiation, and highly segmented modern markets mean that the precise requirements of a particular market segment will impart an equally precise and differentiated definition of quality.

(c)   *Quality is dynamic*

Expectations, and therefore definitions of quality, are highly dynamic - they change over time as a consequence of experience. A ratchet effect is highly likely, so that expectations will rise relatively easily, but will rarely and very reluctantly fall.

5.16   In a series of influential studies, primarily of service delivery, but with implications for marketing practice in general, Parasunam and his colleagues concluded that a key differentiating feature of service quality is that it is judged by the consumer, not simply on the outcome of the service (*what* the service is intended to deliver) but in addition, on the process of delivering the service (the *way* in which the service is delivered). In relation to services marketing, what is emphasised here is the inseparability of services - the fact that services are produced and consumed at the same time. This applies equally to the provision of services internally - this is a key factor in the promotion of a culture of quality, and the proponents of this view do not make a strong distinction between the way in which this affects members of organisations involved in the delivery of a service or product, and the customers who buy and use it.

Quality gaps

5.17   Gap analysis proposes that customer perceptions of the quality of a product or service are determined by the degree to which they believe it meets their expectations. These expectations are created from a variety of inputs. These would include physical aspects service elements and other cues available.

Exercise 2

Gap analysis was introduced in Chapter 4. Explain how it can be used to measure customer satisfaction.

Solution

Gap analysis sets out to measure levels of satisfaction, or dissatisfaction, to identify the source of dissatisfaction when it occurs and to eliminate it. Customer expectations, of course, refer to what *should* be delivered, rather than what they may believe will be delivered. The central issue is how customer expectations develop - what are the sources of unrealistic or inappropriate requirements? Within delivery organisations, this may often involve a careful analysis of the ways in which policies on these issues are implemented, and the communication processes which exist to disseminate official thinking on what the company personnel should be doing about these matters.

5.18   Clearly, what expectations are raised depends on the way in which the supplier treats the deliverer within the chain. A company which is product-oriented starts with its own beliefs about what the customer expects, creates a specification to guide the production or creation process. The product or service which is delivered, then, reflects the perspective of the producer/deliverer rather than any real contact with the needs of the customer for the product or service.

5.19   The major factors which determine customer expectations and perceptions with regard to service quality are:

    (a)   word of mouth communications;
    (b)   personal needs; and
    (c)   past experience.

5.20   The 'gaps' which can cause dissatisfaction are between:

    (a)   customer expectations and marketers' perceptions;
    (b)   management perceptions and service quality specifications;
    (c)   service quality specifications and service delivery;
    (d)   service delivery and external communications;
    (e)   perceived service and expected service.

5.21   This approach argues that external suppliers, standing alongside every other person within the 'quality chain', must be responsive to the standards which are indicated by this analysis. It must be said that, in the future, firms which try to resist the infringements on their autonomy which this will inevitably produce will find it difficult to secure contracts. Decisions made by central policymakers in large companies or institutions such as public utilities who are able to exert this kind of power will certainly do so.

Chapter roundup

- There is a wide range of outside resources. Almost any activity can be outsourced. Typical areas for outsourcing activities are manufacture, distribution, finance and marketing. Marketing activities which can be outsourced include consultancy, marketing research, promotion and 'full service'.

- As a general rule, the use of outside resources can be considered whenever external suppliers can provide better services at the same cost or equivalent services at a lower cost.

- Skilful buying is essential to the profitable operation of any business. Purchasing requires the co-ordination of internal and external factors, including the internal decision to purchase and the external placing of the order. Organisations should develop a formal purchasing policy.

- Just in Time, an inventory control system developed in Japan, is widely used (to varying degrees) in many UK businesses. It significantly affects the operation of the purchasing function.

- Many contracts involve a process of tendering. This is particularly common where contracts are awarded by public/state authorities, but is also of value in the private sector. Sometimes there is a prequalification stage.

- Briefing and working with external suppliers is very important. Good briefing provides a solid foundation for a successful working relationship.

- An organisation using outside resources must ensure that it puts mechanisms for control and review of external suppliers in place.

Test your knowledge

1   Give four examples of outside resources which could be used in manufacturing (see para 1.4)

2   List five types of promotional agency (1.11)

3   What is a 'full-service' agency? (1.12)

4   What are the three key areas involved in agreeing a purchasing price? (2.16)

5   What is Just in Time? (2.22)

6   What criticisms of JIT have been raised? (2.30)

7   What are the EU guidelines on public works contracts? (3.5)

8   Explain the criteria by which pre-qualification bidders might be evaluated. (3.12, 3.13)

9   What problems have been encountered in the use of consultants in the UK health service? (4.14)

10   What factors might a framework for review of outside suppliers take into consideration? (5.9)

11   Summarise Oakland's view of the quality chain. (5.13, 5.14)

Now try illustrative question 9 at the end of the Study Text

MARKETING OPERATIONS IN ACTION

At the end of each part of this Study Text, we take a look at the subject matter covered in the light of real companies, either to offer more detail, or to give an understanding of the wider corporate context.

In this part of the Text we have seen how the organisation can manage outside resources, We looked at the practice of competitive tendering, which is often a feature of the purchasing process. In local government, the focus is not just on competitive tendering, but on compulsory competitive tendering. The example which follows shows an organisation involved in CCT and using a firm of consultants.

Selby District Council, in North Yorkshire, has developed three purpose built leisure centres in recent years, the latest of which cost £4 million. The council had to tender for the contract to provide leisure services before this centre was completed and therefore had to base its tender on estimates. The council won the contract, but the estimates turned out to be over-optimistic.

It became clear that Selby District Council would need to improve its marketing operations. It approached the CIM's Consultancy Services, who recommended a firm of consultants with public-sector experience, Collinson Grant Consultants.

Collinson Grant did the following

(a)   Carry out a marketing audit, focusing on capacity, management systems and competition.

(b)   Carry out research into users in order to help produce a marketing strategy

(c)   Review the results of the marketing audit, which showed amongst other things that potential markets had not been accurately defined and therefore could not be targeted and that there was insufficient knowledge of the competition and of demographic factors.

(d)   Recommend a revision of the figures in the tender (for internal use) and the production of a professional marketing plan.

(e)   Make 44 recommendations, including:

    (i)   writing annual operational plans with quantifiable objectives;
    (ii)   preparing cashflow forecasts;
    (iii)   preparing budget allocations;
    (iv)   setting usage and income targets;
    (v)   introducing a QA programme;
    (vi)   giving centre managers more flexibility;
    (vii)   realigning promotional material with the centre's marketing plan;
    (viii) appointing a sports development officer;
    (ix)   appointing a marketing manager.

Part E
Selected marketing applications

Chapter 9

BUSINESS-TO-BUSINESS, SERVICES AND CHARITY MARKETING

This chapter covers the following topics.

1   Business-to-business marketing

2   Target marketing in industrial markets

3   Marketing mix differences in industrial marketing

4   Services marketing

5   The extended marketing mix for services marketing

6   Charity and not-for-profit marketing

Introduction

This part of the Study Text is concerned with selected marketing applications and covers an area of the syllabus which has a 25% study weighting. A typical exam paper will probably include a question on at least one of the topics covered in this chapter. International applications are covered in Chapter 10, but in this chapter we are interested in three particular areas.

In industrial, or business-to-business marketing, target marketing is easier than in marketing direct to consumers. There are differences in the marketing mix and the creation of competitive edge is increasingly important.

The service sector has grown rapidly in recent years in the UK, both as an employer and in terms of its contribution to GNP. There are certain basic characteristics of service industries which differentiate them from other business operations. The 'people' factor is of great importance.

The objectives of charities and not-for-profit organisations are different from those of most other commercial organisations, and this is reflected in their marketing activities too.

1   BUSINESS-TO-BUSINESS MARKETING

Definition

1.1   Although many of the products involved in industrial markets are the same as those bought within the ordinary consumer markets (for example furniture, motor vehicles, food etc) the reasons why they are being bought will be quite different. Buying motivations, the criteria which consumers apply, and the nature of the buying process itself will be quite different.

1.2   Organisational buyers are buying for their organisations, and what they buy is part and parcel of the business activity of the organisation involved - it is part of the process of earning a profit.

1.3   Where this takes place varies from private sector industry to the public sector, which provides significant markets for goods of all kinds, including government departments, local authorities, boards, quangos, and many operations within the UK which may be partly in both sectors (for instance, health industry organisations). These need supplies, and industrial marketing is about the way in which the goods involved reach their market.

1.4 The professions, banking, the law, financial institutions, architecture etc, also offer marketing opportunities for similar reasons. In addition to these are the growing numbers of not-for-profit organisations which are growing up. All have needs to be met, operating equipment and materials which they need to buy. Industrial marketing, under this view, covers a very wide-ranging sphere of operation. It can be seen that this involves widely varying products and services, so that we cannot simply regard industrial marketing, as in the past, as being about raw materials, or about the selling of specialised, heavy duty machinery or equipment.

1.5 The importance of marketing within the industrial sector is being increasingly recognised. In the past, there has been a reluctance on the part of management to accept this, and it has tended to be regarded as a distinct, separate and actually rather limited function. This attitude is gradually becoming a thing of the past as more and more organisations recognise the importance of placing marketing at the heart of their strategies.

1.6 A good example of an industrial product would be a canning machine. This would be marketed by an industrial machines manufacturer to companies like Heinz for the purpose of producing canned foods and drinks, ie consumer goods. A related industrial service could be the installation of the canning machine and/or a maintenance/repair service.

Products

1.7 Industrial goods and services, then, are bought by manufacturers, distributors and various other private and publicly owned institutions (for example, schools, agricultural organisations, hospitals etc) to be used as part of their own activities, rather than for resale.

1.8 The categories of industrial markets are as follows.

(a) *Capital goods* include such items as buildings, machinery, office furniture and equipment, and materials handling, and record keeping systems. These are treated as 'capital assets' of a business, in terms of accounting procedures. This generally involves recognition of a depreciation in their value, over a period of time.

(b) *Components and materials* include basic raw or partly or wholly processed materials or goods which are used as part of the products which are eventually sold by the company.

(c) *Supplies* are goods which assist production and distribution, although they are not part of the final product or service which is provided. They are not regarded as a capital investment, however; this would include small but important items such as machine oil, computer disks and stationery, mops for the cleaners etc.

(d) *Business services* involve a wide range of intangible elements which could be called upon by the company, from the services of a technical consultant, a market research agency, an office cleaning service or product advertising on television.

1.9 Industrial products are distinctive in several ways.

(a) *Legal conformity*. Industrial products are often bound by legal standards, and as a consequence, products within a particular group are often similar. Differentiation, which is such a key dimension of *consumer* goods, is more difficult here. At the same time, buyers lay down their own specifications to which manufacturers must adhere.

(b) *Technical sophistication*. Many products in this area require levels of complexity and sophistication which are unheard of in consumer products. Often, of course, the industry standard gradually influences the type of features found in the consumer equivalent, for instance, in the case of power tools in the DIY market, or consumer electronics and 'home' computers. Many of these have far outstripped the capabilities of what were the most advanced industrial standards only a few years ago. This complexity entails a high level of R & D, and a very great deal of technical support for the products and services which are being offered to customers. After-sales and maintenance contracts have become a *sine qua non* in certain areas.

(c) *High unit values*. As a consequence of (a) and (b) above, many industrial goods, particularly capital equipment, are very often extremely costly items. Even in the case of supplies, although the unit value of components and materials may be comparatively low, the quantity required frequently means that individual orders and total sales to individual customers usually have a very high value.

(d) *Irregularity of purchase*. Clearly, the machinery which is used in the production of consumer goods is not bought regularly. Materials used to produce the goods certainly are, but components and materials are often bought on a contract basis, so that the opportunity to get new business may not arise very often.

Characteristics of industrial markets

1.10 Three kinds of economic activities have been defined.

(a) *Primary or extractive industries* cover activities like agriculture, fishing, mining and forestry.

(b) *Secondary or manufacturing industries* include manufacturing and construction.

(c) The *tertiary sector* includes the service industries - providing intangible benefits rather than producing and selling 'things'. As we shall see in the next section, services are becoming extremely important within our modern economy and services marketing is exerting a big influence on the way in which marketing is developing. It is becoming more and more difficult to draw a hard line between products and services, and also to distinguish the methods involved in their marketing.

The importance of marketing for the industrial sector

1.11 Attitudes as well as activities are important in the development of effective organisations, and the permeation of a marketing ethic throughout the organisation is important for the achievement of this. Marketing should be something which describes the collective attitudes of management to markets as well as the activity itself. Customer orientation is vital for everyone in the organisation.

Marketing within the organisation

1.12 Customers seek answers to their problems, rather than simply buying products. To sell industrial products, they must be full of 'customer benefits' - providing answers to customers' problems rather than simply producing 'good products'.

The manager within the organisation

1.13 This implies the need for well co-ordinated and focused activity, with organisations working around a common, market-oriented, mission. Managers within these organisations need to accept responsibility for the creation of strong, well resourced marketing management, working together towards common goals. They can:

(a) act as catalysts within the firm
(b) inform technical management about market trends
(c) monitor competitive activity
(d) inform corporate planning decisions
(e) direct R & D

They are not simply concerned with customers, but in linking and co-ordinating various activities within the firm.

Implementation of marketing plans

1.14 'Marketing is not just a business function. It is a consolidating view of the entire business process' (Theodore Levitt). Since many different areas of business activity make an input into corporate performance, these must be integrated in order for the organisation to function effectively and this integration must take place within the marketing plan for the organisation.

1.15 In spite of the increasing complexity of organisations, it is important to retain the focus on the decision-making functions, and to avoid the artificial behaviour which can be produced by people working within 'systems' structured by rules of behaviour.

Special practices

1.16 *Reciprocal trading* is evident in some markets where buying and selling firms engage in reciprocal trading agreements, involving mutual trading in certain products. This closes markets off for newcomers and restricts trading.

1.17 *Joint ventures* often involve large industrial and commercial organisations which pool their resources in order to accomplish particular contracts. This may be necessary because of the scale of the project, or because of cultural, legal or technical advantages which the co-operation confers on both parties.

1.18 *Consortiums* are voluntary industrial associations found typically in the construction industry. Again, they are a useful approach to the management of large projects.

1.19 *Project management*, sometimes also referred to as 'turnkey operations', are large capital investment projects, often overseas which involve the exercise of specialised skills and typically take several years to come to fruition. To finish on time, co-ordination is vital and a turnkey contractor may be appointed to take responsibility for design and construction. Long term planning skills are the vital prerequisite.

1.20 More and more machinery is being *leased* rather than bought to avoid capital expenditure on a large scale. In the construction industry, leasing deals also involve lessors tying the machinery to exclusive purchasing of other items such as raw materials.

1.21 *Licensing* enables new products to be introduced to customers without the great risks and high costs associated with ordinary development and launching of a new product. Since lead time is critical in innovation, licensing can be very enticing, and is being used by more and more companies.

1.22 Industrial marketing has an important role to play in the development of these markets. More and more, it is being realised that in order to be successful, industrial marketing needs to take account of the special features of the industry within which it operates, and of the special characteristics of the environment.

2   TARGET MARKETING IN INDUSTRIAL MARKETS

2.1 Business to business target markets tend to be easier to identify than consumer market segments, mainly because more data is readily available on businesses than on groups of people within the general public. It is very important for marketers of industrial goods to establish a differential competitive advantage. This is more difficult for industrial services owning to their intangibility.

2.2 Quite a lot of information about industrial markets is published in government statistics although these do tend to be in retrospect.

2.3   The production monitors are available monthly and quarterly and give statistics for manufacturing companies broken down into ten major groups known as SICs or the Standard Industrial Classifications, eg 3 represents metal goods, engineering and textiles. These ten major headings are then broken down into smaller groups such as vehicles and further still into types of vehicles, eg lorries, cars, buses. Under each heading is given such detail as number of employees, number of establishments, value of shipments, exports and imports, annual growth rates. All this makes valuable information for segmentation analysis and selection of target markets.

2.4   Then there are the distribution monitors which give statistics on the huge world of retail outlets by type: multiples, independents etc, plus turnover, number of establishments etc.

2.5   Added to the above are all the available business registers and a rapidly increasing databank on EU countries' industrial markets.

2.6   One of the most useful ways of classifying available statistics is as government or private.

Government statistics

2.7   The government is a major source of economic information and information about industry and population trends. Examples of government publications are as follows.

(a)   The *Annual Abstract of Statistics* and its monthly equivalent, the *Monthly Digest of Statistics*. These contain data about manufacturing output, housing, population etc.

(b)   The *Digest of UK Energy Statistics* (published annually).

(c)   *Housing and Construction Statistics* (published quarterly).

(d)   *Financial Statistics* (monthly).

(e)   *Economic Trends* (monthly).

(f)   *Census of Population*. The Office of Population Censuses and Surveys publish continuous datasets including the *National Food Survey*, the *Household Survey* and the *Family Expenditure Survey*.

(g)   *Census of Production* (annual). This has been described as 'one of the most important sources of desk research for industrial marketers'. It provides data about production by firms in each industry in the UK.

(h)   *Department of Employment Gazette* (monthly) giving details of employment in the UK.

(i)   *British Business*, published weekly by the Department of Trade and Industry, giving data on industrial and commercial trends at home and overseas.

(j)   *Business Monitor* (published by the Business Statistics Office), giving detailed information about various industries.

(k)   *Social Trends* (annually).

2.8   Official statistics are also published by other government bodies such as the European Union, the United Nations and local authorities.

Privately published statistics

2.9   Non-government sources of information include the following.

(a)   Companies and other organisations specialising in the provision of economic and financial data (eg the *Financial Times* Business Information Service, the Data Research Institute, Reuters and the Extel Group).

(b)   Directories and yearbooks, such as Kompass or Kelly's Directory.

(c)   Professional institutions (eg Chartered Institute of Marketing, Industrial Marketing Research Association, British Institute of Management, Institute of Practitioners in Advertising).

(d)   Specialist libraries, such as the City Business Library in London, collect published information from a wide variety of sources.

(e)   Trade associations, trade unions and Chambers of Commerce.

(f)   Commercial organisations such as banks and TV networks.

(g)   Market research agencies.

Buying in data

2.10   The sources of secondary data identified above are generally free because they are in the public domain. Inexpensiveness is an advantage which can be offset by the fact that the information is unspecific and needs considerable analysis before being useable.

2.11   A middle step between adapting secondary data and commissioning primary research is the purchase of data collected by market research companies or business publishing houses. The data tend to be expensive but less costly than primary research.

2.12   There are a great many commercial sources of secondary data, and a number of guides to these sources are available:

(a)   *The Source Book*, Key Note Publications;
(b)   *Guide to Official Statistics*, HMSO;
(c)   *Published Data of European Markets*, Industrial Aids Ltd;
(d)   *Compendium of Marketing Information Sources*, Euromonitor; and
(e)   *Market-Search*, British Overseas Trade Board.

2.13   Commonly used sources of data on particular industries and markets are:

(a)   Key Note Publications;
(b)   *Retail Business*, Economist Intelligence Unit;
(c)   Mintel publications;
(d)   *Market Research GB*, Euromonitor.

3   MARKETING MIX DIFFERENCES IN INDUSTRIAL MARKETING

3.1   The industrial marketing mix differs in its detail from the marketing mix characteristically adopted for consumer products. On a broad basis industrial products are not packaged for resale, prices tend to be negotiated with the buyer and distribution tends to be more direct from one business to another. The promotional mix is also generally different in that consumer goods are often advertised heavily on TV and in mass media whereas industrial marketing companies tend to restrict advertising to trade magazines.

3.2   Much more dependency is given to personal selling. Rarely will an industrial buyer purchase off the page, especially where capital goods are concerned. Whereas most FMCG are purchased on a self-service basis, industrial goods involve a great deal more personal contact. After all, the industrial buyer is responsible to his/her company for spending money wisely whereas the average consumer is a free agent to a much greater extent. Industrial marketers also use exhibitions and demonstrations to quite a high degree when promoting their products.

Product

3.3   Most business to business marketing mixes will include elements of service as well as product. Pre-sales services will involve the giving of technical advice, quotations, opportunities to see products in action, free trials etc. After-sales service will include just-in-time delivery, service and maintenance and guarantees. Products will also be custom-built to a much greater degree than for consumer marketing mixes. Special finishes may be requested by industrial customers.

3.4   Frequently, products will have to conform to British Standards specifications and be tested to laid down conditions.

3.5   Packing for protection rather than packaging for self-service is another characteristic of the business to business product-service mix. Some of these elements can comprise a powerful differential competitive advantage. For example ICI offers laboratory testing of various metals so that industrial customers can be assured of the one most suitable for given corrosive conditions.

3.6   When buying machine tools, efficiency features can be the most powerful buying motive. For example, a twin-feed unit offering almost twice the output per hour of a single feed unit will be assured of a good sale. Other product-unique features may be the ease of or safety of operation. If an operator can manage two machines rather than one, his potential output is doubled. Training of operators is another service often provided by manufacturers of industrial equipment.

Price

3.7   Price is not normally fixed to the same degree as in consumer markets. Particularly where products/services are customised, price is a function of buyer specification. Price is negotiable to a much greater extent depending upon the quantity, add-on services/features and sometimes the total business placed per year. Retrospective annual discounts act as loyalty incentives. Mark downs and special offers as used in consumer markets are not normal features of industrial market pricing.

3.8   Trade discounts can apply in those cases where industrial/commercial goods are marketed through middlemen (see below on distribution). In some industrial markets, suppliers bid prices under a tendering system as for example for building a power station or supplying its generators.

Promotion

3.9   Within the promotional mix, personal selling is far more important in business to business marketing. Some industrial products are quite complex and need explaining in a flexible way to non-technical people involved in the buying process.

3.10   More often than not, buying in business to business marketing is a group activity and equally selling can be a team effort. Salespeople are expected to engage in follow-up activities to ensure that the products are working properly and that the business buyer is perfectly satisfied. In this way personal contact is maintained and the salesman has a greater chance of repeat orders. Where an industrial equipment manufacturer markets through an industrial dealer, the manufacturer's salesforce may be required to train the dealer salesforce in product knowledge.

3.11   The partnership approach is present to a much greater degree in industrial selling, where the buyer needs information and services and the seller is seeking repeat business in the long term.

3.12   With regard to advertising and sales promotion, the types of media emphasised differ greatly from those in consumer markets. Mass media such as TV, radio, national newspapers are rarely used. Advertising is usually confined to trade magazines, which reach more precise targets. Direct mail is, however, used to supplement personal selling.

3.13   Industrial exhibitions are also popular as a means of personal contact with particular target markets, and factory visits are used as a means of engendering confidence in the manufacturer's abilities and standards. More industrial marketers are using PR, through agencies, as a means of gaining favourable publicity in the trade media and to build up their corporate images.

Distribution

3.14 Compared to consumer markets industrial marketers tend to deliver direct, ie over half of industrial products are delivered direct from manufacturer to business buyers. Even where agents are used, as in international markets, UK manufacturers will usually deliver direct to overseas business clients.

3.15 Sometimes, however, business to business distributors are employed, particularly for consumable and lower-value goods. Business to business channels are therefore:

(a) Manufacturer → Business buyer

(b) Manufacturer → Agents → Business buyer

(c) Manufacturer → Business distributor → Business buyer

(d) Manufacturer → Agents → Business distributor → Business buyer

3.16 On-time delivery can be an extremely important requirement in industrial markets, especially where valuable contracts can be expensively help up for want of a relatively small piece of equipment. In such circumstances the premium on delivery is so great that penalty clauses for lateness are invoked.

Buyers

3.17 *Organisational buying* is a transaction between a number of individuals rather than an action by one person. Various people within the organisation will be involved in the buying process and those people formally designated as buyers may only be responsible for a small part of the overall process. As with consumer behaviour the study of organisational buying centres around the decision process and the factors that affect this process.

3.18 Differences between consumer behaviour and organisational buying can be summarised as follows from the viewpoint of the *buying centre*.

(a) At an organisational level, the decision process is a *group* buying process, in which the people involved make up the decision-making unit or buying centre.

(b) The complexity of the products is usually greater.

(c) The needs of users are more varied and difficult to satisfy.

(d) The impact of an unsuccessful purchase decision poses much greater personal and organisational risks than the average consumer decision process, for both groups and individuals involved in the purchase.

(e) There is more interdependence between buyer and vendor in industrial markets because there are smaller numbers of goods and customers. Therefore not only are sellers dependent on buyers for an assured outlet for their goods, but also buyers are dependent on sellers for the continued source of inputs for their processes.

(f) Post-purchase processes are much more important.

3.19 There are a number of factors that influence organisational buying behaviour. These include the following.

(a) *Economic*. Interest rates, level of unemployment, consumer and wholesale price index, and growth in GNP. Changes in different economic conditions will impact different sections of the market in differing degrees.

(b) *Political/legal*. Government attitude toward business, international tariffs, and trade agreements and government assistance to selected industries: legal and regulatory forces at the local and national levels which affect the industrial decision-making process.

(c) *Culture*. The means and methods of coping with the environment that are passed from one generation to the next - values, habits, customs and tradition. Corporate *subculture* influences executive behaviour.

(d) *Physical influences*. Climate, geography, locations, labour supply, choice of raw materials.

(e) *Technological influences*. Dynamic nature of modern technological advances influences the way both organisation buying and selling are carried out.

3.20 There are also, of course, organisational forces affecting buying.

(a) *Centralisation*. The physical and managerial location of the locus of influence and decision-making authority.

(b) *Formalisation*. The degree to which certain rules and procedures are stated and adhered to by the employees of the organisation.

(c) *Specialisation*. The degree to which the organisation is divided up into specialised departments according to job function and organisational activities.

3.21 The problem, then, is to deal with how these factors relate to the buying process. The process itself is clearly an important issue. There are a number of stages, and there are clearly relations between them. Webster made the first attempt to define the industrial purchase process in terms of four stages.

(a) Problem recognition
(b) Organisational assignment of responsibility
(c) Search procedures
(d) Choice procedures

3.22 Robinson, Faris and Wind propose an eight stage process called *Buyphase*. This involves the following.

(a) Anticipation of recognition of a problem and a general solution.
(b) Determination of characteristics and quality of a needed item.
(c) Description of characteristics and quantity needed.
(d) Search for and qualification of potential sources.
(e) Requisition and analysis of proposals.
(f) Evaluation of proposals and selection of an order routine.
(g) Selection of an order routine.
(h) Performance and feedback evaluation.

3.23 This has been expanded further by Ozanne and Churchill (the Industrial adoption process model (following the AIDA model of consumer involvement)). Moriarty and Galper propose the purchase decision process model. This combines the internal nature of the buy grid with the external nature of the industrial adoption process model.

3.24 According to Cyert *et al's* study of data processing equipment buying there are three main aspects of the decision process. *Routine processes* that recur within the organisation at various stages in the decision process, *communication processes* which represent the information flow within the organisation and *problem-solving processes* which attempt to locate solutions to the buying problem.

3.25 Recently, a number of different models have recognised the limitations of these process models, and attempted to deal with the complex relations between the factors involved. These represent the attempt to bring together all the facets of the other models are known collectively as 'complex models'. Each incorporates a number of variables and processes, but this complexity poses severe problems in testability and empirical reference (operationalisability).

The American Marketing Association model

3.26 The American Marketing Association model proposes that there are four main influences on organisational buying decisions. These are:

(a) influences within the purchasing department;
(b) interdepartmental influences;
(c) intra firm influences;
(d) inter firm influences.

Departmental influences

	Within purchasing department	Between departments
Intra-firm influence	Cell 1 - Intra-departmental and intra-organisational influences **The Purchasing Agent** Social factors Price/cost factors Supply continuity Risk avoidance	Cell 2 - Inter-departmental and intra-organisational influences **The Buying Centre** Organisational structure Power/conflict processes Gatekeeper role
Inter-firm influence	Cell 3 - Intra-departmental and inter-organisational influences **Professionalism** Word-of-mouth communication Trade shows, journals Supplier purchase reciprocity	Cell 4 - Inter-departmental and inter-organisational influences **Organisational Environment** Technological change Nature of suppliers Cooperative buying

Organisational influences

3.27 The model indicates how these factors relate to each other.

(a) The first cell includes factors relating to the purchase agent (including social factors, price, supply and risk aspects).

(b) The second cell factors relate to the buying centre (its structure, process and the role of gatekeeper).

(c) The third relates to environmental influences on purchase agents, including increased professionalisation within the purchase function in the ways in which communication takes place, how advertising, PR and promotion are done, and the ways in which suppliers and purchases are reciprocally related.

(d) The fourth cell concerns the relation between the organisation and its environment, including the rate of technological change, and how this influences the way in which the organisation functions. Research suggests that as technological change accelerates, the purchasing agent is less likely to be an important influence in the process. The nature of the firm is also, according to this model, likely to influence the buying process, with larger firms presenting less risk to their customers, while smaller firms may be preferable to ensure continuity of supply.

3.28 Although this model emphasises a range of factors, it is concerned with process, and with relationships between factors within a variety of organisational environments. It brings out, however, the centrality of interaction, and also the behaviour of individuals within the organisation, without satisfactorily dealing with the ways in which these can be used to explain or predict outcomes.

3.29 The Sheth model - based on the Howard/Sheth model of Consumer Behaviour (CB), giving a central place to learning following behaviourist S/R principles - is precisely concerned with these processes. This complex model illustrates very well the intricacy of the organisational processes involved, and suggests that the behavioural dimensions of the relationships between the individuals concerned (those which are included in cell number 2 of the American Association model) may hold the key to understanding the process. It differs from the Howard/Sheth CB model in three ways.

(a) It relates only to buyer behaviour.
(b) It takes into account decision making involving more than one person.
(c) Fewer variables are involved.

3.30 Three aspects of organisational buyer behaviour are identified.

(a) Psychological environments of the individuals in the buying decision.
(b) Conditions which precipitate joint decision making.
(c) Joint decision-making process and conflict resolution amongst decision makers.

3.31 This joint aspect of decision making is a very important aspect of the model. It recognises that a number of individuals, and often a number of different departments, are usually involved in the decision to buy. Purchasing agents, quality control engineers, production management - all may be involved, and all have different backgrounds, expertise, and exposure to information. Individuals have very different requirements of the products involved, because of these differences.

3.32 There are five main factors which influence the psychological environments, role requirements and lifestyles of individuals involved in organisational buying decisions. These are as follows.

(a) *Backgrounds* of individuals (education, roles, lifestyles).

(b) *Information sources* available to them (likely to vary considerably according to organisational role, contacts with outside sources and so on).

(c) The degree of *active search* in which they are involved - this is likely to involve purchasing personnel rather more than those in other roles.

(d) *Perceptual distortion* affecting the way they see the problem - backgrounds and training are likely to produce differing values and goals, which influence what information is noticed, how information is interpreted - a kind of selective perception, or distortion.

(e) *Satisfaction* with past purchases - again, backgrounds will influence how satisfactory the performance of the product was judged to be.

3.33 Those expectations determining whether a particular buying decision will be joint or autonomous can be divided into product specific and company specific.

(a) *Product specific* factors include perceived risk, type of purchase and time pressure. Each of these has implications for the degree of risk and joint expectations which the product is expected to satisfy.

(b) *Company specific* factors include company size, degree of centralisation, and company orientation. Clearly, the nature of the company, and the relationships between the individuals and departments involved will all bear on the way in which purchases are approached.

3.34 This model does not examine autonomous buying decisions in any detail, but concentrates on joint decision making. Conflict is seen almost as a natural and inevitable aspect of such decision processes. Resolution is an essential aspect of organisational structure. There are four main ways in which this takes place.

(a) Problem solving
(b) Persuasion
(c) Bargaining
(d) Politicking

3.35 The first two of these are rational, and although time consuming, lead to good decisions, according to this model. The others tend to be used when there are irremediable conflicts between interested parties, and lead to resolution of conflicts, but poor decisions in many cases, since they imply that the requirements of some parties remain unsatisfied or frustrated.

3.36 The model rests heavily on this 'logical process' view of organisational/group processes, and this is obviously an idealistic notion. The model does, at the same time, recognise that in some cases *ad hoc* situational variables (strikes, breakdowns etc) may influence behaviour and affect decision outcomes. The emphasis within this model on the importance of interaction, on negotiation processes and on individual psychology is extremely important, but it raises more problems than it can really deal with - many of the relationships between these variables remain vague and unexplained. More work is needed on these aspects of the model. These behavioural aspects have been acknowledge by other researchers as containing the key to understanding the area.

3.37 Bonoma, Zaltman and Johnson proposed that because industrial marketing is a system of exchange and is an interactive process between two parties, the smallest analysable unit should be the buyer/seller *dyad*.

3.38 Complex models, then, offer an interesting attempt to capture the range of factors which are affecting organisational buying, and promise a great deal. The difficulty comes with the attempt to operationalise the models. At the moment, these are largely abstract and heuristic, rather than substantive and empirical methods of analysis.

Competitive edge

3.39 When competing for business, the industrial product manufacturer is likely to have to conform to laid down standards and/or quote to tight specifications. This means it is more difficult to gain a differential advantage in the product itself.

3.40 Nevertheless, business to business marketers must strive to achieve a distinct competitive advantage and where this is not price, the battleground moves to a variety of add-on services which can be classed as pre-sale and after sale. Technical advice is a valuable pre-sale service and a rapid spares availability is an after-sales service that may tip the balance on who gets the order.

4   SERVICES MARKETING

The rise of the service economy

4.1 There are a number of reasons why services are more important today than they were in the past. These include the following.

(a) *The growth of service sectors in advanced industrial societies*. In terms of employment, more people now work in the service sector than in all other sectors of the economy. In terms of output, the major contributors to national output are the public and private service sectors. 'Invisible' service earnings from abroad are of increasing significance for Britain's balance of trade.

(b) *Increasingly market-oriented trend within service-providing organisation* (eg 'internal markets', 'market testing' and so on).

The extension of the service sector, and the application of 'market principles' across what were previously publicly owned utilities, has made a large number of service providers much more marketing conscious.

4.2 The service sector extends, in Britain, across public provision in the legal, medical, educational, military, employment, credit, communications, transportation, leisure and information fields. Some are not-for-profit, but increasingly, there is a focus on profits in many of these areas. The private sector embraces not-for-profit areas such as arts, leisure, charities, religious organisations, and educational factors, but also, of course, business and professional services involved in travel, finance, insurance, management, the law, building, commerce, entertainment and so on.

Services: some definitions

4.3 The definitions offered of services are:

(a) ' ... those separately identifiable but intangible activities that provide want-satisfaction, and that are not, of necessity, tied to, or inextricable from, the sale of a product or another service. To produce a service may or may not require the use of tangible goods or assets. However, where such use is required, there is no transfer of title (permanent ownership) to these tangible goods.'
(Donald Cowell, *The Marketing of Services*)

(b) ' ... any activity of benefit that one party can offer to another that is essentially intangible and does not result in the ownership of anything. Its production may or may not be tied to a physical product'.
(P Kotler, *Social Marketing*)

Goods and services

4.4 Services marketing differs from the marketing of other goods in a number of crucial ways. Marketing services faces a number of distinct problems, and as a consequence, the approach adopted must be varied, and particular sorts of marketing practices developed.

4.5 While it is difficult to make a judgement which encompasses the wide variety within service types and situations, there are indeed many service organisations which are highly market oriented (for instance, in retailing, transport hire, cleaning and hotel groups) but there are many which remain relatively unaffected by marketing ideas and practices, or have only just begun to adopt them - for example, legal and financial services. This is likely to become much more important as competition within the service sector intensifies.

Marketing characteristics of services

4.6 Characteristics of services which make them distinctive from the marketing of goods have been proposed. These are five major differences.

(a) Intangibility
(b) Inseparability
(c) Heterogeneity
(d) Perishability
(e) Ownership

Intangibility

4.7 Intangibility refers to the lack of substance which is involved with service delivery. Unlike a good, there are no substantial material or physical aspects of a service - no taste, feel, visible presence and so on. Clearly, this creates difficulties and can inhibit the propensity to consume a service, since customers are not sure what they have.

'Ultimately the customer may have no prior experience of a service in which he or she is interested, nor any conception of how it would satisfy the requirements of the purchase context for which it was intended.'   (Morden, *The Marketing of Services*)

4.8   In fact, it would be incorrect to make this a 'black or white' phenomenon. Shostack has suggested viewing insubstantiality not as an 'either/or' issue, but rather as a continuum.

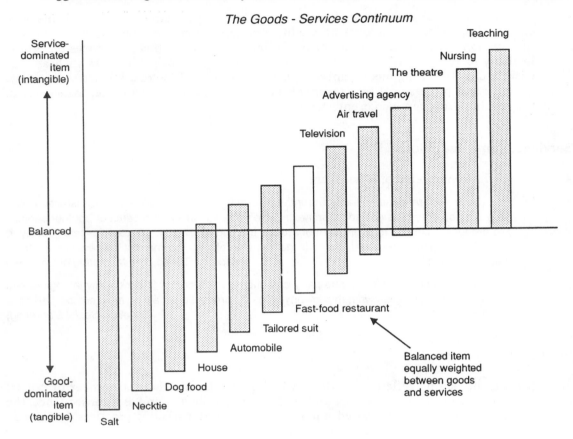

The Goods - Services Continuum

4.9   Shostack has also proposed that marketing entities are combinations of elements, which are tangible or intangible. She uses the metaphor of a molecule to visualise the 'total market entity'. This proposes the elements which make up a product, the interrelationships between them, and the dominance of goods or services, tangible or intangible. A product then comes to be conceived as a 'gestalt', or blend of various elements, which is constituted by combining *material entities* (the aeroplane we are flying in, the airport lounge, etc) with various sorts of *processes* (the courtesy of the airline staff, the frequency of services and so on).

4.10   Clearly, for each service, the number, complexity and balance of the various elements involved will vary a great deal. What is experienced, at the end of the process of the service being delivered, remains insubstantial, although many parts of the process (the machines, buildings and staff of an airline, for instance) are very substantial but still, the actual service itself cannot be owned, but only experienced.

4.11   Marketers and consumers need to try to overcome this problem, and typically seek to do so in a number of different ways, and, of course, for different reasons. The consumer needs information to avoid making a mistake, to form some grounds for judgement, and to cut down risk. The marketer wishes to make the choice of the product 'safer' and make the consumer feel more comfortable about paying for something they do not then own, and which has no physical form.

4.12   This may be countered by:

(a)   the consumer seeking opinions from other consumers;

(b) the marketer offering the consumer something tangible to represent the purchase.

4.13 Intangibility, once again, is a matter of degree, varying from:

(a) intangibles making a tangible product available;

(b) intangibles adding value to a tangible product (house decorating, hairdressing, vehicles or plant maintenance etc);

(c) complete intangibility (entertainment or leisure services).

Marketing implications

4.14 Dealing with the problems may involve strategies in which there is reduction of the level of difficulty to which the intangibility gives rise.

(a) *Increasing the level of tangibility.* When dealing with the customer, staff can use physical or conceptual representations/illustrations to make the customer feel more confident as to what it is that the service is delivering.

(b) *Focusing the attention of the customer on the principal benefits of consumption.* This could take the form of communicating the benefits of purchasing the service so that the customer visualises its appropriateness to the usage requirements within which the principal benefit is being sought. Promotion and sales material could provide images or records of previous customers' experience.

(c) *Differentiating the service and reputation-building.* This is achieved by enhancing perceptions of customer service and customer value by offering excellence in the delivery of the service and promoting values of quality, service reliability and value for money. These must be attached as values to brands, which must then be *managed* to secure and enhance their market position.

Inseparability

4.15 A service often cannot be separated off from the provider of the service. The creation or the performance of a service often occurs at the same instant that a full or partial consumption of it occurs. Goods in the vast majority of cases have to be produced, then sold, then consumed, in that order. Services are only a promise at the time they are sold - most services are sold and then they are produced and consumed simultaneously. Think of having dental treatment or going on a journey. Neither exists until they are actually experienced/consumed by the person who has bought them. Creation of many services is coterminous with consumption.

4.16 Services may have to be, at the same time:

(a) made available;
(b) sold;
(c) produced; and
(d) consumed.

Marketing implications

4.17 Provision of the service may not be separable from the person or personality of the seller. Consequently, increasing importance is attached to the need to instil values of quality, reliability, and to generate a customer service ethic in the personnel employed within an organisation which can be transferred to the service provision. This points up the need for excellence and customer orientation and the need to invest in high quality people and high quality training for them.

Heterogeneity

4.18 Many services face a problem of maintaining consistency in the standard of output. Variability of quality in delivery is inevitable, because of the number of factors which may influence it. This may create problems of operations management. For example, it may be difficult or impossible to attain:

(a) *precise standardisation of the service offered*. The quality of the service may depend heavily on who it is that delivers the service, or exactly when it takes place. Booking a holiday using standard procedures, may well be quite different on a quiet winter afternoon and on a hectic spring weekend, and may well vary according to the person dealing with the client;

(b) *influence or control over perceptions of what is good or bad customer service*. From the customer's perspective, it is, of course, very difficult to obtain an idea of the quality of service in advance of purchase/consumption.

4.19 This points up the need to monitor constantly customer reactions. A common way of addressing this problem involves applying a system to deliver a service which may be *franchised* to operators. The problem remains, however, and almost the only way to address it is by constant monitoring and response to problems.

Marketing implications

4.20 As a marketing policy, this problem illustrates the need to maintain an attitude and organisational culture which emphasises:

(a) consistency of quality control;
(b) consistency of customer service;
(c) effective staff selection training and motivation.

4.21 Note also the importance of:

(a) clear and objective quality measures;

(b) standardising as much as possible within the service;

(c) assume the *Pareto principle* (80 percent of difficulties arise from 20 percent of events surrounding the provision of the service). Therefore, identify and respond most closely to these potential 'troublespots'.

Perishability

4.22 Services cannot be stored, of course. They are innately *perishable*. Seats on a bus or the services of a chiropodist consist in their availability for periods of time, and if they are not occupied, the service they offer cannot be used 'later'.

4.23 This presents specific marketing problems. Meeting customer needs in these operations depends on staff being available as and when they are needed. This must be balanced against the need for a firm to minimise unnecessary expenditure on staff wages. Anticipating and responding to levels of demand is, therefore, a key planning priority. The risks are that:

(a) inadequate level of demand is accompanied by substantial variable and fixed cost;
(b) excess demand may result in lost custom through inadequate service provision.

Marketing implications

4.24 Policies must seek to smooth supply/demand relationship by:

(a) price variations which encourage off-peak demand;
(b) promotions to stimulate off-peak demand.

Ownership

4.25 Services suffer from a fundamental difference compared to consumer goods. They do not result in the transfer of property. The purchase of a service only confers on the customer access to or rights to use a facility - not ownership. Payment is for the use of, access to or the hire of particular items. Often, there are tight constraints on the length of time involved in such usage. In the case of purchasing a product, there is transfer of title and control over the use of an item.

4.26 This may very well lessen the perceived customer value of a service, and consequently make for unfavourable comparisons with tangible alternatives.

Marketing implications

4.27 Possible marketing implications are:

(a) promote the advantages of non-ownership. This can be done by emphasising, in promotion, the benefits of paid-for maintenance, and periodic upgrading of the product. Radio Rentals have used this as a major selling proposition with great success;

(b) make available a tangible symbol or representation of ownership (certificate, membership of professional association). This can come to embody the benefits enjoyed;

(c) increasing the chances or opportunity of ownership (eg time-shares, shares in the organisation for regular customers).

4.28 The issue of how to deal with these problems has occupied many different writers. Some have claimed that the critical factor is the marketing mix which is formulated. Research into the ways in which service quality is evaluated shows that the dimensions of service evaluation are distinctive, and quite different criteria are given emphasis when customers are making a judgement. The following table shows the type of factors on which judgements are based in a particular service sector.

Dimension and definition	Examples of specific questions raised by stock brokerage customers
Tangibles. Appearance of physical facilities, equipment, personnel and communication materials	• Is my stockbroker dressed appropriately?
Reliability. Ability to perform the promised service dependably and accurately	• Does the stockbroker follow exact instructions to buy or sell?
Responsiveness. Willingness to help customers and provide prompt service	• Is my stockbroker willing to answer my questions?
Competence. Possession of the required skills and knowledge to perform the service	• Does my brokerage firm have the research capabilities to accurately track market developments?
Courtesy. Politeness, respect, consideration, and friendliness of contact personnel	• Does my broker refrain from acting busy or being rude when I ask questions?
Credibility. Trustworthiness, believability, and honesty of the service provider	• Does my broker refrain from pressuring me to buy?
Security. Freedom from danger, risk, or doubt	• Does my brokerage firm know where my stock certificate is?
Access. Approachability and ease of contact	• Is it easy to get through to my broker over the telephone?
Communication. Keeping customers informed in language they can understand, and listening to them	• Does my broker avoid using technical jargon?
Understanding the customer. Making the effort to know customers and their needs	• Does my broker try to determine what my specific financial objectives are?

(From Zeithaml, Parasuraman and Berry, *Delivering Quality Service*)

5 THE EXTENDED MARKETING MIX FOR SERVICES MARKETING

5.1 As always, each firm has its own unique concentration of people, processes and problems to deal with and, in that sense, arriving at a marketing mix for services is little different from the process involved for a product.

5.2 It has, however, been pointed out that in the marketing of services, four Ps does not adequately describe the importance of mix elements. It has been suggested that an *extra* three, and perhaps four 'Ps' should be added to the mix for services.

5.3 Booms and Bitner suggest that the standard 4P approach to the marketing of products should be extended for services by the addition of three more Ps, namely:

(a) People
(b) Process
(c) Physical evidence or ambience

5.4 Services are provided by *people* for people. If the people providing the service are wrong, the service is spoiled. In the case of a bus service, a cheap fare, a clean vehicle and a frequent service can be spoiled by a surly driver who takes delight in shaking his passengers sick by driving in a series of jolts.

5.5   With regard to *process*, services are usually systemised, eg you make an appointment with the hairdresser, you arrive a little before time, you wait, you take the chair, the hairdresser asks you how you would like your hair styled (one wit replied 'in complete silence') and so on. At any one of these points in the process, right through to brushing you down and taking your money, the service can be spoiled or enhanced by the provider.

5.6   Finally, there is the *physical evidence* or ambience - how are the hairdresser's premises? Are they pleasant and airy or depressing and stuffy? Is the decor tasteful or vulgar? Are the other customers your sort of people or 'aliens'? Again, ambience can be a maker or spoiler of your experience of the service.

5.7   However, here we will expand on the standard approach by identifying four 'Ps'. These are as follows (you will see some overlap with the above.)

(a)   Personal selling.
(b)   Place of availability (operations management).
(c)   People and customer service.
(d)   Physical evidence.

Personal selling

5.8   *Personal selling* is more important here because it is easier to sell products than services, for reasons outlined above. Because of:

(a)   greater perceived risk involved; and
(b)   greater uncertainty about quality and reliability,

the reputation of supplier may be of greater importance, and there is a perception on the part of the customer of the need for greater reliance on the honesty, sincerity (etc) of the individual salesperson. When consumers seek reassurance, personal contact with a competent, effective representative may provide the necessary confidence. In some cases, however, since the quality of the individual salesperson varies, this may not be achieved.

5.9   Greater contact with the salesperson may potentially generate even more anxiety about the quality of the service. This underlines the need to place even more emphasis on the reduction of customer uncertainty, and to develop standard procedures to minimise customer anxiety ('closing techniques').

Place of availability

5.10   *Place of availability* is really covered by the distribution system, but of course there are special problems for services in the area of *operations management*. The place of availability and the frequency of availability are key service variables, while planning to deal with capacity, and making sure that levels of productivity for the assets to be used are optimised, is essential for efficient and profitable operation.

5.11   The level, and also the quality, of service which is available to the customer is especially sensitive to the efficient organisation of the processes by which services are delivered. Problems with regulating the supply make this a key factor in competitive advantage - a company which 'gets it right' is likely to be clearly differentiated from competitors. Key factors are:

(a)   *capacity utilisation*, matching demand sequences to staff utilisation to avoid unprofitable underprovision and problematic understaffing;

(b)   *managing customer contact*, to avoid crowding and customer disruption, meet needs as they arise, and increase employee control over interactions;

(c)   *establishing objectives within the not-for-profit sector*, for example, standards for teachers or medical staff.

5.12 For marketing service managers, the 'quality control' and 'engineering' of the interactions which take place between customers is a key strategic issue. Customers are often, in the course of service delivery, interacting with other customers to gather information, and form views about the nature and quality of the service of which they are contemplating purchase. Minimising exposure to negative feedback, and promoting the dissemination of positive images and messages about the value of the service, and the quality of customer responses to it, are important objectives here.

People and customer service

5.13 *People*, the personnel of the service deliverer, are uniquely important in the service marketing process. In the case of some services, the physical presence of people actually performing the service is a vital aspect of customer satisfaction. You may think of clerks in a bank, or personnel in catering establishments. The staff involved are performing or producing a service, selling the service and also liaising with the customer to promote the service, gather information and respond to customer needs.

5.14 A key strategic issue for the service marketing mix then is the way in which personnel are involved in implementing the marketing concept, and measures need to be established which will institute a customer orientation in all sectors of organisational activity.

5.15 As we have already remarked with regard to personal selling, customers who lack security and confidence in an intangible service will tend to use cues from the demeanour and behaviour of staff to establish a view about the image and efficiency of the organisation.

5.16 The higher the level of customer contact involved in the delivery of a service, the more crucial is staff role in generating customer service and adding value. In many cases the delivery of the service and the physical presence of the personnel involved are completely inseparable - technical competence and skill in handling people are of equal importance in effective delivery of a service, since, as we have already noted, quality is in the eye of the (consuming) beholder!

Exercise

All levels of staff must be involved in customer service. To achieve this end, it is vital for senior management consciously to promulgate values of customer service constantly, in order to create and build a culture of customer service within the company. How do you think that this might be achieved?

Solution

This means concrete policies and the continuous development of the following.

(a) Policies of selection.
(b) Programmes of training.
(c) Standard, consistent operational practices ('MacDonaldisation').
(d) Standardised operational rules.
(e) Effective motivational programmes.
(f) Managerial appointments.
(g) The attractiveness and appropriateness of the service offer.
(h) Effective policies of staff reward and remuneration.

Physical evidence

5.17 *Physical evidence*, as we have already seen, is an important remedy for the intangibility of the product. This may be *associated with the service itself*, providing cues as to the nature of the service (for example, reports of previous work, or credit cards which represent the service available to customers), building up an association with a particular event, person or object, or building up an identification with a specific individual (a 'listening' bank manager), or *incorporated into the design and specification of the service environment* involving the building, location or atmosphere. Design here can:

(a) convey the nature of the service involved;

(b) transmit messages and information;

(c) imply aesthetic qualities, moral values, or other socio-cultural aspects of a corporate image;

(d) reinforce an existing image;

(e) reassure;

(f) engender an emotional reaction in the customer, through sensory and symbolic blends.

Conclusion

5.18 Marketing mixes for services, then, often place *extra emphasis* on the following.

(a) Personal selling
(b) Operations management
(c) People and customer service
(d) Physical evidence

5.19 In the overall management picture, this greater emphasis on 'people issues' typically involves the management in tight and closely organised practices within the enterprise, in the ways in which personnel are selected and used. Service marketing involves a 'totalitarian' organisational culture, in the same way that is being advocated for philosophies such as TQM, but for this sector, these issues are perhaps even more directly relevant to success. As a consequence, rigorous procedures are typically applied in the areas of the following.

(a) Selection and training

(b) Internal marketing - promulgating the 'culture' of service within the firm

(c) Ensuring 'conformance' in terms of quality procedures, with standards:

   (i) in behaviour;
   (ii) of dress and appearance;
   (iii) in procedures;
   (iv) in modes of dealing with the public

(d) Mechanising procedures where possible

(e) Constantly auditing personnel performance and behaviour

(f) Extending the conscious promotion of image and tangible presentations of the service and its qualities into the design of service environments and the engineering of interactions within and between staff and customers.

5.20 If there is one overall message about the essential quality required in successful service marketing, it is that attention to detail, however small, is the key to success.

6 CHARITY AND NOT-FOR-PROFIT MARKETING

6.1 Although most people would 'know one if they saw it', there is a surprising problem in clearly delimiting what counts as a 'not-for-profit' (NFP) organisation or a charity. Local authority services, for example, would not be marketing in order to arrive at a profit for shareholders, but nowadays they are being increasingly required to apply the same disciplines and processes, and aim for the same practical outcome, as companies which are oriented towards straightforward profit goals.

6.2 Whether there are shareholders involved or not, many organisations seek to arrive at a *close fit*, or a positive surplus for their income and the prices they charge over the costs of operating. Neilsen describes the process of undertaking a non-profit making operation with the intention of making a profit, so that income will exceed expenditure, as 'piggy-backing'. For example Oxfam operates more shops than any commercial organisation in Britain, and these operate at a profit. The Royal Society for the Protection of Birds operates a mail order trading company which provides a 25% return on capital, operating very profitably and effectively.

6.3   Bois suggests that we define NFP enterprises by recognising that their first objective is to be 'non-loss' operations in order to cover their costs, that profits are only made as a means to an end (eg providing a service, or accomplishing some socially or morally worthy objective).

6.4   Bois proposes that a NFP organisation be defined as

> ' ... an organisation whose attainment of its prime goal is not assessed by economic measures. However, in pursuit of that goal it may undertake profit-making activities.'

6.5   This may involve a number of different kinds of organisation with, for example, differing legal status - charities, statutory bodies offering public transport or the provision of services such as leisure, health or public utilities such as water or road maintenance.

6.6   Dibb, Simkin, Pride and Ferrell suggest that non-business marketing can conveniently be split into two sub-categories.

(a)   Non-profit organisation marketing.
(b)   Social marketing.

6.7   *Non-profit organisation marketing* examples cited are hospitals and colleges but the differences here are becoming somewhat blurred as both these types of organisations are beginning to adopt more businesslike stances in a freer market. Nevertheless the basic objective of a hospital could be said to continue to be to provide high quality health care and for a college to provide higher quality education.

6.8   *Social marketing* seeks to shape or grow perceived beneficial social attitudes such as protecting the environment, saving scarce resources, contributing towards good causes etc.

6.9   Kotler clarifies non-business marketing objectives by considering the idea of exchange rather than profit. Thus the police try to serve the public's need for protection with objectives of law enforcement and receive in return funding (through taxes) and a certain degree of support from the public. A charity offers satisfaction and an outlet for compassion and, for some people, a means of reduction of guilt, receiving in return financial contributions from donors and support from voluntary helpers.

Organisational characteristics of NFP organisations

6.10 Marketing objectives of these types of organisation are likely to be derived from the characteristics of the organisation itself. There are five main aspects to such organisations.

Ambiguous goals

6.11 The bodies involved in NFP organisations (voluntary, professional and charitable bodies) often generate conflict over goals. When priorities are being set, it is often difficult to find agreement over fundamentals. Very often, such organisations are relatively 'open' and are founded on values which give members the right 'to have their say'. This may well lead to extended debates when conflicts arise, and make it difficult to arrive at decisions easily. Where full time staff are mixed with volunteers, such conflicts are likely to occur readily.

Lack of agreement on means-ends relationships

6.12   In the case of agreed goals and values, disputes may nevertheless arise over the ways in which these can be achieved. This arises from lack of knowledge, in some cases, and simple disagreement over the efficacy of strategies in others.

Environmental turbulence

6.13   Very often, the aims and goals of NFP organisations are far more specific than those set by straightforward business enterprises. In addition, business organisations have a relatively straightforward principle at their heart - that they must operate at a profit - which affords them the flexibility to switch the nature of their activities, in some cases quite radically, should the environment in which they operate change unexpectedly.

6.14   NFP operations do not have that possibility, so that 'environmental turbulence' is likely to affect them to a far greater degree. In the UK, when an organisation has the legal status of a charity, a very small number of trustees can block any proposed move to alter the way in which it operates. This creates great difficulties when an organisation is faced with changes wrought by technology, the economic realm, social or cultural changes or governmental legislation.

Unmeasurable outputs

6.15   Though goals for NFP organisations are usually agreed upon, it is nevertheless difficult to decide whether or not they are being achieved, or whether the organisation is operating as efficiently or effectively as it can. Sometimes, indicators which are developed as inadequate substitutes for 'true' measures of organisational effectiveness (such as 'throughput' of clients in a welfare agency, for example), can become ends in themselves.

Management intervention effects cannot be calculated

6.16   This is a recurrent problem for all organisations, but is a particular problem for NFP organisations. Where the prime goals of the organisation and its members are not economic, measuring the effects of decisions and actions taken by management becomes particularly difficult.

6.17   Given the distinctive nature of NFP organisations, there are clearly bound to be implications for the pursuit of their marketing goals. In relation to decision making, for example, NFP managerial style is much more likely to be 'judgmental' or 'political' (according to the analysis offered by Hofstede), since important decisions can only be reached by negotiations between groups or individuals within the organisation. These parties are often divided between different interests or value positions.

6.18   The government of NFP/charity organisations is often comprised of bodies composed in the main of officers elected annually from the whole membership, alongside a small number of full-time employees or their representatives. As a consequence, memberships change frequently, owing to the heavy demands on the time of such members. Leadership may well fluctuate as a consequence, and decision making may be erratic or unstable, allowing more politically active or astute groups to achieve power.

6.19   Few NFP organisations develop a hierarchy which permits the resolution of conflicts by imposed solutions, since they do not rest, like profit-based enterprises, on ownership rights. Conflicts here are likely to involve clashes in values; there are seldom dramatic differences in the rationality which is applied by these groups. As a consequence, the outcome of decision making may be very difficult to predict.

The impact on marketing

6.20 Marketing is a purposive activity, the aim of which is to realise an organisation's goals by satisfying the customer's needs. If goals are ambiguous or unclearly formulated, the effectiveness of marketing activity is concomitantly reduced.

6.21 Uncertainty over the stability, and consistency of decisions creates other difficulties. Internal politicking suggests that those decisions which have been taken may well be reversed or altered within relatively short periods of time, as other groups achieve power. Marketing requires consistency over time, for instance pursuing a particular corporate image involves promotional activity over a long period of time.

6.22 The unmeasurability of outcomes makes it very difficult to work with certain key marketing activities. While sales, or customer attitudes to and rating of products, will provide excellent indications to a brand manager that his policies are working, NFP managers cannot look for the same types of feedback data, in many cases. Workers for a heritage collection or famine relief charity will have less clearly defined criteria for success or failure, and can never really benefit from the experience of knowing that they have done particular things wrong and other things correctly.

6.23 There is also a built-in resistance or even antagonism towards marketing in the value system of many of those who are heavily involved in certain types of NFP activity. There is a feeling amongst some involved in charity that commercial approaches to, for instance, promotional activity, are either crass, or actually morally wrong. The idea of responding to 'consumer needs' is, at least in part, in conflict with the idea of 'mission' which underlies many NFP organisations. This makes them less likely to consider consumer choices to be appropriate or valid. Some even hold the view that they know better than their 'customers' what is good for them.

6.24 The dominance of the 'customer orientation' within marketing may challenge the basic mission which the organisation sets for itself. For example, the vegetarian society is dedicated to changing the way in which we eat, and the way in which we use animals and animal products within the food production system. Its basic goals would preclude the use of marketing which responded to the tastes which people have, since it starts from the premise that these are inappropriate, mistaken and misguided.

Objectives

6.25 Possible objectives for a charity include the following.

   (a) Surplus maximisation (equivalent to profit maximisation).
   (b) Revenue maximisation (as for businesses).
   (c) Usage maximisation (maximising the number of users and their usage).
   (d) Usage targeting (matching the capacity available).
   (e) Full cost recovery (minimising subsidy).
   (f) Partial cost recovery (minimising subsidy).
   (g) Budget maximisation (maximising what is offered).
   (h) Producer satisfaction maximisation (satisfying the wants of staff).

Marketing principles

6.26 In conclusion marketing principles of charities might differ in the following ways

   (a) *Strategic visioning.* As with a firm, a charity would have specific ideas of what it wanted to achieve, though these may not be as explicit or formalised as with a business organisation.

   (b) *Marketing audit.* A charity would want to find out how effectively it had been operating but would probably do this in an ad hoc way, and not conform to the marketing audit procedure followed by many firms.

(c) *SWOT and PEST*. Unless a charity is particularly well organised and led by a marketer or someone with contemporary industrial/commercial experience, then it will largely be more re-active than pro-active. It may have a knowledge of the factors constraining it, but its knowledge of itself in terms of efficiency and effectiveness may not enable quality management.

(d) *Marketing objectives, strategy and tactics*. Although staffed by committed individuals, charities usually operate in the short term; rarely are objectives and strategies formally set. Tactics seem to 'evolve' and staff are motivated on the basis of progress made.

(e) *Control, feedback and review mechanisms*. Periodic committee meetings and annual reviews facilitate 'progress and results' communication; very rarely are there clear channels or identified mechanisms for performance measurement as with business enterprises.

Chapter roundup

- Industrial marketing, or marketing business-to-business, is different in nature from consumer marketing. Buying motivations (the criteria which consumers apply) and the nature of the buying process itself are quite different. There are four basic categories of industrial market.

- Target markets for industrial marketing tend to be easier to identify than consumer market segments. Data is generally more easily available on businesses than on consumers. Sources include government and privately-published statistics.

- There are differences in the marketing mix for industrial marketing when compared to the characteristic mix adopted for consumer markets.

- The extension of the service sector, and the application of market principles across many public sector and ex-public sector organisations, has made a large number of service providers much more marketing-conscious. Services marketing differs from the marketing of other goods in a number of crucial ways, and five specific characteristics of services marketing have been proposed.

- An extended marketing mix has been suggested for services marketing. Booms and Bitner suggested an additional 3Ps. Here, we have taken an approach which analyses an additional 4Ps.

- Not-for-profit organisations and charities are usually viewed as a single type, even though this is a varied sector. The marketing objectives of these types of organisation are likely to be derived from the characteristics of the organisation itself. The unmeasurability of outcomes of many of these organisations makes certain marketing activities somewhat problematic.

Test your knowledge

1   What are the four categories of industrial market? (see para 1.8)

2   Give four examples of Government publications which could be used in targeting industrial markets. (2.7)

3   How does 'product' differ in industrial marketing when compared to consumer marketing? (3.3 - 3.6)

4   How does 'distribution' differ in industrial marketing when compared to consumer marketing? (3.14 - 3.16)

5   What is Buyphase? (3.22)

6   What are the four influences on organisation buying as identified by the AMA? (3.26)

7   What are the five factors which influence the *individuals* involved in organisational buying? (3.32)

8   What are the five marketing characteristics of services? (4.6)

9   What issues arise from the heterogeneity of services being marketed? (4.18 - 4.21)

10   How can the problems of lack of ownership be overcome in service marketing?(4.25 - 4.28)

11   What are the additional 'Ps' in the service marketing mix? (5.3, 5.7)

10   Identify five characteristics of NFP organisations. (6.10)

Now try illustrative questions 10 to 12 at the end of the Study Text

Chapter 10

INTERNATIONAL MARKETING

This chapter covers the following topics.

1   International marketing opportunities

2   Marketing information needs

3   Marketing environment differences

4   Regional trade alliances and markets

5   Product

6   Place

7   Price

8   Promotion

9   Structure choices

Introduction

International marketing presents a new set of challenges for the marketer. First, the marketing information needs are great and cannot be satisfied in the same way as domestic needs. The marketing environment is different, and the marketing mix must be adapted. Regional trade alliances and markets present a new set of difficulties and opportunities which must be addressed if the organisation's strategy is to be successful.

---

1   INTERNATIONAL MARKETING OPPORTUNITIES

The nature of international marketing

1.1   Companies will enter into international marketing for a number of different reasons.

(a) *Growth*. If the domestic market is static or growth is slow, or if competition is excessively fierce, a company may seek to explore new areas within which it can hope to compete or operate without competition. It may hope that entry into foreign markets will increase the size of the potential market available to it.

(b) *Economies of scale*. Since the volume of output and unit cost are directly related, lower-than-competitive costs will constitute a very important competitive advantage. Expanding into international markets will provide the level of sales necessary to benefit from economies of scale. Automobile manufacture is one of the most obvious examples of this principle in operation.

(c) *International competition*. Markets of all kinds are becoming globalised, so that fewer and fewer manufacturers and service operations are able to confine themselves to one single market. International trade becomes a necessity. In many industries, those who are unable or unwilling to become 'internationalised' may well become 'screwdriver' (assembly) operations, or find themselves carrying out subcontracts for the main players.

(d) *National necessity*. Where economies are not self-sufficient (as is the case for the majority) they may have to bring in various kinds of goods, services and raw materials. Such imports must be paid for with foreign currency, and exports provide the means of acquiring this currency. This may mean raw materials being exported to pay for manufactured goods, or vice versa. This system of trade means that national economies are closely tied into the terms under which international trade is operated.

The analysis of international marketing opportunities

1.2   Morden (1993) has suggested that the analysis which we carry out in order to make decisions about operating in an international market can be described as the 12Cs. This provides a convenient mnemonic device, although, of course, it might be slightly more accurate to describe these elements in another way. These analytic elements are as follows.

    (a)   Country
    (b)   Culture and consumer behaviour
    (c)   Concentration
    (d)   Communication
    (e)   Channels of distribution
    (f)   Capacity to pay
    (g)   Currency
    (h)   Control and co-ordination
    (i)   Commitment
    (j)   Choices
    (k)   Contractual obligations
    (l)   Caveats

1.3   Marketing into a 'foreign' marketplace presents quite specific problems which should not be under-estimated even when the markets involved appear very similar.

2   MARKETING INFORMATION NEEDS

2.1   In order to develop an effective marketing plan, information about the markets into which the company intends to go is essential. In the case of domestic markets, the normal step would be to undertake research which would provide that information. International marketing, however, requires a different approach to marketing research, and present its own peculiar problems.

2.2   To begin with, the scope of international marketing research is different. A survey of members of the Association of Market Survey Organisations showed that international research grew by 50% between 1989 and 1990, while domestic research in the same period grew by only 18%. The reasons are relatively straightforward. As domestic markets face recession, many of the companies which would have been content to stay 'passive' exporters, have been forced to become vigorous international marketers.

2.3   At the same time, global communications have increased and improved to the point where they have made it irresistibly attractive. There has also been a rapid growth of economies (particularly in South East Asia). As an example, out of 55 projects currently being carried out by Guinness, 30 are in the Far East.

2.4   In other cases, the tastes of China's consumers are proving a magnet. 1993 saw the development of the China Market Research Institute, and connections in consulting companies and market research companies, mostly still foreign, have begun operating in China. These are apparently obtaining excellent data with great potential.

2.5   Although obviously attractive, such research faces a number of challenges which mark it out from home research.

    (a)   Lack of secondary data
    (b)   Difficulty of establishing comparability and equivalence.
    (c)   Cost of collecting primary data
    (d)   Complexity of research design
    (e)   Co-ordination of research and data collection across countries

Secondary data

2.6   In the case of secondary data gathering, for example, it is by no means easy to compare census data gathered in different countries. Different countries gather it in different ways and at different time intervals. For example:

(a)   every 10 years in the USA;
(b)   every 5 years in Japan/Canada; and
(c)   1960 then 1987 in Germany.

2.7   Many countries do not collect income data at all. In some there is a tradition of independence and a suspicion of government interference, plus great cultural differences in attitudes to, for example, tax collection and co-operation.

2.8   Education levels, which may be used to measure socio-economic status, may be misleading since education systems vary between countries. Some countries collect data on 'non citizens' (for example Germany and Switzerland). Others (for example Canada), collect data on religion, but this is regarded as a private and highly sensitive matter in many countries. Comparability and equivalence become sensitive issues when there are no ready agreements as to the definition of a household, for instance, gay and lesbian groups protested when recent research did not accommodate the idea of single sex 'family/household' groups. In some countries, single sex marriages are legally acknowledged. In fact, definitions also vary for 'housewife'/'homemaker', socio-economic groupings, income brackets and customer profiles.

Comparability

2.9   Full comparability seems very difficult to envisage in the foreseeable future in the absence of agreement, and research capabilities also vary from country to country.

2.10   A cross-national comparison of consumer research measures showed that even with the same scales, measuring the same product attributes, different levels of reliability appear. Data may well 'mean' quite different things, even when palpably the same instruments are used in the data collection process.

2.11   The marketing research process conducted internationally is more complex, but the basic approach remains the same as for domestic research.

2.12   The key difference is in implementing some of the steps. For example, problem definition and development of research objectives may take weeks or months, and upon this depends choice of methodology, selection of respondents and decisions about time frame. In a study of market research in Japan, Brizz looked at research objectives. For example, for a bicycle marketer, these will vary according to 'served needs' in different cultures/economies. In a western society, bicycles have to compete with product replacement threats from other 'youth leisure' products such as skis, footballs and the cinema. In less developed countries, the major competition could be motorcycles, mopeds, scooters or small cars, since this product is a major source of serious everyday transport.

Primary data collection

2.13   As noted above, for secondary sources of data in developing countries, both availability and reliability are major problems. Despite the expense, companies may have to commission primary data generation much earlier in a developing country research project.

2.14   As an example of variability, in ten reports on the economies of Eastern Europe, figures varied widely. For the old East Germany, reported GDP varied from per capita $4,000 to $13,000.

2.15   In the case of primary research, participation is often difficult to obtain. In many cultures, men will not discuss shaving habits with anyone, particularly women interviewers, while respondents in the Netherlands and Germany are unwilling to discuss personal finances. The Dutch are more willing to discuss sexual behaviour.

2.16   It is very important to accommodate these differences when gathering information. However, even the process of translation can be a major problem. In *back translation*, for example, questionnaires may need to be translated from the home language to the language of the country where they will be used by a foreign language speaker, then, in order to check their accuracy, translated back to the home language by a bilingual who is a native speaker of the home language. In *parallel translation*, two or more translators translate the questionnaire and then the results are compared.

2.17   Methods of data collection may also vary between countries. For example, face to face interviews at home or work are very popular in the UK and Switzerland, while interviews in shopping areas are favoured in the Netherlands and France. The Japanese consumer prefers personal, face to face discussions to telephone or mail, however.

Research design

2.18   Sample selection is also an important issue. Although normally, probability samples are preferred, because errors can be taken into account, in many countries the market infrastructure and lack of data does not allow probability sampling to take place, because an adequate frame cannot be constructed from which the sample can be selected.

2.19   Overseas data is frequently aggregated, and, as a consequence, does not satisfy the needs of a firm which is focusing on one product. In this case, market assessment by inference becomes a useful tool. This approach uses available facts about related products or other foreign markets as a basis for deriving appropriate information.

According to Reed Moyer, three inference bases are commonly used.

(a)   Inference based on related product (eg replacement tyre market based on auto ownership).

(b)   Inference based on related market's size (eg known need in one country used as basis for estimating countries with similar economic development levels, consumption patterns and generally, scaling down statistics by population ratio).

(c)   Inference based on related environmental factors (eg similar shifts in socio/economic variables).

2.20   In many cases, researchers can use multiple factor indices. Proxies which are known to be correlated to the market potential for the product can also be employed. G D Harrell and R O Kiefer (1981), in a study employing these measures, rated countries by country attractiveness and competitive strength, using multi-factorial measures. This type of approach enables marketers to evaluate the potential of a foreign market using easy to summarise data which is picked out and reduced to a manageable form.

2.21   Despite the problems, market research is able to provide some of the information which managers need in order to make decisions and formulate plans about foreign markets. Even so, other adjustments to the product and mix may need to be made when entering a new market. Entry itself can pose acute problems

3   MARKETING ENVIRONMENT DIFFERENCES

3.1   Even between neighbouring countries (such as France and Spain, or Zimbabwe and South Africa) cultural differences can be very great. Marketing managers should always be aware of the importance of this 'silent language', as Hall referred to it. The main aspects of cultural systems which would be germane to marketing planning would be as follows.

Material culture

3.2   This affects:

(a)   the *level of demand* (eg the lack of electricity will restrict the demand for electronic items. An American firm set out to launch a best selling cake mix in the 1950s to Japan on the basis of rising disposable income and increasing popularity for things western, only to find that Japanese kitchens were not equipped with ovens in which to bake the product);

(b)   *quality and types of products demanded*. Differences in disposable income surely influences the kinds of goods which will be demanded. But note also the *symbolic* importance of particular goods which may be used for exchange but more importantly for *display* (for instance, the popularity of comparatively expensive western cigarettes and sunglasses in Communist China);

(c)   *functional/usage characteristics*. Demand for 'snack food' and the habit of 'grazing' has been stimulated in the UK by changes in the social roles of women, and in the activities which take place within the home;

(d)   the *nature of products demanded*. 'Menu meals' are a product which has been produced to help 'housewives' to prepare quality food when they cannot spare time for shopping and cooking because many are now in full time employment.

Social institutions

3.3   This relates to the social order which gives a society its distinctive form, and refers to the structures which develop around particular aspects of the life experience (for example, the care and training of children, or coping with conflict or suffering). The form of social institutions obviously has profound implications for the ways in which goods are regarded and used, since they provide the foundations for value systems and normative frameworks, and through them, attitudes and behaviour.

(a)   *Social organisation*. Tightly knit family units, in which social roles are bound up with responsibility to the family, are bound to influence both the kinds of products demanded, but also the ways in which purchase decisions are made for many types of product.

(b)   *Political structures*. Through policy, and also through example, the political system sets the agenda for consumption.

(c)   *Educational system*. Literacy is obviously a key factor in consumer access to information, and also to forms of promotional and advertising activity. Also, of course, it is a key means by which consumer tastes and ideas are formed.

(d)   *Family/household roles*. Roles played by family members in decision making are one area in which culture shapes consumption. Also, the way in which the household is actually used and regarded are very important for consumption (the modern household actually forms the focus for leisure activity far more than it did in the past).

Cosmology

3.4   This covers *beliefs and religious, philosophical, and political ideologies*. Generalised belief systems are all pervasive, even in societies which consider themselves secularised. Our holidays and gift giving occasions are formed around the old religious calendar; the foods we eat reflect moral and aesthetic judgements as much as nutritional good sense. Many religions proscribe particular forms of consumption, from coffee and alcoholic drinks, to 'provocative' clothes or licentious music. In Japan, notions of what advertising should aim to do are quite different, and open claims to be 'superior' to other products would be regarded as shocking and in questionable taste.

Aesthetics

3.5   What counts as beauty or ugliness is tied into quite specific values and criteria which a marketer must be aware of in relation to a foreign culture. Marketing to Japan or India, for instance, brings into play different cultural sensitivities on, for instance, sex, where attitudes are quite different to those in the west.

Language

3.6   Marketing literature is full of examples where marketers committed horrendous *faux pas* because of ignorance of the subtleties of language. The marketing of 'Cue' toothpaste in French-speaking Canada failed because the brand name sounds exactly like a very rude French colloquialism. The number 4 (shi) in Japanese also serves as the word for death, and needs to be avoided. In India, numerology is also part of the everyday knowledge, so that numbers have meanings (6, for instance, is 'hijira', the eunuch). Even English speakers may vary in their usage of a common language. A useful electronic monitoring device for small children has yet to be marketed in the UK, but the US brand name will have to be changed. It is called the 'Little Bugger'.

3.7   Advertising slogans, then, need to beware of the pitfalls of the local language games; successful slogans may not work in another language, or may be unintentionally funny or offensive. Since marketers often struggle to find the right language in which to talk to their own customer, this is an ever greater problem for international marketers.

4   REGIONAL TRADE ALLIANCES AND MARKETS

4.1   Trade between nations is of such significance that rules and regulations governing the performance of international trade have to be agreed and established. The experience of the 1930s where protectionism led to depression on a worldwide scale, and the subsequent second World War partly brought about by the depression, has lead the major economic powers to consider the necessity of regulating government intervention in the world market.

4.2   There are two opposing pressures that affect the nature of world trade:

(a)   the desire to expand the domestic economy by trading with other nations; and
(b)   the desire to protect indigenous sources of employment by restricting imports.

Regional trading groups

4.3   Whilst world trading bodies such as GATT encourage free trade, the opposite force of protectionism has led to the creation of regional trading organisations, seeking to encourage trade between members but at the same time introducing barriers to prevent non-members trading within the group. An example is the EU.

4.4   These regional trading groups can take progressively more integrated forms.

(a)   Free trade areas.
(b)   Customs unions.
(c)   Economic unions.

Free trade areas

4.5   The most primitive form of regional trade association, has members who agree to lower barriers to trade amongst themselves. There is little other form of economic cooperation. Examples include, in South America, Mercosur and the Andean Pact. In underdeveloped countries attempts to form such associations have led to problems as members seek to protect their embryo economies, and fear the effects of free trade with member states. A recent example is the North American Free Trade Agreement, comprising Canada, the USA and Mexico.

Customs unions

4.6   Customs unions not only provide the advantages of free trade areas, but also agree a common policy on tariff and non-tariff barriers to external countries and internally attempt to harmonise tariffs, taxes and duties amongst members to encourage free trade. Currently the EU is the leading example of this type of union, and is seen as the prototype for other unions elsewhere.

Economic unions

4.7   The ultimate step is the submission of all decisions relating to trade both internal and external from sovereign member states to the union itself. In effect the members become one for economic purposes. Prior to the dissolution of the USSR, COMECON was perhaps the leading example. The EU has economic union as an aim, although not all members, including the UK, necessarily see this goal as desirable. Economic unions are potentially powerful. The EU has a 'rich' market of over 300 million people and could provide a formidable problem to non-EU countries such as the USA and Japan.

4.8   The effect of regional trade organisations, such as the EU is yet to be felt. On the one hand, trade within the community will no doubt be easier and freer, opening up significant opportunities to importer and exporter alike. On the other hand, those outside the community will find it more difficult to compete on even terms due to the tariff barriers being introduced to protect EU members.

4.9   For a country like the UK membership may then bring mixed blessings.

(a)   Over 50% of UK foreign trade is with other EU members, and the development of the EU will expand such trade and make it easier.

(b)   However our largest market in terms of a single country is the USA, which takes some 13% of UK exports. The EU barriers to non-members such as the USA, may result in retaliatory action, resulting in a reduction in EU member trade with countries such as the USA. The net result could be a trade war between the major economic blocs, and a diminution in world trade.

4.10   One significant effect of regional trade blocs has been the rush to qualify for member status by multinational firms. This has been achieved by the multinationals setting up assembly or manufacturing plant within one or more member states, rather than importing into the EU. Thus France, Germany and the UK have seen considerable inward investment from US and Japanese firms, trying to avoid the barriers being set in place from 1993. In the case of the EU, assembly is not sufficient. EU goods must be 80% sourced within the community to qualify as EU produced and thus avoid tariffs and quotas.

5   PRODUCT

To standardise or to customise?

5.1   Products developed and successfully marketed within one country cannot necessarily be moved 'tout court' into an alien market without problems. Since a product is composed of many different attributes - which will include physical dimensions such as its shape, colour, smell, and so on, but also symbolic and psychological aspects such as the image or personality of the product, the associations and meanings involved in its name or selling proposition, and so on, entry into a market with a different set of cultural, religious, economic, social and political factors may create, at best, infelicities, and at worst, extreme offence in reactions to part or all of a product concept or marketing mix.

5.2   The problem derives from an inherent tension between two important ideas in marketing. Target marketing and segmentation suggest that the way to maximise sales is to identify specific consumer needs (that is, to *adapt* a product for a new foreign market).

At the same time, it is clearly impractical to create separate products for every conceivable segment, since it is more profitable (less costly) to produce a *standardised* product for a larger market segment (composed of different national markets). This is resolved by considering the costs and benefits of alternative marketing strategies, and opting for that which offers greatest profitability.

5.3   Arguments *in favour of product standardisation* include the following.

(a)   *Economies of scale* in

    (i)   *Production*

        (1)   Plant probably confined to one country rather than duplicated.
        (2)   Plant expansion may attract 'home' government grants or other support.
        (3)   Plant used to maximum capacity offers best return on its costs.
        (4)   Exporting rather that difficult licensing deals.

    (ii)   *Research and development*. Product modification, such as that needed to tailor products to specific foreign markets, is costly and time consuming in an area where resources are always jealously husbanded.

    (iii)   *Marketing*. Promotion which can use the same images and theme in advertising is clearly more cost effective when only the soundtrack, or the printed slogan, has to be changed. Similarly, if distribution systems, salesforce training, aftersales provisions, and other aspects of the product mix can be standardised, this saves a great deal of money.

(b)   *Consumer mobility*. Finding a familiar brand name is important for the growing numbers of travellers moving across what are, in any case, diminishing national boundaries.

(c)   *Technological complexity*. The microelectronics market illustrates inherent danger of diversity in technically complex products. Even the endorsement of powerful Japanese companies could not sustain the Betamax VCR system or non-standard PC systems. The international market selected VHS and IBM respectively.

Exercise

What are the arguments in favour of product adaptation?

Solution

Arguments in favour of product adaptation include the following.

(a)   *Greater sales potential*, where this also means greater profitability, which it may not!

(b)   *Varied conditions of product use* which may force a company to modify its product. These may include:

    (i)   climatic variations (corrosion in cars produced for dry climates);

    (ii)   literacy or skill levels of users (languages which can be used on a computer);

    (iii)   cultural, social, or religious factors (religious or cultural requirements for food products - Halal slaughtering of New Zealand lamb for Middle Eastern Markets, for instance - or dolphin-friendly tuna catching methods for Europe and the USA).

(c)   *Variation in market factors*. Consumer needs are in their nature idiosyncratic, and there are likely to be distinctive requirements for each group not met by a standard product.

(d)   *Governmental or political influence*. Political factors may force a company to produce a local product through:

    (i)   taxation;
    (ii)   legislation; or
    (iii)   pressure of public opinion.

(e)   Local competition.

Lack of information on the characteristics of the target markets

5.4   Often, there is little information on the differences between groups within the population towards which advertising and promotion is being targeted. This is, of course, critical for decisions about the medium to be employed, and decisions such as standardisation/adaptation.

New products in international markets

5.5   Product ideas, both internally and externally generated, must be screened in order to identify potentially marketable and profitable products. This involves:

(a)   attracting applicants with new products;
(b)   identifying those which are commercially viable.

5.6   Product screening may be carried out at a centralised location, although this poses the threat of alienating management at remote subsidiary plants at which many ideas may originate. If this does cause problems, some measure of decentralisation in the screening process may be necessary.

Criteria for product screening

5.7   The firm must be capable of:

(a)   *producing the product*. This may involve existing resources (staff and machinery) or involve the firm in realistic diversification;

(b)   *marketing the product*. If this can be accommodated within existing marketing resources, then so much the better. Formulating a new system could involved substantial outlay and disruption;

(c)   *researching the new market*. This might involve the deployment of existing resources, particularly if (as is likely) the firm is already established, and operating in a related area. This will involve economies of scale, and reduce uncertainties through pre-existing awareness of competitor activity. If there is no related market involvement, the criteria for product screening (competition, prices, profitability) remain the same, although there is greater uncertainty and hence risk;

(d)   *marketing internationally*. Orientation to a specific market will reduce the economies of scale involved in multinational marketing. Products are likely to be rejected if they cannot be produced for international markets;

(e)   *motivated to introduce and market the new product effectively*. What are the reasons for the new product being introduced and how well adjusted is the organisation to this process?

(f)   *organisationally suited to marketing the new product*. Are, for example, suitable support and maintenance systems available?

Product screening in practice

5.8   International firms exist because operations spread across several countries reduce risk. The more diverse the operations of the firm, however, the more difficult to co-ordinate; the loss of continuity in the operations of the firm's subsidiaries threatens its existence. This is an important consideration in product screening.

A checklist for new products

5.9   Some factors can be assigned a variable weighting, since they are likely to be of varying important in differing circumstances. Some are critical, and are unlikely to change in that respect. Failure in any of these areas will disqualify a product for international marketing.

5.10 The product must:

(a) fall within a company's term of incorporation (critical);

(b) be profitable in the short term (variable weight);

(c) be profitable in the long term (critical);

(d) have a realistic payback period (1 - 3 years) (variable weight);

(e) be distinct from previously patented products (critical);

(f) be protected by patent or trademark in all overseas markets (variable weight);

(g) comply with all/most national safety standards (variable weight);

(h) be compliant with and profitable when taking into account import duties and regulations (variable weight);

(i) be capable of being produced in a number of countries (variable weight);

(j) be able to be introduced in either a standardised, or suitably adapted form.

5.11 All of these depend on the corporate goals and strategy of the parent company, which may well shift over time. As a consequence, the relative significance of these items is likely to vary markedly.

6   PLACE

Distribution to international markets

6.1 A range of factors affect the selection, establishment, and running of international distribution systems. For example, a wide range of channels can be developed.

6.2 Using an *Export Management Company* can be an attractive alternative.

(a) Key players in this process are the home channel members and the Export Management Company (EMC), which handles all aspects of exporting under contract.

(b) When this strategy is followed, minimal investment and no company personnel are involved. The EMC already has an established network of sales offices, and extensive international marketing and distribution knowledge.

(c) From the company's point of view, however, there is a loss of control.

6.3 Another alternative is *export agents*. These provide more limited services than EMCs, are focused on one country and do not perform EMC marketing tasks; concentrating on physical movement of products. The main problem here is that a company requires several to cover a range of markets.

6.4 *Direct exporting* is attractive in many ways. In-house personnel are used, but the company needs well trained and experienced staff in order to carry out the function adequately. At the same time, the volume of sales must be sufficient to justify employing staff.

6.5 In other strategies, foreign channel members become important. *Import middlemen*, who are experts in their local market needs, can play a key part, being able to source goods from the world market to satisfy local needs. They operate to purchase goods in own name, and act independently of the manufacturer. They are able to exploit a good access route to wholesale/retail networks.

6.6 *Local wholesalers or agents* also play a key role. Here the intensity of transfer to retail/consumer sector is very important.

Developing an international distribution strategy

6.7   As in domestic marketing, there must be consistency of purpose in the way in which elements within the marketing mix operate. Four key strategic decisions are involved, as follows.

(a)   Distribution density (intensity) - exposure or coverage desired.

(b)   Channel length - number of intermediaries to be used.

(c)   Channel alignment and leadership - structure and hierarchy relationships of the channel.

(d)   Distribution logistics - physical flow of product.

Distribution density/intensity

6.8   *Distribution density/intensity* depends on a knowledge of how customers select dealers and retail outlets, by segment. If less shopping effort is involved (as in the case of convenience goods) an extensive system would be appropriate. If more shopping effort is used (eg the case of premium priced goods) then a selective/exclusive system would be required.

Channel members

6.9   *Factors influencing the choice of channel members* are also critical. After strategy has been formulated, marketers must select channel partners capable of implementing the overall strategy. Since it can be difficult to change partners once contracted, this choice is very sensitive indeed. Key selection criteria are likely to include:

(a)   cost;
(b)   capital requirement;
(c)   product and product line;
(d)   control;
(e)   coverage;
(f)   synergy.

6.10   *Cost* falls into three categories. The initial cost of locating and setting up channel, maintenance costs to employ sales people, sales managers, travel expenses, auditing/controlling, profit margin paid to middlemen), and logistics costs - what is involved in transportation, storage, breaking bulk, customs administration and so on.

6.11   W J Bilkey found that the least profitable approach was that of direct exporting to retailers in the host country. The most profitable involved selling to a distributor in a country with its own marketing channels. Capital requirement here - inventories, goods in transit, accounts receivable - is offset by cash flow pattern. In order to arrive at the right decision, these costs must be evaluated between channels. For example, an import distributor will often pay for goods received before they are sold on to the retailer or industrial. An agent, however, may well not pay anything until payment by the end customer.

6.12   *Product and product line* is also relevant. Perishable or short shelf-life products need shorter channels, and this bears on costs and hence profits. High tech products require either direct sales effort or skilled and knowledgeable channel partners.

6.13   *Synergy* is the term often used to describe the complementarity between components within a system which produces more than the sum of their individual parts. In the choice of channel members, such complementarity may increase the total output of the distribution system, if, for example, the chosen partner has some key skill which allows quicker access to the market.

6.14 Compaq's strategy in the internal PC market involves careful selection and training of a network of strongly motivated authorised dealers, rather than depending on 'mail order' and price competition, as have many of their competitors. This results in a highly successful rise to cater for around 10% of the world market at one stage, in spite of IBM dominance.

Logistics

6.15 International logistics management involves very sensitive decisions too. Logistics systems are expensive and can be very damaging to corporate profitability if badly handled. International logistics decision areas are:

(a) traffic/transportation management;
(b) inventory control;
(c) order processing;
(d) materials handling and warehousing;
(e) fixed facilities location management.

6.16 *Traffic/transportation management* deals primarily with the main mode of transport involved in moving goods. Three main criteria are employed in this choice - lead times, transit time and costs.

6.17 *Inventory control* relates to the level of inventory accessible insofar as this affects service levels. Since this involves tying up potential profit in the form of capital, management aim here is to reduce inventories to an absolute minimum. Just in Time (JIT) deliveries of parts and components has become increasingly important, partly due to the influence of Japanese ideas. Rank Xerox used to keep buffer stocks of 40 days and an inventory of finished goods of 90 days. Now, many JIT parts and components are not kept in stock, and the company maintains a finished goods inventory of only 15 days. This is clearly a global trend in distribution systems as markets and money become increasingly squeezed by ever fiercer competition.

6.18 There are five key global trends in international distribution. *Larger scale retailers* are partly a consequence of economic development and growing affluence. Increasing car ownership, increasing fridge/freezer ownership and the changing role of women all make time spent on shopping and 'food provisioning' rather than other activities such as working or leisure, less attractive, and militate towards the growth of larger scale retailing. 'One-stop shopping' in supermarkets is now the order of the day. Tesco has shut down two-thirds of its small in-town stores (less than 10,000 square feet) in favour of larger stores. This is a global trend deriving from a reduction in distribution costs and increased sophistication of retailers.

6.19 *International retailers* have developed for the same reasons. Companies saw limited growth opportunities at home, and moved to overseas markets. This allows manufacturers to build relationships with retailers active in a number of different markets. This internationalisation process is prompted by improved data communications, new forms of international financing, more open international markets and lower barriers to entry. In the EU for instance, the Single European Market motivates retailers to expand overseas, as they see international retailers entering their domestic markets.

6.20 *Direct marketing* is growing rapidly all over the world. This has been encouraged by the visible example of Japanese distribution. Systems demonstrating the possibility of bypassing the wholesale - retail network, and going direct to customers. This is a burgeoning area.

6.21 Non-store retailing in Japan is expected to grow from 10 billion US dollars in 1992 to 62 billion US dollars in 1998, including catalogue sales, door-to-door and on-line shopping by videotex.

Information technology has had an enormous impact. Computerised retail systems allow better monitoring of consumer purchases, lower inventory costs and quicker stock turns alongside a better assessment of product profitability. They also make it possible to extend JIT ideas into the area of retailing.

6.22 Market communications face additional barriers to overcome in non-domestic situations. In developing an effective promotional mix, experience plays a key role. Costs and the overall effectiveness of measures are also important considerations, however. The international environment affects decision making here in several ways. The elements to be considered are as follows.

(a) *Push-oriented strategy*. In a domestic setting, this emphasises personal selling rather than advertising as key factor and may be more expensive if employed abroad. Also, effectiveness may be affected by the preparedness level of foreign prospects, their sophistication and also their product awareness. Purchase effort and task category, for example, may be quite different for non-domestic companies than for domestic companies.

What may involve minor equipment or supplies in large UK firms and limited involvement purchasing, may be 'major equipment' and require more involved personal selling effort when this is used overseas.

The cost of maintaining a salesforce abroad is also a major consideration, as is the length of channel. A long non-domestic channel, involving many non-domestic intermediaries, reduces the effect of personal selling, and poses severe control problems.

(b) *Pull-oriented strategy* is characterised by a greater dependence upon advertising directed at the end user, and is typically employed for FMCG marketing, where very large market segments are involved. It is dictated by the economies involved in the use of mass communication to reach customers, and is generally more appropriate for long channels where relatively simple products are being sold. Self-service is the predominant shopping behaviour here, and clearly there are bound to be variations in its application in international markets. Not all countries have the same access to advertising media, for example, and the quality of media varies greatly. Channel lengths too are likely to play an important role, coupled with the leverage (power in the channel).

7   PRICE

Getting the price right

7.1 Prices in foreign markets are likely to be determined by local conditions, with each market separate. In this way, foreign market pricing is quite distinct from transfer pricing issues.

The degree of control which the firm exercises over pricing is likely to be dependent on whether it has wholly owned subsidiaries in each of the markets (in which case control is greater) or conducts business through a licensee, franchisee or distributor (in which case there is likely to be little control).

7.2 Market conditions are the most important influence on pricing. Other factors would include the following.

(a) *Cost:* full cost of supply goods to consumers. Relevant costs could include administrative costs, a proportion of group overheads, manufacturing costs, distribution and retailing costs.

(b) *Inflation*, particularly in the target market and in raw material suppliers.

(c) *Demand,* which is a product of local taste, price, disposable income and competition. As a consequence, demand curves will be distinct for each individual market. Only the selling price is under the influence of the firm. Important information here is the demand curve and the price elasticity of demand. Profits will be maximised when production reaches a point when MC = MR.

(d) *Official regulations*. Governments may well intervene to prevent the implementation of uniform pricing policies. This may involve *acceptable* measures such as import duties and tariffs, and generally *unacceptable* measures such as non-tariff barriers, import quotas and price freezes. Price controls may also be used, and this will affect the ability of marketers to plan prices effectively.

(e) *Competition*. 'Price leaders' may well be undercut by competitors. The effectiveness of this policy will vary according to the significance of other marketing activities, and the capacity of competitors to match these.

(f) Regional meetings of foreign distributors create related markets, which in turn lead to uniformity in prices.

7.3 The diversity of markets within a country is important. If markets are unrelated, the seller can successfully charge different prices. Pressures for price uniformity often come from large groupings such as free trade areas or the EU. Pressure for price uniformity also comes from increases in international business activity. Control over prices which may be operated by the company would include:

(a) direct distribution to customers;
(b) resale price maintenance;
(c) recommended prices;
(d) agreed margins between parent and subsidiary companies;
(e) centralised control over prices within several subsidiary companies.

8   PROMOTION

8.1 Elements of the promotional mix which may be important include the following.

8.2 *Sales promotions* may be variously affected by different retailing norms and government regulations. For example, coupons, much used in the UK and the USA, are prohibited in Germany and Greece. Frequently 'games of chance' are prohibited but 'games of skill' may be allowed. Reductions in price promotions are often restricted to a percentage of full price. As a consequence, standardising sales promotion tools is extremely difficult. Sales promotions are usually handed over to local experts.

8.3 *Sports promotions and sponsorships* are widely used. The key methods involved are advertising during sports programming on TV, positioning of stadium or arena signs and sponsorship of individuals, teams or events. What type is used depends on the country involved, the circumstances and regulations which they apply. In Germany, for example, TV advertising cannot be used within sports shows so alternative approaches are needed.

8.4 This is an effective approach. During the 1990 football World Cup (in Italy), over the course of eight weeks, 24 national teams were watched by 15 billion viewers with 9 billion exposures for sponsoring companies. Major sponsors, including Coca-Cola, Mars, Gillette, Canon, Fuji-Film, Philips, Anheuser-Busch and Carlsberg, gained excellent exposure. It is important to choose the sport correctly. As the 1994 World Cup has shown, soccer still has limited commercial value in the USA itself, although the programme has proved immensely popular and a powerful vehicle for promotion in most of the rest of the world. Sponsoring teams can be very powerful, as can linking with a sports star such as basketball player Michael Jordan (Nike).

8.5 *Direct marketing*, in which the customer is contacted by direct mail, is used. Door-to-door selling, or telemarketing, doubled in the UK, the Benelux countries, Scandinavia and France during the 1980s. It is also growing rapidly in Singapore, Hong King, Malaysia, whilst in the USA direct marketing accounts for two thirds of total consumer spending, and one third in Europe. Clearly, this will be an important area for international marketing in the future

Advertising abroad - is the message OK?

8.6 International advertising has its own specific problems, as well as sharing those faced by advertisers in one single market. Often conditions vary greatly *within* a country (as they may, for example, in rapidly developing countries with great differences in the levels of wealth and the types of lifestyle enjoyed by the population). If possible, marketing managers would wish to use essentially the same advertising in as many different countries as possible. There are some factors which encourage this.

(a) The widespread international ownership of TV sets

(b) The growing importance of satellite and cable systems

There are, however, factors which encourage local adaptation.

(a) Very localised tastes (eg food and drink)

(b) Differences in the availability of media

(c) Problems in translating advertising messages (an English ad runs 15% longer in French, 50% longer in German)

The general response is to use broadly the same approach, but given a 'twist' which customises the campaign for specific audiences.

8.7 *Media problems* are likely to relate to the following.

(a) *Availability*. Media may be more important and effective in some countries than in others (for instance, cinema in India, radio in the USA), while there may be a lack of specific media in others.

   (i) Newspapers may not be widely available because of low levels of literacy, or even specific policies on the part of the government.

   (ii) Magazines, which are so important for specialist products, such as industrial machinery, may be very restricted.

   (iii) TV commercials are restricted, or even banned in many countries, for instance advertising specifically directed at children is banned in some Scandinavian countries. It is also sometimes very difficult to gauge effectiveness because of missing or incomplete MR data.

   (iv) Billboards, direct mail and other forms of promotion may be unfamiliar or ineffective (there is very limited usage of billboards in some formerly communist countries).

(b) *Financial aspects*. Costs may be very difficult to estimate in many countries, since negotiation and the influence of intermediaries is likely to be much greater. There may also be expectations of gift-giving in the negotiation process.

(c) *Coverage of media (or 'reach' of advertising message)*. This relates to the forms of media employed as well as the physical characteristics of the country. Inaccessible areas may rule out the use of direct mail, or posters; scarcity of telephones may rule out this form of advertising promotion. It may also be difficult to monitor advertising effectiveness.

9 STRUCTURE CHOICES

9.1 There are five basic alternatives when entering a foreign market.

(a) *Simple exporting*, often based on the need to dispose of excess production for a domestic market, is the commonest form of export activity. The main reasons are:

(b) The second main form is *licensing*. This may take a number of forms.

   (i) Patent rights
   (ii) Trademark rights to use technological process

(c) *Franchising* is the third main option. It is very similar to licensing, in terms of advantages and disadvantages, ie, there is minimal risk, but also modest returns. *Joint ventures* are more likely to produce good returns, but they are much riskier.

(d) *Trading companies*

(e) *Manufacturing abroad*

9.2 Circumstances dictate the choice, or the solution forced upon a company making a strategic decision about methods of entry. When considering exporting for the first time a company has to decide upon the degree of involvement which is appropriate and the level of commitment. Some companies get into exporting by default, for example by being asked to supply spares directly to a third party overseas; some companies' commitment to exporting varies according to the condition of the main, home market; and some companies are serious about international marketing to the extent that the majority of their turnover comes from overseas and major investments are made in production facilities abroad.

Exporting

9.3 This approach involves minimum effort, cost and risk. It involves a low level of commitment and is relatively flexible. Exporting can be direct to buyers in foreign countries or (more normally) through export organisations of various kinds. An export agent acts as an intermediary between buyers and sellers, taking a commission from the transactions. Export merchants/export houses buy products from different companies and sell them to other countries.

9.4 In most cases these export organisations have long-established contacts in foreign countries and a purchasing headquarters in, say, London. The exporter thus deals in English, under the English legal system, gets paid by a resident bank, is not involved in shipping and may not have to alter products in any way. It is simple and risk free, but naturally the rewards are not as potentially great as other options.

9.5 Most small companies start exporting in this way before deepening their commitment.

Licensing

9.6 This is where a company, say, in the UK, licenses a company overseas to manufacture and/or sell its goods in the overseas country.

9.7 Benefits are clearcut, for example there is a small capital outlay. This approach is favoured by small/medium companies. It is, however, the least profitable method of entry, although it has the least associated risks, and provides a means of positively approaching export decision making and planning.

9.8 The licensee pays a royalty on every product item produced or sold in addition to a lump sum paid for the license. Licensing is used particularly when local manufacture, technical assistance and market knowledge offers great advantages. It is of course an alternative to investing directly in overseas manufacture/distribution and particularly advantageous if an overseas country should be politically unstable.

9.9 Licensing is also attractive for medium-sized companies wishing to launch a successful home market brand internationally. Fashion houses such as Yves St Laurent and Pierre Cardin have issued hundreds of licenses and Löwenbrau has expanded sales worldwide through this method without having to expend capital building its own breweries overseas.

Joint ventures

9.10 These have become particularly prevalent since the advent of the EC. Typically, they involve collaboration with one or more foreign firms.

(a)   Increasing in popularity

    (b)   Reduced economic and political risks

    (c)   'Ready made' partner's distribution system

    (d)   Access - may be the only way to gain entry to foreign markets

9.11 For example, a German furniture manufacturer may seek a joint venture or partnership with a British furniture manufacturer to sell each others' ranges or indeed to sell a combined range in other EC countries. Control is usually, but not always, split equally. Joint ventures may be used because of government restrictions on foreign ownership.

9.12 Quite a number of vehicle manufacturers have initiated joint ventures or their similar structural form, strategic alliances, including Rover with Honda, Chrysler with Mitsubishi and Alfa Romeo with both Nissan and Fiat.

9.13 In some high technology industries, strategic alliances have been growing at an estimated rate of 20 per cent annually, because of fierce competition and the prohibitive costs of single resourcing.

Trading companies

9.14 This structure avoids involvement in manufacturing. A trading company simply buys in one country and sells to buyers in another country. It will sometimes also act as a consultant advising buyers and sellers on market conditions, quality/price issues etc. For example, long-established trading companies control much of the world's food market for commodities such as cereals or indeed any other items that are able to be stored in bulk and moved rapidly in response to shortages.

Direct ownership

9.15 Where commitment is total and long-term and especially when an overseas country is relatively politically stable and possessing strong growth potential, then direct ownership of an overseas company (manufacturing and/or distributing) becomes attractive.

9.16 Manufacturing abroad has the following features.

    (a)   Establishing manufacturing facility in host country.

    (b)   High level of commitment.

    (c)   Only justified by very heavy demand.

    (d)   Advantages.

        (i)   Lower labour costs

        (ii)   Avoidance of import taxes

        (iii)   Lower transport costs

    (e)   Disadvantages.

        (i)   Significant commitment

        (ii)   Higher involvement levels

        (iii)   Higher levels of risk

9.17 Multinationals, ie global marketers, will have directly owned subsidiaries in many countries. These can offer considerable operating and tax advantages. Some car manufacturers such as General Motors and Ford actually import cars built by foreign subsidiaries.

Chapter roundup

- International marketing is an increasingly important area of marketing, as companies develop their international operations for a number of reasons. There is a range of specific problems to be addressed.

- In order to develop an effective marketing plan, information about the markets into which the company intends to go is essential. In the case of domestic markets, the normal step would be to undertake research which would provide that information. International marketing, however, requires a different approach to marketing research, and presents its own peculiar problems.

- The marketing environment is different in international marketing. Most aspects of cultural systems vary between countries, sometimes quite significantly.

- International marketing operations are affected by regional trade alliances and markets.

- As regards product, the basic question concerns standardisation or adaptation (customisation)

- Distribution is a complex issue in international marketing, and a wide range of channels can be identified.

- Prices in foreign markets are likely to be determined by local conditions, with each market separate. In this way, foreign market pricing is quite distinct from transfer pricing issues.

- Elements of the promotional mix must also be considered.

- There are five basic alternatives for structure when entering a foreign market.

Test your knowledge

1 Why do companies enter into international marketing? (see para 1.1)

2 What are Morden's 12Cs? (1.2)

3 What is the significance of material culture in international marketing? (3.2)

4 What are the two main opposing pressures on the regulation of international trade? (4.2)

5 What are the arguments in favour of product standardisation? (5.3)

6 What is product screening? (5.5)

7 What factors influence the choice of channel members? (6.9)

8 Distinguish between a push-oriented strategy and a pull-oriented strategy. (6.22)

9 What factors influence pricing decisions? (7.2)

10 What media problems may arise in international marketing? (8.7)

11 What is licensing? (9.6 - 9.9)

Now try illustrative question 13 at the end of the Study Text

MARKETING OPERATIONS IN ACTION

At the end of each part of this Study Text, we take a look at the subject matter covered in the light of real companies, either to offer more detail, or to give an understanding of the wider corporate context.

One of the topics which we looked at in this part of the Text was charity marketing. Charity marketing has come a long way from the increasingly outdated view of charity marketers as enthusiastic amateurs, and many charities now employ marketing tactics which commercial organisations could certainly learn from.

Many charities have operated in a market of strict financial accountability for longer than their commercial counterparts. 'Administrative' costs are seen as negative, in that, although clearly essential, they prevent the whole amount donated from reaching the intended beneficiaries of charitable giving. Because the identification and recruitment of new donors is expensive, some charities have concentrated on building databases of existing supporters.

As Anne Masset, writing in *Marketing Business* (March 1995) reports, some charities have concluded that, because some donors give more generously or more frequently than others, they are worth mailing more often. Donor-base segmentation, whereby donors are segmented according to 'recency', 'value' and 'frequency' of gifts, is achieving recognition.

She identifies the following areas as being those in which marketers can learn from charities.

(a)   *Track and score.* 'Fund-raisers carefully track and score their donors, examine what has happened in the past, find out why and use this knowledge to improve future performance. It is not unusual for them to come up with 30 different approaches or timings instead of doing one mailshot to the entire database, as financial marketers would do.'

(b)   *New ways with traditional techniques.* Responses to cold mailings are analysed to target suitable manes and suppress unsuitable ones from cold lists. The St Thomas Blood Transfusion Service tracks whether donors respond at the first, second or third (sometimes up to the ninth) request for blood.

(c)   *A simple and strong message.* Examples include the 'Will you give £15 to save a child's life?' approach and the asthma charity which sent out a drinking straw with a 'Breathe through this for 30 seconds to find out what it's like to have asthma' message.

(d)   *Making the budget work harder.* Charities have to be extremely careful about mailing list selections, as they have no product to sell. They also need to reach potential donors within a couple of days of harrowing media coverage of wars, disasters and natural catastrophes, as memories can be short and the media spotlight does not linger.

Part F
Legal, ethics and wider issues

Chapter 11

MARKETING ETHICS

This chapter covers the following topics.

1 Ethics and social responsibility

2 Ethics and the law

3 Customer service

4 Customer loyalty

5 Ethical issues

6 Ethical codes

Introduction

In this chapter and in Chapter 12 we focus on an area which is of increasing significance to marketers in the UK and in many other countries: the importance of marketing ethics and social responsibility. A lack of ethics can affect customer service and customer loyalty, both of which are central to successful marketing. In Chapter 12 we will develop the themes of social responsibility and the 'green' issue.

---

1 ETHICS AND SOCIAL RESPONSIBILITY

1.1 Whilst the terms marketing ethics and social responsibility are often used synonymously they are in fact quite different in context. *Social responsibility* is corporate rather than functional and concerns current expectations of society at large that organisations will act in a way which makes a maximum contribution to the public's interests. Equally society expects, but does not demand, that organisations will not act in a way which harms the general public or which is thought to be socially irresponsible.

1.2 *Marketing ethics* are on the other hand functionally specific and relate to morality rather than society's interests. Morality is essentially an individual judgement about what is right and wrong. Marketing ethics affect customers rather than society at large. Marketing ethics concern marketing decisions whereas social responsibility is about corporate decisions. It is because corporate decisions subsume marketing decisions that the terms marketing ethics and social responsibility are often used interchangeably.

The well-being of individuals and society

1.3 'It is because of the very success of business, rather than its failure, that corporations are now called upon to be more involved. The price of success for management ... will be very high. We will be expected, as a result of our success, to give leadership and direction in the major problems that face the community.'

(Peter Drucker, *The Future of Corporations*)

1.4 Many of the critics of marketing argue that it is dedicated to selling products which are potentially damaging, either to the health and well-being of the *individual,* or to the *society* in which consumers live. Obvious examples of products which are potentially damaging would include tobacco, alcohol, automobiles, detergents and even electronic goods such as computers and video recorders.

1.5 In some cases, it has been argued that even seemingly beneficial, or at least harmless, products, such as soft drinks, sunglasses or agricultural fertiliser, can damage individuals and societies. In the case of traditional societies, the introduction of new products can disrupt social order by introducing new aspirations, or changing a long established way of life or set of social relations. How should the marketer react to these problems? The main impetus for marketing activity relates to the profit motive, and there appears to be a clear conflict involved here - what is profitable for a business organisation may well not be in the interest of the customer, or the society within which the transaction involved is taking place. What is the ethical position of the marketer? To what extent should marketing be 'socially responsible'?

1.6 Ethics are the first consideration. These are the moral principles and values which guide the thinking, decision making and actions of individuals and groups within society. It is to our ethical framework that we must turn when making decisions which involve moral dilemmas.

2 ETHICS AND THE LAW

2.1 Many of the most important ethical values form the basis for legislation which governs business activity in general including marketing. However, while ethics deals with personal moral principles and values, laws express the standards of a society that can actually be enforced in court. Often, there are fine judgement to be made. If behaviour is not subject to legal penalties and seems 'reasonably' ethical, is it still acceptable?

2.2 For example, is it acceptable for NHS trusts to establish upper age limits for the treatment of resource-hungry medical conditions in order to cope with the pressures of limited budgets? Or for the RJ Reynolds Tobacco Company in the USA to specifically target Afro-Americans for a new brand of cigarette, while public health statistics show that this group has a high incidence of lung cancer and smoking related illnesses. The company maintains that this is still within the law since cigarettes are legal products.

2.3 Clearly, ethics and legality are not necessarily congruent. We can classify marketing decisions according to ethics and legality in at least four different ways.

Marketing decisions according to legality and ethical status

Ethical but illegal	Ethical and legal
Unethical and illegal	Unethical but legal

2.4 A business may be strictly operated on principles which strive to be:

(a) *ethical and legal* (eg the Body Shop);

(b) *unethical and legal* (eg selling arms to brutal military dictators);

(c) *ethical but illegal* (eg publishing stolen but revealing documents about government mismanagement);

(d) *unethical and illegal* (eg the drugs trade, employing child labour).

2.5 Public attitudes to the ethics of business have been in decline for a number of years. ('Greed is good': Gordon Gekko in the film *Wall Street*.) Surveys in both the UK and the USA show that the majority of members of the public think that business has poor ethical standards, and levels of trust are low. In the USA 90% of respondents in a recent survey thought that white collar crime was 'very common', and more than three-quarters of the sample saw tumbling business standards as an important contributor to declining moral standards within society as a whole.

Possible reasons for this perceived decline in standards are as follows.

(a) Increased pressure on business people to make decisions in a society characterised by diverse value systems. For instance, in relation to the use of animals to test products, or to the marketing of goods which have been produced using the labour of children or prisoners there are a variety of different moral and ethical standards within the population at large. This is partly due to greater awareness of such issues, compared to the past, but also because of changes in markets themselves.

(b) More business decisions are now subject to public judgement and scrutiny. There are larger numbers of groups in existence which are concerned to bring the behaviour of business to the attention of the public, more laws which require such decisions to be registered and drawn to the attention of the public, and more government interest in the nature of such decisions and the way in which they are made.

(c) Business is now subject to higher expectations regarding the ethics of its behaviour.

(d) Ethical business conduct may actually have declined.

2.6 Cultures have a strong impact on the kinds of standards which are followed within a particular society. This includes values, ideas and attitudes which have partly been handed down, and partly changed as society develops, so that it represents both a transmitted set of values and a moral standard against which we judge what is right or wrong. Consequently, we should recognise that such standards tend to be relative to specific societies. Thus restrictions on trade or price fixing are morally wrong according to certain cultural presuppositions (in, say, the USA), but look quite different from the point of view of a communist country, or one which is concerned to protect its institutions from the impact of cultural and economic change (for instance, France), or to maintain extra-legal restrictions on its home markets (such as Japan).

2.7 Different cultures view marketing practices differently. While the idea of 'copyright' or 'intellectual property' is widely accepted in Europe and the USA, in other parts of the world, ethical standards are quite different. Unauthorised use of copyrights, trademarks and patents is widespread in countries such as Taiwan, Mexico and Korea. According to a US trade official, the Korean view is that ' ... the thoughts of one man should benefit all', and this general value means that, in spite of legal formalities, few infringements of copyright are punished. This is becoming a massive problem for computer software manufacturers. Within this industry, there are what are referred to as 'one copy countries' where the 'pirating' of software is so widespread and commonplace that sales are reduced to very low levels. In many places, this rests on a general social value which finds it difficult to see this activity as illegal or fraudulent. There are even those within the computer industry who argue that this 'illegal' activity has been an important factor in the growth of that industry, since the market has been driven by the consumer demand for new products when those introduced onto the market have been tried out illegally.

3   CUSTOMER SERVICE

3.1 The idea of *customer service* grew from a focus on 'order-cycle' related activities into a much more general and all-embracing approach which covers activities at the pre-, during- and post-transaction stages. It is seen as a task, separate from proactive selling, that involves various transactions with customers.

3.2 *Customer care* is the preferred term when we are forced to consider activities which are outside the realm beyond direct contact with the customer. One commentator describes it as ' ... the ultimate marketing tool', and a critical factor in the process of differentiating products or services, to develop a competitive edge. It involves ' ... the management and identification of "moments of truth", with the aim of achieving customer satisfaction' (Thomas, 1986). These moments of truth are contacts between companies and customers, where a firm's reputation is at stake. Interaction is still a critical dimension, and the focus has moved away from specific activities to look in a general 'holistic' way at customer satisfaction.

3.3   According to Brown (1989) customer care emphasises the importance of attitude, and covers every aspect of customer/supplier relationships. Customer care is aiming to close the gap between customers' expectations and their experience. The service dimension requires a policy, and a set of activities. Most analysts distinguish between the *concept* and the *scope* of customer care activities. In a definition which covers both these areas, Clutterbuck describes customer care as

> '... a fundamental approach to the standards of service quality. It covers every aspect of a company's operations, from the design of a product or service to how it is packaged, delivered and serviced'.

3.4   The new focus on the service dimension, whether it is referred to as 'customer care or not, involves a *culture change*. It is a core value for all policymaking and strategic thinking. Some see the difference between 'customer care' and the more traditional notion of 'customer service' in the degree of centrality, this is given within the process of formulating corporate policies, objectives and strategies - a difference in emphasis, rather than significant substantive differences in theory or practice.

3.5   Modern strategic marketing begins and ends with the customer - yet service levels may well be overlooked in the pursuit of broader, more abstract objectives. It should be clear that unethical behaviour, even though it may appear beneficial to the company, can only serve to damage the customer relationship in the longer term.

4   CUSTOMER LOYALTY

4.1   Service levels and the pursuit of quality, or TQM, are closely related to each other. Quality programmes, however, cover many topics in addition to those dealing with customers. Customer care programmes, which seek to promote the achievement of service levels, focus on gaining deep knowledge of customers, and aim to identify their needs and improve care provided for them. Care is the outcome of this process, and 'satisfied customers' are the focus of customer care programmes. The challenge is to maintain this emphasis throughout a quality process. Satisfied customers are likely to be *loyal* customers.

4.2   Three principles guide customer-supplier relationships under TQM.

(a)   Recognition of the strategic importance of customers and suppliers.
(b)   Development of win-win relationships between customers and suppliers.
(c)   Establishing relationships based on trust.

4.3   These principles are translated into practice by:

(a)   constantly collecting information on customer expectations;

(b)   disseminating this information widely within the organisation;

(c)   using the information to design, produce and deliver the organisation product and services.

4.4   TQM programmes require the following conditions to be fulfilled.

(a)   *Total involvement from staff.* This is another way of talking about a structural or a cultural change being essential for the achievement of a quality programme. Often, these schemes are presented as 'a philosophy of life' or a 'total way of thinking' rather than just another technique for management. It is a peculiar feature of these systems that they have a religious, or messianic quality - advocates are spoken of as 'evangelists' or, more commonly, 'gurus'. It is perhaps unsurprising that the generation which toyed with transcendental meditation and flower power in the sixties should focus on gurus of a different kind in the nineties!

For this system to work, however, it is a practical necessity for all members to be involved. Those best placed to make quality work are the people who actually carry out the processes which are involved in delivering products or services. In addition, partial quality improvements will constantly face the problems created by those parts of the system which have not been reformed when staff are trying to improve the quality of what they deliver to customers.

(b) *A customer orientation*. As suggested above, each internal group in the quality chain is comprised of a customer and/or supplier to other internal groups, and in some cases to the market. Although programmes can start at any point in this chain, even if the quality of the supply to a group is low, the group should aim to build up its own quality before addressing the shortcomings of its own supplier.

Note how a 'customer orientation' under TQM, focuses not just on the external customer, but on the customer-supplier relationship which is a general feature of marketing *processes*. Customer care programmes, although focused on external customers, are important influences on the way in which such processes are conceived and practised.

(c) *Defining customer requirements and obligations*. From the viewpoint of an organisation, customers can be thought of as an agglomeration of *requirements and obligations*. Customers may be external customers, but also employees, shareholders, top management, government and so on. Requirements will be fitted to resource constraints, and the objectives of the organisation, and must be realistic and obtainable. Obligations need to be clearly defined, and requirements need to be quantified, and accepted by both sides as reasonable. If a customer care programme is to be effective, the relations must be clearly specified on both sides.

(d) *Measurement*. This is extremely important for any quality programme, and in relation to customer care, measurements must be continual and ubiquitous. Required performance needs to be clearly specified in terms which can be measured, and mechanisms must be instituted which provide clear indicators that they have been achieved. These must be in place before programmes are instigated.

Customer care programmes will require survey data on internal and external customers, on customer behaviour, and on the degree to which customer needs are being satisfied. These should permit the application of techniques such as key ratio and trend analysis, and fit into a cycle of assessment and planning.

(e) *Commitment from the top management*. Top management need to ensure that the programme is delivered, and also that it provides the cash payoff from improve quality in customer service.

(f) *Adherence to standard processes and procedures*. Processes and procedures which are developed and specified as an end product of a TQM customer care programme are intended to be followed. Such directions are intended to reproduce proven consistent quality, and should specify administered processes, timing, responsibility and areas of expertise, gathering feedback data. When these strictures are adhered to, the output remains consistent, processes are appropriately monitored, and the data provides the basis for learning and consistent improvement.

(g) *Paying customer objectives*. The end product of any programme must be to satisfy the needs of the paying customer in order to accomplish particular commercial, financial or strategic objectives. To that end, all analysis within customer care programmes must relate to these objectives. Examples of such objectives would be:

(i) increasing sales and profits;
(ii) lowering prices of service provision;
(iii) improving customer perceptions of service;
(iv) shortening waiting lists and prioritising customer needs.

The mission of the organisation, and the corporate values which underlie corporate objectives, must always be clearly and directly related to the formulation of such objectives. If they are not, then TQM programmes will not accord with the strategic direction which has been agreed.

4.5 Again, it should be clear that unethical behaviour can damage customer loyalty.

5   ETHICAL ISSUES

5.1   An ethical issue in marketing can be defined as an identifiable problem, situation or opportunity requiring an individual or organisation to choose from among several actions that must be evaluated as right or wrong, ethical or unethical.

5.2   Examples include the following.

(a)   *Product issues*. When the French company Perrier discovered that its mineral water was in danger of contamination, they immediately withdrew all supplies without quibble, involving huge losses. By acting ethically, the company's market was eventually restored and if anything, its reputation was enhanced.

Motor car manufacturers who try to hide design faults that could be dangerous are acting unethically.

(b)   *Promotional issues*. It was because so many companies were acting unethically with regard to marketing communications that the Trade Descriptions Act 1968 came into being. Estate agents were often greatly exaggerating the attributes of properties to the extent that it almost became accepted as a joke and there is now a Property Misdescriptions Act 1994 designed to curtail their worst excesses. Second hand car dealers were not seen as much better. However, the 'angle' on communications can be more subtle, such as the Spiller's Homepride Flour slogan 'Finer grains make finer flour'. The advertisements gave the impression that the flour was made from smaller grains whereas the grains were actually made larger by a process of coagulation. Upon challenge, Spillers claimed they were using the word 'finer' in the dictionary sense of being better.

In the promotional area of personal selling many people think that persuading people to buy something they don't really want is intrinsically unethical, especially if hard sell tactics are used, or downright deception, such as the switch selling of vacuum cleaners by door-to-door salesmen.

(c)   *Distribution issues*. Some manufacturers have refused to supply retailers who do not carry out their bidding without question or as a means of manipulating the market.

(d)   *Pricing issues*. Petrol companies have been accused of colluding over price increases, deemed to be an unethical practice.

6   ETHICAL CODES

6.1   It is now much more common for businesses to specify what kinds of ethical standards they are following. Some have even published a statement of their *ethical code*, which is a formal declaration of their principles and rules of conduct. This would typically cover matters such as contributions or payments to government officials or political parties, relations with customers or suppliers, conflicts of interest, and accuracy of records which are kept. The Boeing Corporation for example has published such a code since 1964. Yet in 1990, it was charged with using inside information to win a US government contract and fined $5.2m.

6.2   Often such codes do not provide specific guidance on particular issues, and may conflict with the priorities of the commercial world. In such cases, individuals may find themselves torn between the 'moral ideals' which they live by, and the legal obligations, personal or contractual loyalties which bind them to an employer.

6.3   In some cases, ethical standards of individuals may force them to act against the organisation of which they are a part. 'Moral idealism' of this kind involves adherence to certain individual rights or duties which are regarded as universal. 'Whistle blowers' are often individuals who feel that they must adhere to these principles, even when it goes against the interests or policies of their employer. More often, business people are likely to feel that they adhere to moral principles which are 'utilitarian' - that is to say, moral behaviour which produces the 'greatest good for the greatest number', by weighing costs and benefits of the consequences of ethical behaviour. Thus, when benefits exceed costs, the behaviour can be said to be ethical. It is the philosophical position upon which capitalism itself rests, and is often cited to justify behaviour which appears to be unethical or which appears to have socially unpleasant consequences. For example, food production regimes which appear inhumane, or wasteful, or methods of production which result in regional unemployment, are often justified by the claim that these measures produce greater good for the majority of the population.

6.4   A famous case in the USA involved an infant milk food which was advertised as hypoallergenic, designed to prevent or reduce stomach upset caused by allergy to cow's milk. A small percentage of severely allergic infants reacted very strongly to the product. Nestlé, who produced the product, argued that they were not claiming that it was foolproof, but rather that the product involved reduced (hypo) allergic reactions, so that the greatest number of potential consumers benefited. Despite this, the claim was actually dropped from the label.

6.5   The American Marketing Association has produced a statement of the code of ethics to which it expects members to adhere.

Code of Ethics

Members of the American Marketing Association (AMA) are committed to ethical professional conduct. They have joined together in subscribing to this Code of Ethics embracing the following topics.

Responsibilities of the Marketer

Marketers must accept responsibility for the consequence of their activities and make every effort to ensure that their decisions, recommendations, and actions function to identify, serve, and satisfy all relevant publics: customers, organisations and society.

Marketers' professional conduct must be guided by:

1   The basic rule of professional ethics: not knowingly to do harm.
2   The adherence to all applicable laws and regulations.
3   The accurate representation of their education, training and experience.
4   The active support, practice and promotion of this Code of Ethics

Honesty and Fairness

Marketers shall uphold and advance the integrity, honor, and dignity of the marketing profession by:

1   Being honest in serving consumers, clients, employees, suppliers, distributors and the public.

2   Not knowingly participating in conflict of interest without prior notice to all parties involved.

3   Establishing equitable fee schedules including the payment or receipt of usual, customary and/or legal compensation or marketing exchanges.

Rights and Duties of Parties in the Marketing Exchange Process

Participants in the marketing exchange process should be able to expect that:

1   Products and services offered are safe and fit for their intended uses.

2   Communications about offered products and services are not deceptive.

3   All parties intend to discharge their obligations, financial and otherwise, in good faith.

4   Appropriate internal methods exist for equitable adjustment and/or redress of grievances concerning purchases.

It is understood that the above would include, *but is not limited to*, the following responsibilities of the marketer.

In the area of product development and management

• Disclosure of all substantial risks associated with product or service usage.

• Identification of any product component substitution that might materially change the product or impact on the buyer's purchase decision.

- Identification of extra-cost added features.

In the area of promotions

- Avoidance of false and misleading advertising.
- Rejection of high pressure manipulation, or misleading sales tactics.
- Avoidance of sales promotions that use deception or manipulation

In the area of distribution

- Not manipulating the availability of a product for purpose of exploitation.
- Not using coercion in the marketing channel.
- Not exerting undue influence over the resellers choice to handle the product.

In the area of pricing

- Not engaging in price fixing.
- Not practising predatory pricing.
- Disclosing the full price associated with any purchase

In the area of marketing research

- Prohibiting selling or fund raising under the guise of conducting research.
- Maintaining research integrity by avoiding misrepresentation and omission of pertinent research data.
- Treating outside clients and suppliers fairly.

Organisational relationships

Marketers should be aware of how their behaviour may influence or impact on the behaviour of others in organisational relationships. They should not demand, encourage or apply coercion to obtain unethical behaviour in their relationships with others, such as employees, suppliers or customers.

1   Apply confidentiality and anonymity in professional relationships with regard to privileged information.

2   Meet their obligations and responsibilities in contracts and mutual agreements in a timely manner.

3   Avoid taking the work of others, in whole, or in part, and represent this work as their own or directly benefit from it without compensation or consent of the originator or owner.

4   Avoid manipulation to take advantage of situations to maximise personal welfare in a way that unfairly deprives or damages the organisation or others.

Any AMA members found to be in violation of any provision of this Code of Ethics may have his or her Association membership suspended or revoked.

(Reprinted by permission of *The American Marketing Association*)

Chapter roundup

- Ethics are the moral principles and values which guide the thinking, decision making and actions of individuals and groups within society. Many of the most important ethical values form the basis for legislation which governs business activity in general including marketing. However, while ethics deals with personal moral principles and values, laws express the standards of a society which can actually be enforced in court. Ethics and legality are not necessarily congruent.

- A distinction can be made between traditional notions of the product concept and those which emphasise the customer service or customer care dimensions. Customer care aims to close the gap between customer expectations and customer experience.

- Perceptions of quality and service in British products have been lower than in many competitors' products, for example in Japan and Germany. The extension of the service sector has helped to force customer needs into the foreground and improve customer loyalty.

- Ethical issues can arise in relation to any of the elements of the marketing mix.

- Some businesses have published ethical codes, specifying the ethical standards to which they adhere and setting out the standards which they expect all their staff to meet. The AMA has also published a *Code of Ethics*.

- Marketing involves applying a structured approach and applying information about customer needs in order to achieve strategic objectives.

Test your knowledge

1   Distinguish between ethics and social responsibility (see paras 1.1, 1.2)

2   Give an example of a marketing operation which is unethical but legal. (2.4)

3   Give a definition of customer care. (3.2 - 3.4)

4   What are the prerequisites for a TQM programme? (4.4)

5   Give an example of an ethical issue in relation to promotion. (5.2)

6   Give an example of an ethical issue in relation to price. (5.2)

7   List the main areas covered by the AMA's *Code of Ethics*. (6.5)

Now try illustrative question 14 at the end of the Study Text

Chapter 12

MARKETING AND SOCIAL RESPONSIBILITY

This chapter covers the following topics.

1   Social responsibility

2   Consumer issues

3   Community issues

4   Green issues

5   Marketing implications of green issues

6   Green marketing

7   Strategies for social responsibility

Introduction

As we saw in Chapter 11, customer care is essential for successful and effective marketing. Here, we look at care, not for the customer, but for 'society' as a whole.

---

1   SOCIAL RESPONSIBILITY

1.1   In the UK, there is a growing feeling that the concerns of the community ought to be the concerns of business. A survey of executive opinion in the UK by John Humble (1992) found that 'nearly all the [UK] managers think "social responsibility" is important'.   _(Corporate Value; A Survey of Executive Opinion in the UK, 1992)_

1.2   In addition, a number of UK leading companies state that 'community-related concerns' figure in their corporate objectives. For example:

(a)   'The group's strategy is complemented by its continuing caring concern for the community, the environment and its own employees' (John Laing plc Annual Report 1993).

(b)   'Midland continue to play a significant role in the life of the communities in which we operate through our branch staff' (Midland Bank plc Annual Report 1993).

(c)   'Barclays Group operations ... are encouraged to support their local communities, in accordance with general group aims' (Barclays plc Annual Report 1993).

1.3   This is more than posturing. Although cynics might want to say that this kind of corporate activity has little impact on investment itself, recent studies in the US have shown that between 25 and 40% of the financial community take a company's record in social responsibility into account when making investment decisions. Research in the UK suggests that, by 1993, the corresponding figure was around 10%, and rising. Ethics, and the problems which it poses in relation to marketing behaviour are essential to an understanding of how ethical issues arise in the marketing context. This is largely a matter for individual conscience, however, while individuals' decisions are taken within an organisational context. More and more, it is being realised that it is necessary for organisations to develop a sense of responsibility for the consequences of their actions within society at large, rather than simply setting out to provide consumer satisfactions.

1.4   Social responsibility involves accepting that the organisation is part of society and as such, will be accountable to that society for the consequences of the actions which it takes. As with the preceding discussion, it is by no means clear what the nature and scope of social responsibility actually is, as a result of this proliferation of diverse social values and highly diversified organisational cultures. Three concepts of social responsibility which illustrate this diversity and some of its sources are:

(a)   profit responsibility;
(b)   stakeholder responsibility;
(c)   societal responsibility.

Profit responsibility

1.5   *Profit responsibility* argues that companies existing simply to maximise profits for proprietors or shareholders. The arch-exponent of this view is Milton Friedman, and his doctrine of 'monetarism' was particularly influential in Europe and the Unites States under the twin guises of 'Thatcherism' and 'Reaganite Economics' during the 1980s. Friedman asserts:

'There is one and only one social responsibility of business: to use its resources and engage in activities designed to increase its profits so long as it stays within the rules of the game - which is to say, engages in open and free competition without deception or fraud.'

1.6   Thus, drug companies which retain sole rights to the manufacture of treatments for dangerous diseases, or manufacturers who maintain high prices for technology which could be used to relieve suffering or increase the availability of food or clean water, are obeying this principle. The argument, in the case of some socially useful products, is that intervention in such markets, to provide products at affordable prices, will undermine the motivation of groups within the population (such as the 'underclass') to be self-sufficient, or to improve their lot. Proponents of this view argue that unless the market is allowed to exercise its disciplines, groups who are 'artificially' cushioned from deleterious consequences will become victims of 'dependency culture', with far worse consequences for society at large.

Stakeholder responsibility

1.7   *Stakeholder responsibility* arises from criticisms of profit responsibility, concentrating on the obligations of the organisation to those who can affect achievement of its objectives, for example, customers, employees, suppliers and distributors. In a famous recent example of this principle, Perrier recalled 160 million bottles of its water from 120 countries when traces of a toxic chemical were found in 13 bottles. The total cost was more than £50 million, with a further £60 million in lost sales -although there is strong reason to believe that these short term losses might well have been much greater had not this action been taken. Perrier were seen to act in the best interests of the firm's consumers, distributors and employees, at the same time removing all doubts as to the purity and quality of the product. The image of the product, and the firm's reputation for 'square dealing' and concern for customer safety, were immeasurably reinforced.

Societal responsibility

1.8   *Societal responsibility* focuses on the responsibilities of the organisation for ecological matters, and towards the general public. Green marketing - the effort to produce, promote and reclaim environmentally sensitive products - has, as we note elsewhere, become much more significant in recent years. Environmentally friendlier products such as cleaner petroleum products, or biodegradable packaging, or a policy which promotes recycling, such as the design of some models by Citroen, have become familiar over the past few years. While the overall contribution to the problems of environmental degradation are debatable, it is argued by some that these labels are effective marketing strategies, and effectively promote a responsible and caring image for the companies involved - as well as commanding a useful premium price for certain kinds of product.

1.9 Other socially responsible marketing tactics involve cause related marketing, when charitable contributions of a firm are tied directly to the customer revenues produced through the promotion of one of its products. This distinguishes cause related marketing from, for example, the (long established) standard practice of firms making charitable contributions. An example of this approach involves enterprises linking the sale of particular goods to support for a particular cause - for example, Procter and Gamble support for the Special Olympics when particular products are purchased.

The social audit

1.10 Socially responsible ideas may be converted into actions through plans developed in the course of a social audit. Companies develop, implement and evaluate their social responsibility through a social audit, which assesses their objectives, strategies and performance in terms of this dimension. Marketing and social responsibility programmes may be integrated.

1.11 *Social audits* involve:

(a) recognising a firm's social expectation and the rationale for engaging in socially responsible activity;

(b) identification of causes or programmes which are congruent with the mission of the company;

(c) determination of objectives and priorities related to this programme;

(d) specification of the nature and range of resources required;

(e) evaluation of company involvement in such programmes past, present and future.

1.12 In the USA, social audits on environmental issues have increased since the Exxon Valdez catastrophe in which millions of gallons of crude oil were released into Alaskan waters. The Valdez principles were drafted by the Coalition for Environmentally Responsible Economics to focus attention on environmental concerns and corporate responsibility. They encourage companies to:

(a) eliminate pollutants, minimise hazardous wastes and conserve non-renewable resources;

(b) market environmentally safe products and services;

(c) prepare for accidents and restore damaged environments;

(d) provide protection for employees who report environmental hazards;

(e) appoint an environmentalist to their board of directors, name an executive for environmental affairs, and develop an environmental audit of their global operations, which is to be made publicly available.

1.13 Whether or not a social audit is used depends on the degree to which social responsibility is part of the corporate philosophy which the firm endorses.

1.14 Finally, it is worth emphasising that such activities by firms do not remove the onus from the consumer to behave in a socially responsible way. Misusing, misappropriating and fraudulently misrepresenting such matters as finance details and insurance claims are all examples of consumer behaviour which is damaging, and very costly, to business. At the same time, consumers need to be made aware of their responsibility for disposing of environmentally sensitive products such as aerosol containers. While research reveals that consumers are increasingly sensitive to ecological issues, it also shows that they may be unwilling to sacrifice convenience and pay potentially higher prices to protect the environment and also that they are relatively poorly informed with regard to decisions in relation to this product characteristic. In some ways, responsibility for their consumers remains an important issue to which few firms have really faced up.

2   CONSUMER ISSUES

2.1   The consumer movement can be defined as a collection of organisations, pressure groups and individuals who seek to protect the rights of consumers. There has been a surge of interest in consumer matters. As early as 1961, the Moloney Committee on Consumer Protection reported 'a growing tendency for manufacturers to appeal directly to the public by forceful national advertising'. This new method of doing business coincided with the further influence of 'the development of a mass market for extremely complex mechanical and electrical goods ... [whose] performance cannot in some cases be accurately established by a short trial; ... inherent faults may only come to light when the article breaks down after a period of use'.

2.2   These developments were identified as leading to a greater need for consumer protection. The consumer could no longer rely on his own judgement when buying sophisticated goods and services.

2.3   Consumer interests are now served by:

(a)   the consumer movement; and

(b)   consumer protection legislation

The consumer movement

2.4   The main consumer protection body is the *Office of Fair Trading,* although this also deals with disputes within an industry. The Director of Fair Trading:

(a)   has a duty to promote competition;

(b)   encourages the adoption of codes of practice;

(c)   curbs anti-competitive practices;

(d)   issues licences under the Consumer Credit Act (an important piece of consumer protection legislation);

(e)   administers the Estate Agents Act.

2.5   As well as government bodies, there are voluntary associations. Chief of these in the UK is the *Consumers' Association* (CA). This provides the following services.

(a)   *Which?* magazine is published by the CA every month. It contains detailed reviews of products and services, as well as legal hints and tips from members. Each product review typically features one or more 'best buys' recommended for quality, value for money and so forth, although detailed breakdowns of the performance of competing products in a number of tests are also given. Cars, for example, are reviewed for fuel economy, safety, security and so forth. Whilst readership of *Which?* magazine is limited, its findings are widely reported in the media. Business people whose products receive unfavourable reviews might be stung into change.

(b)   Legal advice and help. The CA also provides members with legal advice, even acting on members' behalf in some cases, against malpractice or poor service.

(c)   The CA also lobbies Parliament and ministers on matters such as product safety, labelling, advertising honesty and so forth.

2.6   In addition there are a number of other organisations and groups representing 'consumer' interests.

(a)   National Consumer Council (a government sponsored body)

(b)   National Federation of Consumer Groups

(c)   National Association of Citizen's Advice Bureaux.

2.7   Some industries have panels of individuals appointed to represent the consumer interests. This is particularly true of utilities. There are consumer groups representing users of British Rail services and London Transport for example.

Consumer protection legislation

2.8   Legislation includes the following.

(a)   Trade Descriptions Act 1968
(b)   Fair Trading Act 1973
(c)   Unfair Contract Terms Act 1977
(d)   Food Act 1984
(e)   Weights and Measures Act 1985
(f)   Consumer Protection Act 1987

3   COMMUNITY ISSUES

3.1   Social responsibility also addresses community issues. Marketers are members of a community which expects the marketer to contribute to the well-being of the community in some way. Areas which the marketer might consider as suitable for supporting community growth and increasing community satisfaction include the following.

(a)   Education
(b)   Arts
(c)   Disadvantaged community groups

3.2   The organisation also has a 'community' responsibility towards its own employees. This responsibility is recognised by modern employment protection legislation and health and safety regulations.

3.3   Recognition of community issues can also have a long-term benefit for the organisation. It can generate goodwill and publicity and perhaps affect the attitudes of potential customers.

4   GREEN ISSUES

4.1   The increasing importance of green issues reflects, more than anything else, a new focusing of the marketing concept - an absolute necessity to respond to consumers' needs. Companies now realise that in order to compete, one must be aware of what it is about the product or service that is important to the consumer. Discerning, quality conscious, sophisticated consumers are also looking at how products and services fit into a society which is becoming more and more anxious about the possible consequences of needless and escalating consumption. Public awareness of the connections between industrial production, mass consumption and environmental depletion and damage is higher than it has ever been, with scientific information flooding out through the mass media and sometimes generating profound public reaction.

4.2   Food scares, when badly handled, have caused great damage to primary producers and retailers in the UK food sector - when handled well (as, for instance, in the scare over the mineral water Perrier (see above)), little damage to sales is caused, and the company may even emerge with an enhanced reputation. Modern marketing practice, then, needs to reflect awareness of these concerns, and is being changed by the issues that they raise and the practices that they recommend.

Green concerns

4.3   Marketing, and business activities in general, were formerly regarded as problems for the environmental movement, but now it is being recognised that the two are complementary, in many ways. In 1990 26% of all new products marketed in the USA were marketed using a 'green' approach.

4.4   The modern Green Movement is animated by concerns over pollution and overpopulation which are centuries old, but studies carried out in the 1970s into the effects of massive growth on the finite resources of the earth, underlined by disruptions in the supply of oil and other raw materials due to wars and economic conflicts added to public reactions to their lobbying and other activities.

4.5   A series of ecological disasters, notably the emission at the Union Carbide plant at Bhopal, India, the Chernobyl Nuclear reaction in the former USSR, the Exxon-Valdez oil spill in Alaska, and the torching of the Kuwaiti oilfields at the end of the Iraqi invasion, along with scientific reports about the state of the North Sea, the forests of Central Europe, and the droughts which afflicted several regions, all highlighted links between environmental damage and modern industry.

4.6   More recently, saturation TV coverage of environmentally-linked catastrophes such as the famines in sub-Saharan Africa, and the opening up of countries in Eastern Europe, South America and Asia through events such as Live Aid and through the new satellite communications systems have all elevated general concerns about common dangers and conflicts which threaten our environment.

4.7   More than ever, consumers are aware of the importance of green issues. Unsurprisingly, products and services, and the way in which they are marketed, are changing as a consequence.

4.8   The *Green Movement* is concerned with mankind's relationship to the environment, as a consequence of exploitation of natural resources and modern ways of living.

4.9   A major concern is with the study of ecology, the systems of plant and animal life which exist, and the relations between them. Major themes of this way of thinking include:

(a)   the environment is a web of complex interconnected living systems;
(b)   everything, including pollution, goes somewhere into this system;
(c)   the balance of nature reflects a natural wisdom which is benign;
(d)   all exploitation of nature will ultimately have a cost.

4.10   Conventional economics, according to green thinkers, has failed to deal with the problems of economic overproduction. It fails to differentiate the growth-generation of the goods and services produced in response to society's need to replace and renew, from the consequences of decay and destruction, and positive growth. Also, markets do not inhibit pollution; this is only limited by statute. Consumers, however, are assumed to have endlessly expandable and insatiable desires which provide the assurance of constantly expanding markets. Green economists have tried to put together an economics based on alternative ideas. These include:

(a)   monetary valuation of economic resources;
(b)   promoting the quality of life;
(c)   self reliance;
(d)   mutual aid;
(e)   personal growth
(f)   human rights.

5   MARKETING IMPLICATIONS OF GREEN ISSUES

The impact upon marketing practices

5.1   *Environmental impacts on business* may be:

(a)   *direct* through:

  (i) changes affecting costs or resource availability;

  (ii) impact on demand;

  (iii) effect on power balances between competitors in a market;

(b) *indirect* as legislative change may well affect the environment within which businesses operate; and finally pressure from customers or staff as a consequence of concern over environmental problems.

5.2 Some examples of the effects of ecological issues on businesses are the following.

(a) *Resource depletion* impacts on the availability of raw materials.

(b) *Genetic diversity* affects the potential development of many important new plants, animals, medicines, while the new bio-technology promises the development of commercially valuable materials of all kinds from these resources - high yielding and disease resistant plants, for example.

(c) *Pollution concerns* create more pressure on business to curtail their impact on the water table, the seas and the oceans. Recent concern over the quality of drinking water has generated growth rates of around 20% pa in the UK bottled water market.

(d) The *quality of air* may well have a bearing upon business's road distribution policies. Other concerns affecting business include:

  (i) *pollution of the land*, through landfill policies and operational damage;

  (ii) *noise pollution*.

(e) The '*polluter pays principle*' was adopted by OECD in the early 1970s to relate the damage done by pollution involved in the production of goods and services to the prices of those goods, in order to deter potential polluters by making their activities uneconomic.

(f) Problems such as *acid rain* and *ozone depletion* have so far resisted such attempts at resolution, however, owing to the difficulty of establishing culpability and the precise scale and extent of the damage.

(g) *Waste* of all kinds is increasingly becoming the target of national and international legislation by governments concerned about the effects on marine life and beaches.

(h) *Climatic change* is still debatable. Increasing average temperatures and rising sea levels, involving disastrous effects on agriculture and flooding of low lying areas, have yet to become firmly established trends, although the threat seems clear. In the event of acknowledgement of this, great changes in laws would be enacted in a wide range of business and marketing related areas to enforce such restrictions as were thought appropriate.

(i) *Energy resources*, and the environmental impacts of energy usage are related to the concern over climatic change. Some energy sources used at the moment are yielding far less of their potential than seems possible - coal, for example, typically gives up only 40% of its potential. Energy saving programmes and new *energy efficient* products are also being developed. The ways in which buildings, cars and electrical devices are designed will undoubtedly change as a consequence.

(j) *Recycling* is already widespread, and the demand for products and packaging made from recycled materials, or from materials which lend themselves to recycling is increasing steadily. Car manufacturers such as Mazda and Citroen are using plastic components to reduce vehicle weight and recycling used components.

(k) '*Food scares*' related to the safety of food are closely linked to the use of chemicals and drugs are used in intensive husbandry and crop production, as well as the forms of feeding and management which have been employed. 'Mad Cow Disease' (bovine spongeform encephalopathy) has been tentatively linked to the use of recovered proteins from waste meat products in animal feed. The mistreatment of animals in food production, and concern over the inhumanity of certain kinds of animal husbandry techniques has produced a strong reaction amongst consumers. Vegetarianism is on the increase in the UK, and this has had a significant impact on the demand for meat, eggs and other animal based products and a significant impact on the sales of cosmetics and other products in which animals are used in product testing.

Green pressures on business

5.3 Pressure for better environmental performance is coming from many quarters. Consumers are demanding a better environmental performance from companies - in recent surveys, it has been demonstrated that around three-quarters of the population are applying environmental criteria in many purchase decisions.

(a) *Green pressure groups* have increased their influence dramatically during the late 1980s. Membership of the largest 13 green groups in the UK grew to over 5 million, with staff of over 1,500.

(b) *Employees* are increasing pressure on the businesses in which they work for a number of reasons - partly for their own safety, partly in order to improve the public image of the company.

(c) *Legislation* is increasing almost by the day. Growing pressure from the 'green' or green-influenced vote has led to mainstream political parties taking these issues into their programmes, and most countries now have laws to cover land use planning, smoke emission, water pollution and the destruction of animals and natural habitats.

Part of this increased pressure is coming from the media. Large scale disasters and more technical, less dramatic issues such as global warming have become common theme for newspaper and television stories, and have generated very widespread public awareness of the issues concerned. Surveys have found that coverage of these issues increased by a factor of 10 between 1985 and 1989. As a result, the criteria applied by the public at large, and investors in particular, have undergone change. *Ethical investment* has grown in popularity, standing at around £200 million in the UK in the late 1980s.

(d) *Environmental risk screening* has become increasingly important. Companies in the future will become responsible for the environmental impact of their activities.

Social responsibility and sustainability

5.4 Green marketing is founded on two main ideas; one is a response to and *responsibility for the community*; the other is *sustainability* - the idea that we must be aware of the need for resources to be marshalled and monitored so that the environment can continue to provide inputs and absorb the products of consumption.

5.5 Social responsibility rests on:

(a) *the moral responsibilities of businesses*. Businesses exist within society, and depend on it for continued existence. While business controls many of the resources available to society, the majority of the population actually contribute to the production of wealth, and justice demands that they share in its benefits. Business therefore has a moral obligation to assist in the solution of those problems which business causes. Businesses and businessmen are also socially prominent, and must be seen to be taking a lead in addressing the problems of society;

(b) *the benefits to business of 'enlightened self-interest'*. In the long term, a business concern over the possible damage which may result from certain types of business activity will safeguard the interests of the business itself. In the short term, responsibility is good for the image of the company - it is a very valuable addition to the public relations activities within a company. In addition, as pressure for legislation grows, 'self-regulation' can take the heat out of potentially disadvantageous campaigns.

5.6 Opponents of the idea, such as Milton Friedman, argue that social responsibility is no part of a company's remit, since it should only be concerned to protect the interests of its shareholders, rather than protect society's interests. Friedman believes that since unfettered market forces are most likely to produce the greatest degree of affluence, this is what will provide the basis for social welfare programmes. More extreme proponents of this view in the USA have even succeeded, in some states, in having businesses legally prevented from making charitable donations.

5.7   Sustainability involves developing strategies so that the company only uses resources at a rate which allows them to be replenished in order to ensure that they will continue to be available, while at the same time, emissions of waste are confined to levels which do not exceed the capacity of the environment to absorb them. In relation to the development of the world's resources, policies based on sustainability seek to:

(a)   pursue equity in the distribution of resources;
(b)   maintain the integrity of the world's ecosystems;
(c)   increase the capacity of human populations for self-reliance.

5.8   Recent involvement of the business community through the World Industry Conference pointed out that business policy was an essential ingredient of the solution to environmental problems, as well as a cause; and that a concern for the environment did not simply present businesses with constraints, but also represented considerable business opportunities, and the possibility of generating considerable competitive advantage.

While early ideas about sustainability were derived from the idea that depletion of resources and environmental damage would 'push' companies into sustainability policies, the power of consumers and the behaviour of society could 'pull' companies towards the idea of the *conserver society*.

5.9   As will be apparent from the above, sustainability is a general aim rather than a truly practical proposition for business managers. However, new standards have been developed which are beginning to have a significant impact on business practices.

Environmental standards: ISO 19000 and BS 7750

5.10   Emphasis is moving away from 'end of pipe' pollution control to preventing problems at source. Laws setting standards for products such as packaging materials and manufacturing processes are likely to become more prominent. Faced with growing legislation and public pressure, companies have begun to develop new standards themselves. These are referred to as 'environmental management systems'.

5.11   Potential benefits include:

(a)   reduced insurance premiums;
(b)   easier conformance with environmental legislation;
(c)   reduced fines for infringing regulations;
(d)   cost savings through more efficient resource use;
(e)   improved public relations;
(f)   reduced likelihood of environmental accidents;
(g)   increased staff motivation;
(h)   improved ability to attract and retain staff.

5.12   The world's first standard for environmental management systems, BS 7750, developed by the British Standards Institution, follows in the footsteps of the increasingly successful, although controversial, quality standard BS 5750. BS 7750 is now being followed by a European regulation, the European Eco-Management and Audit regulation.

5.13   BS 7750 provides the basis for a structured, documented system. According to the Environment Business Supplement (1992), main characteristics are that it is:

(a)   generic: it can be applied to all kinds of organisations;

(b)   pro-active: to prevent problems at source;

(c)   on-going: directed towards continual improvement;

(d)   voluntary: there is no legal requirement to adopt the standard and no specified performance targets;

(e)   systems-based: involves carefully documented procedures and policy directives.

6   GREEN MARKETING

6.1   As previous sections have emphasised, there are strong reasons for bringing the environment into the business equation, but the strongest reason is the consumer, and the need to make responsiveness to and responsibility for the consumer the central principle of marketing activity.

The 'green consumer' must be the driving force behind changes in marketing and business practices. If new practices do not meet consumer needs, they will fail.

6.2   Green consumption can be defined as the decisions directly or indirectly related to consumer choice and usage which involve environmentally-related beliefs, values, attitudes, behaviour or choice criteria. That this is important is evident from:

(a)   surveys which indicate increased levels of environmental awareness and concern;
(b)   increasing demand for, and availability of, information on environmental issues;
(c)   green product concepts and green substitute products;
(d)   value shifts from consumption to conservation;
(e)   effective PR and marketing campaigns by environmental charities and causes.

Nevertheless, of course, levels of greenness vary across the population.

Segmenting the green market

6.3   Profiles of green consumers show that the force of green concern varies according to product class, prevailing market conditions and attitudes and beliefs about the product in question. Many consumers have not resolved the complex, confusing and often contradictory messages which are being sent out by various interest groups in this area. Broadly, females are more environmentally-aware than males, and families with children (particularly young children) are more likely to be concerned about making green consumption choices. The evidence also shows that consumers are taking the issue on board, and are becoming both more aware and more sophisticated in their approach.

6.4   Marketing diagnostics has developed a typology of green consumers which identifies four main groups.

(a)   *Green activists* (5 - 15% of the population) are members/supporters of environmental organisations.

(b)   *Green thinkers* (30% includes activists) seek out green products and services, and look for new ways to care for the environment.

(c)   *Green consumer base* (45 - 60%) includes anyone who has changed their behaviour in response to green concerns.

(d)   *Generally concerned* (90%) claim to be concerned about green issues.

6.5   A behaviourally-based *psychographic typology* by Ogilvy and Mather involves a range of factors. Four categories of consumers are identified in terms of tendencies and characteristics.

(a)   *Activists* (16%) are:

   (i)   aware of the issue;
   (ii)   likely to buy green products;
   (iii)   concerned for their children;
   (iv)   optimistic about technological change;
   (v)   people oriented;
   (vi)   home owners with children;
   (vii)   Conservative voters;
   (viii) likely to be upmarket consumers.

(b)   *Realists* (35%) are:

   (i)   the youngest group - those with young children;
   (ii)   worried about the environment;
   (iii)   consider profit and environmental protection as conflicting

    (iv)   are pessimistic about a solution
    (v)   are sceptical about a 'green bandwagon'
    (vi)   vote Labour.

(c) *Complacents* (28%):

    (i)   are upmarket consumers with older children;
    (ii)   are optimistic about mankind, business and government;
    (iii)   see this as someone else's problem;
    (iv)   are not very conscious of green issues;
    (v)   are right wing politically.

(d) *Alienated* (22%):

    (i)   less well educated, downmarket consumers;
    (ii)   young families/senior citizens;
    (iii)   unaware of green issues;
    (iv)   see greenness as a fashion or a fad;
    (v)   are pessimistic about a solution;
    (vi)   are left wing politically.

6.6   Studies show that consumer behaviour varies in greenness according to the information which is available to them about the product, the regularity of purchase, the price-sensitivity of the purchase involved, their degree of brand loyalty to existing brands, the availability of substitutes and the credibility of green products which are available. The importance of this issue, and the different factors which are impelling marketers to take it on board will force a new role for the marketer, in which a greater account is taken of the world outside the company and its priorities, but also how the company functions internally, and what role the marketer plays in linking these things.

6.7   A successful green marketer needs to:

(a)   understand the customer's wants and needs;

(b)   understand the environmental issues which are relevant to the company, customer, products and market environment;

(c)   evaluate the degree to which green product attributes fit consumer needs;

(d)   match price to consumer demand;

(e)   develop strategies which identify and effectively meet consumer needs and competitor challenges in relation to green issues;

(f)   consumers and product/service performance throughout the company.

Principles of green marketing

6.8   How are we to resolve the seeming contradiction between the reduction in consumption which lies at the heart of the idea of green marketing, and the extra consumption which has been the primary aim of marketing as previously conceived? Green marketing begins from the premise that marketing *as such* is not environmentally unfriendly, and that the products and services with which it deals will necessarily become greener to reflect more general awareness of the need to counter the effects of environmental degradation and develop sustainable management strategies.

6.9   A number of barriers have to be overcome.

(a)   *Costs* are likely to be incurred with the need to develop new products and services.

(b)   *Technical and organisational barriers* have to be overcome in developing, for instance, practical applications of green energy sources, and in reshaping organisations and their workforces into new ways of carrying out their work roles and promoting new attitudes to their jobs.

(c)   At the moment, many of the problems which will need to be addressed are highly *complex*, and there seem to be *conflicts* between the various alternatives available. How do we choose between fuels which create acid rain, and those which produce atomic waste? What about the human consequences of dismantling environmentally unfriendly industries in areas where there are no alternative sources of employment?

(d) Many of the policies pursued by a particular enterprise will have implications for the environment in countries *beyond national boundaries*. Conversely, changes which promote beneficial effects, for example, on the ozone layer, may well not have *visible effects*, and may as a consequence be resisted. The fact that problems are generally created, and have to be treated, over a relatively long timescale, also creates difficulties in promoting policies and mobilising groups to implement them.

(e) One of the main problems faced by those seeking to implement these green policies is the *lack of certainty* about the nature of the problem, about the *effectiveness* of the remedies proposed, and about the *reactions* of the public towards which these policies are ultimately directed. In some cases, companies have introduced supposedly environmentally friendly policies and products simply as a means of paying a token allegiance to the idea, or to try to garner extra sales from the gullible. One possible consequence of this is *moral fatigue* - as with other issues in the past, the public may become jaundiced and *disenchanted* with the whole idea, or sceptical about claims to greenness which are made, in various ways, by almost every manufacturer or service provider.

Developing the policies

6.10 Green marketers argue that these policies are very close to the spirit of total marketing advocated by Peter Drucker, and latterly by advocates of the Total Quality Concept, where managerial principles are related strictly to the generation of customer satisfaction. This requires a particular kind of manager, treating all of the company's activities as a holistic entity, and seeking to rethink the ways in which corporate aims - traditionally, the pursuit of customer satisfaction and profit through meeting a clearly defined need - can be reconciled with a responsible and sustainable means of achieving them. A new, green, managerial orientation is involved. This will include:

(a) rethinking the balance between efficiency and effectiveness;
(b) rethinking attitudes to and relationships with customers;
(c) rethinking the balance between our needs and our wants;
(d) redefining 'customer satisfaction';
(e) refocusing onto the long term objective, rather than short or medium term;
(f) 'less is more';
(g) rethinking the value chain;
(h) new corporate culture(s).

6.11 Processes for green marketing differ from conventional marketing in:

(a) the *information* which is fed into the process;

(b) the *criteria* against which performance is measured;

(c) the *values* against which objectives are set;

(d) the extent to which the process need to be *holistic* - to permeate and involve the whole organisation.

Marketing information

6.12 At the heart of green marketing is an appreciation and thorough understanding of the way in which the company impacts on the customer, the society and the environment. An audit of company performance is therefore essential.

6.13 Customer needs, and their sensitivities to particular environmental issues, need to be closely researched, along with the activities, strategies and policies of competitors. A typical mode of analysis, such as the SCEPTICAL list, could be applied to green issues.

Social factors
Cultural factors
Economic factors

Physical environment
Technological factors
International factors
Communication and infrastructure factors
Administrative and institutional factors
Legal and political factors

For each of these areas, we can examine which 'green issues' are raised for the company in question.

Marketing planning

6.14 Marketing plans need to be reconsidered in the light of new environmental priorities. Those areas which will required redefinition include:

(a) financial, strategic product/market and technical objectives;

(b) markets;

(c) strategies and action plans, including market share, customer satisfaction and competitor comparisons;

(d) performance and technical aspects of product performance and quality.

Performance

6.15 All of these aspects will have to be fitted within a view of the company's performance which takes account of environmental responsibilities. In addition, the traditional criteria for evaluating success or failure, and the parameters within which they operate, may well have to be redrawn.

Time

6.16 Timescales also have to be lengthened considerably, since products are now evaluated in terms of their long-term effects, as well as the impact of the processes by means of which they have been produced. Programmes designed to clean up environmental impacts often take a long time to become fully operational.

Judging success

6.17 Getting marketing's 4Ps (Price, Place, Promotion and Product) right leads to profit, according to orthodox ideas. Green marketing insists that the mix must be evaluated in the terms of four Ss.

(a) *Satisfaction* of customer needs.

(b) *Safety* of products and production for consumers, workers, society and the environment.

(c) *Social* acceptability of the products, their production and other activities of the company.

(d) *Sustainability* of the products, their production and other activities of the company.

Competitors and suppliers

6.18 Since greenness will be an important competitive factor, it will be important for companies to have information about their performance here in comparison with major competitors and to be assured that their suppliers are meeting green standards.

A model of the green marketing process

6.19 As we have argued, green marketing process requires the matching of those internal variables which the company can control with the strictures of the operating environment which the commercial decision maker faces. Like conventional marketing, green marketing needs to sort out, not the four Ps of the conventional mix, but a blend of internal and external factors. Peattie (1992) describes these as internal and external 'green Ps', to be used as a checklist to diagnose how well the company is succeeding in living up to targets for green performance.

The Green Marketing Process
(from Ken Peattie, *Green Marketing*)

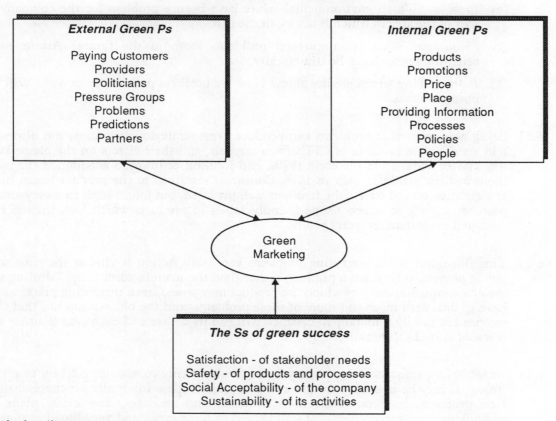

Analysing the process

6.20 Inside the company, marketers need to attend to the following 'internal green Ps'.

(a) A green audit needs to look at how safe *products* are in use, how safe they are when disposed of, how long they last and what are the environmental consequences of materials used in manufacturing and packaging the product.

(b) Green messages should be used in *promotion*. There is a need to establish standards of accuracy and reliability.

(c) *Prices* set for green products must reflect differences in demand; price sensitivity is also an important issue.

(d) *Place*. How green are the methods by which distribution takes place?

(e) *Providing information*. This needs to relate to internal and external issues bearing on environmental performance.

(f) *Processes*: energy consumed, waste produced.

(g) *Policies*. Do they motivate the workforce and monitor and react to environmental performance?

(h) *People*. Do they understand environmental issues, and how the company performs in relation to these issues?

6.21 Outside the company, a different set of factors need to be addressed. These might be referred to as 'external green Ps'.

(a) *Paying customers*. What are their needs in relation to green products and services? What information are they receiving about green products?

(b) *Providers*. How green are suppliers of services and materials to the company?

(c) *Politicians*. Public awareness and concern over green issues is beginning to have a strong influence on the legislation which appears, and this directly impacts on the conduct of business. A modern organisation must make this part of its concerns.

(d) *Pressure groups*. What are the main issues of concern? Which groups are involved and what new issues are likely to concern them?

(e) *Problems*. Which environmental issues have been a problem for the company, or part of the area in which it works, in the past?

(f) *Predictions*. What environmental problems loom in the future? Awareness of scientific research can be strategically vital.

(g) *Partners*. How green are my allies? How are business partners perceived? Will this pose problems?

6.22 Being able to predict problems can produce great strategic advantages, but also some odd results. The problem of CFCs from aerosols, and their effects on the ozone layer, was known about from the early 1970s, and Johnson & Johnson abandoned the use of them in their products back in 1976. Consumer reactions to the product began in the late eighties, and of course the firm was well prepared, but found itself in a very strange position, having to attach 'ozone friendly' labels to products which had, in fact, been modified more than ten years before.

6.23 This illustrates green marketing problems very well. Action is vital at the time when public *perceptions* threaten a product, rather than the manufacturer simply dealing with the environmental dangers which the product may pose. Green marketing practices will have to deal with more and more of these problems, and the old assumption that these worries are simply a 'moral panic' which will run its course and disappear is surely now revealed as wishful thinking.

6.24 Nevertheless, resistance to green marketing within many companies is likely to remain strong. It may be necessary for marketers to market ideas internally for these changes. New products, new communications strategies and messages, new 'clean' plant and technology, new appointments of staff skilled in these areas, and very broad changes in organisational culture will all have to be 'sold' to powerful individuals and groups within organisations. Obviously, the internal politics of business organisations need to be taken into account by green practitioners.

6.25 Green marketing needs to be accepted not just into the present policies of the company, but into the way in which it plans and acts far into the future. It is necessary to institutionalise the ideas, to change the culture of the company by:

(a) building a *basis for understanding* by setting up frameworks for disseminating information;

(b) formulating systematic plans for the *implementation* of green marketing;

(c) setting aside *resources*;

(d) requiring demonstrations of managerial *commitment*;

(e) encouraging *participation* and contributions throughout the company;

(f) sustaining an internal relations *public relations* programme which creates a healthy response to green ideas.

Mix variations for different industries.

6.26 (a) *Product*. For *primary industries*, products are often relatively bulky and undifferentiated. One producer may well have only a single product or a number in their portfolio. Manufactured goods are highly variegated in value, complexity, and degrees of differentiation. Service and not-for-profit industries offer intangible products which present particular marketing difficulties.

(b) *Place*. Primary products are often bulky and perishable, and as a consequence, distribution is a key factor. The nature of the product, and the pure volume of the market, as for instance in foodstuffs, places particular demands on the technologies involved in storage and transportation. For example, FMCGs face very different distribution problems, given the variety and complexity of the market segments towards which they are targeted.

(c) *Price*. Primary product prices are usually fixed in commodities markets. Food product prices are often the end product of complex support mechanisms. Prices set amongst manufacturers are typically cost-based, while services tend to be priced according to demand. Not-for-profit organisations do not, as is commonly thought, simply aim to cover costs. Profits here mean better ability to function, and lead to all manner of organisational gains.

(d) *Promotion*. Promotional activity may be inappropriate and entirely ineffective for primary producers, and what is done tends to be generic. This contrasts strongly with the intensive promotional campaigns mounted by large scale producers of manufactured goods, and service providers. NFP organisations are finding promotional campaigns and public relations to be increasingly important, but their funding and expertise in these areas is often severely limited.

Green marketing contexts

6.27 *Primary industries* use up a country's natural resources, and may involve industries as varied as multinational food companies and peasant sharecroppers. These are major concerns for green marketing. They are under constant scrutiny with regard to environmental legislation, and are the target of international concerns about the destruction of natural ecosystems and wildlife habitats. Concerns here will relate to:

(a) deforestation;
(b) threats to wild creatures;
(c) replacing natural habitat with monocultures (eg cattle, wheat etc);
(d) pollution;
(e) health and safety of produce;
(f) poor working conditions and wages.

Green policies here would aim to promote efficiency and effective use of finite resources, diversification and recycling where appropriate, and the urgent need to develop alternatives to the materials which are being used up.

6.28 Manufacturers of *consumer goods* may be seen as:

(a) damaging the environment or social institutions to meet consumer demand;
(b) producing 'dirty' products;
(c) using up scarce and/or environmentally significant raw materials (eg rare woods).

6.29 Some manufacturers are already making products which contribute environmental improvements (biodegradable packing, for example) while larger manufacturers are under pressures to act in a socially responsible manner because of their size and social prominence.

6.30 They tend to use green marketing strategies which are more customer oriented and opportunity driven. White goods manufacturers have begun to produce washing machines and dishwashers which use less water; car manufacturers are producing models which have a high degree of recyclability and durability, and detergent manufacturers are making products which are kinder to animal species, or which perform more effectively with smaller amounts.

6.31 *Industrial*, or *business-to-business marketers* are finding themselves having to fit in with the policies of customers who are producing green products. MacDonalds, for example, adopts a green strategy which draws in products conforming to green standards and which is worth more than £100 million (1991 figures).

6.32   In retailing, the green consumer is dealing directly with the enterprise. They act too as a 'filter' deciding which products will actually get to the customer.

6.33   *Service providers* have traditionally thought that green issues are less relevant to them than to other types of business enterprise. Although service enterprises typically do have less environmental impact than other types of business, they still consume resources and generate waste. They still face the same choices in their selection of suppliers, their investments and their contribution to the welfare of staff and customers. In fact, the very proliferation of green marketing practices is creating a growing demand for business services such as environmental auditing, green training, waste management and pollution control specialists.

6.34   The *not-for-profit sector*, since it seems devoid of the 'profit motive' which has been blamed for generating wasteful and environmentally damaging over-consumption, would seem to be endemically greener. Free market enthusiasts argue that a missing profit motive is more likely to promote waste and inefficiency, lacking the discipline of competition. Even within the NFP sector, there are likely to be varying factors at work, for instance government departments are more likely to feel a responsibility for the environment than smaller organisations.

6.35   *Small businesses* face a different scale of environmental challenges than large scale enterprises producing large environmental impacts by consuming large amounts of raw materials and producing large volumes of waste. Despite this difference, green issues are becoming more significant for small businesses because:

(a)   small companies may be able to develop products for green 'niches' more effectively than large enterprises, and can take advantage of flexibility to create green processes and systems;

(b)   many are using traditional methods of manufacture, which are often greener than more modern processes - using less energy and non-renewable resources. Demand for such products is increasing;

(c)   in areas where demand for green products is increasing, competition with larger companies may be difficult for smaller companies faced with the power and resources at the command of the larger organisation.

6.36   Since the publication of Schumacker's *Small is Beautiful*, small companies have been believed to embody the spirit and future of green production. Gurus such as Tom Peters have been arguing that, for other reasons, industry will be downsizing to meet the challenges of the future. Green marketing may well be assisted by this process, and it may be easier, and more attractive strategically, for such companies to adopt and implement green marketing processes.

Exercise

You should, as part of your studies, read a quality daily newspaper so as to keep abreast of current marketing developments. But keep a special look out for articles about marketing and social responsibility. The examiner will be impressed if you are able to give up-to-date examples in your exam.

---

7   STRATEGIES FOR SOCIAL RESPONSIBILITY

7.1   An organisation can adopt one of four types of strategy for dealing with social responsibility issues.

Proactive strategy

7.2   A proactive strategy is a strategy which a business follows where it is prepared to take full responsibility for its actions. Proactive behaviour implies taking action before there is any outside pressure to do so and without the need for government or other regulatory intervention. A company which discovers a fault in a product and recalls the product without being forced to, for example, before any injury or damage is caused, acts in a proactive way.

Reactive strategy

7.3   This involves allowing a situation to continue unresolved until the public, government or consumer groups find out about it. The company might already know about the problem. When challenged, it will deny responsibility, while at the same time attempting to resolve the problem. In this way it seeks to minimise any detrimental impact.

Defence strategy

7.4   This involves minimising or attempting to avoid additional obligations arising from a particular problem. Defence tactics include:

(a)   legal manoeuvering;
(b)   obtaining support from trade unions;
(c)   lobbying government.

Accommodation strategy

7.5   This approach involves taking responsibility for actions, probably when one of the following happens.

(a)   Encouragement from special interest groups
(b)   Perception that a failure to act will result in government intervention

7.6   It can be seen that this strategy falls somewhere between a proactive and a reactive strategy. McDonalds developed a nutrition-centred advertising campaign in an attempt to appease nutritionists and dieticians who were pressing for detailed nutritional information to be provided on fast food packaging. Action before the pressure arose would have been proactive; action after government intervention in response to the pressure would have been reactive.

Chapter roundup

- In the UK, there is a growing feeling that the concerns of the community ought to be the concerns of business. Social responsibility involves accepting that the organisation is part of society and, as such, will be accountable to that society for the consequences of its actions.

- Three key areas of social responsibility which have implications for marketers are consumer issues, community issues and 'green' issues.

- The increasing importance of green issues reflects, more than anything else, a new focusing of the marketing concept - an absolute necessity to respond to consumers' needs. Companies now realise that in order to compete, one must be aware of what it is about the product or service that is important to the consumer.

- Green marketing is founded on two main ideas; one is a response to and *responsibility for the community*; the other is *sustainability* - the idea that we must be aware of the need for resources to be marshalled and monitored so that the environment can continue to provide inputs and absorb the products of consumption.

- An organisation can adopt one of a number of different strategies for dealing with social responsibility issues.

Test your knowledge

1   What is profit responsibility? (see paras 1.5, 1.6)

2   What is societal responsibility? (1.8, 1.9)

3   What does the Consumers' Association do? (2.5)

4   List ten issues on the green agenda. (5.2)

5   What is sustainability? (5.4)

6   What is BS 7750? (5.12, 5.13)

7   What are the four 'green' character types in Ogilvy and Mather's psychographic typology. (6.5)

8   What are the four Ss of green marketing? (6.17)

9   Why are green issues particularly significant for small businesses? (6.35)

10 What does a proactive strategy for social responsibility involve? (7.2)

Now try illustrative question 15 at the end of the Study Text

Chapter 13

WIDER ISSUES

This chapter covers the following topics.

1   Marketing as a profession

2   Management

3   Information technology and marketing operations

4   Information systems

5   Databases

6   Privatisation

7   Internal marketing

8   Marketing techniques for internal marketing

9   Problems with the internal marketing concept

Introduction

In this chapter we examine some of the 'wider' issues of marketing operations: firstly marketing as a profession and the responsibilities of the marketing professional, secondly the contribution of IT to marketing operations, and, thirdly, the topical issues of privatisation and internal marketing.

---

1   MARKETING AS A PROFESSION

1.1   Marketing has been a popular and burgeoning career choice for the past 20 years, but few appreciate what is actually involved, and what becoming a marketer actually entails. What skills are needed? What personal qualities are required? What do marketers actually do? There is a great variety of marketing positions, many of which can be found either in a large company or in a specialist organisation which provides services to many clients. The main categories are as follows.

Marketing research

1.2   Marketing researchers obtain and analyse data to assist marketing decisions on strategy and the marketing mix. This is an essential first step, namely finding out what people want *before* you provide it. Duties can range from asking people in the street, to computer analysis, to survey and questionnaire design.

1.3   The sort of person likely to succeed in marketing research is educated, thoughtful, numerate and literate, the latter not least on account of being required to write lucid reports for senior managers.

Personal selling

1.4   There are many different types of selling used, including telesales, pioneer selling, technical sales, special account executives as well as sales managers and sales trainers.

1.5   The duties of a salesforce are first and foremost to sell the company's products, to present a favourable image, to provide feedback and to handle customers' problems/complaints.

1.6   To do this, a salesperson needs to be presentable, articulate, persuasive, likeable and determined. Sales managers need the extra attributes of leadership qualities and sales trainers should be good teachers, demonstrators and motivators.

Public relations

1.7   This covers a host of activities designed to maintain favourable relations between a company and its various publics - shareholders, employees, customers, society at large etc.

1.8   Duties include writing press releases, articles, speeches, reports etc for a variety of media and audiences. Public relations personnel need to be good diplomats, sensitive to the moods of others, good writers, creative, excellent hosts and smoothly articulate. They need good acumen.

Advertising

1.9   We all know what advertising is, since we are bombarded with it in our daily lives: on television, on posters, on radio, in the cinema, in the press and, today, on electronic media. Advertising clearly needs a variety of people with diverse skills such as creative artists and copywriters. Imagination and persuasion are essential personal attributes. Managerial skills and the ability to meet deadlines are also important qualities.

Product management/ brand management

1.10   Product/brand managers are in fact marketing managers for a given product or brand. They are responsible to senior marketing managers for the effective marketing of a product/brand including profitability, sales, product formulation, packing, pricing, promotion, marketing research, brand image etc.

1.11   These people need to be problem solvers, able to deal with multi-faceted situations. Product/brand managers have to be able to brief, work and control advertising agencies, marketing research agencies, packaging designers etc. They should also be creative and, most important of all, have a keen sense of balance.

Distribution management

1.12   A distribution manager is responsible for the safe transit of company goods to retailers. This individual has to choose from a variety of transport modes and carriers against criteria of cost, reliability, speed and security.

1.13   Distribution adds time and place values to our products. A distribution manager has to supervise company personnel, and also the carrier's personnel, and maintain adequate records. The right sort of person has to be adept at handling technical data, be highly computer literate and good with people from other functions: accountants, production managers, marketing managers and personnel managers. An interest in law is also appropriate.

Marketing managers

1.14   A marketing manager has all the duties described for product/brand managers above, multiplied by all the products in the range for which he is responsible.

1.15 The distinguishing feature is, however, that of being able to manage people. A close second is the ability to recruit and motivate the right staff. A marketing manager must like responsibility and enjoy problems. He/she also needs to be highly responsible and ethical.

Marketing management

1.16 *Marketing managers* - marketing is a province of management - are responsible for putting the marketing concept into practice. This means that they must:

(a) make sure that all of the activities of the business - from production and finance through to personnel training and all the various branches of the work which organisations of many different kinds carry out - are actually oriented towards identifying, anticipating, and satisfying customer needs. While this is what the marketing concept involves, at the same time, businessmen - especially managers - are in business to make a profit, so that this must be carried out as proficiently as possible, but also as profitably as possible;

(b) make sure that every activity within the business is carried out in a manner which is directed to the markets which the business is seeking to serve so that the company will move towards satisfying its financial objectives and obligations.

1.17 Marketing managers, like all others, have responsibility for:

(a) planning;
(b) organising;
(c) motivating, guiding and directing;
(d) controlling.

1.18 They may also be involved in either:

(a) profit making; or
(b) not-for-profit organisations,

each of which has its own particular culture, including distinctive values, objectives, priorities and moral code. The challenges facing particular managers, then, are likely to vary, according to the profile of the particular company within which they find themselves operating.

1.19 To some extent, of course, they find themselves facing the same issues and problems faced by every manager in the modern business environment. Organisations of all kinds share common features, and create the same sorts of problems for all managers.

The role of marketing management

1.20 The definition of marketing management as laid down by the American Marketing Association in 1985 says:

'Marketing (management) is the process of planning and executing the conception, pricing, promotion and distribution of ideas, goods and services to create exchanges that satisfy individual and organisational objectives.'

This definition clearly identifies the need for analysis, planning, implementation and control, activities involved in the role and functions of any manager.

1.21 The marketing manager has not only the responsibility of managing the marketing resources of the organisation to achieve agreed objectives, but will also be expected to play a part in agreeing the *overall* objectives, strategy and direction of the business.

1.22 It is also worth clarifying the precise and fundamental task of the marketing activity and therefore responsibility of marketing management that is essentially an economic role, since this can influence the level, timing, nature and composition of demand.

2   MANAGEMENT

2.1   You may already be familiar with management theory from elsewhere in your studies, but because most of the roles described above involve management in one way or another, we provide here a brief summary of some of the main issues.

The nature of management

2.2   The real development of a systematic approach to management seems to have arisen when business organisations grew beyond a size where control by the owner or partner was no longer possible or effective (ie after the industrial revolution).

2.3   Views of management are constantly changing and evolving. Arguably this is a desirable state of affairs. As managers work in a constantly changing business environment, it is clearly important to be flexible, creative and open minded about how best to 'manage' an organisation's resources. Management thinking, then, is certainly affected by fashion.

2.4   It is still not even certain how best to develop the managers of the future. In Germany and Japan, business schools and programmes of the Harvard, London or Insead variety are unknown. Only in 1987, reports by Handy and Constable were highly critical of the standards of management education in the UK. They were the catalysts for once more putting issues of management development firmly on the agenda of both politicians and business people.

2.5   The process of managing and the functions of management have been analysed many times, in various ways and by various writers, who have taken the view that:

(a)   management is an operational process, which can be understood by a close study of management functions; and

(b)   the study of management should lead to the development of certain principles of good management, which will be of value in practice.

2.6   Management theory and studies often recognise two distinct parts to management.

(a)   Managing *the process*, ie forecasting, planning, monitoring and controlling.

(b)   Managing *the people* encompassing motivation, leadership, delegation etc and relationship management in general both within the organisation and with groups outside it.

2.7   As an activity management is the essential core of any organisation. It is responsible for the effective and efficient use of the available resources. The quality of management in any endeavour is a critical factor in the success of that operation. Managerial skills involve a range of aptitudes - part art, part science. These are sometimes referred to as *competences*. To be a competent manager you need knowledge of the tools of management - analysis, decision making, planning and control, as well as the opportunity to practice and use that knowledge and to perfect these skills.

The role and functions of managers

The classical view of the management process

2.8   The ideas of Henri Fayol (1841-1925), the French industrialist and management theorist working in the early decades of this century, represent one of the first systematic approaches to defining the manager's 'job'. According to Fayol, the process of management consists of five functions.

(a)   *Planning*. This involves selecting objectives and the strategies, policies, programmes and procedures for achieving the objectives, either for the organisation as a whole or for a part of it. Planning might be done exclusively by line managers who will later be responsible for performance; however, advice on planning decisions might also be provided by 'staff' management who do not have 'line' authority for putting the plans into practice. Expert advice is nevertheless a part of the management planning function.

(b) *Organising*. This involves the establishment of a structure of tasks, which need to be performed to achieve the goals of the organisation, grouping these tasks into jobs for an individual, creating groups of jobs within sections and departments, delegating authority to carry out the jobs, providing systems of information and communication and co-ordinating activities within the organisation.

(c) *Commanding*. This involves giving instructions to subordinates to carry out tasks over which the manager has authority for decisions and responsibility for performance.

(d) *Co-ordinating*. This is the task of harmonising the activities of individuals and groups within the organisation, which will inevitably have different ideas about what their own goals should be. Management must reconcile differences in approach, effort, interest and timing of these separate individuals and groups. This is best achieved by making the individuals and groups aware of how their work is contributing to the goals of the overall organisation.

(e) *Controlling*. This is the task of measuring and correcting the activities of individuals and groups, to ensure that their performance is in accordance with plans. Plans must be made, but they will not be achieved unless activities are monitored, and deviations from plan identified and corrected as soon as they become apparent.

2.9 Other functions which might be identified, for example, are *staffing* (filling positions in the organisation with people), leading (unlike commanding, 'leading' is concerned with the interpersonal nature of management) and acting as the *organisation's representative* in dealing with other organisations (an ambassadorial or public relations role).

Many theorists now reject Fayol's concept of 'commanders', arguing instead that managers function by being *communicators*, *persuaders* and *motivators*.

This view is held by those who advocate the *internal marketing* of plans whereby employees are treated as 'customers of change'. Total quality management which emphasises the importance of internal customers and the role of teams, strongly supports this notion.

2.10 Another important role not included in Fayol's model is that of sustaining of corporate values (ie the creation and maintenance of the *culture* of the organisation). Recent theorists see this as the vital role of management in today's business environment, since it determines how planning, organising, control and the other functions are carried out.

> 'A company is more than a legal entity engaged in the production and sale of goods and services for profit. It is also the embodiment of the principles and beliefs of the men and women who give it substance, it is characterised by guiding principles which define its view of itself and describe the values it embraces. Such values have, for our company, existed implicitly for very many years - (the company) is what it is and as good as it is because a great many individuals over a long period of time have contributed their own best efforts to preserving and enhancing the values that cause it to endure.'
>
> (*Ethics and Operating Principles Handbook*, United Biscuits plc)

2.11 Corporate culture, as a dimension of management theory, has only attracted attention since the 1970's. In companies such as Body Shop the culture is obvious and is used as a marketing platform. It is sustained through the selection of new franchisees with similar cultural values and ideals.

The approach of Peter Drucker

2.12 Peter Drucker worked in the 1940s and 1950s as a business advisor to a number of US corporations, and was also a prolific writer on management. Drucker adds to Fayol's version that the manager's task is to communicate ideas, orders and results to different people, both within and outside the organisation. Communication is essential for planning, organising, motivating and controlling.

2.13 Drucker grouped the *operations* of management into five categories.

(a) *Setting objectives* for the organisation. Managers decide what the objectives of the organisation should be, and quantify the targets of achievement for each objective. They must then communicate these targets to other people in the organisation.

(b) *Organising the work*. The work to be done in the organisation must be divided into manageable activities and manageable jobs. The jobs must be integrated into a formal organisation structure, and people must be selected to do the jobs.

(c) *Motivating employees* and communicating information to them to enable them to do their work.

(d) The *job of measurement*. Management must:

(i) establish objectives or yardsticks of performance for every person in the organisation;

(ii) analyse actual performance, appraise it against the objectives or yardsticks which have been set, and analyse the comparison;

(iii) communicate the findings and explain their significance both to subordinate employees and to superiors.

(e) *Developing people*. The manager 'brings out what is in them or he stifles them. He strengthens their integrity or he corrupts them'.

All managers perform all five of these operations, no matter how good or bad a manager they are. A bad manager performs these functions badly, whereas a good manager performs them well.

2.14 Drucker has also argued that the management of a *business* has one overriding function - *economic performance*. In this respect, the business manager is different from the manager of any other type of organisation. Management of a business can only justify its existence and the legitimacy of its authority by the economic results it produces, however significant the non-economic results which occur as well.

2.15 He called attention to the fact that the jobs of management are carried out within a *time dimension*.

(a) Management must always consider both the short-term and longer-term consequences of their actions. A business must be kept profitable into the long-term future, but at the same time, short term profitability must be maintained to avoid the danger that the long term will never be reached. The cause of many business failures is cash flow problems rather than an inherent lack of profitability.

(b) Decisions taken by management are for the future, and some have a very long 'planning horizon': the time between making the decision and seeing the consequences of that decision can be substantial. For example a decision to develop market opportunities in China or Japan may take a number of years to implement and still longer to achieve profitable sales.

Managerial 'roles'

2.16 Another way of looking at the manager's job is to observe what managers actually do, and from this to draw conclusions about what 'roles' they play or act out. This is known as the *managerial roles* approach. Henry Mintzberg identified ten managerial roles, which may be taken on as appropriate to the personality of the manager, the subordinates and the nature of the task in hand.

(a) *Interpersonal roles*

(i) Figurehead   performing ceremonial and social duties as the organisation's representative, for example at conferences

(ii) Leader   of people, uniting and inspiring the team to achieve objectives

(iii)	Liaison	communication with people outside the manager's work group or the organisation

(b) *Informational roles*

(i)	Monitor	receiving information about the organisation's performance and comparing it with objectives
(ii)	Disseminator	passing on information, mainly to subordinates
(iii)	Spokesperson	transmitting information outside the unit or organisation, on behalf of the unit or organisation

(c) *Decisional roles*

(i)	Entrepreneur	being a 'fixer' - mobilising resources to get things done and to seize opportunities
(ii)	Disturbance-handler	rectifying mistakes and getting operations - and relationships - back on course
(iii)	Resource allocator	distributing resources in the way that will most efficiently achieve defined objectives
(iv)	Negotiator	bargaining, for example for required resources and influence

2.17 The mix of roles varies from job to job and situation to situation: a manager will, as it were, put on the required 'hat' for each task. A manager will, however, wear some hats more than others: senior officials (say, the branch manager of a retail store at local level, and the directors and general managers at corporate level) are more likely to be called upon to act as figureheads than sectional managers and supervisors, who will be more concerned with resource allocation and disturbance-handling.

2.18 In modern management theories, particular emphasis has been placed on leadership and entrepreneurship, at *all levels* of management. The cultural effects of both work at team as well as organisational level requires involving and committing employees to achieving goals, and focusing on creative action and resource mobilisation to get things done.

2.19 The differences between the jobs of management and employees can be expressed in terms of the *functions* and *roles* (discussed above) which are the prerogative of management.

However, there are also particular *characteristics* of a managerial job which also distinguish it from an employee's job. Also, of course, particular types of manager have their own distinctive set of responsibilities, tasks and routines.

Characteristics of managerial work

2.20 The characteristics of the managerial job include the following.

(a) *A high level of activity*. Managers are very 'busy' in the sense that they tend to perform a high number of separate activities, and have a high number of interpersonal contacts, in the course of a day.

(b) *Discontinuity*. As the number of activities suggests, managers tend not to be able to spend long on single, continuous tasks. They are constantly interrupted by personal contacts and matters arising for their attention: telephone calls, meetings, people bringing information or problems, and 'deskwork' resulting from all of them. Managerial activity tends to be a rather unpatterned mixture of routine/planned and unplanned tasks.

(c) *Variety*. The nature and diversity of the managerial roles mean that managers have more job variety than most of their subordinates, covering differing types of activity including:

(i) paperwork (dealing with it *and* generating it);

(ii)   telephone calls (taking and making);

(iii)   meetings (formal - especially in more senior posts - and informal);

(iv)   interpersonal contacts - (internal and - especially in senior and marketing posts - external).

For each of these types of activity, the potential range of matters to be dealt with - ie job *content* - is extremely wide, since it is management's responsibility to handle the unforeseen and discretionary areas of business as well as the routine.

(d)   *Separation* from the location and detail of operational work. The more senior the manager, the less he or she will be involved 'at the coal face' (relying on feedback through subordinates) and the more time will be spent outside the office, the department and even the organisation and the more time will be spent planning the future direction and strategy of the business.

(e)   *Talking and thinking*. Managers are expected (and paid) to perform much more 'brain' activity (such as thinking, planning, decision-making and problem-solving) than subordinates. They are not, in other words, expected to be as immediately and visibly productive as workers. In addition, up to 90% of total work time may be taken up in primarily oral activity: telephone calls, discussions, meetings etc.

(f)   *Time span of discretion*. This was a term devised by Elliot Jaques to describe the amount of time between a decision or action taken by an individual, and the checking up on it and evaluation of it by the individual's superior. Low level employees are frequently monitored - in so far as they are allowed to exercise their own discretion at all - but managers perform actions and take decisions whose consequences may not emerge for a long time.

(g)   *Networks*. The more senior a person is - and the more 'broad' their concerns in the organisation - the wider is the network of information in which they participate. Lower employees 'network' with peers in their immediate sphere of work, and with immediate superiors and subordinates. At higher levels, information for decisions, planning and control will be drawn from a wider set of contacts, including many sources outside the organisation.

The humanistic approach

2.21   The classical approach to management as characterised by Henri Fayol has given way to a more humanistic approach. Here managers are seen as persuaders and motivators rather than as commanders.

2.22   Organisations are, in effect, collections of individuals grouped together in departments or teams responsible for a function or task within the business. These groups have to be linked together if the organisation is to work. How they link together represents the structure of the organisation and exists both formally and informally.

2.23   As we saw in our earlier discussion of marketing organisation, different structures have different characteristics and cultures.

2.24   The design of the formal organisation structure influences both the effectiveness of the operation and its culture. The development of matrix organisation structures reflects the growing recognition of the importance of organisational flexibility and adaptability.

2.25   The style of management and the 'atmosphere' of an organisation reflect its culture. Although intangible, 'the way we do things around here' is fundamentally important in influencing the effectiveness of the business and how it adapts to challenges and changes.

2.26   Neither managers nor students can afford to ignore the cultural dimension of the business when developing and implementing plans.

2.27 The role and nature of management as well as the specific techniques and competences of the manager are all relevant in understanding marketing as a career. Marketing managers do not carry out their tasks in isolation but are a central aspect of the way in which modern business operates.

3   INFORMATION TECHNOLOGY AND MARKETING OPERATIONS

Information and the new management age

3.1 Theorists such as Peters and Drucker see modern business as serving increasingly fragmented markets, with customers able to pick and choose from ever more varied and diverse product assortments. Failure rate amongst new products is very high, and growing. Competitive, unstable and rapidly changing markets have increased business's need for information, to monitor and 'target' their segment of the market by identifying needs, formulating products and communicating with consumers. Competition has created enormous pressures to cut margins and make every decision count. *Information reduces the risks involved*. Commercial success can only rest on a *marketing orientation*.

3.2 At the same time, large organisations contain many decision makers with widely varying types and levels of expertise, so that the information they need must be rendered into *many different forms*.

3.3 The range, quality and amount of information has increased enormously with the electronic storage, retrieval and manipulation of data on stocks, purchases, and a whole range of information about customers. *Direct marketing* (sometimes called 'precision', 'database' or 'niche' marketing), uses this information to identify market segments by *combination* (with, for example, census information) or *projection* (making inferences, for example, about attitudes, opinions or interests based on limited information, such as postcode or first name). Markets are subjected to *psychographic segmentation* according to differences between consumers lifestyles, using socio-demographic, behavioural and attitudinal data. *Strategic analysis and corporate strategy* must take into account not simply 'market facts' but the macroeconomic environment, political factors, social and cultural changes.

3.4 The idea that marketing simply means selling is oversimplistic, and dangerously misleading. Businesses pursue different objectives at different times. Long-term objectives (for instance, market dominance) may very well necessitate short-term strategies which do not involve profit (such as loss leader price cutting, improving public relations, developing consumer awareness, repositioning a product).

3.5 *Good decisions* depend on comprehensible and actionable information about these markets being *accessible* to decision makers - from sales personnel dealing face to face with retailers or customers, through research/development and production staff concerned with product form or uses or satisfactions they must deliver, to marketing staff, concerned with identifying customer needs and wants and communicating with those customers.

3.6 *Management information systems* accomplish this purpose. Market information - about sales, about customers, about competitor activity, trends in the market, financial movements and government policies - can be accessed and used, perhaps incorporated into databases and software which enables non-specialists to perform complex projections and analyses, as well as monitoring their own and competitors' performances.

3.7 Information, then, is produced in a variety of forms for members of business organisations making decisions about their operations. This has become more important with the rise of the marketing concept.

3.8   Generally, data gathered for other reasons by a variety of agencies includes company reports, government statistics, newspaper and journal articles, and reports produced by commercial market research agencies. Most secondary data is quantitative, gathered by government or industry in accounting and record keeping. Thanks to IT, most of this is now available to marketers through direct interrogation, or else can be accessed through CD-ROM systems.

What is information technology?

3.9   Developments in information technology (IT) have played a major role in effecting many of the changes taking place in marketing operations. IT may provide for cost reductions and increased efficiencies in producing and delivering products, but it also affects the structures of markets, the patterns of competition and conditions of entry into markets. IT provides marketing opportunities through the ability to construct and interrogate databases, through enabling marketing communications to be targeted at particular consumer groups and through innovations in the process of delivering financial services. In considering the impact of IT particular attention is drawn to its use in computerised databases for marketing purposes (such as for targeting direct mail shots) and in electronic transfer of funds (such as through automatic cash dispensers, home banking, EFTPOS and debit cards).

3.10   IT is the integrated use of computing, micro-electronics and telecommunications technology. Its impact on:

(a)   design;
(b)   manufacturing processes;
(c)   information processing;
(d)   record keeping;
(e)   data management; and
(f)   communications

cannot be overestimated. We are in the midst of a revolution.

3.11   Three areas are particularly important to marketers.

(a)   The use of low cost electronics to facilitate the rapid storage, processing and retrieval of information relating to such items as customer accounts, interest rates, foreign exchange rates and share prices.

(b)   The automation of routine functions such as cheque clearing and order processing and the direct control of systems for processing accounts and other data.

(c)   The use of electronic means to effect rapid communication to customers.

The impact and use of information technology

3.12   The impact of IT may be identified at various levels.

(a)   IT changes the nature of production processes, and therefore reduces transaction and associated costs. Ultimately, this effect may be seen in the creation of the paperless office, although this has probably yet to be achieved. IT has a particular impact upon delivery systems by reducing costs and increasing efficiency.

(b)   IT is also important in new product development, especially in respect of product modification. IT may also enable entirely new products to be developed which were not previously possible.

(c)   IT introduces the possibility for revolutionary changes in the way in which marketers communicate or interact with their customers.

(d)   IT also affects links between organisations.

The Dangers Of Machine-Based Information

Information architectures: **Human-centred approaches:**

Information architectures	Human-centred approaches
Focus on computerised data	Focus on broad information types
Emphasize information provision	Emphasize information use and sharing
Assume permanence of solutions	Assume transience of solutions
Assume single meaning of terms	Assume multiple meanings of terms
Stop when design is done or when system is built	Continue until desired behaviour is achieved enterprisewide
Build enterprisewide structures	Build point-specific structures
Assume compliance with policies	Assume compliance is gained over time through influence
Control users' information environments	Let individuals design their own information environments

From *Harvard Business Review,* March/April 1994

3.13 At one level IT may affect *market structure* that is the number, relative size and degree of integration of the firms in the industry.

(a) *Economies of scale* may be possible where costs of producing greater volumes decline as a result of the application of IT.

(b) However, *economies of scope* resulting from IT may also be highly important in, for example, the banking and financial services sector. Economies of scale arise where the cost of producing two or more products is less than the cost of producing them separately. IT developments in financial services are often not confined to a single use. For example, a cash dispenser (automatic teller machine, ATM) network can be used for withdrawals and deposits. Having established a network to facilitate withdrawals, the extra cost of a deposit facility is small so that it costs less to have both together rather than separately. To achieve some of the economy of scale benefits of IT it may be necessary for firms to undertake joint venture arrangements rather than incur costs which would be prohibitive for all but the very largest firm. The use of shared ATM networks is a clear example where economies of scale can only be realised through joint arrangements.

3.14 The groups of banks and building societies which come together to form a particular joint venture may be strongly influenced by technological compatibilities and such issues may also have a future bearing on the structure of the industry as they may be a key factor in determining whether a proposed merger between two institutions is feasible or not. IT may also be important in enabling links between different kinds of financial services firms to take place. For example, banks may be able to offer customers on-line quotes for insurance policies. The relative importance of these various impacts of IT is identified in the table below which reports the results of a survey of banks and building societies.

3.15 The most important factors for banks in particular are seen to be the impact of IT on improving *customer databases* and improving management information systems. The need for adequate management information systems relates to several levels and functions in an organisation. Of particular importance may be the increased needs to monitor product performance and integrate the various parts of an organisation. There may, however, be very severe problems in integrating different functions. The problem is especially acute where the information required is more subjective and difficult to codify. A key issue concerns the need to distinguish matters which relate to the information system as such and those which have an IT dimension. IT may provide appropriate solutions in some cases, but in others the fundamental problem to be solved may be related to managerial issues rather than to data manipulation.

The direct use of IT for selling products was found in the research to be very important for a substantial proportion of banks and building societies. However, as is discussed shortly, there has been considerable concern as to the adequacy of databases for marketing purposes.

4   INFORMATION SYSTEMS

4.1 The kind of marketing information system referred to earlier may be developed in an IT context as shown in the following diagram. Routine contact with customers, for example, provides a crucial source of data. Together with other marketing information on general trends, it is possible to construct a computerised database to aid various marketing functions. The marketing information system so developed is shown to be a sub-system of the firm's overall management information system and is required to be consistent with and able to co-ordinate with the firm's overall corporate strategy.

An IT-based MIS with emphasis on marketing

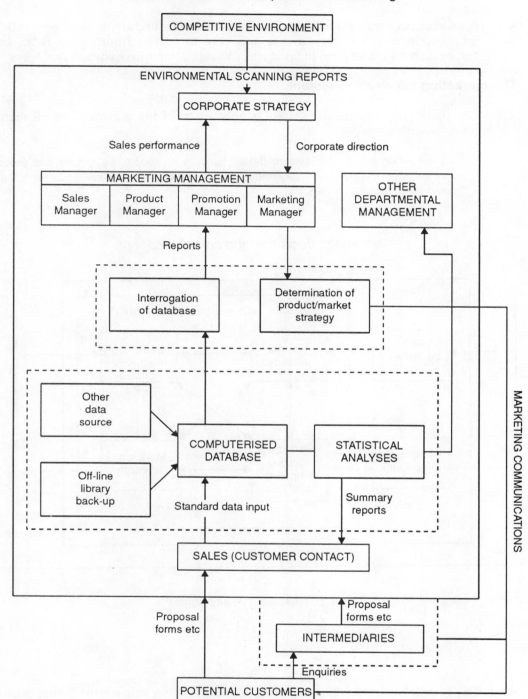

4.2   In the development and use of such as system there is a need to ensure quality control of the information which is inputted. A general issue in the development of databases using significant amounts of personal details for marketing purposes concerns the need for accuracy and other security issues.

4.3   Managers need easy access to good quality, relevant and up to date information as a meaningful basis for planning. It is only possible to maintain an up-to-date picture of the competitor's strength and weaknesses, changes in the environment and a realistic picture of your own organisation's effectiveness if such information is readily available, and widely disseminated. This information must cover both internal performance and external variables, not only in respect of historical results and trends, but also providing a forecast of future changes.

4.4 A management information system or database aims to provide managers with relevant information which is easy to use and easy to access. Information is an important corporate resource and can provide considerable competitive advantage.

The marketing information system

4.5 The marketing information system is only a part of the company overall management information system.

> 'A marketing information system (MkIS) consists of people, equipment and procedures to gather, sort analyse, evaluate, and distribute needed, timely and accurate information to marketing decision makers.'
> (Kotler)

Marketing decisions and communications

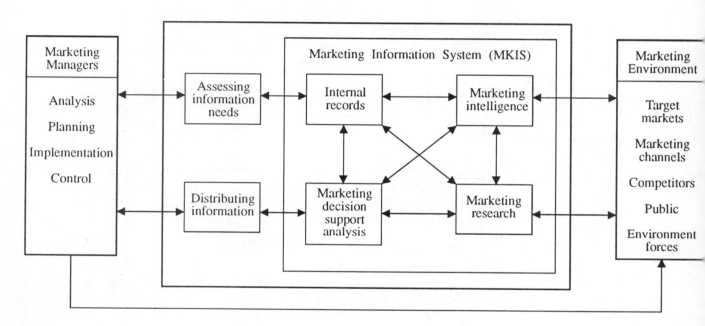

From Kotler: *Marketing Managment Analysis Planning, Implementation and Control*

4.6 The complexity of the planning process, and the systematic approach that is essential in what rapidly becomes a multi-aspect and multi-dimensional planning model, lends itself readily to the use of computers and computer databases. The diagram which follows suggests the position of the database within the planning and control system.

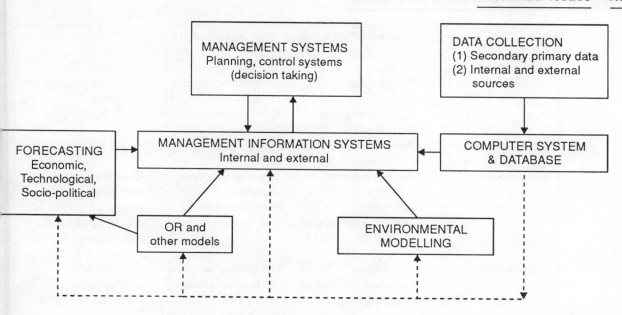

'It is possible, as just one example, to ask the database to show, over a five-year rolling period, manufacturers and their country of origin of commercial vehicles defined by the number of axles, vehicle weight, torque or power output, or cubic capacity - or a combination of these.'
(Financial Times)

Collecting and using marketing information

4.7   Marketing managers usually keep their own internal records which provides the most basic form of marketing information. Examples include number of brochure requests against orders taken, sales call against order value, records of where enquires are generated from, average order sizes and so on.

4.8   This can be used to provide user friendly and relevant source of information. It is important to remember that in any information system too much information is often as bad as too little.

4.9   Avoiding information overload starts with a clarification of what information is needed and when. 'Work on what we *need* to know, *not* on what it is *nice* to know.'

(a)   What decisions are made?
(b)   What information is needed?
(c)   What is already available?
(d)   What are the gaps?

The typical needs of staff from an information system are shown in the following table.

Information needs of large organisations			
	Recurrent	*Monitoring*	*Requested*
Directors	Regional economic data	Competitor product changes	Customer profiles
	Competitor prices/ promotions	Customer acquisitions	Customer needs/satisfactions
	Regional market share	New entrants	
Sales managers	Product margins	Regional economic changes	Contribution per customer
	Costs per call per customer	New competitive activities	Salesforce effectiveness vs competitors
	Share by salesperson		
Brand managers	Brand share	Competitor activities	Test of new formulation
	Customer satisfaction	Technology changes	Price elasticity data
	Feature preferences	Government regulations	
Advertising managers	Advertising awareness	Media rates	New commercial theme test
	Media habits of target audience	Ad themes of competitors	Communications impact of competitor's ad
		Media effectiveness studies	
Public relations manager	Key public attitudes towards the firm	Legislative activities	Impact on buyers' attitudes of strike by the union
	Company plans that affect the public	Trade and popular publications	Impact on firm of other industries' responses to safety problems
Sales and marketing	Net contribution by product line	New competitors	Impact on related products of dropping one product line
	Market share by product line	Developments in related markets	Price and advertising elasticities across products
	Customer satisfaction levels	New product launches by competitors	

4.10   The information 'facts of life' can be characterised as follows.

(a)   The most important information in an organisation is not available from a computer.

(b)   Managers prefer to obtain information from people and not from machines.

(c)   Value can be added to information by interpreting it.

(d)   The more information there is available on a subject, the less likelihood there is of agreement on the nature of the subject.

(e)   Managers who sense the importance of information may wish to retain a feeling of power by becoming reluctant to share it.

(f)   Managers are more likely to use information if they played a role in generating it.

(g)   Face-to-face communication is more important than electronic communication.

Marketing intelligence

4.11 There are two distinct systems both collecting information from the external environment. One is marketing research activity, the other marketing intelligence. Marketing intelligence systems are designed to tell you *what is happening*.

(a) *Marketing research* is used to collect information on an 'ad hoc' basis, used to help make a specific decision.

(b) *Marketing intelligence* is derived from a continual monitoring of the market and external environment, on a continuing basis, providing data to identify trends and alert managers to changes or happenings.

4.12 This would include external environmental factors, like population changes, which affect the size of our target market, but so too would 'mystery shopping' undertaken on a regular basis to quantity and compare levels of customer service in both our own and our competitors' operations. Some specialist external suppliers provide marketing intelligence, for example A C Nielson with details of retail sales etc. The summary below sets out the main British consumer panels.

British consumer panels

4.13 These are continuous research services, offered by the largest research organisations.

(a) *Audits of Great Britain (AGB) Ltd* operates the household consumer panel which was the first to operate in the UK (1948, as Attwood Statistics Ltd). It comprises a panel of 8,500 households who are equipped with electronic scanners to record price, place of purchase and selected brand. This is used to supply trend analyses to clients.

(b) *Neilsen: Homescan* was launched in the late 1980s as a grocery consumer panel based on 7,100 homes, derived from the Neilsen establishment survey of 80,000 households. A wand scanner records all items purchased after shopping trips, and the data, along with programmed questions, is transferred weekly over a modem called up by the remote data store. Core data vary slightly, but typically include:

(i) purchases by value, volume and expenditure
(ii) percentage of homes buying ('penetration')
(iii) average weight of purchase; average bought by each home buying
(iv) average purchase occasions (number of times each home bought)
(v) average price

Clients can design particular questions or analyses.

(c) *Taylor Nelson*

(i) *Family Food Panel*, established in 1974, monitors family eating habits and behaviour. All food and drink, home made or bought is surveyed continuously by means of a bi-weekly diary. The country wide survey involves the collection of 2,000 diaries quarterly. These are stratified by constituency/ward. There are over 200 sampling points. Data includes

(1) types of food and drink consumed
(2) brands
(3) methods of preparation
(4) packaging
(5) meal occasions
(6) demographic profiles of households

Used by the National Dairy Council to monitor trends in consumption, particularly those in home made foods.

(ii) *Monitor* is a continuous survey of social trends and their relation to consumer opinion and purchasing behaviour, using qualitative interviewing based on a random sample of 1,500 aged 16 - 65. This is linked to a whole network of similar studies carried out internationally and co-ordinated in Switzerland.

(d) *Research International* incorporates ad hoc research groups on a wide range of fast-moving consumer goods including food and drink.

(e) *Telephone panels* are offered by:

(i)   Capital Radio/Marplan - 2,000 residents from Capital's broadcast area; includes advertising, recognition, and public opinion topics

(ii)   Facts International and Martin Hamblin Research are both medical panels, involving 500 GPs.

(f) *Shop audit panels*

Neilsen has operated a Retail Index service in the UK since 1939. These 'Neilsen Index Reports' are based on a sample of stores audited every two months for information on purchases, stocks, sales promotions, and price levels. Stores are selected by classifying them by type of organisation, (co-operatives, multiples, large independents, small independents), concentrating on those stores which sell most products, and using a principle of disproportionate sampling. The resulting data are projected from the sample to national population figures to produce estimates of market size, market share, geographic distribution of market, effectiveness of pricing, promotional policies etc. 52,000 items are audited each month. A typical report will include the following, each shown for UK as a whole, by region (according to nine areas in which Neilsen operates based roughly on TV areas), by shop size and type

(i)   Consumer sales (value and volume)
(ii)   Market shares
(iii)   Retail deliveries
(iv)   Retail stocks
(v)   Distribution
(vi)   Out of stock
(vii)   Average price to the consumer
(viii) Average stocks and sales
(ix)   Average expenditure (manufacturer and brand)

5   DATABASES

5.1   *Database marketing* is a new phenomenon which has been described as:

'An interactive approach to marketing communications, which uses individually addressable communications media (such as mail, telephone and sales force).'

(a)   to extend help to a company's target audience;

(b)   to stimulate their demand;

(c)   to stay close to them by recording and keeping an electronic database memory of customer, prospect and all communications and commercial contacts, to help improve all future contacts.

5.2   The aim is to promote three main benefits.

(a)   Strategic improvements through the better use of marketing information internally, leading to increased efficiency and effectiveness.

(b)   Identification of strategic advantage through better use of customer and market information leading to the development of new and unique products and services.

(c)   The development of long-term customer relationships to increase customer loyalty, reduce brand switching and enhance cross-selling opportunities.

5.3   There is a range of market research classification systems. The use of databases comprised of routinely gathered information is described in the following table.

Database marketing
Uses of customer information in database marketing

Information	*Marketing use*
Customer title	Sex, job, description identification
Customer first name	Sex, coding, discriminates households, MONICA[1] analyses
Customer surname	Ethnic coding
Customer address	Geodemographic profiling and census data - ACORN, PINPOINT, SAGACITY
Date of sale	Tracking of purchase rates, pre-purchase identification
Items ordered	Benefit/need analysis, product clusters
Quantities ordered	Heavy/light user. Crude segmentation
Price	Life time value calculation of profitability
Discount (if any)	Price sensitivity
Terms and conditions	Customer service needs, special requirements

[1] MONICA is a system offered by CACI which claims to predict psychographic profiles of consumer households simply on the basis of first names (eg 'Reginald' and 'Hilda' are likely to be over 50, working class, etc; 'Tracey' and 'Wayne' are likely to be under thirty, lower class etc. CACI claim 95% accuracy. Based on the Census.

Market research classification systems

5.4 All of these systems depend on electronic manipulation and merger of official census data with market research information. Economic and demographic systems used included the following.

(a) ACORN profile (CACI) - stands for 'A Classification of Residential Neighbourhoods'. Based on the census statistics, it categorises housing in terms of neighbourhood type. There are 11 groups (eg 'Group A - Agricultural areas; Group B - Modern Family Housing, high income etc') and 38 ACORN types (A1 = agricultural villages; B6 = new detached housing, young couples, etc)

(b) PINPOINT is a similar system with 12 general level PIN types, and then further subclassifications into 25 or 60 PIN types, with progressively smaller percentages of the population in each group.

(c) SAGACITY Life Cycle grouping - based on the idea that people have different aspirations and behaviour patterns as they go through their life cycle. Four main stages of the cycle are defined, subdivided by income and occupation groups.

5.5 Lifecycle definitions are as follows.

(a) Dependent - mainly under 24s living at home or full-time students

(b) Pre-family - under 35s who have established their own household but have no children

(c) Family - housewives and heads of household under 65 with one or more children in the household

(d) Late - includes all adults whose children have left home or who are over 35 and childless

---

Exercise

The table in paragraph 5.4 above is missing the most commonly used market research classification system. We looked at this system in detail earlier in the text. Let's test your memory. What is the system and what are the classifications?

Solution

Distribution by JICNARS National Readership Survey provides breakdown by categories based on occupation of the main wage earner in the household. The classifications are as follows.

Social grade	Social status	Occupation
A	Upper middle class	Higher managerial administrative or professional
B	Middle class	Intermediate managerial, administrative or professional
C1	Lower middle class	Supervisory or clerical and junior administrative or professional
C2	Skilled working class	Skilled manual workers
D	Working class	Semi and unskilled manual workers
E	Those at the lower level of subsistence	State pensioners or widows (no other earner), casual or lowest grades of workers

---

5.6 A great deal of data about the marketing environment is likely to be secondary data, such as government statistics, economic forecasts by economic forecasting groups, the published reports and accounts of competitors, and information obtained from the financial press, national newspapers or professional magazines etc. The table below describes a range of secondary data sources. Most of this information is available 'on line', on CD ROM or in electronic form.

(a) Subscription services
(b) Yearbooks etc
(c) On-line data

Subscription services

5.7 These include the following.

(a) Mintel Market Intelligence Reports - monthly

(b) Retail Intelligence - quarterly

(c) *Mintel Digest* - monitors national newspapers, trade journals, and a selection of international newspapers

(d) *ADMAP* - monthly journal with information and statistical data on advertising expenditure. Three times annually publishes a summary of advertising expenditure by product category and media.

(e) *Media Expenditure Analysis* (MEAL) monitors advertising expenditure by media; details by product group and individual advertisers.

(f) *The Economist Group* (or *Economist Intelligence Unit*) reports periodically on industrial sectors, including retailing and distribution, in addition to occasional special reports.

(g) *Retail Business and Marketing in Europe* - monthly indexes of specific aspects of markets. Swift detection of market trends.

(h) *Euromonitor* - publishes *Market Research Great Britain* monthly, covering ten specialist topics per issue (many food products are covered).

(i) *Financial Times Business Information Service* (est 1971) provides a wide ranging service. Detail can include brand shares, advertising expenditure, production, import, export, sales figures, demographic analyses of purchasing patterns. With *Extel*, FT is the major provider of business information to electronic information services (on PRESTEL).

Yearbooks, directories and statistical summaries

5.8   These include the following.

(a) *KOMPASS:* names and addresses of companies (eg possible competitors) by company and product category.

(b) *Kellys Guide* lists industrial, commercial and professional organisations in the UK, giving a description of their main activities and addresses.

(c) *Key British Enterprises:* a register of 25,000 UK companies. Includes basic financial data, including sales, number of employees and Standard Industrial Code (SIC).

(d) *UK trade names:* lists trade names and parent company.

(e) *Who Owns Whom* lists firms and their parent organisations.

(f) *Business Monitor:* gives statistics for different products, eg number of manufacturers, industry sales and import levels.

(g) *Henley Centre for Forecasting:* projects future social attitudes, lifestyles, income and expenditure.

(h) *Market Intelligence (MINTEL):* monthly reports on profile of different markets (customers and competitors). Also publishes special reports on individual markets (eg fresh fish, hamburgers, carbonated drinks) which are commercially available and much used.

(i) *Retail Business:* monthly reports on the profiles of different retailing markets.

(j) *The Retail Directory:* details of trade associations and retail companies according to type and geography.

(k) *Target Group Index (TGI):* annual profile of most product markets in terms of who buys what; 34 volumes each year.

(l) *National Readership Survey:* profile of readers of newspapers and magazines (for advertising readership selection).

(m) *BRAD (British Rate and Data):* costs of advertising in various mass media.

(n) *Trade Associations:* information on numbers of competitors and size of market.

(o) *Local Chambers of Trade:* statistics on companies in their trading area and information on trading conditions.

On-line data

5.9   On-line data includes the following.

(a) *Viewdata* (PRESTEL): general purpose on-line database, including some market and company information. Specialist on-line data services can provide much more specialised information (eg Textline provides a keyword search of newspapers and journals for specialist information on specific topics; food and farm data.

(b) *Pergamon Infoline:* 29 databases covering marketing and sales prospects, finance and credit checking, business intelligence and news, trademarks and British Standards.

(c) *Kompass On-line:* covers 23,000 companies including names and addresses, telephone/telex numbers, descriptions of businesses, numbers of employees, executive names and sales figures.

(d) *Textline* offers abstracts from British and European Newspapers plus some marketing journals.

5.10   Secondary data is relatively cheap, usually easily available, and can cover sample sizes and geographic areas which it would not be possible for a single firm to do for itself. The census of population, for instance, is now used extensively as a basis for much market segmentation analysis.

Using internal databases

5.11   A database can be built up of internal data about the business itself. The data can be used in the initial stages of strategic planning as follows.

(a)   To carry out a *resource audit*.
(b)   To assess and plan *resource utilisation*.
(c)   To *control* the use of resources.

5.12   A resource audit is a survey of what resources the business has in each of its functions or divisions. There are four groups of resources.

(a)   Physical resources.
(b)   Human resources.
(c)   Systems.
(d)   Intangibles (for example company image).

Efficiency

5.13   Efficiency can be measured and recorded in a database in a number of ways.

(a)   *Profitability*. Commercial organisations must, at the end of the day, make a profit. The efficiency of the use of resources in achieving profit can be measured in the context of cost of capital, return on finance, and how the competition is doing.

(i)   The PIMS approach (Profit Impact of Market Strategy), which we looked at in Chapter 4, identifies in this context company size, return on investment (ROI), profit ratios, earnings per share (EPS), dividend rates, market price of equities, liquidity ratios, size of monetary assets balances, use of assets, leverage ratios, and the intensity of investment. This latter measure identifies the amount of investment being put in by a company.

(ii)   There are two ratios to measure the intensity of investment: investment/sales and investment/value added.

(iii)   Capital intensive organisations, with a strong commitment to more investment, often have poor ROI ratios, and it is argued that capital investment is not necessarily a sign of company health, but rather a situation where hardware has become an end in itself.

(iv)   For the public sector, such as a local authority, the ratios must hinge upon the efficient stewardship of resources, since there is no profit motive.

(b)   *Labour productivity* and the use of human resources. Efficiency records will cover the cost of labour (white as well as blue collar workers), levels of absenteeism, labour turnover, days lost through stoppages and strikes, the balance of functional expertise in the workforce, the equality of employees and the degree of unionisation and the attitude of the unions.

(c)   *Production and marketing performance*. In a production context, this refers to yield and productivity ratios, while in the marketing context, product sales analysis, sales growth, market share, width of product line, sales per employee, number of customers, rate of new product development and quality of production will be important items of data.

(d)   Other measures that can be recorded are as follows.

(i)   *Capacity-fill*, ie actual volume as a percentage of full capacity. This is vitally important in a capital-intensive service industry, such as hotels and restaurants.

(ii)   *Working capital utilisation*. It may be that the competition is controlling working capital better and in consequence has lower financing charges.

(iii) *Operating systems*. As an example, does the company move goods in the most efficient way, minimising excessive handling, and taking advantage of any new methods of goods handling that may become available. The ability to respond quickly to delivery requests is an increasingly important element in customer decisions, particularly in business to business markets.

Effectiveness

5.14 Effectiveness may well be less easy to measure and obtain data for than efficiency. Nonetheless, it embraces such areas as the following.

(a) *The use of people*. The question must be 'are you getting out of the people what is wanted?'

(b) *Use of capital*. Is capital being raised and used to achieve its purpose? For example a hotel represents a considerable capital investment, which requires a high level of occupancy. Thus, its performance in the business market in the week, its share of the holiday market, however defined, and if appropriate, its share of the conference market will all be measures in this context.

(c) *Use of research knowledge*. Again this is an area that borders on the intangible, but the extent to which R & D is creating new products (and that market research is identifying realist new market opportunities) should be assessed.

(d) *Use of operating systems or logistics*. Is the organisation using its systems of operating to a good purpose or could they be used better to do other things?

(e) *Use of intangibles*. Is the company making use of its intangible assets, such as brand image, trademarks and patents, to develop its products and markets?

The database and control of resources

5.15 Johnson and Scholes suggest that once a database has been built up which recognises what resources the organisation has at its disposal and how efficiently and effectively they are being used, management can draw on information to control the use of the resources.

5.16 Where good resources are well deployed, it is possible that the actual performance is poor because of poor control. Areas that will come under review are as follows.

(a) Control of physical resources
(b) Control of key personnel
(c) Costing
(d) Quality of materials
(e) Market outlets
(f) Stock control and production control

5.17 Most of this information will be of relevance to the marketing decision-making process.

6   PRIVATISATION

6.1 Various areas of the public sector (eg water, gas, electricity, telecommunications) have been delivered to the private sector in a process of privatisation. This process had a number of sometimes conflicting objectives. These are outlined below.

(a) Short-term *reductions in public sector borrowing* and expenditure to finance tax cuts.

(b) *Greater investment*. A reason for deregulating the water industry was that the government at the time was unwilling to finance the necessary capital investment to maintain and improve the system from general taxation.

(c) Privatising was a way of removing industries from the *control of civil servants*. Privatised utilities are free to borrow (previously restricted by Treasury controls) and spend as they wish. Unpopular commercial decisions or operating practices are no longer held to be the government's fault. The utilities are free to expand elsewhere.

(d) *Efficient management.* It was believed that the private sector is necessarily more efficient than the public. However, as many efficiency savings were made before privatisation to make the industries attractive to private investors, perhaps it was the threat of privatisation that carried out this task.

(e) *Competition.* Privatisation was held to encourage competition, but criticism has been levelled in some cases as public utilities were sold off as private monopolies.

(f) *Contracting out* work to private firms, where the work was previously done by government employees - eg refuse collection, hospital laundry work, even prison management. This is supposed to save money.

NHS Trust marketing

6.2   Although the NHS has not been privatised, it offers a useful example of how marketing is relevant to traditional public sector organisations which now operate in a competitive environment. A new internal market has been created in healthcare and there is a split between:

(a)   purchasers (the health authorities and GP fundholders); and
(b)   providers (hospitals).

6.3   Hospitals are no longer directly managed units, but have become autonomous trusts with their own boards and directors. They have to contract with their purchasers for the provision of healthcare. Hospitals are therefore exposed to risk and must focus carefully on the services which they wish to provide. The relationship has become a commercial one and customer satisfaction is an important concept.

6.4   Marketers therefore need, on behalf of hospitals, to understand the new marketing environment, which is a highly political one, and perform well from the start in a short-term culture.

7   INTERNAL MARKETING

7.1   The initial impetus underlying the development of the internal marketing concept was a concern that employees in contact with customers - engaged in so-called 'interactive marketing' - should be responsive to customers' needs. One of the pioneers of the movement, Christian Gronroos, argued that the objective of *internal* marketing is to get motivated and customer-conscious personnel. Effective service delivery, he argues, is not guaranteed by customer-conscious employees. It is also important to develop co-ordination between contact staff and background support staff.

7.2   The internal marketing concept also functions to integrate different functions at the core of customer relations within service companies.

7.3   Berry provided an early definition, as 'viewing employees as internal customers ... jobs as internal products that satisfy the needs and wants of these internal customers while addressing the objectives of the organisation'.

7.4   The basic implication is that to have satisfied customers, a firm must have satisfied employees. Radical proponents of this 'personnel' view, such as Sasser and Arbeit, assert that personnel is the first market of a service company.

7.5   Berry and Parasuranam take this view to greater lengths, explicitly appropriating for marketing many activities which are traditionally the province of the personnel function, maintaining that

'Internal marketing is attracting, developing, motivating and retaining qualified employees through job-products that satisfy their needs. Internal marketing is the philosophy of treating employees as customers ... and it is the strategy of shaping the job-products to fit human needs.'
(Berry and Parasuranam, *Marketing Services*)

7.6 This broadening of the sphere in marketing has been led by Kotler, who sees marketing as relevant to the way in which organisations relate to all their 'publics', employees as well as external customers. Gronroos has also extended his own concept to encompass the motivation of personnel towards customer consciousness by applying 'marketing-like activities internally' and that employees' ... are best motivated for service-mindedness and customer oriented behaviour by an active marketing-like approach, where marketing-like activities are used internally'.

7.7 An alternative approach is advanced by the total quality management approach, with the focus upon relationships between employees themselves rather than between the organisation and the employee. Under the idea of the internal customer, everyone is both a supplier and a customer, and organisational processes are comprised of 'quality chains'. TQM sees the primary need as motivation for employees to view each other as customers/suppliers, and to achieve performance to measurable standards, which can be set either internally or externally. BS 5750 in the UK has provided such a 'benchmark'.

7.8 It is increasingly recognised within firms of all kinds that in order to be effective when marketing to external customers, internal marketing, or marketing to staff within the firm, is essential. There is general agreement that this seems to involve two key aspects.

(a) Every employee and department in an organisation have roles as both internal customers and internal suppliers. To create high quality external marketing, they must set out to create quality in the service which they give to others, and look to receive that quality of service themselves.

(b) This objective must be stated in the organisation's mission, in the strategies which it follows, and in the goals which it sets. In order to achieve this objective, effective teamwork is vital.

7.9 This aims to ensure that all the staff provide the best possible contribution to the overall marketing activities of the company. For instance, when communications are taking place, both within the organisation and in contacts with customers, adherence to the internal marketing principle 'adds value' to all service encounters and enables the function to be carried out all the more effectively.

7.10 Research suggests that although the principles involved may be acknowledged by a large number of companies, formalised internal marketing programmes in the UK are still fairly uncommon. Initial findings suggest that:

(a) internal marketing is implicit in other strategies such as quality programmes and customer care initiatives, rather than standing alone as an explicit policy in its own right;

(b) where it is practised, internal marketing tends to involve a core of structured activities surrounded by less rigorously defined ad hoc practices;

(c) to operate successfully, internal marketing relies heavily on good communication networks;

(d) internal marketing is a key factor in competitive differentiation;

(e) conflicts between functional areas are significantly reduced by internal marketing;

(f) internal marketing was felt by employees to be a valuable learning experience;

(g) internal marketing evolves and changes over time;

(h) internal marketing dissolves barriers between organisational elements;

(i) internal marketing has a vital role in balancing marketing and operations;

(j) internal marketing promotes innovatory initiatives;

(k) internal marketing depends heavily on commitment at the highest level of management, on general, active, widespread co-operation, and on the presence of an open management style.

7.11 In the research which was carried out, internal marketing was thought to contribute in a major way to the 'people element' of the marketing mix, and was a very strong influence on the development of 'customer-focused' organisations. The main impact of this approach was on communications within the organisation, and it was shown to promote significant improvements in the degree of responsiveness, responsibility and unity of purpose which was manifested.

7.12 Internal marketing, for obvious reasons, also plays an important part in fostering good employee motivation.

7.13 The fundamental aims of internal marketing are:

(a) to develop awareness of customers, both internal and external to the organisation;
(b) to remove functional barriers to organisational effectiveness.

7.14 Companies using this approach to great effect include SAS (Scandinavian Airline Systems), who have increased the involvement of employees in the decision-making process to achieve the highest levels of satisfaction, empowered them to make decisions appropriate to the requirements of particular customers, and trained them to feel a responsibility towards customers of all kinds. As a consequence the company culture fosters a caring relationship internally and externally.

7.15 Marks and Spencer concentrates on recruiting and retaining the highest calibre staff, and promotes a corporate philosophy in which quality is the biggest single factor in the success of the company. Great emphasis is placed on the manifestation of this philosophy in all aspects of the organisation, from the meals in the staff canteen to contacts with customers.

7.16 Internal marketing is also important because of the way in which it fits into other strategic developments. For example, here internal marketing is concerned with the development of a customer-orientated policy, the specific integration of internal and external marketing facilitates the development of a general policy of 'relationship marketing'.

7.17 'Relationship marketing' refers to the attraction, maintenance and, in multi-service organisations, the enhancement of customer relationships. Contrary to the conventional view of marketing, attracting new customers here is only the first step of the process, and relationship marketing moves the emphasis from 'transaction' to long term customer retention, to the development and enhancement of more enduring relationships with other external markets such as suppliers, recruitment, referral and influence, as well as internal markets, and a serious attempt to bring together quality, customer service and marketing activities in other to release their combined 'synergistic potential' (after Christopher, Psayne and Ballantyne, *Relationship Marketing*).

7.18 Several commentators argue that a major problem in the dissemination of an approach that is broadly accepted within industry, and whose value is widely acknowledged, is the difficulty of arriving at a clear and precise definition of what is involved in this approach. As we saw earlier, some formulations suggest that traditional personnel functions - attracting developing and motivating staff - should be integrated within the marketing function.

8   MARKETING TECHNIQUES FOR INTERNAL MARKETING

8.1 To what extent is it possible to apply marketing techniques to develop customer oriented behaviour and to motivate employees? If we examine the extended marketing mix (the 7Ps of People, Price, Promotion, Place, Physical evidence, Process and Participants) we see that the integrated effort of the internal marketing programme is a product of the inter-functional interdependence and integrated marketing activity which this concept proposed.

8.2   *Product* is the job under the internal marketing concept and the *price* is the psychological cost/benefit of adopting the new orientation and those things which have to be given up in order to carry out the new tasks (opportunity costs). Difficulties here relate to the problem of arriving at an accurate and adequate evaluation of psychological costs.

8.3   Communication and *promotion* for external marketing are concerned with getting messages across to existing or potential customers. Many of the same methods need to be employed to motivate employees and influence attitudes and behaviour. Existing HRM practices are beginning to employ techniques developed within marketing, such as multi-media presentations and in-house publications. Presentational skills are also being borrowed from personal selling techniques, while incentive schemes - cash bonuses, awards, recognition programmes, prize draws and competitions - familiar to below-the-line marketers, are being employed to generate changes in employee behaviour. These can also be used to overcome short term resistance, increase productivity or produce consistent behaviour.

8.4   *Advertising* is increasingly used to generate a favourable corporate image amongst employees as well as external customers. The proliferation of 'narrow casting technologies' makes communication by television a much more cost effective proposition. Federal Express has the largest corporate television network in the world, with 1,200 sites in the UK, Paris and Brussels as well as the USA, able to receive transmissions world wide. In lieu of a conference for the top executives, a recent three hour broadcast was watched by all employees who were then able to ask questions. This method shows every sign of expanding exponentially as the medium itself undergoes constant and continuing development.

8.5   *Distribution* for internal marketing probably means meetings, conferences and so on, which can be used to announce policies and refer to third parties (eg consultants and training agencies) used, for example, to deliver training programmes.

8.6   *Physical evidence* refers to the environment in which a product/service is delivered and where interaction takes place between contact staff and customers, as well as any tangible goods with facilitate delivery or communication of the product. For internal marketing, the environment in which the product is delivered is not as important as for services in general because this will generally be the same as the normal working environment. Tangible clues may be even more important, however; documentation of policies and changes in policies are important because they provide a clear way of measuring whether employees are meeting the standards involved. Quality standards such as BS 5750/ISO 9000, for instance, place great emphasis on documentation. Other tangible elements might involve training sessions, which would constitute a manifestation of commitment to standards or policies.

8.7   *Process*, which refers to how a 'customer' actually receives a product, relates to the internal marketing context through the medium of training which may be used to promote customer consciousness.

8.8   *Participants*, or the people involved in producing and delivering the product, along with those receiving the product who may influence the customer's perceptions, are clearly important within the internal marketing process. Communications must be delivered by someone of the right level of authority in order to achieve their aims. In internal marketing, the source of these programmes is a critical factor influencing whether or not they will be effective. The way in which employees act is strongly influenced by fellow employees, particularly their immediate superiors. Inter-departmental or interfunctional communications are likely to be least effective, because they have equal status or lack the authority to ensure compliance.

8.9 To improve the performance of contact staff, communication through immediate superiors, directed by strategic management, is likely to be the most effective. Direct communication from the level of management which is directing the formulation of management strategy is likely to be less effective.

8.10 Segmentation and marketing research can also be very important techniques for use in internal marketing. Employees may be grouped according to their service characteristics, needs, wants or tasks in order to organise the dissemination of a service orientation. Research will monitor the needs and wants of employees, and identify the impact of corporate policies. This kind of occupational research has a long history.

8.11 Clearly, marketing concepts and techniques are potentially very valuable indeed in the process of implementing corporate goals, and promoting employee motivation.

9   PROBLEMS WITH THE INTERNAL MARKETING CONCEPT

9.1 Assumptions, that, for instance, effective use of inwardly directed marketing techniques can solve all employee related quality and customer satisfaction problems are clearly over-optimistic. Departments need to co-operate, rather than looking for one function to solve all these problems. Research clearly shows that actions by the personnel department, or effective programmes of personnel selection and training, are likely to be more effective than marketing based activities.

9.2 Internal marketing clearly has limits too. In the UK retail sector, for example, while many large scale operations have begun Sunday trading, there has been significant resistance from employee organisations. Internal marketing would argue that employees should be persuaded by means of a well-executed communications campaign and by the offer of proper incentives. Although these strategies have been tried, they have met with little success, or (in the case of incentives) have been too expensive. Employers have solved the problem by specifically recruiting employees who are required to work on Sunday, who may be paid slightly higher wage rates for the time in question. Rather than internal marketing, external recruitment proved to be the solution.

9.3 Claims by some marketers (George, Berry and Parasuranam) that marketing can replace or fulfil the objectives of some other functions are clearly overstated. Rather than attempt to apply an internal marketing programme from the marketing department alone, such programmes need to involve the co-operation and activity of the full range of internal departments. The internal marketing concept has a major role to play in making employees customer conscious. The most effective and widely adopted programme at the moment appears to be TQM, although there are very few models of how internal marketing should be implemented available at the moment.

9.4 The simple transfer of marketing concepts and techniques is unlikely to produce the necessary results. It seems necessary to identify what kinds of results are required, and what the involvement of other departments should be.

Chapter roundup

- Marketing has been an increasingly popular career choice for the past 20 years. The role of the marketing manager involves all the activities typically carried on by managers.

- A number of theorists have written extensively on the role and function of managers. They include Fayol, Drucker and Mintzberg.

- Developments in IT have played a major part in effecting many of the changes taking place in marketing operations. Management information systems provide a wide range of market information, and databases and other software enable non-specialists to carry out complicated analyses.

- The marketing information system can be seen as a subset of the organisation's overall management information system.

- Internal marketing is the concept that employees in contact with customers should be responsive to customer needs. It has been adopted by a number of companies.

Test your knowledge

1   What does public relations involve? (see paras 1.7, 1.8)

2   What is marketing management? (1.20)

3   According to Fayol, what does the process of management involve? (2.8)

4   What are Drucker's five categories of management activity? (2.13)

5   What are Mintzberg's three basic management rules? (2.16)

6   What is the impact of IT on marketing? (3.12)

7   What is a marketing information system? (4.5)

8   What is database marketing? (5.1)

9   What is PIMS? (5.13)

10   What is internal marketing? (7.1 - 7.4)

11   What are the drawbacks inherent in internal marketing? (9.1 - 9.4)

Now try illustrative question 16 at the end of the Study Text

MARKETING OPERATIONS IN ACTION

At the end of each part of this Study Text, we take a look at the subject matter covered in the light of real companies, either to offer more detail or to give an understanding of the wider corporate context.

In the chapter on social responsibility, we analysed the effect of the green movement on marketing operations. A recent report from Mintel, entitled *The Green Consumer*, suggests that the green consumer base has remained fairly static since 1990. The report is summarised in *Marketing Business* (July/August 1995) as follows.

'The percentage of respondents who buy environmentally friendly products has increased slightly to about 60 per cent.

The balance between dark green and pale green consumers - between those who make an effort to buy such products and those who only buy when they see them - has remained the same at 40 per cent and 20 per cent respectively. The percentage of respondents who admit they do not care about - nor have an opinion on - environmental issues has fallen, but the proportion of armchair greens - those who are concerned but have not changed their spending habits - has increased.

The Mintel report reveals that J Sainsbury has the highest proportion of green customers, with nearly seven in 10 putting themselves in this category. About two-thirds of Marks & Spencer, Tesco and Gateway shoppers are green - they at least buy environmentally friendly goods when they see them. Kwik Save, with a more C2DE-biased profile, has the fewest green shoppers - 56 per cent - and the largest proportion in the unconcerned category.

The proportion of green shoppers at J Sainsbury is the same as in 1990, but Tesco's percentage has increased. The store now has the highest proportion - 47 per cent - of the most committed, dark green shoppers. The biggest increase in the proportion of green shoppers has been among those who shop at the Co-op, with an increase of seven percentage points to 60 per cent. This may seem low for a store with strong environmental and ethical commitments, but could be partly because of its high proportion of older shoppers.

Both Kwik Save and Asda have fewer green shoppers than in 1990. These stores have traditionally been associated with price-cutting, and their customers may have lost interest in environmental issues as the recession squeezed their budgets.

Mintel found that shoppers at J Sainsbury and Safeway are more likely than others to mention the ozone layer as a concern. River and sea pollution are especially important to Gateway customers. Forest destruction and recycling are higher on the agendas of regular Safeway shoppers than other.

Overall the highest level of environmental concern - measured in specific issues that might prevent a purchase - is exhibited by Safeway shoppers, 63 per cent of whom mentioned at least one such issue.

Environmentally friendly products are as effective as standard products, according to 45 per cent of respondents to the Mintel survey; but 25 per cent thought they did not work as well. One in three felt unable to judge - possibly because they have not used environmentally friendly cleaning and laundry products, or because they do not use cleaning and laundry products at all.'

Illustrative questions and suggested solutions

1   SWOT

Distinguish clearly between a marketing audit and a SWOT analysis, indicating where, why and when they should be used.

2   SEGMENTATION

Using appropriate examples, illustrate the nature and usage of the major types of segmentation variables in marketing consumer and industrial goods.

3   AUDIT (25 marks)   *45 mins*

The following is an extract from a letter sent by a management consultancy company to a UK industrial company. The consultancy company has undertaken a series of interviews with senior managers on the organisation of marketing activities with a view to helping in the preparation of the current year's marketing strategy.

Mr G A Brown
Managing Director
Brown Industrial plc
Northington

Dear Mr Brown

Further to my recent visits and interviews with managerial personnel, please find a brief resume of our consultant's findings.

1   Poor communication of marketing information between and within departments.

2   Insufficient interaction between marketing and sales functions.

3   Limited understanding of customer needs.

4   Low awareness of the nature of competitive threats.

In view of these observations it is our recommendation that your company conducts a full marketing audit prior to the preparation of this year's marketing plan. This exercise should identify information gaps and help you appraise future marketing opportunities.

Yours sincerely

J A Smith
Senior Consultant

Draft out the contents which Brown Industrial should cover in the marketing audit and explain why it is a useful technique for the company to use.

4   PLANNING

Explain and illustrate the relationship between planning at corporate level, and planning a marketing strategy. Show how the two types of planning are interconnected.

5   ENVIRONMENT (25 marks)   *45 mins*

Assume that you are the Marketing Manager for an international airline. In order to take advantage of marketing opportunities your company needs to have a sound understanding of its internal capabilities and of the marketing environment in which it operates.

Your company's board of directors has already assessed the organisation's internal capabilities and now wishes to become better informed about the marketing environment. You have been given the task of preparing a document for the board, which identifies the elements of the marketing environment that your company needs to understand and explains why each is of importance.

6   **IKEA (50 marks)**   *90 mins*

Swedish furniture manufacturer and retailer IKEA was formed in 1943 by Ingvar Kamprad. Between 1954, when the first store opened, and 1990 the company underwent massive expansion from a single Swedish outlet to more than 80 spread through 21 different countries, with over 70% of revenue generated outside Scandinavia. The IKEA concept comprises large retail outlets (around 80,000 square metres) situated on the edge of sizeable towns and cities, selling a full range of furniture and furnishings. From beds to lounge suites, kitchen utensils to carpets, curtains, pictures and lighting everything the customer needs to set up and update the home. The stores also offer instore restaurant and child care facilities to make the shopping experience a pleasant one. To help in the selling effort, the company produces an extensive catalogue, giving details of the items for sale, prices, colours, measurements and availability. In 1990 alone, around 35 million US dollars were spent producing 40 million copies in 12 different languages.

IKEA operates with an up market brand image, linked to stylish and sophisticated Swedish taste, but its products are aimed clearly at the mass market. The company is not a market nicher and to maintain its growth must attract large numbers of customers of low as well as high incomes. To keep its prices low, IKEA must keep costs down. This is achieved by a clever combination of buying in bulk, making buying centres compete for orders, having large stores with self-service facilities and products which are flat packed, for self assembly at home.

The IKEA company mission is clearly stated 'We shall offer a wide range of furnishing items of good design and function, at prices so low that the majority of people can afford to buy them'. This philosophy is backed up by the following aims.

- IKEA should keep costs low and assist customers

- products should combine good quality, durability and be functional

- profit should be used to build and expand

- a keen understanding of the company's cost base must be maintained and good results achieved with careful investment

- energy must be concentrated carefully and time used efficiently

- simple solutions should be found to product and company problems

- IKEA should take responsibility and put things right

- IKEA should find alternative solutions to problems by experimenting

Currently IKEA seems to appeal particularly to customers aged in their 20s and 30s who are furnishing a home for the first time. These customers want their homes to look stylish and smart, but with relatively low disposable incomes must carefully consider price. The company is also keen to attract other customer types, from many different countries and of all ages and lifestyle stages. Although IKEA does not formally use demographics and psychographics to segment its market, it divides its markets into different geographical areas, each with a standard product range but having the flexibility to include products which match local, cultural requirements.

Answer the following questions with reference to the IKEA case.

(a)   Briefly define marketing planning and say why it is important for IKEA to use it.   (10 marks)

(b)   How should the marketing planning process relate to IKEA's corporate planning?   (10 marks)

(c)   Describe the elements of a detailed marketing plan and show within this framework what types of information might be included in a marketing plan for IKEA.   (25 marks)

(5 marks will be allocated for presentation.)

7   **ORGANISATION**

Explain the difference between the organisation of marketing on the basis of function and the use of matrix organisation systems.

8   **THE MARKETING MIX**

What are the elements of the marketing mix? Outline some of the factors to be considered for a company to arrive at an appropriate marketing mix.

9   SUPPLIERS

What are the main problems likely to be encountered in the relation between marketing managers and external suppliers? Why is this becoming a more pressing issue for modern managers?

10   SERVICES

Which characteristics of services have the most important marketing implications? Why might this be more important for marketing practices in general?

11   SERVICES MARKETING (25 marks)   *45 mins*

Services marketing is often said to involve extending the marketing mix to include the three additional elements of people, process and physical evidence.

Assume you are a marketing analyst acting for the board of a company in a service industry of your choice. Prepare a report which explains why the marketing mix is extended in this way. You should pay particular attention to the role of people in delivering service and maintaining service quality.

12   CHARITY (25 marks)   *45 mins*

You have recently taken up a new position with a well-known national charity. Your job is to oversee and organise marketing activities for the charity. Your previous work experience has been entirely in the commercial sector so not-for-profit marketing is new to you.

Your new boss, the charity's director, has asked you to make some notes on the similarities and differences you expect to find between your new and old positions. Prepare a document which does this and explains how these contrasts will affect the marketing activities which you carry out.

13   PRODUCT STANDARDISATION

Some products tend to be required in a standardised form in several countries; while others emphasise local variations. What particular conditions lead to:

(a)   greater standardisation; and
(b)   greater variation?

14   QUALITY

What are the implications of quality management for relations between marketing departments and personnel within and outside of the organisation?

15   ETHICS AND SOCIAL RESPONSIBILITY (25 marks)   *45 mins*

Major multinationals such as PepsiCo, McDonald's, Lever Brothers and Proctor and Gamble must increasingly consider marketing ethics and social responsibility when making marketing decisions.

Adopt the role of marketing manager for *one* of these companies and prepare a report which explains what the key ethical and social responsibility issues are and discuss how the company might go about handling them.

16   INFORMATION TECHNOLOGY

Why is information technology so important to modern managers?

1   **SWOT**

There is often confusion between a marketing audit and a SWOT analysis, yet there is a very clear distinction between them.

(a)   A *marketing audit* is a process or activity carried out periodically, usually annually, to assess the effectiveness of the organisation's marketing activity.

(b)   *SWOT analysis* is a management tool or technique, used to help sort information and clarify the current situation.

A *marketing audit* involves a review of current marketing activity. It is a systematic and thorough analysis of the whole marketing operation, including an assessment of the company's attitude to marketing and the marketing philosophy on the one hand and on the other a review of the marketing organisation, methods and procedures. A rigorous evaluation should be made of the marketing objectives, policies and the effectiveness of strategies to achieve them. A marketing audit attempts to assess the marketing process and how well it performs. It could be seen as the equivalent of an annual 'MOT test' for marketing. A marketing audit is therefore best undertaken by an independent outsider who can review the marketing activity objectively. It can be undertaken by a consultant or perhaps by someone in the company who does not work in the marketing function.

A marketing audit should be undertaken at the start of the planning cycle. It represents an important element of the corporate situational analysis.

SWOT stands for Strengths, Weaknesses, Opportunities and Threats.

(a)   Strengths and weaknesses represent internal controllable factors which management can influence.

(b)   Opportunities and threats represent external, uncontrollable factors which influence the business but cannot be controlled by management.

This simple technique provides a method of organising information and identifying a possible strategic direction. The basic principle of SWOT analysis is that any statement about an organisation or its environment can be classified as a Strength, Weakness, Opportunity or Threat. An opportunity is simply any feature of the external environment which creates conditions which are advantageous to the firm in relation to a particular objective or set of objectives. By contrast, a threat is any environmental development which will present problems and may hinder the achievement of organisational objectives. What constitutes an opportunity to some firms will almost invariably constitute a threat to others. An increased presence in domestic financial markets by overseas banks might be regarded by them as the pursuit of an opportunity but will be perceived as a threat by domestic banks. By contrast, the recent changes relating to State pension schemes might be regarded as an opportunity for building societies, banks and insurance companies in relation to personal customers.

A strength can be thought of as a particular skill or distinctive competence which the organisation possesses and which will aid it in achieving its stated objectives. These may relate to experience in specific types of markets or specific skills possessed by employees. A strength may also refer to factors such as a firm's reputation for quality or customer service. A weakness is simply any aspect of the company which may hinder the achievement of specific objectives such as limited experience of certain markets/technologies, extent of financial resources available. The lack of experience within building societies of money transmission facilities could be regarded as a weakness when considering the development of current accounts, while banks may consider their experience in wholesale money markets to be a strength in relation to the development of mortgage services.

This information would typically be presented as a matrix of strengths, weaknesses, opportunities and threats. Effective SWOT analysis does not simply require a categorisation of information, it also requires some evaluation of the relative importance of the various factors under consideration. In addition, it should be noted that these features are only of relevance if they are perceived to exist by the consumers. Listing corporate features that internal personnel regard as strengths/weaknesses is of little relevance if they are not perceived as such by the organisation's consumers. In the same vein, threats and opportunities are conditions presented by the external environment and they should be independent of the firm.

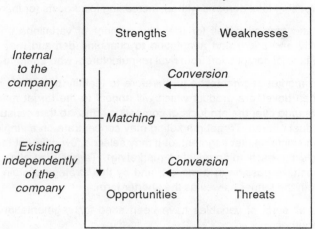

SWOT Analysis

Having constructed a matrix of strengths, weaknesses, opportunities and threats with some evaluation attached to them, it then becomes feasible to make use of that matrix in guiding strategy formulation. The two major options are as follows.

(a) *Matching*. This entails finding, where possible, a match between the strengths of the organisation and the opportunities presented by the market. Strengths which do not match any available opportunity are of limited use while opportunities which do not have any matching strengths are of little immediate value from a strategic perspective.

(b) *Conversion*. This requires the development of strategies which will convert weaknesses into strengths in order to take advantage of some particular opportunity, or converting threats into opportunities which can then be matched by existing strengths.

Although SWOT provides some guidance on developing a match between the organisation's environment and its strategic direction, it is also necessary to consider more specific aspects of strategies such as how best to compete, how to grow within the target markets etc. To aid this process there are a number of analytical techniques which can be used; the role of these techniques is not to offer definitive statements on the final form that a strategy should take, but rather to provide a framework for the organisation and analysis of ideas and information.

2   SEGMENTATION

The market is not a homogeneous mass, but is made up of individual consumers or organisations each with its own unique set of needs. Dealing with each customer individually would be the ultimate in customer orientation. Whilst this may be possible in the personal service markets like bespoke tailoring, and it may be a future development in consumer durable markets (eg where cars can be 'finished' to specific requirements), for most manufacturers segmentation of the market is an acceptable middle ground.

Segmentation is the process of dividing the market into differing groups of buyers, as smaller groups have broadly similar patterns of need and so are more easily managed at a strategic level. These groups can then be targeted and their needs are more likely to be satisfied. The logic of this approach is straightforward. The critical factor in putting it into practice lies in the way in which the market is segmented.

Segments have to be significant enough to be worthwhile, easily identifiable so their members can be isolated from the rest of the population, and accessible so they can be reached. Over twenty years or so writers and practitioners have invented suitable methods of segmenting different markets. This practical task has been made both easier and more sophisticated by improvements in technology and the growth of data bases etc.

Segmentation, an aspect of product policy, is the variation of the design of a single basic product (or service) so that different types of the same product (or service) are produced and marketed. Each variation is intended to appeal to a different sort of customer (and therefore different market segments) within the total market for the product or service.

Segmentation is based on the desire or need to maintain markets large enough to achieve a unit cost of output which enables the product to be sold at a profit. High fixed costs of production (a feature of modern manufacturing) make it necessary to sell high levels of output to be profitable.

As the same equipment and administration can be used for all segment products, segmentation is a means of increasing total demand without increasing fixed costs (or increasing them only a little).

Changing demand may also call for the development of variations on a product (for example high/lower quality and price) and adaptation to changing demand may be necessary to stay in business in the face of competition from rival manufacturers who adapt to the changes themselves.

The purpose of market segmentation is therefore to identify potentially profitable target markets. The firm can then develop a product which will appeal to the target market as having a tangible differential advantage over the products of competing firms, so that consumers in the target market will buy the product offered. Target marketing may concentrate on a single product (or small range of products) and single market segment, or it may select a few different target markets and develop 'unique' products for each (differentiated marketing). Target marketing should enable a firm to achieve a competitive position in a market, and by this strategy sustain adequate sales volumes and profits in both the longer as well as the shorter term.

Over the years all sorts of variables have been sued for segmentation, sometimes in isolation, more usually together.

(a)   Demographic.
(b)   Geographical.
(c)   Behavioural.
(d)   Psychographic.

Segmentation decisions for individual goods vary according to the nature of the market. For example

(a)   Diesel engines are an industrial good, so a manufacturer would probably segment the market on a 'typical' industrial basis, namely by industrial user segments or by individual customers. Diesel engines are used in a variety of industries, such as mining and quarrying, vehicles, mechanical engineering, marine engineering etc. Different types of diesel engine will be required in each industry, so that a manufacturer can produce 'specialist' machines for each segment of the market. The industries mentioned above can also be divided into sub-categories, so that market segments and sub-sub-segments could be identified and established as target markets.

An alternative form of segmentation might occur if the market for diesel engines is dominated by a few major buyers. If this is the case, the engine manufacturer might decide to identify each major buyer as an individual target market.

(b)   Breakfast cereals are consumer goods, therefore segmentation of the market will be according to perceived sub-groupings of consumers. Possible segments might be on the basis of any of the following.

(i)   *Age:* it is possible that many households buy cereals in order to feed children, although some cereals could be clearly targeted at adults.

(ii)   *Family life cycle:* large families may consume cereals quickly and market segmentation on family size had led to the sale of 'family-sized' and 'economy' packets.

(iii)   *Geographical area:* there may be a preference for certain cereals over others in each geographical region. It is possible, for example, that porridge oats are more popular in Scotland than in the rest of Britain.

(iv)   *Occupation:* people in some occupations may breakfast more regularly than others and therefore eat cereals more frequently. Conceivably, segmentation based on occupation might help a firm to identify a target market.

(v)   *Race or nationality:* the eating preferences of different nationalities are likely to create variations in taste for cereals. A firm might be able to produce a cereal product which appeals particularly to one country's population or to one racial group.

(vi)   *Usage rate:* this is perhaps a similar basis for segmentation as item (ii) above. Large users may want 'family-size' packets, whereas occasional users may prefer small one-meal packets of cereal.

(vii)   *Customer buying habits:* market segments may relate to brand loyalty or those consumers who buy on impulse. Groups which are not brand loyal might become the target market of cheaper cereal brands (for example supermarket's own brand labels), and groups which buy on impulse might become a target market by means of sales promotion and display planning.

(viii)   *Life-style:* high-fibre low-sugar cereals are fashionable amongst healthy eaters.

Life style segmentation fits into the psychographic category and it is increasingly popular. Lifestyle techniques considers more than income or social class, and more than personality. They try to develop group profiles as to how people relate with, and respond to, the world.

A number of models of categorising lifestyle have been developed over the years. One of the best known is Young and Rubicam's Cross Cultural Consumer Classifications, developed to help with targeting marketing and advertising campaigns. It identifies three groups:

(a)   *the constrained* of resigned and struggling poor;

(b)   *the middle majority* of mainstreamers, aspirers and succeeders;

(c)   *the innovators* of reformers and transitionals.

Lifestyle analysis has proved to be significant in marketing terms. 'Yuppies' of the 80s might have provided plenty of material for comedians, but also led to massive new product developments for items like Filofax and car phones. Recognition of lesser known lifestyle groups like Glams, (greying leisured affluent middle aged) are likely to be of great importance to the marketing strategists of the late 90's looking for high potential growth market opportunities. As a firm's ability to pinpoint such specific groups improves, so its targeting and use of marketing resources should become more effective.

3   AUDIT

In order to develop an effective marketing strategy, Brown Industrial plc will first need to undertake a *full evaluation of current marketing activity. This will be done through the marketing* audit. The marketing audit will focus on the following.

(a)   How effectively the company is currently performing in terms of its product/market strategy.

(b)   How appropriately the company is structured to implement current strategy and realise current objectives.

(c)   How efficiently the company is currently managing its resources to meet its objectives.

(d)   The required changes needed to (a), (b) and (c) in order to increase competitiveness through increased profitability and productivity.

The marketing audit can be divided into two parts - the *task audit* (concerned with factors internal to the organisation; concerned with 'doing things' and largely within its sphere of control)l and the *macro audit* (concerned with external factors, largely outside the organisation's sphere of control but to which the organisation must respond).

Possible factors impacting upon Brown Industrial

(a)   *Macro specific factors*

   (i)   Impact of economic climate
   (ii)   Impact of population changes
   (iii)   Impact of technical innovation of self and competitors
   (iv)   Impact of political changes
   (v)   Impact of new laws or statutory instruments
   (vi)   Impact of social changes, trends or fashion

(b)   *Task specific factors*

   (i)   Type and characteristics of market segments addressed after research

   (ii)   Nature of customer profiles identified from research

   (iii)   Nature and strengths and weaknesses of competitors requiring to be addressed

   (iv)   Quality of relationships with company suppliers, dealers and intermediaries

   (v)   Effectiveness of external communication system

   (vi)   Quality of market intelligence system

It is within these above six areas that the company will need to improve its performance if it wishes to grow the business. Initially it must ensure that it has developed a marketing-orientated culture to deliver the decided strategy; this can only happen once management have addressed current issues concerning 'people management'. These issues will relate to the following.

(a)   Having the right staff with the right skills in the right jobs.

(b)   Having an appropriate structure through which to deliver a marketing orientation.

(c)   Having an effective management style.

(d)   Developing effective management information systems to serve the strategy.

(e)   Developing effective, clear and appropriate communication channels and identifying and removing barriers to communication.

(f)   Identifying information needs in terms of priorities and establishing a system to deliver this.

(g)   Implementing a series of controls to measure the effectiveness of people, systems and procedures and to guide the development of the organisation between planning cycles.

(h)   Ensuring there is a sense of shared values - that people believe in, and own the strategy!

Brown Industrial plc will need to embark upon a programme of 'relationship marketing' with all key stakeholders both internal to, and external to, the organisation, as it is the poor quality of relationships, in conjunction with poor quality information and communication systems, which currently impede the firm's development.

4   PLANNING

Marketing can and should play a very significant part in the corporate planning process of a market-oriented organisation. In such a business the needs of the customers will be central to all decisions and so they are an essential starting point from which all plans should evolve. As marketing information and research provides the bridge between the customer and the firm, so its role can be seen as fundamental.

However we should recognise that not all companies are market driven. Finance, operations or R&D may represent the driving force. In these more product-oriented cultures, the role of marketing in the corporate planning process is likely to be much more re-active than pro-active.

With that caveat we can consider in more detail the possible role that marketing planning and control may adopt.

Planning at corporate level

The corporate planning process can be split into a number of stages.

(a)   Where are we now?
(b)   Where are we going?
(c)   How can we get there?
(d)   Which is the best route?
(e)   Developing our plan.
(f)   Implementation and control.

We need to evaluate the contribution of marketing at each of these stages.

Where are we now?
The audit stage is based on information about the current strengths and weaknesses of the organisation, including its market position and image etc, and opportunities and threats. This environmental audit is most likely to be informed by marketing information systems which have been set up to monitor the market place and the evolving market opportunities and threats.

Where are we going?
Although set normally in financial terms of profit and return, the activity of corporate objective setting of 'Where are we going?' should be influenced by all the functions. Perhaps most importantly, marketing will provide the sales forecasts which will ensure that corporate objectives are realistic and perceived to be achievable.

How can we get there?
Identifying alternative strategies and selecting the one best suited to the organisation's strength and weaknesses is also likely to be strongly influenced by marketing. An organisation which wants to develop and change has options related to product/market opportunities as illustrated by the Ansoff matrix.

Products
Existing   New

		Existing		New

M
a
r
k
e
t
s

Existing

New

Quantification and calculation of the potential benefits of each of the identified opportunities will be the responsibility of marketing, informed by the information available from marketing research.

Developing our plan
Developing the plan means turning corporate objectives and strategy into operational plans. With other functions, marketing has a part to play in developing a marketing plan which is designed to deliver the agreed corporate objectives.

Implementation and control
The success of the corporate and marketing plans is determined by the skill of the managers implementing them. Communication is essential at this stage and marketing has an increasingly important part to play in developing plans to ensure the effective internal marketing of corporate plans and changes.

Control is the feedback of actual performance results to allow the modification of plans as the environment changes and as better information becomes available. The acid test will be the market reaction to the company's offering, therefore marketing control is critical to ensuring that the demand can be satisfied by the firm's capacity to supply.

Marketing's role as the voice of the customer within the organisation puts it in a special position, able to influence, inform and contribute to the success of the corporate planning process.

Planning a marketing strategy

The term strategy, whether used at corporate or marketing level has the same meaning. It describes the basic approach, the 'how' of how we will achieve a given objectives. It is usually a broad brush statement, but its role is critical as it ensures that those involved in implementing a plan are not just aiming for the same target, but are approaching it from the same direction. Simply, strategy ensures the co-ordinated use of resources resulting, hopefully, in a synergy of effort.

The words 'corporate' or 'marketing' preceding 'strategy' convey the level within the planning framework at which you are working. The corporate level strategy is responsible for co-ordinating all the resources of the organisation - productive, administrative, financial as well as marketing resources. It is the statement which tells everyone in the organisation not just where the firm is going but *how* it will achieves its objectives.

At lower operational planning levels, functional areas like marketing will translate corporate objectives and strategy into objectives and strategies relevant to these levels. In the marketing department these marketing objectives and strategy will become the cornerstone of the marketing plan.

Despite the similar terminology there does appear to be a distinct difference of level in the planning frameworks, so it may be hard to see how marketing and corporate strategy could ever be taken as the same. However, if you consider how central the customer is to the success of the business and that in marketing orientated businesses the customer is likely to be the driving force behind change and growth, it is easy to see that the role of marketing and an evaluation of the best market opportunity is likely to be a factor critical to the development of the corporate strategy.

If you consider that the only strategic options for revenue growth (often the key to increased profits) can be expressed by the Ansoff Matrix.

	Product	
	Current	New
Current	Market penetration	Product development
New	Market extension	Diversification

(left axis label: *Market*)

This matrix is also often used to communicate marketing strategy expressed in terms of product/marketing opportunities.

However, whilst marketing has a key role in providing management with evaluation of these alternatives, it should be noted that a decision for the organisation to move into quadrants 2 and 4 has as much implication for production and research resources as it does for marketing.

Decisions about moving into new geographical markets, or investing in new product development, are so important that while informed by marketing and based on the options which look the best from the marketing view point, they must be taken at corporate level. This could then, in a sense, be described as the corporate marketing strategy.

In the context of the marketing plan, the marketing strategy is concerned with how best to achieve the marketing objectives, using the variables controlled by the marketing function (ie the 4Ps of the marketing mix).

Marketing strategy can best be summarised as evaluating and deciding the best positioning strategy for the organisation and/or one of its brands.

Decisions which are in essence to do with the balance of marketing mix variables, in turn become the dimensions and detail of the marketing plan. Whilst it is easy to see the role of marketing at corporate level, and whilst the process of strategic development may be similar at both levels, there is a difference, and managers need to be clear about the context in which they are considering marketing strategy.

5   ENVIRONMENT

Report to the Board

Introduction

We need to focus on the marketing environment. One way of achieving a full appreciation of it is by means of a marketing audit. This will help focus on business planning. We need to make definite assumptions about how the airline should respond to the marketing environment in terms of marketing objectives, strategies, tactics, contingency plans and of course the control mechanisms which test the degree to which forecasted performance is being realised. We have used a PEST analysis, as follows.

(a)   *Economic factors.* The level of economic activity in a country will influence the demand for both passenger and cargo air transport. Economic stability and growth would stimulate demand, while recession and economic crisis would act as a disincentive to demand.

(b)   *Political factors*, such as the level of government regulation, the type of economy (free or mixed), and the degree to which the country is part of a trading bloc such as the European Union are all factors which will influence demand for the airline's services. For example, an international operator may be preferred for cargo or passenger services on a national air route, given favourable rates and effective service.

All these factors will therefore have an impact on the airline's marketing and promotional mixes used to segment and target customers.

(c)   *Social factors*. The degree to which air transport is the 'preferred method', the distance travelled and habits of the populous, will all influence the degree to which the airline should seek a 'foothold in the market'.

(d)   *Technological factors*. The degree to which the airline can utilise technology to provide quality service (such as bookings, baggage administration, same day delivery for cargo, and customer servicing) will all influence the extent to which it can gain a competitive edge.

(e)   *Relationship marketing*. The quality of relationships developed with suppliers, employees, and customers will do much to enhance both the corporate image and corporate identity of the business and will be factors influencing future growth prospects in a highly competitive industry.

(f)   *Competitive factors*. The airline will need to identify the nature of competitor companies.

(i)   Who are they?
(ii)   What market segments do they target?
(iii)   What are their competitive strengths and weaknesses?
(iv)   How can this line's services portfolio be differentiated from that of competitors?

The answers to these questions will help the airline position its services in the market, and to devise appropriate marketing and promotional mixes.

(g)   *Legal factors*. The airline will need to be fully conversant with regulations binding its activities in the different countries in which it has operations. These regulations might cover:

(i)   licensing and route operations;
(ii)   safety, inspection and maintenance;
(iii)   mergers with other airline operators;
(iv)   nature of business activity and information availability for 'public record'.

Summary

A marketing orientated approach to the marketing environment of the airline, where objectives and strategies are devised after a detailed consideration of all influential forces, should ensure growth for the business and a prosperous future in one of the world's most competitive industries.

(*Note*. You would not be expected to reproduce the diagram below in an examination.)

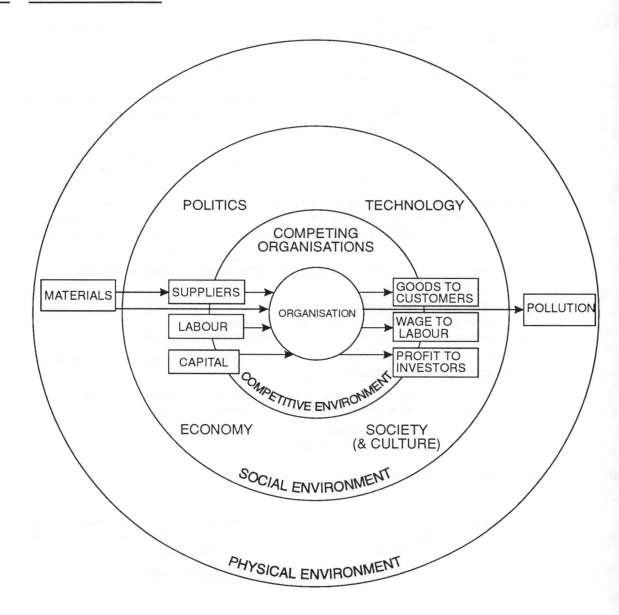

6 **IKEA**

(a) Marketing planning is the regular, systematic, customer-centred and controlled series of activities a company will undertake to meet business objectives, secure long-term profitability and realise its product/market strategy effectively and competitively. Planning activity exists over the short term (1 year), the medium term (2 - 3 years), and the long term (3 - 6 years). Marketing planning is an essential 'management tool' for IKEA to use because:

(i) planning pre-supposes an organised and structured approach to business - essential for IKEA to stay competitive;

(ii) marketing plans, effectively implemented, can be a spur to action for all concerned with their execution;

(iii) marketing planning provides a market orientation to customers, and a control mechanism to keep corporate activity 'on track' so that customer needs are continually satisfied;

(iv) marketing planning helps stimulate the 'corporate vision', and as such may contribute to the creation of an open, action-centred culture;

(v) marketing planning focuses all organisation outwardly, towards the customer, and as such helps the organisation become more pro-active towards such constraining forces such as economic and technical change.

(b)   The marketing planning process should be fully integrated with the IKEA corporate planning process. This is due to the following.

(i)   Marketing is an 'organisation-wide' function. Marketing can no longer be 'compartmentalised' into a department.

In the 1990s, successful organisations are those that realise everyone is marketer; that there are internal as well as external customers, and that successful marketing is reflected in the quality of relationships people have with each other and with customers.

(ii)   Marketing strategy is developed from corporate objectives, and therefore the results of it must feed the corporate planning process.

Successful marketing planning requires leadership - this can only come from the top in terms of direction-setting.

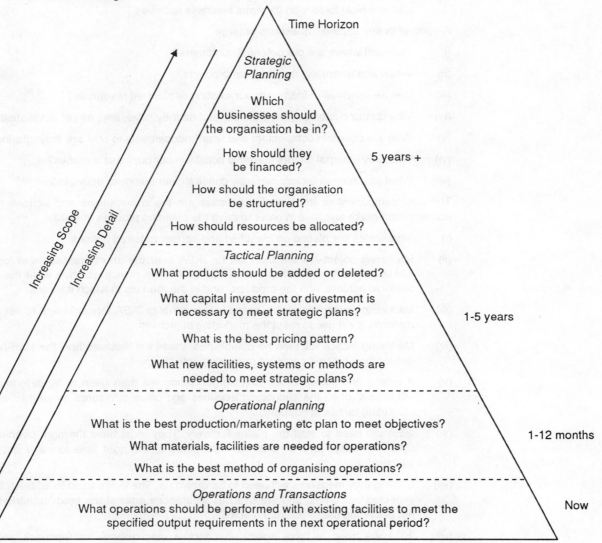

The following approaches will facilitate the integration of marketing planning with IKEA corporate objectives.

(i)   Ensure marketing is represented at senior executive level (within a directional post).

(ii)   Create a culture where participation, motivation and self-development are encouraged, and where there is a sincere interest in, and dedication to, customer servicing.

(iii)   Ensure the management information systems within IKEA are linked to a market intelligence system, to facilitate speedy and reliable information flow back to the organisation.

(iv)   Develop marketing tactics (what to do) from marketing strategy and test them against the requirements of corporate objectives; they should be in 'sync'. If they are not, there is not currently a full integration between marketing planning and corporate planning.

(v) The control mechanisms used to test the effectiveness of marketing planning should also be able to be used as tools to indicate to what extent corporate objectives are being achieved.

(c) The marketing plan will begin with a marketing audit which will examine in full the business environment of the firm. Additionally, it will examine the internal marketing system of the firm, and the specific marketing activities which are currently being carried out. IKEA management will use the information gathered from this exercise to gain an overall picture of the firm's current trading and to ultimately improve marketing effectiveness. Two specific marketing tools are used.

(i) SWOT analysis - which will indicate to IKEA the company's current strengths, weaknesses, business opportunities and competitive threats.

(ii) PEST analysis- which will indicate to IKEA the influences of political, economic, social and technical factors on the firms business activities.

A number of key strategic questions emerge.

(i) Who and where are our potential customers?

(ii) When and where will they buy our products?

(iii) Can we reach all of them with our existing or planned resources?

(iv) Why do our customers buy from us, and do they have, any, as yet unsatisfied needs?

(v) Who are our main competitors and what 'inducements to buy' are they offering?

(vi) What key external factors currently constrain our business activities?

(vii) What key internal factors currently constrain our business activities?

The next component of the planning process are the assumptions and actions that IKEA management make and take in order to drive the planning process forward.

(i) Timescales are placed on identified and agreed required actions.

(ii) Marketing objectives are then set for IKEA over the short, medium and long terms. These should be quantifiable where possible. The objectives state what the company seeks to achieve with the products, and in the markets in which it trades.

(iii) Marketing strategy is clearly set out. This enables IKEA management to set down the methods it will use to meet the marketing objectives.

(iv) Marketing tactics will then be established; these will illustrate how the staff (who must deliver the plan) will carry out marketing activities.

(v) A selling and sales management organisation will then need to be determined. This will consist of all the supporting activities and office structures needed to enable the marketing tactics to happen.

(vi) IKEA will need to staff the plan effectively. They must have the right people with the right knowledge and skills in the right place at the right time to carry out the plan successfully.

(vii) Contingency measures will need to be drawn up. These are used to address failures in expected outcomes, and are used as insurances against the product/market strategy not delivering the forecasted results.

(viii) IKEA will need to have drawn up effective mechanisms for feedback and review. These are controls such as targets (individual objectives), budgets (used to finance the plan) and audits (used to test its effectiveness). Feedback information will feed both the marketing planning and corporate planning activities and will be used to initiate the next planning cycle.

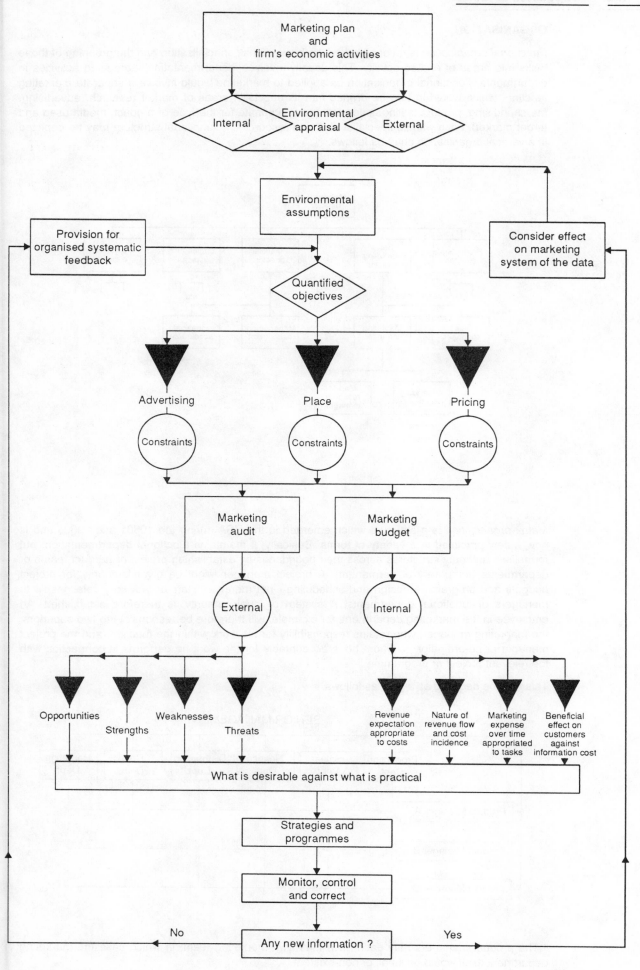

7   ORGANISATION

Functional organisation is rationalised on the basis of task specialisation and the grouping of those tasks into areas of related activity. This usually involves 'departmentation' - grouping activities in departments. Functional organisation as applied to marketing would involve a separate marketing function, which would in turn be divided into its specialist areas of market research, advertising, merchandising, product testing, sales etc. (as appropriate for the type of product, media used and target market), each with its specialist staff and resources. A functional structure may be depicted in a vertical organisation chart as follows.

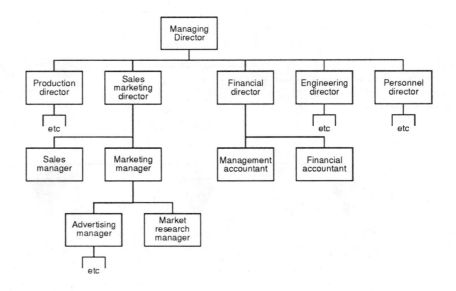

Matrix organisation is a structure which emerged in the USA during the 1950s and 1960s and is now widely practised in a variety of forms. Basically, it maintains functional departmentation, but formalises authority structures across their boundaries by establishing project or product teams or departments (temporary or permanent). A project manager might be given authority for project budgets and programme design and scheduling - not merely a 'staff' or 'advisory' relationship to managers of functional departments. A system of 'dual authority' is therefore established. An employee in the marketing department, for example, will therefore be responsible to two superiors: the marketing manager, who retains responsibility for his work within the function, and the project manager or co-ordinator, to whom he is accountable for the work he performs in connection with the relevant project or programme.

This may be depicted as a grid, as follows.

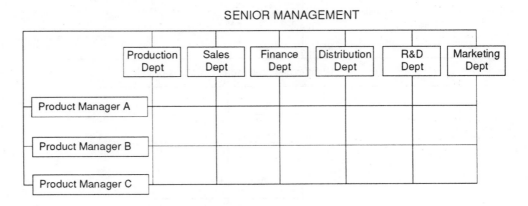

* The product managers may each have their own marketing team; in which case the marketing department itself would be small or non-existent.

8   THE MARKETING MIX

A company's marketing mix includes all the tools that come under the organisation's control to affect the way products and services are offered to the market. Borden coined the phrase 'the marketing mix' from the idea that business executives were mixers of ingredients. From observing industries and individual firms it can be seen that there are wide ranging applications of the tools of marketing. The elements of the marketing mix are often described as the 'four Ps', Product, Price, Place and Promotion. It includes all the policies and procedures involved in each of these elements. This can be on a strategic level: for instance, whether to adopt a penetration or skimming pricing policy for a new product. It can also be on a more tactical level, for instance special price discounts. Each element is looked into in more detail below.

Product

Decisions to be made regarding products include the product lines that are produced, product improvements, new product development and which market(s) to sell them in, including whether to adopt a market segmentation approach.

Pricing

Decisions include the appropriate price level to adopt, the specific prices, price strategy for new products and price variations.

Place

The 'place' aspect of the four Ps is often also called 'channels of distribution'. This includes the way in which goods are passed from the manufacturer to the final consumer.

Promotion

Promotional aspects include personal selling, advertising, publicity and sales promotions. Each of these must be looked into to give an overall consistent message to the public. For example, it is not good to stress service quality in advertising if the actual personal selling of the organisation is not of high calibre. Decisions have to be made on the amount of time and money spent, media selection, desired image and length of campaign.

This is obviously not an exhaustive list. Some elements of the marketing mix do not easily fall exclusively into one category. Packaging, for example, has promotional aspects and product aspects.

There are many factors that come into play when the organisation is considering the most appropriate marketing mix. Some of these are market forces and some are product specific.

Many product areas are dominated by players that excel in one area of the marketing mix. A market may be typified by price competition for example, whereas in another branding may be of importance. This dominance of one aspect of the marketing mix will have an influence on competitors in the industry. This does not mean to say that all firms within the industry successfully differentiate themselves from the competition by focusing on neglected areas of the marketing mix. The stage in the product life cycle also has an influence on the appropriate marketing mix. In the introductory stage any design problems with the actual product should be solved. Price will depend on the costs of developing the product and the strategy regarding required market share. Promotion may concentrate on creating awareness and distribution may be selective. Throughout the other stages in the product life cycle the objectives of the marketing mix may change and during the growth and maturity stage product differentiation, image building and quality may be concentrated on; whilst in the decline stage rationalisations may occur.

Other factors that should be taken into account when designing a marketing mix include the following.

Buyer behaviour

The behaviour of consumers and the behaviour of intermediaries should be taken into account. The actual number of buyers in a market is important as is the motivation for purchase and their buying processes. It is of no use providing products by mail order, for example, if there is a strong resistance from buyers to purchasing products in this way. Whether the firm is providing goods or services will have an influence on buyer behaviour, as will whether the purchaser is in the consumer or industrial market. All these aspects will have an influence on marketing mix decisions.

Competitors

To a certain degree this has been dealt with above. However, the influence of competitors on marketing mix decisions is far reaching. Companies must analyse competitor strengths and weaknesses and their likely response to any marketing tools used.

Government

The government impose some controls on marketing that would affect decisions made regarding the marketing mix. These include regulations on advertising (eg cigarette ban), product specifications, pricing and competitive practices.

Company specific

All the above factors have to be taken into account when designing an appropriate marketing mix. However, it is easy to overlook one important consideration, company resources. The amount of money and staffing resources that marketing is allocated will determine to a large extent the elements of the marketing mix that are viable. The efficiency and effectiveness of marketing programmes need to be constantly monitored and built into the marketing planning process for the future.

All these factors should be taken into account when marketers are designing marketing mix programmes taking into account the size and resources of the organisation.

9   SUPPLIERS

Outsourcing of functions - particularly the management of previously internally managed facilities - has grown faster than any other aspect of middle management during the past ten years. Companies have begun to 'farm out' their non-essential activities in order to concentrate on what they see as the core activities of their business. The main reasons are:

(a)   a large scale re-sourcing of support services;

(b)   the extension of highly professional standards to the management of the key resources upon which the basic performance of company business depends;

(c)   changing circumstances and the nature of markets;

(d)   technologies are becoming more complex and this has created new needs amongst an increasingly knowledgeable and demanding set of customers.

These services must be well managed, so the outside suppliers who are called upon to carry out these tasks are a key aspect of the overall functioning of the organisation. People within organisations interact not only with each other but also with their working environment, and are strongly affected by the services provided by outside suppliers.

Downsizing, the name for shakeouts and privatisations which took place in the UK during the 1980s, encouraged many functions related to marketing (those providing intermittently needed functions such as market research information) to set up as separate external enterprises, on a contract basis.

The advantages include:

(a)   removing the costs of staffing, training and manning such functions on a long term basis;

(b)   the function could be fulfilled on a competitive basis.

This practice has been widely extended, and simple subcontracting has been supplemented by the 'outsourcing' of management functions too. In the UK, a continued commitment to these practices in the 'privatisation' of what were previously public services and utilities sees this development continuing well into the 1990s.

The degree of outsourcing varies from business to business. Companies vary in what they see as their core business. Smaller companies may actually source many of the functions associated with marketing from outside the company. Examples would include:

(a)   market research services;

(b)   advertising;

(c)   design of packaging;

(d)   specialist aspects of product testing (for example, sensory testing of new food products, or safety tests on new electrical goods).

Other aspects of organisational function upon which marketing activity depends are also typically subcontracted. For example:

(a)   promotional campaigns;
(b)   'leafleting';
(c)   free samples; and
(d)   in-store promotional exercises.

The reasons for outsourcing have been discussed. The main advantages are:

(a)   cost savings;

(b)   specialism of the company;

(c)   accountability tied to specific performance;

(d)   introduction of desirable outside qualities (such as imagination, fresh ideas etc) into particular sorts of activities);

(e)   risk shedding.

The main problems related to 'outsourced functions' include:

(a)   degree of control over outsourced companies;
(b)   lack of response to client input.

There are some mechanisms - such as staged payments, and incentive structures - which attempt to address this issue by making the outsourced function responsible for meeting particular targets, and holding back payment. This may be seen as a somewhat excessive measure if applied too insensitively.

Control depends on the market power of the client, and on the quality of the management control system which is being operated within the client organisation. New developments in this area include the bundling or grouping of outsourced functions, for example those working to supply promotional services may also offer market research information, since that kind of information is the lifeblood of such companies. This may also create pyramid effects, with suppliers subcontracting and downsizing in order to cut costs and shed risk, and this can raise great problems in the articulation of the functions which are being served by external suppliers including severe problems of control and responsiveness to customer needs.

Within a service economy the perceptions of the company are shaped by the way in which they are treated by personnel. There has been a movement consequently to regulate contacts between customers and provider-organisation personnel. Outsourcing creates the need for new systems in order to bring this about, and raises important issues about the internal dynamics of the relationships involved. Privatising public utilities within the UK provides a useful illustration of one of the dangers involved in working with external suppliers. The management of, for example, the National Health Service has led to massive increases in the number of managers employed by the new 'Hospital Trusts', coupled with a reclassification and redeployment of staff previously employed in direct provision of health services. There was also huge expenditure on the employment of management consultants in order to make recommendations concerning the most efficient deployment of the new management within the organisation. Despite a remit to develop efficient and competitive units based on competition within internal markets, a number of mistakes were made, including the following.

(a)   *Consultants were given inadequate briefs.* Reports showed that too often, consultants would be called in to 'fix' an organisation without real guidance as to the areas which needed to be addressed, and without any limits on the scope of the problem with which they were involved. As a consequence, the reports they produced were often inappropriate, unrealistic or ineffective. Often, recommendations were too broad to be implemented, and were used as ammunition when particular interests were being aggressively pursued within the organisation.

(b)   *Consultants were given too much power.* Managers employing consultants in these circumstances were inclined to delegate too wide a range of decisions to them.

(c)   Public perceptions were not considered sufficiently.

'Enterprise culture' produced by Thatcherism and Reaganomics in the 1980s generated a movement towards downsizing and risk shedding. Many large organisations have now shed or hived off functions to the control of independent managers. Companies retain only 'core' activities, and can subcontract virtually every other function which they need in order to operate, from cleaning and building security to the plant and fitting which they use from day to day - all maintained in the most appropriate and cost effective way by subjection to 'market discipline'.

This notion of autonomous decision making within a downsized free market actually conflicts with the idea that responsiveness to customer needs necessarily produces a more flexible and varied process of service provision.

10   SERVICES

The characteristics of services which have the most important marketing implications are:

(a)   intangibility
(b)   inseparability
(c)   heterogeneity
(d)   perishability
(e)   ownership.

Intangibility refers to a lack of substance; services typically involve no taste/feel/visible presence etc. According to Morden, the customer may have no prior experience of a service in which he or she is interested, nor any conception of how it would satisfy the requirements of the purchase context for which it was intended.

This may be countered by:

(a)   seeking opinions from other consumers;
(b)   offering the consumer something tangible to represent the purchase.

Intangibility is a matter of degree varying from:

(a)   intangibles making a tangible product available;

(b)   intangibles adding value to a tangible product (house decorating, hairdressing, vehicle or plant maintenance etc)

(c)   complete intangibility (entertainment or leisure services).

This may create problems of operations management - for example, it may be difficult or impossible to attain precise standardisation of the service offered and influence or control over perceptions of what is good or bad customer service.

Marketing implications of this intangibility involve a reduction of the level of difficulty to which the intangibility gives rise by *increasing the level of tangibility*, (eg by physical or conceptual representations/illustrations) or by focusing the attention of the customer on the principal benefits of consumption (eg communicating the benefits of purchasing the service so that the customer visualises its appropriateness to the usage requirements within which the principal benefit is being sought).

Another possibility involves differentiating the provision of the service and the building of a reputation, for example enhancing perceptions of customer service and customer value by offering excellence of quality, service reliability and value for money. These must be attached as values to brands, which must then be managed to secure and enhance their market position.

Inseparability refers to the fact that the creation of many services is coterminous with consumption (eg medical). Services may have to be, at the same moment of time:

(a)   made available;
(b)   sold;
(c)   produced
(d)   consumed.

Provision of the service may not be separable from the person or personality of the seller. Consequently, an increasing importance is attached to the need to instil values of quality and reliability, and to the promotion of a customer service ethic which can be transferred to the service provision.

The main marketing implications are:

(a)   a need for excellence and customer orientation;
(b)   a need to invest in high quality people and high quality training for them.

Heterogeneity refers to the fact that services often involve extremely diverse and varied elements delivered in widely varying circumstances at different times, with widely differing elements. The main problem for marketers is that of maintaining consistency of output standard. To some extent, variability of the quality in the delivery of a service is inevitable. There is also a need to monitor customer reactions. The main marketing implications involve the need to maintain an attitude and organisational culture which emphasises:

(a) consistency of quality control
(b) consistency of customer service;
(c) effective staff selection training and motivation.

It is extremely important to:

(a) establish clear and objective quality measures;

(b) standardise as much as possible within the service;

(c) assume the Pareto principle (80% of difficulties arise from 20% of events surrounding the provision of the service).

Perishability refers to the fact that services cannot be stored in advance of demand. Demand may fluctuate, especially for person-centred services, but operational capacity may have to anticipate a level of demand which may not arise.

This involves a number of risks, including:

(a) inadequate level of demand: substantial variable fixed cost;
(b) excess demand: lost custom through inadequate service provision.

The main marketing implications involve smoothing supply/demand relationship by:

(a) price variations which encourage off-peak demand;
(b) promotions to stimulate off-peak demand.

Ownership is a key issue, since purchase of a service only confers on the customer access to or rights to use a facility, and not ownership (unlike the case of purchasing a product in which there is transfer of title and control over the use of an item). This may lessen the perceived customer value of a service, and consequently make for unfavourable comparisons with tangible alternatives. Main marketing implications involve the need to promote the advantages of non-ownership (eg paid-for maintenance, periodic upgrading) and make available a tangible symbol or representation of ownership (certificate, membership of professional association). It is also a good idea to increase the changes or opportunity of ownership (eg time-shares, shares in the organisation for regular customers).

The marketing mix for services as a whole involves an increased emphasis on:

(a) personal selling
(b) operations management
(c) people and customer service
(d) physical evidence.

Quality in marketing practices

Recent work has suggested that this has implications for marketing practice in general. Parasuranam and his colleagues argue that a key differentiating feature of service quality is that it is judged by the consumer, not simply on the outcome of the service (what the service is intended to deliver) but in addition, on the process of delivering the service (the way in which the service is delivered). The inseparability of services - the fact that services are produced and consumed at the same time - is given prominence equal to the provision of services internally. They see this as a key factor in the promotion of a culture of quality, and the proponents of this view do not make a strong distinction between the way in which this affects members of organisations involved in the delivery of a service or product, and the customers who buy and use it.

Gap analysis argues that customer perceptions of the quality of a product or service are determined by the degree to which they believe it meets their expectations, created from a variety of inputs including physical aspects, service elements and other cues available.

To identify the source of dissatisfaction when it occurs and to eliminate it, gap analysis set out to measure levels of satisfaction, or dissatisfaction. Customer expectations refer to what should be delivered, rather than what they may believe will be delivered. The central issue is how customer expectations develop - what are the sources of unrealistic or inappropriate requirements? Within delivery organisations, this may often involve a careful analysis of the way in which policies on these issues are implemented, and the communication processes which exist to disseminate official thinking on what the company personnel should be doing about these matters.

Expectations depend on the way in which the supplier treats the deliverer within the chain. A product oriented company starts with its own beliefs about what the customer expects and creates a specification to guide the production or creation process. The product or service, then, reflects the perspective of the producer/deliverer rather than the needs of the customer.

Customer expectations and perceptions with regard to service quality are determined by:

(a) word of mouth communications;
(b) personal needs; and
(c) past experience.

'Gaps' occur between:

(a) customer expectations and marketers' perceptions;
(b) management perceptions and service quality specifications;
(c) service quality specifications and service delivery;
(d) service delivery and external communications;
(e) perceived service and expected service.

Every person within the 'quality chain' must be responsive to the standards which are indicated by this analysis. Clearly, decisions made by central policymakers in large companies or institutions such as public utilities who are able to exert this kind of power will dictate much of what goes on behind their own companies or institutions.

11   SERVICES MARKETING

For any product or service, application and use of the *marketing mix* can be a useful tool for a company to expand its business. With services, the provider and the service provided are one and the same, and increasingly services appear to be surpassing manufacturing as the dominant business sector within the UK.

The marketing mix and services

It is suggested that with services marketing, the marketing mix needs to be extended to include three additional elements:

(a) People
(b) Process
(c) Physical evidence

These are perceived to complement the accepted, *product, place, price, promotion* and are specifically added because of the *nature of services* themselves. This has happened because research into the effective provision of services has shown the following.

(a) *Reliability of a service* for customers revolves around a consistent commitment to quality service from providers, in short, providers can be depended upon to deliver on promises.

(b) *Responsiveness* is held in high esteem by customers; this involves willingness, readiness and timeliness on the part of providers.

(c) *Competence* is considered a critical success factor by customers; it refers to the skills and abilities of the service provider's staff. *'Distinctive competence'* is a measure of the firm's degree of competitiveness in its market segment.

(d) *Access* is thought by many customers to be important; the service provider must be easily accessible and approachable.

(e) *Courtesy* is thought to be important - this involves politeness, consideration and the degree of friendliness shown by the service provider's staff.

(f) The *quality of communication* is another essential ingredient to successful service provision; this is also a two way process; communicating regularly and clearly with clients and also taking account of their feedback - ie 'listening'.

(g) *Credibility* is considered a critical success factor as service consumers (both industrial and private) are increasingly becoming more discerning, complex, and quality conscious. Credibility involves the provider being honest, trustworthy, believable and possessing a reputation for professionalism.

(h) Customers of service providers wish to feel *secure*; this means to be free of doubt, not to be taking a risk, or even being subject to danger, through partaking of the provider's service.

(i) Firms that demonstrate a *knowledge of customer needs and customer servicing* will become market leaders. Services can become 'customised' to the individual requirements of the client. Firms who offer this level of service are likely to succeed.

(j) Customers perceive *tangible* factors as being important to successful service provision. This could imply the quality of the provider's equipment, his personal appearance and dress as being influential 'selling factors'.

	Dimensions of client service quality	
1	Problem solving creativity	looking beyond the obvious and not being bound by accepted professional and technical approaches
2	Initiative	includes anticipating problems and opportunities and not just reacting
3	Efficiency	keeping client costs down through effective work planning and control
4	Fast response	responding to enquiries, questions, problems as quickly as possible
5	Timeliness	starting and finishing service work to agreed deadlines
6	Open-mindedness	professionals not being 'blinkered' by their technical approach
7	Sound judgement	clients want business advice not just accounting advice
8	Functional expertise	need to bring together all the functional skills necessary from whatever sources to work on a client project
9	Industry expertise	clients expect professionals to be thoroughly familiar with their industry and recent changes in it
10	Managerial effectiveness	maintaining a focus upon the use of both the firm's and the client's resources
11	Orderly work approach	clients expect salient issues to be identified early and do not want last minute surprises before deadlines
12	Commitment	clients evaluate the calibre of the accountant and the individual attention given
13	Long-range focus	clients prefer long-term relationships rather than 'projects' or 'jobs'
14	Qualitative approach	accountants should not be seen as simple number crunchers
15	Continuity	clients do not like firms who constantly change the staff that work with them - they will evaluate staff continuity as part of ongoing relationship
16	Personality	clients will also evaluate the friendliness, understanding and co-operation of the service provider

Source: *Marketing News*, 28 May 1990

12   CHARITY

Managing the marketing activities for a charity may seem radically different from that of managing marketing in a profit-orientated enterprise. However, marketing a charity may offer a more creative arena for marketers and often considerably greater challenges.

Goals

Often goals of business organisations are formulated in quantitative statements; for a non-profit organisation, goals may be stated in contribution value terms, or in terms of levels of support over a given period.

Structure

Within business organisations, there is usually a formalised structure of operating. In charities, more of an informal approach may prevail; there may be many more 'interests', perhaps individual (rather than collective groupings as with business) with a lack of agreement about how to move the charity forward. Opinion leaders in charities may have no formal management training, or may be retired; they may possess a 'fixed mindset' and be highly resistant to change. Hence charities may be fairly slow moving organisations with fixed 'norms' of operating.

Results

One can measure the effectiveness of business organisations by the 'bottom line' result - profit. In a charity, no such measure exists and it can therefore be very difficult to measure results.

Intervention

With a charity, the effects of management intervention are largely unknown, as most charities operating today are structured for human/social non-profit ends rather than for strategic reasons, like most business organisations. Businesses are often structured into levels of 'hierarchy' and 'accountability'. Charities are frequently much more informally structured.

Possible objectives for a charity

(a) Surplus maximisation (equivalent to profit maximisation).
(b) Revenue maximisation (as for businesses).
(c) Usage maximisation (maximising the number of users and their usage).
(d) Usage targeting (matching the capacity available).
(e) Full cost recovery (minimising subsidy).
(f) Partial cost recovery (minimising subsidy).
(g) Budget maximisation (maximising what is offered).
(h) Producer satisfaction maximisation (satisfying the wants of staff).

Marketing principles and charities

(a) *Strategic visioning.* As with a firm, a charity would have specific ideas of what it wanted to achieve, though these may not be as explicit or formalised as with a business organisation.

(b) *Marketing audit.* A charity would want to find out how effectively it had been operating but would probably do this in an ad hoc way, and not conform to the marketing audit procedure followed by many firms.

(c) *SWOT and PEST.* Unless a charity is particularly well organised and led by a marketer or someone with contemporary industrial/commercial experience, then it will largely be more re-active than pro-active. It may have a knowledge of the factors constraining it, but its knowledge of itself in terms of efficiency and effectiveness may not enable quality management.

(d) *Marketing objectives, strategy and tactics.* Although staffed by committed individuals, charities usually operate in the short term; rarely are objectives and strategies formally set. Tactics seem to 'evolve' and staff are motivated on the basis of progress made.

(e) *Control, feedback and review mechanisms.* Periodic committee meetings and annual reviews facilitate 'progress and results' communication; very rarely are there clear channels or identified mechanisms for performance measurement as with business enterprises.

13   PRODUCT STANDARDISATION

(a) *Factors encouraging greater product standardisation*

It is probably true to say that the impetus for standardisation normally comes mostly from the producer rather than the consumer. The principal benefit of standardisation comes from cost savings, which gives a producer greater scope in setting an appropriate price as part of his marketing mix. In particular, cost savings may be derived from:

(i) manufacturing economies of scale;
(ii) lower inventory levels;

(iii)   simplified distribution;

(iv)   standardised packaging; and

(v)   interchangeable components.

Cost reduction techniques such as these all encourage standardisation. So too does any international technical specification, for example the European Community CE mark for 'essential requirements'.

Although the principal impetus towards standardisation comes from direct benefits to the manufacturer, there is also some pressure from the market for some goods, particularly those such as 'fast food' and electronic consumer products, that are associated with a modern, cosmopolitan lifestyle. A second pressure comes from the modern increase in consumer mobility. Consumers find it attractive to find identical products when they travel to those they know at home, since it obviates the need to make trial purchases to confirm that a product meets their requirements.

(b)   *Factors encouraging greater product variation*

While there are many individual influences that can lead to variation in products, they mostly fall into three broad groups: compulsory product changes, 'voluntary' changes dictated by the market and company policy.

The most important type of compulsory product change is that required by legal regulation. These can occur in numerous guises but common ones concern national health and safety laws and local content regulations (to protect local employment). In these circumstances standardisation is not legally possible; if the producer wishes to compete in these markets his product must be adapted to meet local law.

A much more widespread product change is caused by quasi-legal and indirect legal influence. For example many countries have technical standards or specifications for products which, although not legally enforced, have widespread acceptance. Failure to observe them will mean failure for the product in that market. Indirect legal influence often concerns taxation. Tariffs (and thus price to the consumer) may be altered by changes, sometimes very minor ones, in the product specification. Differing levels of taxation on similar goods (for example cars with different engine sizes) encourages modification to ensure that the exact product maximises the consumer benefits.

Market influences toward local adaptation commonly centre on economic and cultural factors. Particularly for culturally sensitive goods, such as food and clothes, the product may have to be adapted to meet local norms. A physical change to the product is not necessarily needed; it may be a question of changing the brand name to make the product appear more local or associated with an origin that is well thought of.

Most product innovations and international marketing come from the developed world. It is thus usual for product modifications to take the form of changes that adapt them to less developed countries. Cars and bicycles, for instance, normally require different designs for sale in high income and low income economies. In the former they need to display attributes which give the customer a feeling of wealth and social status. In less developed countries they are more likely to be rugged in design, with the accent on practicality and reliability. Account also has to be taken of levels of education (where use of the product requires technical knowledge) and the availability of maintenance and repair facilities (for sophisticated, high value durables).

Occasionally physical differences also encourage product variation. Diet and genetics ensure that people are not identical in shape all over the world, which is important, for example, to the clothing industry. Similarly climate can effectively enforce product modification. Soft topped cars would be unlikely to sell well in Greenland!

Although companies' efforts to reduce costs have been a major influence in encouraging standardisation where the economic benefits have been high, companies have also taken advantage of technology, such as computer controlled equipment and software, to reduce the cost of making local adaptation. This shows their desire to position their products as close to customers' requirements as they can, providing the cost of doing so is not so high that customers choose a lower cost alternative from a competitor.

14   QUALITY

An important part of TQM is concerned with the way in which managers, including those concerned with the marketing function, deal with outside suppliers, with customers and with each other. To assure quality, everyone with whom we deal must be treated as either a customer for the services or functions we provide for them, or else suppliers of services or functions to us. This then forms a 'quality chain', with the guidelines for the provision of customer service being applied internally as well as externally - and, by implication, extended to the way in which managers relate to the suppliers of external services. The quality chain extends out into 'satellite companies'. The award of contacts to external suppliers may depend on commitment to these standards of service and responsiveness to customer needs. There is a danger here that market power is used to extend the authority and autonomy of this policy into (smaller) external companies.

Oakland argues that meeting customer requirements is the main focus in a search for quality. The main aspects would include:

(a)   availability;
(b)   delivery;
(c)   reliability
(d)   maintainability;
(e)   cost effectiveness.

First priority is to establish what customer requirements actually are. If the customer is outside the organisation, then the supplier must seek to set up a marketing activity to gather this information, and to relate the output of his organisation to the needs of the customer.

Internal customers for services are equally important, but seldom are their requirements investigated.

The quality implementation sees all the supplier customer relationships within the 'quality chain' as marketing exercises. Each customer should be carefully consulted as to their precise requirements from the product or service with which they are to be provided, and the following questions asked.

Of customers

(a)   Who are my immediate customers?

(b)   What are their true requirements?

(c)   How do or can I find out what the requirements are?

(d)   How can I measure my ability to meet the requirements?

(e)   Do I have the necessary capability to meet the requirements? (If not, then what must change to improve the capability?)

(f)   Do I continually meet the requirements? (If not, then what prevents this from happening, when the capability exists?)

(g)   How do I monitor changes in the requirements?

Of suppliers

(a)   Who are my immediate suppliers?
(b)   What are my true requirements?
(c)   How do I communicate my requirements?
(d)   Do my suppliers have the capability to measure and meet the requirements?
(e)   How do I inform them of changes in the requirements?

The main problems related to this process are as follows.

(a)   _Quality is subjective_

   (i)   If quality is relative to customer expectations, it cannot be measured in an absolute sense.

   (ii)   Different customers will want, need or expect different things from the same product-type.

(b)   _Quality is distinctive._ Product differentiation, and highly segmented modern markets mean that the precise requirements of a particular market segment will impart an equally precise and differentiated definition of quality.

(c) *Quality is dynamic.* Expectations, and therefore definitions of quality, are highly dynamic - they change over time as a consequence of experience. A ratchet effect is highly likely, so that expectations will rise relatively easily, but will rarely and very reluctantly fall.

15 ETHICS AND SOCIAL RESPONSIBILITY

During the 1970s and latterly during the 1980s, companies have increasingly produced codes on 'public responsibility'; particularly with the advent of business environmentalism in the 1990s, organisations which are conscious about *'how they do what they do'* have been able to *add value to their corporate images* through active policies not to damage the environment through the effects of their production processes and to recycle their resources where practicable. *Social responsibility* can therefore also save money as well as contribute to *increasing efficiency*.

However, it is not just important to be socially responsible; for maximum corporate benefit, those stakeholders who stand to gain most by this initiative need to know the organisation has such a policy. An effective corporate communications strategy is therefore crucial if the firm's policy of public responsibility is to achieve maximum effect.

An organisational stakeholder is anyone who has a personal interest in the firm's activities. Anyone who can be affected by, or interacts with the firm in a significant manner can be termed a 'stakeholder' or part of the firm's range of 'publics'. Stakeholders can be internal or external, they may be shareholders, employees, customers, suppliers, or the local community - each 'want something' from the organisation. The firm with a policy of public responsibility will have developed business objectives relating to each of its major stakeholders.

Responsibility to employees

In addition to its legally binding responsibilities to employees under employment legislation, an employee-orientated firm will wish to underline that employees are the most important asset of the business; they will do this through a commitment to training, equality, empowerment and equality of opportunity.

Staff development programmes will be developed for all groups of employees, and quality circles, a company newspaper (designed and edited by the workforce) and participative managerial approaches will reflect a desire in the firm to create a successful corporate culture where all staff are motivated to give of their best.

The firm will be committed to providing a healthy and safe environment in which to work and will have developed an *employee communications* policy to ensure that staff are able to play an active role in the firm's strategic direction.

One could argue that a policy of public responsibility is about 'making money', because a happy and motivated staff are likely to be more productive, hence profitability would improve.

Responsibility to customers

This part of the firm's public responsibility policy would be concerned with providing customers with products of good value and of high quality. The firm would set high standards of sales and after-sales service, product safety and reliability would be important, as would integrity in advertising and promotion.

The organisation would wish to establish quality relationships with suppliers, perhaps moving towards a 'just in time' buying system or seeking reciprocity (turning a supplier into a buyer for the final product). A publicly responsible firm would avoid using its economic power to influence supplier and customer relationships and would be seeking always to enhance its market reputation through developing a high profile corporate image. A truly effective firm would be one where the organisation's successful corporate identity was reflected through its corporate image.

The firm's corporate image could also be strengthened by well-developed links with local schools and colleges (for example, through provision for industrial visits or work experience placements).

Responsibility to shareholders

Social responsibility is increasingly being raised by shareholders at company annual general meetings, covering such matters as political sensitivity to world events (for example, company trading relationships with Iraq or other countries where human rights or imperialistic military objectives are of world concern) and environmental matters.

Shareholders impress upon management the need to produce written codes on their position with regard to such matters. The degree of success shareholders have is often related to the 'value of lost business' traded against 'the value of image enhancement' - firms often take the view that 'doing business' is their lifeblood and whilst they will empathise and do their best to meet shareholder expectations, they would not be willing to lose a lot of business to achieve this.

Generally, a public responsibility policy inclusive of shareholders would highlight the drive towards sustainable profits, corporate growth, a good return on and security of investment, effective communication with shareholders and a sound management of the firm's assets.

Such a multi-stakeholder policy can be an effective management tool designed to integrate and underline the common interest of the company, its employees and the wider society to which they both contribute.

Key summary ethical and social responsibility codes

(a)   *On the environment*

Not to damage the environment through the effects of productive or trading activity

(b)   *On employees*

Commitment to training and development
Commitment to involvement and participation

(c)   *On customers*

Commitment to customer servicing
Commitment to quality products

(d)   *On shareholders*

Commitment to honesty and integrity
Commitment to professionalism

16   INFORMATION TECHNOLOGY

New management theorists such as Peters and Drucker see modern business as serving increasingly fragmented markets, with customers able to pick and choose from ever more varied and diverse product assortments. Failure rate amongst new products is very high, and growing. Competitive, unstable and rapidly changing markets have increased business's need for information, to monitor and 'target' their segment of the market by identifying needs and communicating with consumers. Competition has created enormous pressures to cut margins and make every decision count.

Information reduces the risks involved. Commercial success can only rest on a *marketing orientation*, an approach which places the needs of the consumer, and the process of gathering information about the consumer, at the heart of the business. At the same time, large organisations contain many decision makers with widely varying types and levels of expertise, so that the information they need must be rendered into *many different forms*. Thus, for example, a study which reveals a consumer preference for a product which is 'strong tasting' will have quite different implications for those concerned with design of the packaging, formulation of the recipe, or development of TV advertising.

The range, quality, and amount of information available has increased enormously with the electronic storage, retrieval and manipulation of data on stocks, purchases, and a whole range of information about customers.

Direct marketing (sometimes called 'precision', 'database' or 'niche' marketing) uses this information to identify market segments by *combination* (with, for example, census information) or *projection* (making inferences, for example, about attitudes, opinions or interests based on limited information, such as postcode or first name).

Markets are also commonly subjected to *psychographic segmentation* according to differences between consumers' lifestyles, using socio-demographic, behavioural and attitudinal data.

Good decisions depend on comprehensible and actionable information about these markets being *accessible* to decision makers - from sales personnel dealing face to face with retailers or customers, through research/development and production staff concerned with product form, to marketing staff, concerned to identify customer needs and wants, and communicate with those customers.

All of these systems make heavy use of information technology in order to improve the quality of decision making. *Management information systems* accomplish this purpose. The marketing research system is one of four components of the marketing information system. The others are the following.

(a) The internal accounting system
(b) The marketing intelligence system
(c) The marketing management science system

Marketing information - about sales, about customers, about competitor activity, trends in the market, financial movements and government policies - can be incorporated into databases and software which enables non-specialists to perform complex projections and analyses, as well as monitoring their own and competitors' performances.

Information, then, is produced in a variety of forms, for members of business organisations making decisions about their operations. This has become more important with the rise of the marketing concept.

Secondary data - generally, data gathered for other reasons by a variety of agencies - includes company reports, government statistics, newspaper and journal articles, and reports produced by commercial market research agencies. Most secondary data is quantitative, gathered by government or industry in accounting and record keeping. Thanks to IT, most of this is now available to marketers through direct interrogation, or else can be accessed through CD ROM systems.

Information technology, particularly the advent of optical codes and the means to store, handle and process the immense amounts of data which they generate is revolutionising marketing research and management information systems. In the area of food choice, the richness, accuracy and immediacy of the information which they offer about stock levels, ordering patterns, product distribution, customer profiles, and so on, is readily apparent. When this information first began to appear, there was such an immense volume, that many enterprises, and even the Grocery Distribution Institute itself, could not use more than a fraction.

Database marketing has grown out of this new potential. It has been defined as

'An interactive approach to marketing communications, which uses individually addressable communications media (such as mail, telephone and sales force)

- to extend help to a company's target audience

- to stimulate their demand

- to stay close to them by recording and keeping an electronic database memory of customer prospects and all communications and commercial contacts and to help improve all future contacts.'

The aim is 'to promote *strategic improvements*, *identification of strategic advantage* through better use of customer and market information leading to the development of new and unique products and services and *development of long term customer relationships*'.

These new developments are, to some degree, *de-skilling* market research and analysis, by making it possible for non-specialists to access and manipulate data very quickly, and at very low cost.

This information is becoming more important because:

(a) the range, volume and detail is enormous and increasing;
(b) new methods of analysis are developing fast;
(c) data is now becoming more accessible and widely used.

The cheapness and ubiquity of IT has encouraged the development of management information systems generating a two way flow of information.

Glossary
and
Index

> *Tutorial note.* In this subject, it is not always easy to arrive at exact definitions of certain words, as different authors use them in different ways. So treat this glossary as a memory jogger, not as the definitive answer to your query. If in any doubt after you have used this glossary, consult the index and go back to the relevant section of this Study Text.

4 Ps See marketing mix.

Activities What an organisation does. Primary activities (eg manufacturing) directly add value to inputs. Support activities (eg R & D) support primary activities.

Advertising Any paid form of non-personal presentation and promotion of ideas, goods or services by an identifiable sponsor.

Ansoff matrix Approach to product-market strategies based on new or existing products and new or existing markets.

Applied research Original research with a definite application in mind.

Avoidable costs The specific costs of an activity or sector of a business which would be avoided if that activity or sector did not exist.

Benchmarking Technique by which a company tries to emulate or exceed standards achieved or processes adopted by another company.

Brand A name, term, symbol or design (or combination) which is intended to signify the goods or services of one seller or group of sellers and to differentiate them from those of competitors. Also, a particular make of a product form.

BS5750 A standard of quality assurance.

Business process re-engineering Management technique which aims to enhance productivity and responsiveness by changing organisation structures and deployment of resources around key business processes.

Business strategy How to approach a particular product and/or market.

Buyer behaviour The process a buyer goes through, and the weight given to various factors, in arriving at a decision to purchase a product. Models of buyer behaviour include Howard-Sheth (consumer) and Webster and Wind (organisational).

Cluster Geographically proximate collection of related businesses and industries. Clusters are supposedly a key factor in the competitive advantage of nations

Cognitive theories Approach to ethics which holds that these are moral truths to which we can have access, irrespective of personal psychology or prejudice.

Competitive advantage Factor which enables a firm to compete successfully with competitors on a sustained basis

Competitive forces/five forces Porter's model of the competitive environment of any firm, consisting of the threats of new entrants and substitute products, the bargaining powers of customers and suppliers, and the rivalry amongst current competitors

Competitive position The market share, costs, price, quality and accumulated experience of an entity or product relative to competition.

Competitor analysis Analysis of competitors' strengths and weaknesses, strategies, assumptions, market positioning, etc from all available sources of information in order to identify suitable strategies.

Competitor intelligence system Procedures to obtain data for competitor analysis.

Concentrated marketing Sell your product to one segment only.

Concentration ratios The proportion of firms holding most of the market (eg the top two firms hold 20%).

Conglomerate diversification Making new products for new markets.

Consensus Organisational objectives result from a consensus of the views of different stakeholders (Cyert and March).

Consequentialism Approach to ethics suggesting that the goodness or badness of the action can be judged only by the consequences of the actions (as opposed to the state of mind or intention of the person carrying out the action).

Constraints Rules restricting managers' freedom of action.

Consumer goods Goods made for the household consumer, which can be used without any further commercial processing. Convenience goods are generally purchased in small units or low value (eg milk). Shopping goods have higher unit values and are bought less frequently (eg clothes, furniture). Speciality goods are those of high value which a customer will know by name and go out of his or her way to purchase. These distinctions are broad and blurry; there is no point in logic-chopping.

Consumer The end user of a product service. May or may not be the customer.

Consumers' Association UK interest group representing consumers; conducts product tests and comparisons, lobbies government etc.

Corporate appraisal A critical assessment of the strengths and weaknesses, opportunities and threats (*SWOT analysis*) in relation to the internal and environmental factors affecting an entity in order to establish its condition prior to the preparation of the long-term plan .

Corporate culture Culture residing in an organisation

Corporate objectives Objectives for the firm as a whole

Corporate strategy Strategy for the business as a whole (Johnson and Scholes)

Cost leadership See generic strategies.

Cost-focus See generic strategies.

Culture The sum total of beliefs, knowledge, attitudes of mind and customs to which people are exposed in their social conditioning.

Customer The purchaser of a product/service. May or may not be the consumer.

Departmentation An organisation structure whereby an organisation's activities are grouped into departments in order to be managed efficiently, such departments being based on some common factor such as area or region (geographic departmentation), type of work done (functional departmentation), product or brand, customer etc.

Desk research The collection of secondary data in marketing research.

Differentiated marketing Introduce several versions of a product, each tailored to a particular segment.

Differentiation See generic strategies.

Differentiation-focus See generic strategies.

Direct distribution Supply of goods to customers without an intermediary (eg direct sales, mail order in some cases).

Direct exporting Exporting to overseas customers, who might be wholesalers, retailers or users, without the use of export houses etc. See also indirect exporting.

Direct mail Means of promotion, whereby selected customers are sent advertising material addressed specifically to them (eg by post and/or fax).

Direct selling The use of a salesperson to sell a product, as opposed to advertising etc.

Distribution channel Means of getting the goods to the consumer.

Diversification Extension of a firm's activities to new products and/or new markets.

Divisionalisation Arrangement of a business into autonomous units each with its own revenues, costs, capital expenditure programmes.

DMU Decision-making ie the people in a business who decide whether to buy a product.

Effectiveness Doing the right job.

Efficiency Deployment of resources in the right way; outputs per unit input.

Emergent strategy Strategy developed out of a pattern of behaviour not consciously imposed by senior management.

Entry barriers These discourage firms from entering an industry.

Environment Anything outside the boundary of a system.

Ethics The enquiry into morality (ie what is right and wrong, and the yardsticks by which people assess what is right or wrong); business ethics is an enquiry into the moral dimensions of business activities; descriptive ethics merely describes moral matters; prescriptive ethics passes judgement on them.

EU (European Union) Formerly called the European Community (EC) itself formerly called the European Economic Community (EEC); has 15 member states.

Exit barriers These make it difficult for firms to withdraw from an industry.

Field research The collection of primary data in market research.

Flexibility Ability to respond to change, new circumstances etc.

Focus See generic strategies.

Forecasting The identification of factors and quantification of their effect on an entity, as a basis for planning.

Formal goals Goals imposed by dominant individual or group. People work to achieve these goals in order to satisfy their own.

Franchising Popular in retail and service industries, the franchisee supplies capital and the franchiser supplies expertise, a brand name and national promotion.

Freewheeling opportunism Approach to strategy which eschews planning processes.

Functional strategy Strategically important decisions made at lower levels eg product pricing (Johnson and Scholes).

Gap analysis The comparison of an entity's ultimate objective with the sum of projection and already planned projects, identifying how the consequent gap might be filled.

GATT General Agreement on Tariffs and Trade; organisation which exists to promote free trade on a multilateral basis between members. Shortly to be superseded by the World Trade Organisation (WTO).

Generic strategy Term which Porter uses to describe the strategy a firm takes to pursuing competitive advantage in an industry. There are three generic strategies and Porter argues, although others have disputed his conclusion, that a firm must choose one of them: cost leadership (become the lowest cost producer); differentiation (make your product different), focus (only serve a segment of the market, through cost leadership - a cost-focus strategy - or differentiation - a differentiation-focus strategy - within that segment).

Globalisation Blanket term which refers to a number of trends in world trade, including global products and services (eg foreign exchange which can be bought anywhere,) global markets (ie no effective boundary between the domestic and international market, so that domestic firms enjoy no particular advantage in their own country) and global companies (which supposedly have no national basis).

Goal congruence In a control system, the state which leads individuals or groups to take actions which are in their self-interest and also in the best interest of the entity.

Goals Often not quantified, these interpret the mission to the needs of different stakeholders. Non-operational goals cannot be quantified as objectives; operational goals can (Mintzberg).

Growth Stage of product life cycle characterised by increasing sales volumes, profitability and competition.

Horizontal integration Firm acquires more businesses delivering similar products to similar markets.

Indirect distribution The use of intermediaries, such as wholesalers and retailers, to supply a product to the customer.

Indirect exporting Use of intermediaries such as export houses, specialist export management firms, complementary exporting (ie using other companies' products to pull your own into an overseas market); ie the outsourcing of the exporting function to a third party.

Industrial markets Business-to-business market (eg the sale of machine tools, consultancy advice etc).

Insider groups Interest group regularly consulted by government.

Interest group Pressure group or defensive group (eg trade union) promoting the interests of a group in society.

JIT (just in time) A technique for the organisation of work flows to allow rapid, high quality, flexible production whilst minimising manufacturing waste and stock levels. An item should not be made or purchased until it is needed by the customer or as input to the production process.

Joint venture An arrangement of two or more firms to develop and/or market a product/service; each firm provides a share of the funding and has a say in management.

Management control The process by which managers assure that resources are obtained and used effectively and efficiently in the accomplishment of the organisation's objectives (Anthony).

Market positioning The attempt by marketers to give the product a distinct identity or image so that it will be perceived to have distinctive features or benefits relative to competing products (Economist Pocket Marketing).

Market research Sometimes used synonymously with marketing research; strictly speaking, however, it refers to the acquisition of primary data about customers and customer attitudes for example, by asking a sample of individuals to complete a questionnaire.

Market segmentation See segmentation.

Market share One entity's sales of a product or service in a specified market expressed as a percentage of total sales by all entities offering that product or service. A planning tool and a performance assessment ratio.

Marketing The management process which identifies, anticipates and supplies customer requirements efficiently and profitably.

Marketing audit Part of the position audit which reviews the organisation's products, markets, customers and market environment: 'a comprehensive, systematic, independent and periodic examination of a company's or business unit's marketing environment, objectives, strategies and activities, with a view to determining problem areas and opportunities and recommending a plan of action to improve the company's marketing performance '(Kotler).

Marketing mix The set of controllable variables and their levels that the firm uses to influence the target market. The mix comprises product, place, price, promotion (the 4 Ps). In service industries, this can be expanded to include people, processes, and physical evidence.

Marketing orientation Identify what your customers need; only then produce goods and services to meet those needs.

Marketing research The objective gathering, recording and analysing of all facts about problems relating to the transfer and sales of goods and services from producer to consumer or user. Includes market research, price research etc. Marketing research involves the use of secondary data (eg government surveys) in desk research as well as field research (which the firm undertakes itself) to acquire primary data.

Maturity Stage of product life cycle characterised by relatively stable sales volumes and profitability.

Media Non-personal means of communication (eg TV, newspapers etc).

Mission An organisation's rationale for existing at all and/or its long term strategic direction and/or its values.

Mission statement Document in which the mission is formally stated.

MKIS Marketing information system.

Non profit marketing Marketing activities undertaken by non profit making organisations such as charities, government departments etc.

Outsourcing Buying products, components, subcomponents or services from outside suppliers, which might otherwise have been supplied or made in-house.

Pareto (80/20) distribution A frequency distribution with a small proportion (say 20 per cent) of the items accounting for a large proportion (say 80 per cent) of the value/resources.

People Marketing mix element for services, to highlight the fact that the quality of many services depends on the quality of the people delivering it (eg a play can be ruined by bad acting).

Personal selling The presentation of goods or services in person by a sales representative.

PEST factors Factors in an organisation's environment (political-legal, economic, social-cultural, technological).

Physical evidence Marketing mix element for services denoting the environment in which the service is delivered (eg seating comfort and lighting in a restaurant).

PIMS Profit impact of marketing strategies.

Place Element of the marketing mix detailing how the product/service is supplied to the customer (distribution).

Planning The establishment of objectives, and the formulation, evaluation and selection of the policies, strategies, tactics and action required to achieve them. Planning comprises long-term/strategic planning, and short-term operation planning. The latter is usually for a period of one year.

Position audit Part of the planning process which examines the current state of the entity in respect of: resources of tangible and intangible assets and finance; products, brands and markets; operating systems such as production and distribution; internal organisation; current results; returns to stockholders.

Positioning See market positioning.

Primary data In market research, this is data collected specifically for the study under consideration (eg by questionnaire).

Processes Marketing mix element for services denoting how the service is actually delivered.

Product life cycle A model which suggests that sales of a product grow and mature and then decline as the product becomes obsolete and customer demands change. Applicable in some cases (eg horse-drawn transportation) but perhaps less so in others (eg corn flakes); use with caution.

Product orientation Customers will always buy a good product at a reasonable price.

Promotion Element of the marketing mix which includes all communications with the customer, thus including advertising, publicity, PR, sales promotion etc.

Quality The totality of features and characteristics of a product or service which bears on its ability to meet stated or implied needs; fitness for use

Quality assurance Arrangement whereby a supply guarantees quality of goods supplied by enabling the customer to review the production process or suggest techniques, or by adoption of an externally monitored quality standard such as BS 5750.

Quality management Ensuring products are made to design specification.

Resource planning Process which identifies resources need by strategy, reviews existing resources and assesses the fit between them.

Responsibilities Obligations a company undertakes which are not part of its guidance or control mechanism.

Risk Volatility, often measured by standard deviation. Also taken to mean general uncertainty, which cannot be quantified (eg political risk, personal risk to managers' careers).

S/L trade-off Balance of organisational activities aiming to achieve long term and short term objectives when they are in conflict or where resources are scarce.

Sales orientation Customers have to be persuaded to buy a product.

Sales promotion Marketing activities other than personal selling, advertising and publicity aimed to stimulate purchasing by customers. Examples include money-off coupons, free flights, competitions etc.

Secondary data In marketing research, data neither collected directly by the user nor specifically for the user, often under conditions not known to the user. Examples include government reports.

Segmentation (market segmentation) The subdividing of the market into distinct and increasingly homogeneous sub groups of customers, where any subgroup can be selected as a target market to be met with a distinct marketing mix.

Services Distinguished from products because they are generally produced as they are consumed, and cannot be stored or taken away. For example, a bus is a product which is used to provide a service (transportation); the service is provided as you are consuming it (ie your trip from A to B). Also the standard of service differs each time it is produced (eg one bus driver may be a better or faster driver than another).

Short-termism Preference supposed to exist in the UK, US and similar business cultures, as opposed to Japan or Germany, in which short-term results take priority over long-term benefits (ie the S/L trade off is weighted towards the short term). Used by industrialists to blame the City institutions' alleged reluctance to invest in high risk high-tech ventures, and investors' preferences for high dividend payouts. Use this phrase with caution, as empirical evidence to support it is shaky, and there are many other reasons which explain the UK's poor economic performance, in relative terms, in comparison with its former adversaries.

Social responsibility cost Tangible and intangible costs and losses sustained by third parties or the general public as a result of economic activity, eg pollution by industrial effluent. See also externalities.

Stakeholder Person or group with an interest in organisational activities (eg shareholders, employees, customers, government etc).

Strategy A course of action, including the specification of resources required, to achieve a desired objective. Note that different authors use the word to mean different things.

Strategic business unit Similar to a division, but far more autonomous, so much so that it is not affected by other parts of the business.

Strategic control Strategic control should concentrate on targets that measure strategic process, just as budgetary control focuses on annual profit targets. The strategic control process should ensure that there is a clear agreement on the strategic targets that businesses are pursuing and a means of monitoring achievements against them. It should also provide incentives for business managers who achieve their targets, and should prompt central intervention where necessary to close gaps between planned and actual results (Goold and Quinn).

Strategic management The implementation and control of an agreed strategy.

Strategic planning The formulation, evaluation and selection of strategies for the purpose of preparing a long-term plan of action to attain objectives. Also known as *corporate planning* and *long range planning*.

SWOT analysis See Corporate appraisal.

Target market Market, or market segment to which an organisation offers goods/services; one or more segments selected for special attention by a business.

Test marketing Samples of a proposed new product are tried out in areas which are supposed to be representative of the market as a whole.

TQM (Total quality management) An approach to production, and also management, aimed to prevent defective manufacture and to promote continuous improvement. CIMA defines it as 'the continuous improvement in quality, productivity and effectiveness obtained by establishing management responsibility for processes as well as outputs. In this, every process has a process owner and every person in an entity operates within a process and contributes to its improvement'.

Undifferentiated marketing Hope as many people as possible will buy the product, therefore do not segment.

Utilitarianism Ethical theory which suggests that what is right is determined by the greatest good for the greatest number of people.

Value chain Concept which describes the relationships between an organisation's value activities from input to output; a model of value activities.

Values Basic, perhaps unstated, principles and assumptions. In organisational terms this can relate to issues such as secrecy, market orientation.

Vertical integration A firm acquires a business or carries out a business which makes it its own supplier, or its own distributor.

Wholesaler Intermediary between manufacturers and retailers.

FURTHER READING

For further question practice on Advanced Certificate *Marketing Operations* BPP publish a companion Practice & Revision Kit. The 1995 edition contains a bank of questions, many of which are drawn from past examinations, plus a full test paper. Fully worked suggested solutions are provided for all questions, including the test paper. A new edition will be published in February 1996.

To order your Practice & Revision Kit, ring our credit card hotline on 0181-740 6808. Alternatively, send this page to our Freepost address or fax it to us on 0181-740 1184.

To: BPP Publishing Ltd, FREEPOST, London W12 8BR   **Tel: 0181-740 6808**
Fax: 0181-740 1184

Forenames (Mr / Ms): _____

Surname: _____

Address: _____

_____

Post code: _____   Date of exam (month/year): _____

Please send me the following books:	Quantity	Price	Total
Marketing Operations Kit	....	£7.95	....

Please include postage:

UK: £1.50 for first plus £0.50 for each extra book	....	....
Europe (inc ROI): £2.50 for first plus £1.00 for each extra book	....	....
Rest of the World: £4.00 for first plus £2.00 for each extra book	....	....
Total		....

I enclose a cheque for £ _____ or charge to Access/Visa/Switch

Card number ☐☐☐☐ ☐☐☐☐ ☐☐☐☐ ☐☐☐☐ ☐☐☐☐

Start date (Switch only) _____ Expiry date _____ Issue no. (Switch only) _____

Signature _____

To order any further titles in the CIM range, please use the form overleaf.

ORDER FORM

Any books from our CIM range can be ordered by ringing our credit card hotline on 0181-740 6808. Alternatively, send this page to our Freepost address or fax it to us on 0181-740 1184.

To: BPP Publishing Ltd, FREEPOST, London W12 8BR
Tel: 0181-740 6808
Fax: 0181-740 1184

Forenames (Mr / Ms): _____

Surname: _____

Address: _____

_____

Post code: _____   Date of exam (month/year): _____

Please send me the following books:

	Price		Quantity		Total
	Text	Kit/ Workbook	Text	Kit**/ Workbook	£
Certificate					
Marketing Environment	16.95	7.95	....	....	....
Understanding Customers	16.95	7.95	....	....	....
Business Comunications	16.95	7.95	....	....	....
Marketing Fundamentals	16.95	7.95	....	....	....
Advanced Certificate					
Promotional Practice	16.95	7.95	....	....	....
Management Information for Marketing and Sales	16.95	7.95	....	....	....
Effective Management for Marketing	16.95	7.95	....	....	....
Marketing Operations	16.95	7.95	....	....	....
Diploma					
Marketing Communications Strategy	17.95	8.95	....	....	....
International Marketing Strategy	17.95	8.95	....	....	....
Strategic Marketing Management: Planning and Control	17.95	8.95	....	....	....
Strategic Marketing Management: Analysis and Decision	24.95	16.95*	....	....	....

* Subject to availability

** Please state whether you want the current edition of the Kit or the new edition to be published in February 1996. Prices are for 1995 editions.

Please include postage:

UK: Texts £2.50 for first plus £1.00 for each extra	....	....	....
Kits £1.50 for first plus £0.50 for each extra.	....	....	....
Europe (inc ROI): Texts £5.00 for first plus £4.00 for each extra	....	....	....
Kits £2.50 for first plus £1.00 for each extra.	....	....	....
Rest of the World: Texts £7.50 for first plus £5.00 for each extra	....	....	....
Kits £4.00 for first plus £2.00 for each extra.	....	....	....

I enclose a cheque for £ _____ or charge to Access/Visa/Switch

Card number ⬚⬚⬚⬚⬚⬚⬚⬚⬚⬚⬚⬚⬚⬚⬚⬚⬚⬚⬚

Start date (Switch only) _____   **Expiry date** _____   **Issue no. (Switch only)** _____

Signature _____

REVIEW FORM

Name: _____

How have you used this Text?

Home study (book only) ☐   With 'correspondence' package ☐

On a course: college_____ ☐   Other_____

How did you obtain this Text?

From us by mail order ☐   From us by phone ☐

From a bookshop ☐   From your college ☐

Where did you hear about BPP Texts?

At bookshop ☐   Recommended by lecturer ☐

Recommended by friend ☐   Mailshot from BPP ☐

Advertisement in _____ ☐   Other _____

Have you used the companion Kit for this subject?   Yes/No

Your comments and suggestions would be appreciated on the following areas

Syllabus coverage

Illustrative questions

Errors (please specify, and refer to a page number)

Structure and presentation

Other

Please return to: BPP Publishing Ltd, FREEPOST, London W12 8BR